# CORK'S
# REVOLUTIONARY
## DEAD

### 1916–1923

## BARRY KEANE

MERCIER PRESS

IRISH PUBLISHER – IRISH STORY

I gcuimhne ar mo mháthair
18.12.1925–5.11.2016

MERCIER PRESS

Cork

www.mercierpress.ie

© Barry Keane, 2017

ISBN: 978 1 78117 495 1

10 9 8 7 6 5 4 3 2 1

A CIP record for this title is available from the British Library

Printed and bound in the EU.

# CONTENTS

List of Abbreviations     4

Acknowledgements     5

Introduction     7

Part 1: Significant Incidents in the War     13

   The Irish Revolution and Civil War, 24 April 1916–24 May 1923     15

   Cork 1916–1919     20

   The Murder of Lord Mayor Tomás MacCurtain and the 'Stolen' Jury     25

   The Death of Colonel Smyth     30

   The Disappearance of John Coughlan     33

   The Funeral of Terence MacSwiney     35

   The Kilmichael Ambush     39

   The Burning of Cork     51

   The Incident at Mallow Station     55

   Cascading Death     58

   The Clonmult Shootout     62

   28 February 1921     65

   The Crossbarry Ambush     69

   The Destruction of Rosscarbery Police Barracks     76

   Tom Barry's Trench Coat     81

   Massacre in West Cork     85

   Michael Collins: 'The Man Who Couldn't Be Killed'     90

   The Door to Madness     99

Part 2: The Dead     103

Possibles     368

Addendum     372

Endnotes     374

Bibliography     424

Index     432

# LIST OF ABBREVIATIONS

| | |
|---|---|
| ASU | Active Service Unit |
| BMH | Bureau of Military History |
| CCCA | Cork City and County Archives |
| DI | District Inspector |
| GHQ | General Headquarters |
| GPO | General Post Office |
| HMSO | His Majesty's Stationery Office |
| IPP | Irish Parliamentary Party |
| IRA | Irish Republican Army |
| IRB | Irish Republican Brotherhood |
| IRP | Irish Republican Police |
| MAI | Military Archives (Ireland) |
| MSPC | Military Service Pensions Collection, MAI |
| NAK | National Archives Kew (UK) |
| NCO | Non-Commissioned Officer |
| O/C | Commanding Officer |
| RAF | Royal Air Force |
| RIC | Royal Irish Constabulary |
| UCDA | University College Dublin Archives |
| UDC | Urban District Council |
| WS | Witness Statement |
| YMCA | Young Men's Christian Association |

# ACKNOWLEDGEMENTS

I am indebted to a great many people who have contributed in no small way to the final result. No book is ever the product of one person and it is through conversations with other researchers, and holders of important documents and information, that the fullest story can be fleshed out. Each and every one deserves my deep gratitude for the time and effort they put in to help me tell this story. I can only hope they will not be disappointed with the result.

Some individuals and groups deserve particular acknowledgement. First among these is David Grant, who has conducted an enormous amount of detailed and accurate research in his two linked websites dealing with the 'Cairo Gang' and the Auxiliaries, without which the task of tracing details of the British casualties of this war would have presented an almost insurmountable challenge. Such is his generosity that when I asked him for formal permission to use his research he simply replied, 'You can use anything you want.'

Equally, the staffs of the various archives and libraries have been extraordinary in their willingness to assist in this work. These include the staffs of the Cork City Library, Cork County Library, Cork City and County Archives, National Library of Ireland, National Archives of Ireland, National Archives UK, Military Archives of Ireland, Roman Catholic Dublin Diocesan Archives and University College Cork Archives. Once again their knowledge and willingness to help made it a pleasure to work with all of them. To each and every one I am deeply grateful.

My own friends have encouraged and supported this work, either by listening to parts of the story or proofreading it, or simply offering encouragement. However, I must again give thanks to my long-standing partner in crime, Henry O'Keeffe, whose keen intellect and sharp analysis has often nudged me in the right direction. Our much put-upon wives, Mairead O'Reilly and Louise Crockett, have literally travelled this long road together and without their grace under pressure it is doubtful if this book could have been finished.

Mercier has taken a risk in publishing this book, and Mary Feehan and the brilliant team have put a proper structure and polish to the original manuscript. Without brave independent publishers like Mercier few, if any, history books would be published in Ireland and they deserve to be supported.

Finally, Louise and my daughter, Ella, have put up with an awful lot over the years and remain my two greatest supporters. Ella has grown up listening to this topic and there is no doubt that research can often be all-consuming. Neither has complained (too often) and I will always owe them a great debt for this.

Barry Keane

June 2017

# INTRODUCTION

The origin of this book is simple. Over the past five years, while doing research for my book *Massacre in West Cork* and articles dealing with the Protestant decline in Cork between 1911 and 1926, I have been collecting information about the dead of the revolutionary period. As I published my initial research on the Internet, I was surprised by the number of responses I received from the families of the dead who were tracing a relative's story. Too often, the information I published was the first confirmation for them that a family story was true. It was obvious that the victims of the war were in danger of being forgotten as folk memories faded, memorial cards lost their meaning and documents were mislaid. Equally, as many of the victims were British troops, their records were in danger of becoming lost simply because there appeared to be little or no British or Irish interest in recording their deaths.

The Internet has proved to be a uniquely powerful tool in tracing the victims of the revolutionary era in Ireland from 1916 to 1923. Previously sealed archives such as the Irish Bureau of Military History (BMH) witness statements and the Military Service Pensions Collection are now available free online and in searchable formats. These have proved to be invaluable for identifying IRA victims and those who killed them. With the advent of paid and free searchable newspaper archives, the monumental task of working through these to look for victims has been reduced to manageable proportions. This does not mean that it is easy, and trawling through thousands of 'hits' still takes an enormous amount of disciplined and focused work. Often a newspaper record is little more than a single line, especially in reports from the most violent years, 1921 and 1922, and in the latter year first names are often omitted, increasing the difficulty of the task. More recently the online launch by the British National Archives of their Easter Rising and War of Independence documents means that the details of practically every death can be read and cross-checked against the newspaper and Irish archives, creating a fuller picture of how each of these events came about.

However, a serious difficulty arises from the variable quality of the sources. *The Southern Star* is an excellent source for the periods when it was published, but it was forcibly closed by the British for the latter part of 1920, leaving a large gap in the record at a crucial moment. Fortunately, it was re-opened by Michael Collins in January 1921 with an Irish government loan. However, because he placed his cousin in charge to exert more control over the content, the paper takes on an increasingly Sinn Féin tone and its value as an unbiased source diminishes from that time.[1]

Other sources are unquestionably biased. The records of courts martial in cases where it is stated that IRA members were shot 'while trying to escape' are challenged by IRA records where witnesses state that the prisoner was shot out of hand. Both cannot be right, but it is often difficult to say beyond reasonable doubt who is telling the truth. However, it is noticeable that 193 of the 577 shootings attributable to British forces recorded in the martial law area (mostly Cork, Kerry and Limerick) between 7 August 1920 and 11 January 1922 were described as 'civilians attempting to escape from military' outside of armed conflict situations.[2]

In much of the commentary about the war the focus is very much on the Irish side of the story, particularly in relation to the trail of destruction, arson and looting wrought by the Auxiliaries and Black and Tans once they were introduced in 1920. Historians are constrained by the relative paucity and lack of availability of sources on the British side. There is, for example, no single official list of British casualties. Because the British refused to recognise it as a war, the War of Independence did not even merit its own medal or commendation on the British side, in stark contrast to the commemoration of the struggle by the Irish government and the Irish armed forces.[3] However, David Grant has traced most of the British victims in two linked websites.[4] The first deals with the so-called 'Cairo Gang', an intelligence-gathering squad operating in Dublin. Many of its men were assassinated by Michael Collins' 'Squad' on 21 November 1920, in the first action of Bloody Sunday.[5] The second concentrates on the Auxiliary Division of the Royal Irish Constabulary (RIC), popularly known as the Auxiliaries or Auxies. David has recently expanded these websites to include all members of the British forces killed in Ireland. This book has, with David's permission, relied heavily on his work and cross-checked all of his entries to ensure that all the names are recorded.

Even more bizarre than the British attitude, the winning side of the Civil War between Free State forces and the anti-Treaty IRA erected no monument to those soldiers who lost their lives in the service of the state. While it is true that many of the names are inscribed around Michael Collins' grave in Glasnevin Cemetery, that source is in no way comprehensive. In contrast, Co. Cork is sprinkled with monuments to the anti-Treaty (Republican) dead. While it is understandable that the successors of the anti-Treaty IRA, Fianna Fáil, who dominated the state from 1932 to 2011, would have little interest in commemorating their enemies, it is now perhaps time that such a monument was constructed, although there is little doubt that any such suggestion would meet with opposition. Recent suggestions that the seventeen Auxiliaries killed at the Kilmichael ambush and its aftermath might be commemorated in a redevelopment of the site caused such an uproar that strenuous denials were made that this had ever been contemplated.[6]

Part 1 of this book is a brief introduction to the period and examines the more important events which epitomised the conflict in the county from 1916 to 1923. Part 2 is a list of every death that surviving records show can be ascribed to the war, including crossfire and some accidental deaths that can be linked to one side or the other. Some individuals who did not die in the county, but who were central to the conduct of the war there, are also included. One such example is Terence MacSwiney, who died in Brixton Prison in London in October 1920, but was both head of the IRA in Cork and lord mayor of the city, having assumed the role after his predecessor, Tomás MacCurtain, had been assassinated earlier that year.

Sources are usually quoted without comment. This can lead to the semblance of bias in some entries, but this would be an incorrect inference. Clearly, if a British or unionist source is used then the shooting of a member of the RIC, for example, is inevitably referred to as murder. In the BMH witness statements, the same death will be described as a shooting or an execution. The reverse is also true. Pedants will also be disappointed by some of the nomenclature employed. I use Free State, for example, to describe the period from the handover of Dublin Castle in January 1922 to the state's formal creation in December 1922, rather than create a technically correct but turgid construction like proto or nascent Free State. Irregular is rejected in favour of anti-Treaty IRA, as the former was a derogatory term used by the Free State. Using 'Republican' to identify the anti-Treaty IRA is also rejected, because many on the Free State side would also have regarded themselves as republicans. Equally, National Army is preferred to Free State Army, as this is what the soldiers themselves called it.

Richard Kent
*(Author's collection)*

Choosing a start date for the book was simple. On the morning of 2 May 1916 an attempt to arrest the Kent brothers led to the only three deaths in Cork resulting from the Easter Rising. When the RIC arrived at the family home at Bawnard, outside Castlelyons, the resulting shootout left Head Constable Rowe and Richard Kent dead. Rowe was shot in the head while he took cover behind a low wall and Richard was shot in the back when he tried to escape after the family surrendered. Thomas Kent was court-martialled and hanged in Victoria Barracks. Deciding on a date to end the list proved more problematic. Professor Eunan O'Halpin understandably decided to end his national list at the end of 1921.[7] As this clearly leaves out the Civil War, it appeared to me that to stop there would leave out half the story. I further decided that the generally accepted end date for the Civil War in May 1923 was too early, as there were sufficient politically inspired incidents after that to justify continuing until the end of that year. This, of course, omits some politically motivated deaths in 1924 and 1925, but as normality returned, these events became almost as rare as they had been before the war.

The fragmentary Civil War reportage, in comparison to that of the War of Independence, makes the task of identifying the victims of that time period more difficult. This may be partially due to the apparent willingness of both sides to draw a veil over these events and to various attempts to destroy and censor the press. Equally, a certain war-weariness can be detected in the reportage by 1922, where the amount of coverage an individual killing gets can be as little as one sentence. The same event two years earlier would have garnered banner headlines for days.

For each victim recorded, I provide the precise date of death (if known) and the source, the location of the source, the name(s) of the people involved and the outcome for them. Where possible an extract from the original source(s) is quoted. Despite detailed research, it is possible that some individuals have been missed due to the large volume of material available. Where this is the case they will be added to the database for inclusion later. I am confident that the number of omissions, if any, is small. Some names were not included because the decision was taken to exclude 'ordinary' deaths unless the circumstances were such that they suggested the death could, in some way, be linked to the conflict.

I originally intended to include photographs of the dead, but few, if any, of the surviving images were of sufficient quality, so photographs have only been included in Part 1.

Finally, as there were more than 700 deaths during the revolutionary period in Cork city and county, I decided that to expand the book beyond

Cork would be unreasonable. I intend to continue this project and hope to publish the results for other counties in due course. I would also like to encourage other historians to take up this challenge, especially in the under-researched Civil War period, before the folk and family memory of these events is lost forever.

# PART 1
## SIGNIFICANT INCIDENTS IN THE WAR

# THE IRISH REVOLUTION AND CIVIL WAR
## 24 APRIL 1916–24 MAY 1923

When Patrick Pearse surrendered to General William Lowe at 3.30 p.m. on 29 April 1916, the small rebellion of 1,200 Irish Volunteers, Irish Citizen Army and Cumann na mBan that had resulted in the destruction of much of the centre of Dublin and almost 500 deaths was over. The final surrender of arms took place the following day. What became known as the Easter Rising had lasted little more than five days and had been a complete military failure. Unsurprisingly, in England's capital in Ireland, the revolutionaries were spat at as they were marched to Richmond Barracks after their surrender.[1]

The newly appointed military governor, General John Maxwell, immediately commenced courts martial of the leaders, and British Prime Minister Herbert H. Asquith informed the House of Commons on 3 May that 'P. H. Pearse, Thomas J. Clarke, and Thomas MacDonagh, were tried by court martial, found guilty and sentenced to death by being shot. The sentence was duly carried out this morning.'[2] A further eleven executions took place in Dublin over the next nine days, and Thomas Kent was executed in Cork on 9

Thomas Kent
*(Courtesy of Mercier Press)*

May.[3] On 3 August Roger Casement was executed by hanging in Pentonville Prison in London after a trial for treason against the British Crown.[4] A further 3,500 Irish Volunteers and Sinn Féin members were arrested, and approximately 1,300 of them were interned. Many of them were released over the following months, with the final 600 internees from Frongoch Internment Camp in North Wales freed at the end of December. However, around fifty ringleaders were kept in English prisons until the middle of 1917.[5]

The rebellion came while an Irish Home Rule Act was on the statute books. The Act had been passed, although it was suspended in September 1914 for the duration of the Great War. In the circumstances many Irish nationalists were incredulous that anybody saw a need to rebel. Indeed, one of the reasons for the initial success of the Rising was that the British authorities ignored intelligence reports of a possible rebellion, having checked with Irish Parliamentary Party (IPP) leaders John Redmond and, more importantly, John Dillon. Dillon was in Ireland more often than Redmond and his opinion was trusted by Augustine Birrell, the chief secretary for Ireland. Both men assured the authorities that nothing serious was happening. This, combined with the capture of the German arms ship *Aud* off the Kerry coast and the cancellation of Easter Sunday manoeuvres by the Irish Volunteers' leader Eoin MacNeill, had persuaded Birrell, who was in London, that the planned rising had been called off.[6] Indeed, his under-secretary, Sir Matthew Nathan, having eventually agreed the night before to arrest the Irish Volunteer leadership, was sitting in his office in Dublin Castle waiting for permission from Birrell when the building was attacked. Incredibly, he had not thought it necessary to increase the guard on either the castle or the vice-regal lodge, both of which were guarded by little more than ten men. According to the evidence of Lord Lieutenant Lord Wimborne at the subsequent inquiry, once the Irish Volunteers had shot Constable James O'Brien at the castle gate, 'They could walk right in, of course.' If they had, they would have captured Major Price, the director of military intelligence, who 'was talking to Sir Mathew [*sic*] Nathan in his office not 25 yards from the gate when the firing commenced'.[7] Arthur Hamilton Norway, head of the Irish Post Office, had also just arrived at the castle.[8]

A plaintive dispatch sent to Birrell by Wimborne on Easter Monday afternoon set out the situation:

... the worst had happened just when we thought it averted. The Post Office is seized – Nathan still besieged in the Castle, but I hope he will be soon out. Almost all wires cut. Bridges blown up. Everybody away on holiday.[9]

The reaction of the British government in the aftermath of the Rising was understandable, but they failed to listen to John Redmond or to Edward Carson, leader of the Ulster Unionist Party, who were both urging leniency and extreme caution.[10] The executions changed the public mood in Ireland and the IPP lost ground to a re-emergent Sinn Féin, which had gained credibility by being blamed (in the wrong) for the Rising. From 1916 to 1918 various attempts were made to reach a political settlement, most notably the Buckingham Palace Conference of 1916 and the Irish Convention of 1918, but came to nothing.[11] The public continued to turn away from the IPP as a result of these repeated failures. In the general election of 1918 Sinn Féin swept the IPP out of power everywhere except in parts of Ulster.

On 21 January 1919 twenty-seven of Sinn Féin's sixty-nine TDs (some of whom held more than one seat) met at the Mansion House in Dublin and ratified a Declaration of Independence. Separately, on the same day two members of the RIC were killed in Soloheadbeg, Co. Tipperary – the Irish War of Independence had 'officially' begun.[12]

In comparison with the industrial slaughter of the Great War, what happened in Ireland during the War of Independence is best summed up by British Lord Chancellor F. E. Smith, who told the House of Lords on 21 June 1921:

In judging whether noble Lords are right, or whether the Government are right, in this matter, do not, at least, let us add to all our other errors, errors in which all Parties and sections have shared, this further error that we did not look around us now and with clear and undeceived eyes realise what is going on at this moment in Ireland. It is no longer even, in a phrase once used by an illustrious predecessor of mine, 'a kind of war'. It is a small war that is going on in Ireland.[13]

This is not in any way to diminish the effect of the war on the countryside, the combatants or the civilians caught in the crossfire, who numbered in their tens of thousands. However, the raw figures of 2,819 homicides between January 1919 and December 1923 show how little it affected the majority of the population in a country where the average number of deaths in any one year was in excess of 75,000.[14] To put it in further perspective, on the first day of the Battle of the Somme on the Western Front (1 July 1916) the Ulster Division lost 2,069 officers and men killed and missing, which is only 750 less than the total for five years of war in Ireland. The figures also point to the central position Cork occupied in the revolution. More than 30 per cent of all the homicides recorded took place in this one county. During the most violent years, 1921 and 1922, there was at least one violent death every second day on average in the county.[15] Not for nothing did Cork earn its nickname, the 'Rebel County'.

On 6 December 1921 a Treaty was signed between an Irish delegation and a British delegation which set out the future constitutional relationship between the two countries. Ireland would have dominion status within the British Empire, while six northern counties that already had a Home Rule parliament in Belfast would have the option of seceding from this Irish parliament, pending the demarcation of both parts by an ill-defined Boundary Commission.[16] Crucially, this new Free State dominion was to have fiscal independence. Six weeks later the Provisional Government of Southern Ireland was inaugurated at Dublin Castle when Michael Collins handed an endorsed copy of the Treaty to the British viceroy, Lord Fitzalan, who then relinquished control to the Provisional Government. Collins had been nominated as chairman of the new government at a meeting of the Parliament of Southern Ireland on 14 January.[17] A few hours later he issued a statement announcing the 'surrender of Dublin Castle', much to the chagrin of the British government and members of the House of Lords.[18]

Early on the morning of 14 April 1922 forces opposed to the Treaty and the creation of the Free State occupied the Four Courts in central Dublin. Led by Rory O'Connor, who described himself as leader of the 'left wing of the IRA', the stated aims were to maintain the Republic, end the Provisional

Government, retain the IRA under the control of an independent executive, disband the new Civic Guard in favour of the Irish Republican Police (IRP), pay the army's bills and ensure that no elections were held while a threat of war with England existed.[19] The leaders of the anti-Treaty IRA had not sanctioned the occupation and it is likely that it was a response to Churchill's speech in the House of Commons, which had been reported on 13 April:

> Whatever happens in Ireland, however many years of misfortune there may be in Ireland, whatever trouble, the Treaty defines what we think should be the relations between the two countries, and we are prepared, and will be prepared, to hand over to any responsible body of Irishmen capable of governing the country the full powers which the Treaty confers. Further than that, in no circumstances will we go, and if a republic is set up, that is a form of government in Ireland which the British Empire can in no circumstances whatever tolerate or agree to.[20]

The occupation resulted not in an immediate attack but in negotiations. These continued throughout the months of May and June, when proposals to unify the army were put to the 'Four Courts' Executive and finally narrowly rejected on 22 June 1922. A proposal by Tom Barry to this meeting to declare war on the British was defeated after a recount and those anti-Treaty IRA who had supported Barry's suggestion retreated to the Four Courts and closed the doors.[21] Early on the morning of 28 June, after an ultimatum to quit the building had been ignored, the National Army attacked the building and the Civil War commenced. The conflict soon drew in many other members of the anti-Treaty IRA, including Liam Lynch, who returned to the role of chief of staff after the capture of Joe McKelvey on 29 June.[22]

The Civil War effectively ended on 30 April 1923, shortly after the death of Lynch and a subsequent order to 'dump arms' issued to anti-Treaty forces by the new leader, Frank Aiken, on 23 May 1923. This was to come into effect the following day. For good or ill, after eight years the British had left Southern Ireland and the government of the Irish Free State had secured control over its territory.

# CORK 1916–1919

The period between Easter Monday 1916 and the meeting of the First Dáil on 21 January 1919 was virtually non-lethal in Cork city. During the week of the 1916 rebellion no shot was fired in the city by either side. After 'shuttle diplomacy' by Roman Catholic coadjutor Bishop Daniel Cohalan and Lord Mayor Thomas C. Butterfield, the Volunteers agreed to surrender all of their weapons into the lord mayor's custody by agreement of the British commander in the city. Breaching the agreement that the surrendered weapons would eventually be returned to their owners, the military confiscated them, much to the annoyance of Bishop Cohalan, who wrote to the *Cork Free Press* outlining the sequence of these events.[1]

Outside the city, Volunteers had assembled at Macroom on Easter Sunday. Their original objective had been 'the obstruction and delaying of British forces at Millstreet and Rathmore by cutting the railway line' in order to protect the arms shipment, which, as far as they knew, was to be landed from the *Aud* in Tralee Bay. They had been mobilised despite being informed on the night of Good Friday that the arms had been captured. The Volunteers returned to Cork city by train after hearing of MacNeill's command to cancel all manoeuvres for Easter Sunday.[2]

In due course inquiries were set up by the Irish Republican Brotherhood (IRB) and the Irish Volunteer Executive to inquire into the failure of Cork, Limerick and Waterford to rise. Both inquiries found that as a result of nine countermanding orders, the sinking of the *Aud* and the loss of the vital arms it carried, it had been impossible for Cork to rise.[3]

This did not mean that Cork was generally pliant. After the majority of internees were released from Frongoch in December 1916, the Volunteers and Sinn Féin in the county spent much time reorganising. However, with the exception of the incident at the Kent family home in May 1916, only one other individual died between 1916 and 1919 who might reasonably be described as having been killed for political reasons. This was Abraham Allen, who died after being bayonetted during a riot on 24 June 1917. Republican prisoners had been granted a general amnesty and their return had resulted in pro-Sinn Féin demonstrations across the city centre. Around 9 p.m. police with rifles and fixed bayonets clashed with a huge crowd near St Patrick's Bridge, which had spent the previous hour on Patrick's Street destroying the recruiting office and fighting off a counter-demonstration by 'separation women', whose husbands were at the Front. Reinforcements under RIC District Inspector Oswald Ross Swanzy managed to contain the situation, but the police were unable to regain control until the military arrived from Victoria Barracks. The threat of machine-gun fire eventually persuaded the crowd to disperse.[4]

This was the first, and most serious, of the riots in the city which continued until the end of the year. Yet the Irish Volunteers remained a small force. For example, until the conscription crisis of April 1918, the Queenstown/Cobh Company of Volunteers had no more than forty members.[5]

The attempt to extend conscription to Ireland was a disastrous error of judgement by the British government. In March 1918 the British Army was desperate for fresh troops to replace the men lost during Operation Michael, the German offensive on the Western Front that drove a wedge between the British and the French. On 9 April British Prime Minister David Lloyd George had announced the conscription policy, but it had the unintended consequence of pushing Sinn Féin towards respectability when the party joined forces with the Roman Catholic hierarchy and the IPP to oppose the move.[6] In Cork, Patrick Murray, who later became a member of the Volunteers' Cork City active service unit (ASU), noted that there was only one Volunteer brigade in the city and county, with six battalions, until the conscription crisis; by January 1919 the organisation had rapidly expanded to twenty battalions.[7] At this stage the IRA divided into three brigades roughly equating to the three main river valleys in the county: Blackwater

(Cork No. 2 Brigade), Lee (Cork No. 1 Brigade) and Bandon (Cork No. 3 Brigade).

Conscription was never introduced to Ireland and by the end of the Great War the voluntary recruitment campaign designed to paper over the cracks of the debacle had managed to persuade only 840 Cork recruits to join up out of an initial target of 5,250. The initial total of 50,000 for the whole country had been reduced to a paltry 10,000 and the figures for Cork show that it did not even reach its equivalent proportion of the reduced total. Those who did join up flocked to the RAF and the navy, both of which were safer than the army.[8]

The general change in mood towards the war from the initial optimism of 1914 was palpable, as this motion passed by the workhouse Board of Guardians in response to its Church of Ireland chaplain's call to arms shows:

> That the Cork Board of Guardians have seen with surprise that the Reverend Treasurer Nicholson have [sic] made a public declaration in favour of Conscription … in order to put his martial spirit to the test we are willing to offer him every facility to join the colours … we are sure his Four [sic] sons … will follow his example.[9]

While the conscription crisis had eased by early May, with the containment of the German advance outside the strategic railway junction of Hazebrouck between 12 and 29 April, the British viceroy provided Sinn Féin with a second propaganda victory almost immediately. On the night of 16–17 May, 150 senior members of the party were arrested and interned in England as part of the 'German Plot'. According to British Intelligence the Germans had contacted Sinn Féin and were planning an expedition to Ireland. The information had come from John Dowling, who had been arrested in Clare having been landed from a U-boat.[10] While there is some evidence that the Germans were attempting to contact Sinn Féin, the arrest of the leaders kept the focus on the party in the lead-up to the general election in December

1918. Inevitably, Michael Collins, who had warned the leadership of their imminent arrest but was not believed, escaped. As he was one of the few party leaders not in prison, he chose many of the prisoners to represent the party in the election.[11] The slogan 'Put them in to get them out' was coined for the occasion.[12]

Exactly seven days after the armistice of 11 November 1918 brought the Great War to a close, Lloyd George announced the much-delayed general election. For the first time every male over eighteen and every female over thirty would be entitled to vote. The electorate in Ireland had increased from just over 700,000 to almost 2,000,000.[13] The national result was extraordinary. Across Ireland two parties achieved landslides: Sinn Féin took seventy-three of the 105 seats available, while the Ulster Unionists took twenty-two seats, the majority of which were in the north-east. The IPP, which had dominated nationalist politics since 1880, was practically wiped out.[14] Sinn Féin was in such a strong position in Munster that their candidates in nineteen of the twenty-five constituencies were unopposed. The only Munster constituency which was contested by a unionist was Cork city, where Sinn Féin received 41,308 votes, the IPP 14,642 and the unionists 4,773.[15] Patrick O'Keeffe (Pádraig Ó Caoimh) for Cork North and Thomas Hunter for Cork North East were in prison at the time of their election.

By the time the House of Commons assembled in London in early February 1919, the situation in Ireland had been transformed. The Sinn Féin members who were at liberty had assembled at the Mansion House in Dublin on 21 January and proclaimed independence. Out of nine Cork TDs, only J. J. Walsh and Seán Ó hAodha answered the roll call.[16] One of the Dáil's first acts was to send Seán T. O'Kelly to the Paris Peace Conference seeking recognition of the 'Provisional Government' from the American president, Woodrow Wilson, and to press the French premier, Georges Clemenceau (the official host), for 'the international recognition of the independence of Ireland'.[17] His attempts were rebuffed and, in an article dripping with condescension, *The New York Times* suggested that O'Kelly might be 'cooling his heels for a very long time' if he was waiting for a reply from President Wilson.[18] Not a single word of this was mentioned in the British parliament: it was as if it hadn't happened.[19]

Collins engineered a spectacular propaganda coup when he and Harry Boland rescued Éamon de Valera, Seán McGarry and Seán Milroy from Lincoln Prison on 3 February 1919. De Valera literally took a taxi to freedom and returned to Dublin on 20 February, where he was elected president (Príomh Aire) of Dáil Éireann on 1 April.[20] Unsurprisingly, the escape made international news and the British looked particularly foolish as the prisoners had apparently walked through locked doors. It was three hours before the escape was discovered.[21]

This was the most spectacular escape organised by Collins, but others included Robert Barton from Mountjoy Prison on 16 March, followed a few weeks later by Piaras Béaslaí, J. J. Walsh, Thomas Malone, Paddy Fleming and fifteen other prisoners, who escaped over the wall of the same prison. Warders were kept at bay by other prisoners armed with 'revolvers', which turned out to be spoons. In October Austin Stack and Béaslaí (who had been re-captured) escaped with four others from Strangeways Prison in Manchester. All of this kept the Irish story on the front pages in Britain and around the world.[22]

Inevitably, the standoff between the Irish and British parliaments would have to be resolved. Already, in Tipperary, Dan Breen and Seán Treacy had shot dead RIC constables Patrick MacDonnell and James O'Connell during a raid for gelignite at Soloheadbeg. On 1 February 1919 *An t-Óglách* (the internal newspaper of the Irish Volunteers) declared war on the British. It was unambiguous: '[Dáil Éireann] claims the same power and authority as any other lawfully constituted Government; it sanctions the employment by the Irish Volunteers of the most drastic measures against the enemies of Ireland. The soldiers and police of the invader are liable to be treated exactly as invading enemy soldiers would be treated by the native army of any country.'[23] Thus the stage was set for the War of Independence.

# THE MURDER OF LORD MAYOR TOMÁS MacCURTAIN AND THE 'STOLEN' JURY

On 19 March 1920 Sinn Féin Lord
Mayor of Cork Tomás MacCurtain
wrote to his colleague Liam de Róiste,
TD, arranging to meet Bishop Daniel
Cohalan the following day. Signifying
the profound change that had occurred
in the local elections, when Sinn Féin
and their allies in Labour obtained an
overall majority despite the use of the
new proportional representation elec-
toral system, the letter and the lord
mayor's headed notepaper were in Irish.

Tomás MacCurtain
(*Courtesy of Mercier Press*)

Later that night Constable Joseph
Murtagh of the RIC was shot dead on Pope's Quay by members of the IRA
as he returned from the funeral of his colleague Constable Charles Healy,
who had been shot in Toomevara, Co. Tipperary, on 16 March. According
to Patrick Murray, O/C of 'C' Company, 1st Battalion, Cork No. 1 Brigade,
Murtagh was killed 'by two members of my company (Christy MacSwiney
and — O'Connell) on instructions from the brigade'. He continued:

> It was reported that Detective Murtagh was endeavouring to get information
> from Martin Condon who had been captured by the British in an attack on
> a barrack in Liam Lynch's brigade area. Condon was being held prisoner in
> the military barracks in Cork at the time, and it was known that this detective
> was using extreme methods on him in order to procure information regarding
> Volunteer activities.[1]

After the shooting, the gunmen went to Blackpool, to the house of Peg Duggan at 49 Thomas Davis Street, which was directly opposite MacCurtain's home. Duggan and her sister had taken the two men to Sunday's Well and when returning home had noticed 'queer looking fellas' on Blackpool Bridge, within yards of the lord mayor's house. Duggan described what happened next:

> We went to bed and noticed the gas lamps being put out, my sister passing a remark: 'There is old Keane putting out the gas lamps.' This fixed the time at about 12.30 a.m. Very shortly afterwards, we heard a thundering knock at a door, followed by shots up and down the street. My sister Annie looked out a window and said: 'They are at Tomas's house.' Next we heard another few shots ring out and then a cry: 'A priest, a priest, will someone go for a priest?' Annie and I jumped out of bed and put on coats over our night attire. We could hear a woman's voice crying: 'A priest, a priest.' We ran up to the presbytery attached to the Cathedral and met Rev. Father Burts, one of the curates ... Father Burts did not know where Tomas lived and asked us to show him the way. The priest, my sister Annie and myself arrived at McCurtain's [*sic*] in a very short time and were met by Mrs. McCurtain who said: 'Thank God, Father, you are in time.' Father Burts heard Tomas's confession on the stairs landing. Tomas was lying there where he was shot, but was conscious. We were present while he was being anointed and, after the anointing, he died where he lay.[2]

Shortly after MacCurtain was killed in front of his wife and children, the house was raided by the military, who conducted a detailed search, including under the bed where the lord mayor's body lay. Of course, Tomás MacCurtain was not only lord mayor, but also the brigade commander of the IRA, and his funeral on 22 March was used as a major demonstration of IRA strength, with thousands marching in the cortège and a volley of shots being fired over his grave.

Immediately after his murder, the British suggested that MacCurtain had been killed by members of the IRA because he was not radical enough and had fallen out with them.[3] This was despite the mountain of evidence from witnesses that linked an RIC-led gang to the attack. According to ex-RIC officer Michael Feeley, on the morning of 19 March the military had linked MacCurtain to an attack on Viceroy Lord French in December 1919. It was decided to arrest and intern the lord mayor. At the meeting the Cork RIC, led by District Inspector Swanzy, had stated that MacCurtain was a moderate, so the revelation that he was an active gunman must have come as a shock to them.[4] The inquest into the killing went through the events of the night in minute detail. A gas lamplighter working on King Street provided crucial evidence which proved that the police had, against regulations, left King Street Barracks, which was only a few minutes from the MacCurtains' house, after the killing of Murtagh.

Only seven people had answered the coroner's initial summonses for the inquest. Corkonians of all creeds and classes were traditionally well known for avoiding jury duty, so this would have been of little surprise. However, at this stage of the war Sinn Féin had begun to ban people from any involvement with the British state and it was proving difficult to hold assizes courts, especially in Munster.

Minutes before the inquest was supposed to open, the coroner was still under pressure to find jurymen after an ex-RIC man, Mr Sherman, had asked to be excused, stating: 'I have a summons in my pocket signed by you, but if there is no objection I'd rather be off.'[5] Finally, the coroner managed to find a jury of sixteen to take on the task, despite the potential threat.

So who were these brave souls? The foreman was W. J. Barry, and the other members were Michael J. Grace, Melville McWilliams, Jeremiah O'Callaghan, Joseph Kiely, Florence O'Donoghue, Daniel Barrett, Thomas O'Shaughnessy, D. Hennessy, Patrick McGrath, Peter O'Donovan, Tadhg O'Sullivan, Padraig O'Sullivan, Wilfred Perry, Richard Barrett and Harry Lorton. Some of these names will be readily identifiable to those familiar with the War of Independence in Cork. Tadhg O'Sullivan was shot on Douglas Street by the police while trying to escape from a raid on an IRA brigade meeting in April 1921. He had just returned from London after an abortive attempt to assassinate Essex Regiment Intelligence Officer Major Arthur Percival. He was the captain of 'C' Company, and at the time of his death it was noted that he was on the MacCurtain jury. Harry Lorton (sometimes written Loreton) was a founder member of the Irish Volunteers, while Wilfred Perry had joined that organisation on its first day.[6] Although there was a Florence O'Donoghue on the jury, which also happened to be the name of the chief IRA spymaster in Cork, and while the person on the left of a contemporary photograph of the jury looks very similar to him, there is no corroboration that this was in fact the IRA spymaster.[7] Of the other jury members, Daniel Barrett had joined the Irish Volunteers in 1914, Richard Barrett was a member of the Young Ireland Society, Patrick McGrath was an IRA member and a future lord mayor of the city, and Peter O'Donovan was the O/C of the Cork City ASU in April 1922. That all these men were sitting on the same jury was an extraordinary coup for the IRA.

The result of the inquest, announced on 10 April, was shocking and made headlines around the world.[8] The sixteen-man jury concluded:

> We find that the late Alderman MacCurtain, Lord Mayor of Cork, died from shock and hemorrhage [*sic*] caused by bullet wounds, and that he was willfully [*sic*] murdered under circumstances of the most callous brutality, and that the murder was organised and carried out by the Royal Irish Constabulary, officially directed by the British Government, and we return a verdict of willful murder against David Lloyd George, Prime Minister of England; Lord French, Lord Lieutenant of Ireland; Ian McPherson, late Chief Secretary of Ireland; Acting Inspector General Smith of the Royal Irish Constabulary; Divisional Inspector Clayton of the Royal Irish Constabulary; District Inspector Swanzy and some unknown members of the Royal Irish Constabulary. We strongly condemn the system at present in vogue of carrying out raids at unreasonable hours. We tender to Mrs. MacCurtain and family our sincerest sympathy. We extend to the citizens of Cork our sympathy in the loss they have sustained by the death of one so eminently capable of directing their civic administration.[9]

The propaganda value of the jury calling Lloyd George a murderer was immense.[10]

The jury that sat on the inquest into Tomás MacCurtain's death.
(*Courtesy of Mercier Press*)

# THE DEATH OF COLONEL SMYTH

Lieutenant Colonel Gerald Brice Ferguson Smyth, the divisional police commissioner for Munster, returned to Cork from Co. Kerry on 17 July and checked into the Cork County Club on the South Mall. As he was not expected, he telegraphed ahead. This message was intercepted in the telegraph office in Cork by a telegraph officer who was also an IRA courier and passed on to Volunteer Seán O'Hegarty.[1] Ned Fitzgerald, a waiter who worked in the club, confirmed that Smyth was staying there.[2] A squad was quickly assembled consisting of 'Daniel ("Sando" [sic]) Donovan, Jack Culhane, Cornelius O'Sullivan, Seán O'Donoghue, J. J. O'Connell and myself [Daniel Healy]'.[3]

At approximately 10 p.m. Colonel Smyth was sitting in the lounge of the club with RIC County Inspector Craig. Seán Culhane described what happened next:

> The five whom I have named above [Donovan, O'Sullivan, O'Donoghue, O'Connell and Healy] remained at the opposite side of the street and I went across to the entrance of the Club and met 'Bally' [Fitzgerald], who told me that Smyth was still inside. I took off my cap and ran my fingers twice through my hair, which was the signal arranged with my comrades. They immediately came to the Club entrance and with 'Bally' in front of us, as if at the point of the gun, he moved to where Smyth was sitting in the room and faced him. This was arranged to ensure that we got the right man.
>
> We opened fire simultaneously, without any preliminaries, and most of our shots hit the target. Smyth made an effort with his one arm to make for his gun but collapsed in the attempt – he must have died at once.[4]

The shooting of Smyth had its genesis in a speech he had given to quell a mutiny among RIC officers in Listowel Barracks on 19 June. He had arrived in Listowel with 'Police Advisor' Major General Henry Hugh Tudor, as part of a tour of Kerry.[5] The speech, which was written down by the leader of the rebellion, Constable Jeremiah Mee, and published in *The Freeman's Journal* on 10 July, outlined Smyth's version of what the British government intended to happen over the coming months. According to Mee, Smyth said:

> Police and military will patrol the country roads at least five nights a week. They are not to confine themselves to the main roads but take across country [*sic*], lie in ambush, take cover behind fences, near the roads, and, when civilians are seen approaching, shout 'hands up'. Should the order be not immediately obeyed, shoot, and shoot with effect. If the persons approaching carry their hands in their pockets or are in any way suspicious looking, shoot them down. You may make mistakes occasionally and innocent persons may be shot, but this cannot be helped and you are bound to get the right persons sometimes. The more you shoot, the better I will like you, and I assure you that no policeman will get into trouble for shooting any man. In the past, policemen have got into trouble for giving evidence at coroners' inquests. As a matter of fact, inquests are to be made illegal so that in future no policeman will be asked to give evidence at inquests. Hunger strikers will be allowed to die in jail, the more the merrier.[6]

Mee, who had already persuaded his colleagues to disobey an order to turn over the barracks to the military, replied:

> 'By your accent, I take it you are an Englishman. You forget you are addressing Irishmen.' He checked me there and said he was a North of Ireland man from Banbridge in the County Down. I said, 'I am an Irishman and very proud of it.' Taking off my uniform cap, I laid it on the table in front of Colonel Smyth and said, 'This is English, you may have it as a present from me.' Having done this, I completely lost my temper and, taking off my belt and sword, clapped them down on the table, saying, 'These too are English and you may have them. To Hell with you, you are a murderer.' At this, Colonel Smyth quietly said to District Inspector Flanagan, 'Place that man under arrest.'[7]

To Smyth's surprise, fourteen of Mee's colleagues also resigned and proceeded to rescue Mee, while at the same time threatening the senior officers, who withdrew rather than exacerbate the situation. Colonel Smyth's party went on to Tralee, where they were refused a hearing, and then to Killarney, where they were met with shouts of 'Up Listowel' according to Mee, who had apparently tipped off his comrades there.[8] Irish Chief Secretary Sir Hamar Greenwood explained to the House of Commons that Smyth had not exceeded what the attorney-general for Ireland, Denis Henry, had said on 22 June.[9] Yet all Henry had said was, 'If they have reason to suspect that a person approaching them is in possession of deadly weapons they are to call on him to put up his hands, and, failing his doing so, they are to fire upon him. It is impossible to give more explicit instructions.'[10] Smyth's version of his address to the men, which could at best be said to be a generous interpretation of what Henry actually said, was printed in *The Irish Times* after his death, and it is hard not to conclude that Mee's recollection of what was said is correct.[11]

Smyth's death led to indiscriminate reprisals by British forces over the following two days. These resulted in at least three deaths (James Bourke, William McGrath and John O'Brien) and a host of civilians being treated in all the Cork hospitals for gunshot wounds. The official report stated that there had been rioting in the city, but all the local newspapers described armoured cars being driven through the streets and firing wildly around Parliament Bridge and along the nearby South Mall. Indeed, William McGrath was killed by a bullet fired from an armoured car, having just saved a child from being run over in the middle of North Main Street.[12]

# THE DISAPPEARANCE
# OF JOHN COUGHLAN

In August 1920 John Coughlan, who lived in Cottrell's Row in Queenstown (now Cobh), was kidnapped by the IRA and taken across Cork Harbour to Aghada on the south side. Two of his daughters were 'keeping company' with British soldiers stationed in the town and, as the IRA had issued warnings against fraternising with the enemy, this was always going to be a risk. Years later Ernie O'Malley, who was recording the recollections of participants in the War of Independence, interviewed Michael Leahy. Leahy had been the head of the IRA in the area. O'Malley records Leahy as saying:

> The strangest thing about the first spy who met his death through us was that we didn't shoot him. In Cobh we arrested this fellow ... and we took him to Aghada and we wanted to scare him for a while. He was kept in Mary Higgins' in a loft and there was a young girl there. She was bringing him his breakfast when she found him hanging from a rafter, dead. We were in a jamb [*sic*] then, for he had been arrested in broad daylight, so I got 4 lads to bury him. Paddy Sullivan from Cobh who was later executed in Cork gaol after he had been caught in Clonmult. [*sic*] Later on he asked me 'did you see "the Examiner".' And when I read it I found that a body which had been tied to an axle had been washed up on Inch Strand. The lads had not buried him. They had tied him to an old car axle and had flung him out into the sea. He was in a morgue in Middleton [*sic*], I was told, in the workhouse. 'Did you search his clothes?' I asked. 'No, but we knew his face.'[1]

Like many of the stories told by the IRA, the huge problem with this was that it lacked verification. Certainly there was no doubt that John Coughlan had been abducted from Cobh, as a war office file in the National Archives at Kew discussed prosecuting individuals who had been involved in the abduction.[2] The problem lay with being able to find any public record that confirmed the story of the recovery of his body. However, the digitisation of newspapers across the world has created a revolution in historical research. A tiny reference in the *Lincolnshire Post* mentioned a body tied to a cartwheel found five miles from Cloyne.[3] After a meeting with his grandchildren, who had heard the same story, a search of *The Irish Times* found two linked articles, which confirmed all the details of Leahy's story. John Coughlan's body had been found on Ballybranagan beach in East Cork.[4] The body had been taken to the nearest town with a morgue (Midleton) and, when nobody claimed it after two days, it was buried in St James's, the workhouse cemetery at Knockgriffin.[5]

# THE FUNERAL
# OF TERENCE MacSWINEY

OUTSIDE BRIXTON PRISON 23. 10. '20.
Diary of week of Terry's greatest torture and of the English Government's
and English Doctor's low malice in excluding us from his deathbed.

Áine MacSwiney[1]

On Saturday 23 October 1920 Terence
MacSwiney's sisters, Máire and Áine,
were banned from their brother's bedside
by the Home Office, which had become
increasingly frustrated at their continuing
belligerence towards the doctors and with
the regular press conferences they held
for the Irish and international media
outside the gates of Brixton Prison in
central London. They were ushered out of
the gates at 10.55 p.m. and driven down
Brixton Road. They would not see their
brother alive again.

Terence MacSwiney
(*Courtesy of Mercier Press*)

Alderman Terence MacSwiney, Tomás MacCurtain's successor as lord
mayor of Cork and commandant of Cork No. 1 Brigade of the IRA, passed
away in Brixton Prison at 5.20 a.m. on 25 October, after a hunger strike
lasting seventy-four days.[2] On the same day Joseph Murphy died in Cork,
having survived for three hours longer, but it was MacSwiney's dramatic
gesture in the centre of London that captured the world's attention.[3]

While the Cabinet had set its face against the release of the hunger
strikers, it was aware of the impact of MacSwiney's death and feared
repercussions among the British public and the possible effect on American

public opinion in the run-up to the presidential election that year. The Irish side (including MacSwiney) had been interested in keeping the spectacle going for as long as it could, certain in the knowledge that every day the lord mayor survived the Irish revolution would stay centre stage in world news. However, outside these narrow political calculations was the appalling human tragedy of a man deliberately starving himself to death in pursuit of a political goal, which *The Irish Times* ungraciously described on the morning after his death as 'a thing of folly and crime which is sacrificing Ireland's peace and progress to the pursuit of an impossible dream'.[4]

MacSwiney's death presented the British government with a practical problem: how to dispose of the body. If they buried MacSwiney in the prison grounds, his sisters were likely to continue their vigil outside Brixton Prison with all the inevitable bad press that would bring. However, if they handed the body over to the family, then the procession through Dublin and Cork would be an enormous propaganda opportunity for the IRA and Sinn Féin to exploit. This could not be allowed.

After the inquest on the following Wednesday, at 11 a.m., the Home Office declined to release the body, informing the family 'that a government vessel would be placed at [their] disposal, free of all expense, and every facility offered if [they] would go straight to Cork'.[5] Assisted by Sinn Féin's press representative in London, Art O'Brien, the family refused. MacSwiney's wife, Muriel, asked to see Home Secretary Edward Shortt and demanded her husband's body. Initially, Shortt refused, allegedly seeking more time to consider whether he had the legal authority, but in the face of mounting pressure (and not a little embarrassment according to O'Brien) the body was released at 7 p.m. and taken to Southwark Cathedral. Following Requiem Mass on Thursday morning, the funeral procession went to Euston Station through crowded and silent streets, passing in sight of Westminster Palace on the way.[6] The family left Euston at 6 p.m. on a special train accompanied by three carriages full of police, Deputy Lord Mayor of Cork Donal O'Callaghan, Bishop Mannix of Australia, Art O'Brien and other supporters.

After the train had passed Crewe, they were informed that the police had orders from Chief Secretary Hamar Greenwood to take the body directly to Cork. This was done to avoid a funeral procession in Dublin, which would undoubtedly have been far larger than the London event.

At Holyhead the family attempted to prevent the police taking the body. Áine MacSwiney's diary recalled:

> Sean and Min were at the end nearest the entrance; next were Fred and myself. Art O'Brien, Fr. Dominic, Fr. Dan Walsh and Desmond Murphy were at the other side. Mid O'Hegarty, Geraldine O'Sullivan, Aileen O'Sullivan and May Foley were all there ... Sean (our own Sean) and Min got the brunt of it, they were dragged from the coffin; Min was lifted off her feet and thrown out of the van. Sean tried to protect her; he had his arm around her, and three huge police attacked him in front; one of them struck Min in the face, while a military officer jumped at him from behind, caught him by the collar and tried to choke him ...
>
> I was still in the van at the time; after Min and Sean had been dragged out, the police came at the rest of us. I was pushed from behind away from the coffin and, having nothing to catch on to, they got me easily away. I tried to get back again, but a cordon of police surrounded the coffin, and it was impossible to get back. In the same way, everyone was either pushed or dragged from the coffin.[7]

The police took their trophy and headed to the waiting steamer, *Rathmore*. The coffin was 'picked up by a crane and was silhouetted against the midnight sky for a moment as it was swung over the side. It was then lowered into the hold.' Two hours later the family boarded the ferry for Kingstown (Dún Laoghaire), having told the stationmaster that they refused 'to accompany you and your nefarious expedition'.[8] On their arrival in Dublin, Sinn Féin held a funeral procession for the lord mayor, with his family following an empty hearse through the streets to Kingsbridge (Heuston) Station.

The *Rathmore* reached Queenstown (Cobh) early the following morning and the lord mayor's body was brought by tug to the Customs House Quay at Cork to be handed over to the deputy lord mayor. As he was with the family in Dublin, Cork Corporation officials refused to accept the body, stating that 'No one had any authority to receive the Lord Mayor's body in the absence of the Lord Mayor's relatives.'[9] The tug lay at anchor outside City Hall with the coffin surrounded by Auxiliaries, soldiers and police. Eventually, at 10 p.m., the family took possession of their brother's body and he was laid in state in City Hall. On Sunday 31 October, following Requiem Mass, he was brought through Cork to St Finbarr's Cemetery and buried in the Republican plot. A volley of shots was fired over the grave, but the military did not intervene.

The funeral of Terence MacSwiney. (*Courtesy of Mercier Press*)

While the death of Terence MacSwiney blunted the weapon, there is no doubt that his sacrifice and the subsequent events were a huge victory for the Irish in the propaganda war.[10] The Irish war had gone from being ignored to being on the front pages of the world's newspapers and, more importantly, it had become a central issue in the United States election.

# THE KILMICHAEL AMBUSH

The Kilmichael ambush, lasting 30 minutes, is one of the most controversial topics in the history of this period.[1] An ambush in West Cork by the newly formed Cork No. 3 Brigade IRA flying column resulted in the death of sixteen Auxiliaries on 28 November 1920. Since the Auxiliaries had been introduced to Ireland as a special gendarmerie to combat the growing rebellion and take the fight to the IRA, their slaughter at Kilmichael was a shock to the British and a major morale boost for the Irish.

After the late Peter Hart described the leader of the ambush, Tom Barry, as 'vain, angry and ruthless', claimed that 'Barry's "history" of Kilmichael' was 'riddled with lies and evasions' and said that 'there was no false surrender', which Barry had used to explain the annihilation of the Auxiliaries, the debate over what happened at Kilmichael has attracted historians of the period like no other.[2] Controversy still rages over whether the Auxiliaries were gunned down in cold blood after surrendering, or whether, as Barry claimed, they started shooting again after supposedly surrendering – the so-called 'false surrender' – thus justifying the IRA's actions.

Confusingly, while Hart accepted that versions of the false surrender story were circulating as early as 1921, a fact specifically mentioned in General Frank Crozier's *Ireland Forever*, he insisted that changes in Barry's story over time suggest that the story entered the narrative only after Crozier's book was published in 1932.[3] (Crozier had been head of the Auxiliaries at the time of the attack.) This is not in fact the case, as the false surrender was part of the story used to explain the savagery of the ambush in the first published account by Lionel Curtis, in *Round Table* in June 1921.[4]

Exchanges in the debate have been robust, but one of the difficulties has been that few of the 'combatants' have returned to the core sources to reconstruct what actually happened in the fight, preferring to criticise each others' interpretations of various single items of evidence. This re-examination con-centrates on the BMH witness statements, written thirty years after the event, published eyewitness accounts, a map drawn by the British Army on the day after the ambush (the Fleming map), a sketch map drawn by Tom Barry after the event, and the record of injuries to the Auxiliaries, the first version of which was published three days after the ambush.

Following the Toureen ambush in October 1920, where the first British lorry had simply driven at speed through the attack before anyone could react, Tom Barry, Michael McCarthy and Sonny Dave Crowley scouted possible locations where the same thing could not happen again, in order to attack the Macroom Auxiliaries, who had been raiding the area since their arrival there in late August.[5] The IRA noticed that individual Auxiliary commanders had fallen into a pattern of following the same routes while on patrol, and so the location chosen was on one of these routes, just south of Kilmichael, on the Macroom to Dunmanway road, where two sharp bends meant the lorries had to slow down.

Michael McCarthy
(*Courtesy of Mercier Press*)

On the chosen day, the IRA contingent arrived at approximately 8 a.m. Barry then divided his force into five groups.[6] He set up a command post at the eastern bend with his second-in-command, Michael McCarthy, 150 metres to the west. Just north-west of Barry's command post, ten men were placed on a low hill to provide flanking fire once the lead lorry was stopped. As the road was narrow, stopping the first lorry would inevitably halt the convoy. It was the job of Barry's group at the command post to do this. Another squad of six riflemen was placed 50 metres opposite them on the south of the road, at a point from which they could fire on both ambush sites if the Auxiliaries attempted to take cover south of the road. Scouts kept watch to the north and south of the site. Another group of six riflemen was placed well behind and above McCarthy's section, in case the patrol consisted of three lorries instead of the expected two – these men would engage the third lorry. They took no part in the actual fighting as they could have hit their own men.

The nature of the terrain meant that McCarthy's group of three was low down and very close to the side of the road, with six men behind them and Ned Young across the road. McCarthy sent Young to the south side of the road before the ambush to prevent the Auxiliaries taking cover around a farm lane opposite his position. Jack Hennessy, John Lordan and Michael McCarthy had no cover as they lay on their low rock metres above the road, so they built a low wall while they were waiting. Because the column had broken camp just after midnight, the men had had no food since the day before, apart from a 'bucket of tea' from a nearby farm.

Half an hour before sunset, at around 4 p.m., approaching Auxiliary lorries were spotted by the scouts.[7] Tom Barry was most likely talking to Michael McCarthy, either about two late arrivals or about calling the ambush off, when news of the lorries was signalled to him. He directed the pony and trap driven there by the two late Volunteers up the farm lane to the south and sprinted back to his command post. When the first lorry neared the eastern bend, Barry threw a grenade into the body of the lorry and opened fire, killing the driver and the Auxiliary commander, Lieutenant Colonel Crake.[8] Simultaneously, the lorry was blasted at point-blank range by the ten riflemen to the north. Barry described what happened at the first lorry after the initial grenade:

> Revolvers were used at point blank range, and at times, rifle butts replaced rifle shots. So close were the combatants, that in once instance the pumping blood from an Auxiliary's severed artery struck one attacker full in the mouth …[9]

The Auxiliaries in the first lorry stood no chance and all nine were killed.

At the same time the second lorry had been engaged by McCarthy's men. The Auxiliaries from that lorry dismounted at the start of the ambush and spread out on the road, south of and just to the east of McCarthy's section. As the 'driver to the second tender tried to get back out of it all, his differential broke completely and the tender just ran off the edge of the road and slipped into the bog' to the west of the IRA position.[10] Ned Young left his position when he saw the driver and another Auxiliary make a run for it to the west. He fired at both men and mistakenly believed that he had killed the driver, Guthrie, who actually escaped. He then pursued the other man, who had taken shelter under the Crossley tender, and shot him dead.

Jack Hennessy, who was in the most exposed position, less than 5 metres from the Auxiliaries, described the rest of the fight:

> I was engaging the Auxies on the road. I was wearing a tin hat. I had fired about ten rounds and had got five bullets through the hat when the sixth bullet wounded me in the scalp. Vice Comdt. McCarthy had got a bullet through the head and lay dead. I continued to load and fire but the blood dripping from my forehead fouled the breech of my rifle. I dropped my rifle and took Ml. McCarthy's. Many of the Auxies lay on the road dead or dying. Our orders were to fix bayonets and charge on to the road when we heard three blasts of the O/C's whistle. I heard the three blasts and got up from my position, shouting 'hands up'. At the same time one of the Auxies about five yards from me drew his revolver. He had thrown down his rifle. I pulled on him and shot him dead. I got back to cover, where I remained for a few minutes firing at living and dead Auxies on the road. The Column O/C sounded his whistle again. Nearly all the Auxies had been wiped out. When I reached the road a wounded Auxie moved his hand towards his revolver. I put my bayonet through him under the ribs. Another Auxie tried to pull on John Lordan, who was too near to use his bayonet and he struck the Auxie with the butt of his rifle. The butt broke on the Auxie's skull.[11]

John Lordan, who had been next to Hennessy, had stood up at the same time as him and been shot in the ear. Pat Deasy also stood up and was shot in the abdomen and subsequently in the chest.[12] It is claimed that Jim O'Sullivan

Pat Deasy
(*Courtesy of Mercier Press*)

had apparently died earlier when he was killed by the bolt action of his rifle, which exploded and lodged in his skull.[13] However, Dan Hourihan, who was next to him, told Meda Ryan in 1971 that 'after they shouted that surrender, it was silence! Jim lifted himself. Thought it was all over' and it was at this point he was shot. This evidence has great weight, as it was given by a witness who ended up positioned between two of the dead IRA men.[14] What is certain is that O'Sullivan died from a head wound.

According to another veteran, Tim Keohane, some of the Auxiliaries appeared to surrender, only to open fire again when the IRA fighters emerged from cover to take them prisoner:

> The enemy party in the leading lorry was disposed of in about five or six minutes, but the survivors from the second lorry continued to fight for about 20/30 minutes. At this stage Tom Barry blew a blast on his whistle as a signal that all men should get on to the road. At the same time he moved with his section along the road from the east to take the survivors in the rear. Tom Barry then called on the enemy to surrender and some of them put up their hands, but when our party were moving on to the road the Auxiliaries again opened fire. Two of our men (John Lordan and Jack Hennessy, I think) were wounded by his fire. Pat Deasy had been wounded, while Jim Sullivan [*sic*] and Mick McCarthy (V/C Dunmanway Battn.) had been killed prior to this happening. The O/C (Tom Barry) immediately ordered an all-out attack, and after a few sharp bursts the enemy forces were silenced. We then found that everybody on the road had been killed.[15]

Indeed Stephen O'Neill, who had a good vantage point (and therefore was in a prime position as a witness), stated:

The O/C, with three of the section responsible for the destruction of the first lorry, came to our assistance, with the result that the attack was intensified. On being called on to surrender, they signified their intention of doing so, but when we ceased at the O/C's command, fire was again opened by the Auxiliaries, with fatal results to two of our comrades who exposed themselves believing the surrender was genuine. We renewed the attack vigorously and never desisted until the enemy was annihilated.[16]

Other participants do not mention a surrender call, most noticeably Paddy O'Brien and James 'Spud' Murphy, who, being next to Barry, is as important a witness as Stephen O'Neill.[17] However, both make clear how intense the fighting was:

Some of the men of the second lorry got out on the road and took up positions by the fence and started firing back on the men in No. 3 section. We were ordered out on the road – Tom Barry first – and we followed. We got down on our knees and we opened fire on the men that got out of the lorry at the other end (west) of the position. After an exchange of fire lasting about ten minutes, they were all killed with the exception of one man who jumped into the bog and ran about 50 yards before being shot.[18]

According to Jack O'Sullivan, at least one Auxiliary was killed having surrendered, but no other IRA witness mentions this.[19]

The results of the Auxiliary post-mortems, which were publicised during the inquest into the events of Kilmichael, appear to back up the evidence in the Volunteers' witness statements:

- William Barnes: Gaping wound in axilla and four other bullet wounds in various parts of the body. Post mortem wounds. Large bullet wound over heart.[20]

- Cecil J. W. Bayley: One bullet wound in head; bullet wound behind right ear which entered skull; one bullet wound on right hand.

- Leonard Douglas Bradshaw: Big perforating wound over liver (fired at close range), wound at right shoulder with fracture of humerus, wound in left axilla, fracture of femur.

- Francis W. Crake: Gunshot wound through head, which entered at point of lower jaw and came out at back of skull. Gunshot wound clean.

- James Chubb Gleave: Gunshot wound over heart; wound on upper portion of chest and large gaping wound in chest (fired at short range) with scorching; large lacerated wound on left side of pelvis, probably from a bayonet.

- Philip Noel Graham: Explosive wounds through head.

- Stanley Hooper-Jones: Two wounds, one in groin and one in axilla. Death due to shock and haemorrhage.

- Frederick Hugo: Compound fracture of skull, compound fracture of femur and extensive lacerated wounds.

- Albert G. J. Jones: Bullet wound in axilla. Six bullet wounds in limbs and body. Fracture in femur.

- Ernest W. Lucas: Gunshot wound in head; severe gunshot wounds in neck and body. Fracture of femur.

- William Pallester: Large wound through middle of chest over heart, small wound of right hand. Post mortem wounds: compound fractures of skull (brains protruding) caused probably by an axe or some fairly sharp metal implement.

- Horace Pearson: Bullet wound in head; lacerated wound on forearm; bullet wound in leg.

- Arthur Poole: Five bullet wounds in neck and shoulder, which were the cause of death. Post mortem wounds, extensive depressed fracture of bones of face head and skull.

- Frank Taylor: Large wound on chest (bayonet or gunshot), large wound on left shoulder with fracture of joint, one wound in upper right chest, three other gunshot wounds.

- Christopher Wainwright: One bullet wound on right side of chest; one abdominal wound; two wounds back of right side of chest (fired at short range).

- Benjamin Webster: Gaping wound in shoulder; fracture of femur; three rifle bullets through back.[21]

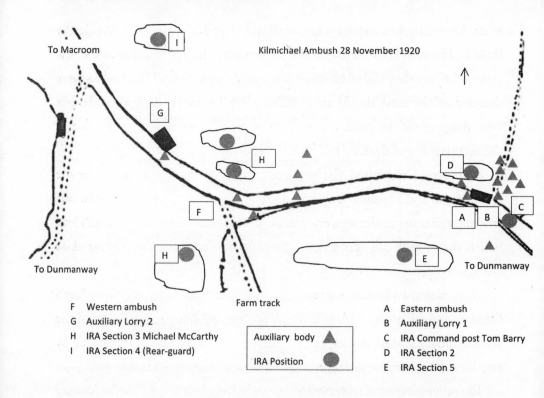

To Macroom

Kilmichael Ambush 28 November 1920

G

H

D

F

A B C

To Dunmanway

H

E

To Dunmanway

Farm track

F   Western ambush
G   Auxiliary Lorry 2
H   IRA Section 3 Michael McCarthy
I   IRA Section 4 (Rear-guard)

Auxiliary body ▲

IRA Position ●

A   Eastern ambush
B   Auxiliary Lorry 1
C   IRA Command post Tom Barry
D   IRA Section 2
E   IRA Section 5

It should be noted that gaping wounds to the underarms do not mean that the Auxiliaries had their arms raised in surrender. In fact, Dr Kelleher, who outlined these wounds at the inquest, stated that he believed at least some of these injuries actually came from the grenade thrown by Tom Barry into the first lorry.

The surviving contemporary records of the ambush site and where the Auxiliaries' bodies were found also appear to confirm many of the details in the witness statements. Turning first to the Fleming map, it should be noted that Michael McCarthy, Jack Hennessy and John Lordan were at the western ambush location as stated. Annotations by Tom Barry on a copy of this map held in a pub at nearby Coppeen show this to be the case. Pat Deasy and Jim O'Sullivan were above and behind them. The soldier that Ned Young shot under the western lorry was presumably Barnes from the location of the body. The Auxiliary who ran across the bog and was shot in the back is likely to be Hooper-Jones from the wounds and position of the body. All the IRA casualties – Deasy (killed), O'Sullivan (killed), McCarthy (killed), Hennessy (wounded) and Lordan (wounded) – occurred where the statements say they did. Although Tom Barry later said all the bodies were dragged off the road, the Fleming map shows that while the eastern bodies were dragged off the road, the western were not. This was probably due to the fact that it was dark by the time the IRA had regrouped.

Moreover, I measured the distances at the ambush site based on the locations on the Fleming map and there is less than 15 yards between one side and the other at the western end of the ambush and probably much less, which shows that this was a face-to-face fight. The combatants were close enough to each other to see clearly what their enemy was doing.

There were two British survivors of the Kilmichael ambush: Cadet Cecil Guthrie and Lieutenant H. F. Forde. Cecil James Guthrie, the driver of the second lorry, escaped during the battle, but was captured later that day by two local IRA members, disarmed and killed with his own revolver.[22]

The other survivor, Lieutenant Forde, was described at the court of inquiry in January 1921 as being 'utterly incapable of giving evidence'. However, somewhat miraculously, a week later he was pictured sitting up in bed in Millbank Hospital, London, having his lunch and describing in great detail what had happened to him. The *Irish Independent* reported on 17 January:

> Lieut. H. F. Forde, M.C, the sole survivor of the Auxiliary Cadets in the Macroom ambush on Nov. 28, has arrived at Millbank Hospital from Cork, and yesterday the 'Observer' published his story of the episode.
>
> Lieutenant Forde in his description of the ambush in the 'Observer' says:– 'A heavy fire broke out from both sides of the road. I could see little puffs of smoke from here and there amongst the rocks. I saw the first lorry slow up and then run on again and run into a ditch or trench across the road. At the same time as our lorry was pulling up, I heard cries from the other occupants and could see that most, if not all of them, had been more or less severely hit. However, as soon as the lorry stopped all managed to scramble out and we took up position at each side of the road, lying down to return the fire.

'After about ten minutes I felt as though struck by a heavy blow above my eye, and all at once began to feel very sick, I believe it was about ten minutes later than this that I suddenly heard a whistle blown loudly, and a cry to cease fire. Then a large number of the attackers from both sides rushed into the road, shouting in the foulest language. They wore the uniform of British soldiers. These men proceeded to handle us all very roughly, not excepting even those who were by this time dead. After knocking us about they called on us all to stand up and hold our hands up.

'There was no response for a time, but after about two minutes two of the party were able to stagger to their feet, and were immediately shot down again at very close range by the Shinners. Then one of the Cadets quite near me, who had been lying on his back, groaned heavily and turned over. One of the civilians, who had a rifle and bayonet, immediately walked up to him and plunged the bayonet into his back as near as I could see between the shoulder blades.

'I could see the others going through the clothes of the Cadets, and I could, see they were being treated brutally. Then one of the civilians came up to me and tried to pull a gold ring off my finger. He failed to do this, and in view of the treatment of the others I fully expected him to cut my finger to get it off. This, however, I am glad to say, he did not do. The next thing I remember was that one of them came up to me and rolled me over roughly to see, I suppose whether I was not dead. He swung his rifle and gave me a blow with the butt end of it on the back of my head. When I woke up again it was pitch dark, and I must have been conscious, and unconscious alternately throughout the night. The ambushers had retired to their previous positions, and I only remember that now and again, presumably when they saw or heard any movement amongst us, they fired a few shots. It was in the afternoon of the following day when the rescuing party arrived and I was taken in a state of semi-consciousness to a hospital at Cork.'[23]

While the first part of the testimony (up until he was shot) is corroborated by IRA testimony and the positions and conditions of the Auxiliaries' bodies, it is likely that there is an amount of inaccuracy operating in the second half, given his described wounds were:

… the result of a rifle bullet which entered on the left side of the middle line of the forehead, and passed out at the back of the head. Also two long wounds on the back of the head, evidently caused with a blunt instrument like a rifle butt. Paralysis of the left face and arm, which to some extent would cause permanent effects. Wound complicated with crysipelas, and still discharging. Large amount of very fine pieces of metal in brain.[24]

Some of the elements, such as the IRA firing shots in the night (no IRA men remained in the vicinity), are clearly wrong.

It is worth looking again at the controversy in the light of all this evidence. First let's look at the facts that are known about Kilmichael. It is a fact that Tom Barry would have seen Jack Hennessy, John Lordan and Pat Deasy stand up after he blew the first ceasefire signal as described by Hennessy. It is also a fact that John Lordan was shot in the ear and Pat Deasy was shot in the chest at this time.[25] Both Jack Hennessy and Tim Keohane heard the ceasefire signal before being attacked again by some of the Auxiliaries. Hennessy states he threw himself back on the ground when an Auxiliary who had thrown away his rifle drew his revolver after the first ceasefire signal from Tom Barry. It is also known that there was a second ceasefire order after further firing. There is little doubt that some of the Auxiliaries at the western lorry were shot after death and some were shot at close range according to their inquest reports. Both Jack Hennessy and Ned Young say they shot men at close range at the western site. John Lordan smashed his rifle butt on the skull of an Auxiliary – an Auxiliary called Pallester at the western site had a wound consistent with this, as did Lieutenant Forde. While there is a dispute about when Michael McCarthy died, there is no dispute that he was incapacitated from the first moments of the ambush. Both Tom Barry and Hennessy, who was next to him, said he was dead early. Others say he was still alive at the end of the ambush and died on the way to Buttimers, but either way he could not have stood up during or after any ceasefire.

It is also a fact that the false surrender was part of the story used to explain the savagery of the ambush in the first published account by Lionel Curtis in *Round Table* in June 1921.[26] General Crozier also referred to being told about the false surrender in *Ireland Forever*.[27] Equally, when *The Irish Press* published an account of the ambush in 1932, Barry objected to the fact that it made no mention of a false surrender. Finally, it is also a fact that some veterans mention a false surrender and some do not.

Was Hart justified in stating that Barry's version of events changed over time and that the false surrender is only a later addition to the story? I leave that to the reader to decide in light of the evidence as it survives and is presented here. However, in truth it should not matter, as the purpose of an ambush with two killing zones is to wipe out the enemy before they have an opportunity to respond. How that is done is irrelevant.

# THE BURNING OF CORK

At 8 p.m. on 11 December 1920 the IRA ambushed a British Auxiliary patrol at Dillon's Cross, within 100 metres of the entrance to Victoria Barracks, the British headquarters in Munster. Twelve members of the newly formed 'K' Company became casualties when an IRA grenade was lobbed into the second of two Crossley tenders. One member of the patrol, Spencer Chapman, was mortally wounded. His friend Vernon Hart stayed with him until he died the following day.[1]

At 9.30 p.m. lorries of Auxiliaries and British soldiers arrived at the scene of the ambush. They set fire to the surrounding houses and watched while they burned. Seven homes and businesses were destroyed. Shortly after this the city fire brigade, answering a call to help at Dillon's Cross, noticed that Grants on St Patrick's Street, one of the city's largest department stores, was on fire. Alan Ellis of *The Cork Examiner* witnessed the events of the night. His is the most succinct account:

> I soon became aware that something unusual was happening. There had been sporadic gunfire all evening and my ears had grown so accustomed to it that I did not really notice it. I then became aware of the thud of nearby explosions. I knew by then what a bomb sounded like. There were numerous groups of Auxiliaries, men recruited to make up numbers in the depleted Royal Irish Constabulary. The Auxiliaries were former British officers sent to Ireland in June, 1920, and were as vicious a bunch of thugs as ever I would encounter. There were also regular soldiers about. I could hear sporadic rifle fire and small arms from every direction.
>
> At first I thought it was an engagement between republicans and the military. Then I noticed, further down Patrick Street, the Auxies and soldiers were driving people from the streets and firing over their heads to make them disperse into the buildings.

Grant's drapery store appeared to be on fire but there was a small unit of the Fire Brigade on hand …

I was then joined by a man who swore that earlier he had seen a patrol of Auxiliaries marching up the street with an officer at their head. He said that they had halted in disciplined fashion and on a word of command had broken into Grant's and set it ablaze. My informant said one of them noticed him and came across, shoving a gun in his face and had told him to leave or else! …

Now I realised that all the principal buildings along Patrick Street had suddenly burst into flame. There is no doubt who was causing the fires. At Munster Arcade, a residential block, the British military ordered people out at gunpoint, shots were fired at the windows and incendiary bombs were thrown in. Some of the attackers, while not hiding their uniforms, wore scarves over their faces.

I saw Fred Huston, chief of the Cork Fire Brigade, who I knew slightly, who had just arrived from Sullivan's Quay and was valiantly trying to organise his men. He told me bluntly that all the fires were being deliberately started by incendiary bombs, and in several cases, he had seen soldiers pouring cans of petrol into buildings and setting them alight. He had telephoned an appeal to the military commander of the regular troops in the city, Brigadier Higginson, but without any response. Already two of his firemen had been wounded by gunfire from the military.

I hurried down the street to Patrick's Bridge. On the bridge I saw a deserted tram, set on fire. This was the very one for St Luke's Cross … Lorries full of regular soldiers, members of the Oxfordshire Regiment, were moving along Merchant's Quay. A crowd of them stood in front of Wickham's shop, which sold Primus stoves, on Merchant's Quay. There was little discipline among them. The soldiers were yelling abuse at anyone they saw and now and then firing off a round into the air. Any stragglers were now being halted searched and threatened …

After heading to the *Examiner*'s office and then venturing back out onto the streets, Ellis was arrested by the military. Released at around three in the morning, he continued his account:

There was still gunfire about the city. I heard it not far away at Bandon railway station [now Albert Quay station] and my idiocy drew me along the quay to see what was going on. I found a unit of the City Fire Brigade actually pinned down by gunfire. When I asked who was firing on them, they said it was Black and Tans who had broken into the nearby City Hall next to the station. One fireman told me that he had also seen 'men in uniform' carrying cans of petrol into the Hall from the very barracks on Union Quay that I had just been released from.

Around four o'clock there was a tremendous explosion. The Tans had not only placed petrol in the building but also detonated high explosives. The City Hall and adjoining Carnegie Library, with its thousands of priceless volumes, was suddenly a sea of flames.

The firemen with me managed to get a hose on the Carnegie Library as the Tans had evidently given up their game of firing at the firemen. Instead they turned off the fire hydrant and refused to let the fire crews have any access to water. Protests were met with laughter and abuse. Soon after six o'clock the tower of the City Hall crashed into the blazing ruins below. I heard that elsewhere in the city soldiers ran their bayonets through the Fire Brigade's hose pipes.[2]

More than sixty business premises, 300 homes, the City Hall and the Carnegie Library were destroyed. Over £2,000,000 worth of damage was done, thousands were left jobless and many of the poorest people in the city were made homeless.

The burning and looting of Cork was started by 'K' Company members according to evidence given to the British Cabinet on 15 February 1921, which stated that the seven ringleaders were under arrest for various offences in Dunmanway.[3] The subsequent British Army report on the burning of the city was suppressed by the government.[4] While there is little doubt that 'K' Company started the fires in revenge for the Dillon's Cross ambush, there also appear to have been plans to burn buildings in the city in reprisal for the capture of British informant George Horgan by the IRA.[5] It seems reasonable to conclude, based on the available evidence, that it was a planned 'official' reprisal, which descended into an orgy of drink and looting and did far more damage than was originally intended. After all, many buildings had been burned in the city over the previous weeks, so there was nothing unusual about the night's events except for the scale of the damage.[6]

The aftermath of the burning of Cork. (*Courtesy of Mercier Press*)

In a final postscript to the night's events, at 2.30 a.m. on 12 December unarmed IRA Volunteers Jeremiah and Cornelius Delaney were shot in their bedroom at Dublin Hill just north of the city by a group of Auxiliaries. Jeremiah died immediately; Cornelius survived until 18 December. The men who carried out the ambush at Dillon's Cross had been tracked to the Delaneys' house (apparently by bloodhounds), but had left before the Auxiliaries arrived.[7]

On 13 December 'K' Company was ordered to Dunmanway. Three months later the company was disbanded.

# THE INCIDENT AT MALLOW STATION

Between 28 January and the end of February 1921, eighty-two people were killed in Cork as a result of War of Independence violence. To put this in perspective, more than one in ten of all those killed in the entire revolutionary era in Cork died in a single thirty-day period.

February started with a horrific incident at Mallow Station, where all the casualties were non-combatants. The incident began when the IRA noticed that at the same time every evening the Black and Tans stationed at Broadview House in the town took dispatches to the railway station, 250 metres away on the edge of the town, for the Cork to Dublin mail train. The IRA decided to set up an ambush in the apparently unguarded station to attack the party as they walked up the hill to the platform.[1] There seemed to be little likelihood of civilian casualties as there was a curfew in the town and only military or police were allowed on the streets. According to Jeremiah Daly, they were positioned in two groups:

(a) Four – Jack Moloney ('Congo'), Denis Mulcahy, Jeremiah Daly (witness) and the Column O/C. (Jack Cunningham) took up a position behind a wall facing the road to the station entrance. They were armed with revolvers.

(b) Two – Leo O'Callaghan and Ned Murphy – were on duty on the road at the opposite side of the railway in order to cover off any approach from the rear. They also carried revolvers.

When a party of Black and Tans was seen to approach, the ambush party at (a) opened fire. There was no reply from the Tans.[2]

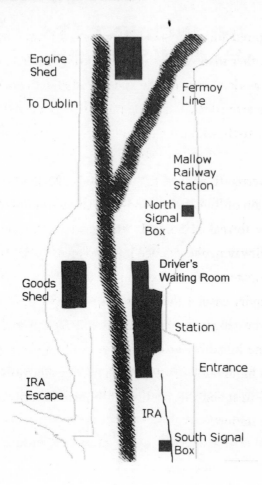

The reason for the lack of response was simple. The IRA men had mistaken RIC Inspector William H. King and his wife, Alice, for the Black and Tans. Inspector King was injured and Alice was fatally wounded, dying in her husband's arms.

The ambush party retreated west across the railway line as Black and Tans rushed towards the station. The British forces raided the north signal box at the opposite end of the station from the ambush and arrested its occupants. Joseph Greensmyth, aged seventy, was thrown down the steps and badly injured. The Tans then went to the drivers' waiting room and arrested the occupants. The fifteen railwaymen were marched out of the station and told to run, 'but before they had got 12 yards away a volley was fired into them'.[3]

Seven men were injured and two, Denis Bennett and Daniel Mullane, were killed outright. Another man, Patrick Devitt, died a couple of days later in hospital. Other rail workers were beaten and assaulted in the police barracks. When a goods train arrived the following morning it was fired on. The final casualty was Greensmyth, who never recovered from his injuries and died a few months later.[4]

Uniquely, the investigation into what happened at Mallow was conducted by the National Union of Railworkers and raised by the union's leader, James Thomas, during the formal opening of parliament on 15 February 1921. Thomas read the railwaymen's evidence into the record and challenged the government to instigate an immediate public enquiry into the events.[5] A military court of inquiry ensued, though its report gave little impression that its members knew the geography of the station. In particular, the claim that the rail workers were killed by crossfire between the south signal box and the station exit was highly unlikely given the known direction of the IRA's retreat to the south-west and the location of the rail-drivers' quarters at the opposite end of the station.[6]

# CASCADING DEATH

By the end of November 1920 the IRA had set a trap for one of its own members, Din-Din O'Riordan, who was suspected of passing information to the British. Once the British reacted to the information they had fed O'Riordan, they knew they had their man. He was taken to the Chetwynd Viaduct, just outside Cork city near the main Bandon road, where senior IRA officer Mick Murphy, playing on his weaknesses, promised him fifty pounds and free passage from Ireland if he gave information about his paymaster.[1] Din-Din confessed and said that he had been recruited by another IRA man who worked for Woodford Bourne, a local wine and spirits company. His confession also implicated the owner of the firm, James Nicholson, and subsequently some of the other leading businessmen in the city, including Alfred Reilly, manager of Thompson's Bakery, and George Tilson. The alleged paymaster was an Englishman called Charles Beale, who had come to manage Woodford Bourne eight years previously.[2] After he finished his confession Din-Din was shot and buried at the viaduct according to senior IRA officer Frank Busteed.[3]

Around the same time, according to his BMH witness statement, Mick Murphy had picked up a teenage suspect called Parsons (no first name given). Murphy claimed that Parsons admitted he was a spy and that he had informed Detective Inspector Swanzy about Tomás MacCurtain's location on the night he was killed. Parsons also claimed that there was a spy ring in the YMCA and Freemasons, and apparently identified the Blemens family as being members of the spy ring.[4] However, Gerard Murphy has shown that the only Parsons kidnapped and killed by the IRA was William Parsons (15) who was captured in July 1922 eighteen months later. Either Mick Murphy was wrong about the name of the person who gave him the information about the Blemens family, or his suspect was a different person also called

Parsons about whom no further information has survived. An alternative but highly implausible theory is that Mick Murphy was trying to throw people off the scent of a series of secret murders of Protestants in 1922 by misdating the capture of Parsons by more than eighteen months.

According to Busteed, letters passing through the hands of Josephine Marchment Browne (the IRA spy in the office of Captain Kelly, the intelligence officer for the British in Cork) also identified two interlinked spy rings centred on Woodford Bourne. The first consisted of businessmen, bankers, merchants and clergymen of high social standing, and the second consisted of members of the YMCA who had been recruited by the senior spy ring.[5]

Retribution was swift. Father and son James and Fred Blemens were kidnapped separately from their home on 29 November, held for a few days and shot. Fred worked in Woodford Bourne. The men were buried in Carroll's bog to the south of the city according to Murphy.[6] Blemens' other son, James Junior, had also worked in the company and his daughter Sarah had worked there before she married James Charles Beale.[7]

The next killing was even more shocking as it struck at the heart of Cork polite society:

> As the result of information received by our Brigade Intelligence Service it became known that an organisation run by the Free Masons and The Young Men's Christian Association had been formed in Cork to spy on the movements of I.R.A. men in the City and to report on them to the British Authorities. One of the principal men in this organisation was named Riley [*sic*], who was Manager (so far as I can recollect) of Thompsons [*sic*] Bakery, Cork, and lived in Rochestown, County Cork. This man was reputed to be the paymaster for the Spies.
>
> Early in February 1921 I received instructions from the Brigade to take into custody Riley and have him executed. On the evening of the 10th February, 1921, as he was returning from work in King Street (now MacCurtain Street) in his pony and trap, four of us, armed with revolvers, got into the trap

and drove him to his home at Rochestown. We shot him outside the gate of his house and affixed a card to the body with the words 'Spies and Informers Beware' written on it.[8]

Meanwhile, in the middle of January 1921 two men had called to the house of James Charles Beale at 7 Laurelhurst, College Road, Cork, looking to speak to the 'man of the house'. Sarah, his wife, grew suspicious of the two men and said he was not at home, which was true. The men left. On 16 February Beale was kidnapped on his way home from work, having been spotted on the South Gate Bridge. His body was found in a field almost opposite Wilton church, then a mile outside the city and currently in the grounds of Cork University Hospital. He was face down with his arms outstretched. His head was a tangled mass of blood. On the body was a note 'Spies and informers beware'.[9] His funeral service was held in St Fin Barre's Cathedral and was conducted by Bishop Dowse. He was afterwards buried in Douglas. Sarah died on 20 December 1921 and is also buried at Douglas. She had lost her father, brother and her husband within a year.

According to the IRA, information found on Charles Beale's body cracked the spy ring open and other members of the Anti-Sinn Féin League were picked up and 'suitably dealt with'.[10] This doesn't mean that all these people were shot; they may have been warned to stop or told to get out of the country at short notice. Certainly, neither James Nicholson, nor his brother who owned the company with him after their father died in 1920, was harmed, but one more death shocked London:

On the morning of Saturday the 19th of February 1921, George Tilson was found on the Fishguard Express train at Old Common Station near Acton [just outside] London on the Great Western Railway. A piece of paper found in his possession read *Shadowed from Ireland*. He was taken to St. Mary's Hospital Paddington where he died at 3.20 on Saturday afternoon. Tilson was 36 years old and from Blackrock, County Cork. He was the son of the late Robert

Tilson, Justice of the Peace, Cork and brother of Richard H. Tilson, Justice of the Peace, Lisnalee, Blackrock, County Cork.[11]

The inquest was told that Tilson had received a threatening letter 'charging him with spying on the IRA'. While he had decided to ignore it, he was persuaded to go to his uncle who lived in Hastings. Somewhere between Cork and Paddington, George became convinced that he was about to be murdered and cut his own throat.[12]

# THE CLONMULT SHOOTOUT

On 12 December, after escaping from British forces in Cloyne that same day, the East Cork flying column moved northwards and took over a disused farmhouse just outside the village of Clonmult in the hills above Midleton.[1] At this stage of the war it seems that many of the IRA columns had become confident that they had the upper hand in the fight, and this led them to relax their vigilance when in camp. Many of the incidents which resulted in IRA casualties, such as Crois na Leanbh in Kilbrittain, Mourneabbey and Nadd, were a result of scouts not spotting British forces in time to give warning, combined with improved intelligence gathering on the British side.

The farm at Clonmult is on the side of a gentle hill with a road running north–south along the top of the hill. To the east was the village of Clonmult. Between the village and the farm, at the bottom of the hill, was a stream also running north–south. The IRA column was resting in the old thatched farmhouse. Part of the daily ritual was to draw water from the stream. It appears that some of the column was noticed doing this and this information was conveyed to the British at Fermoy.[2] On 20 February 1920 the Hampshire Regiment dispatched a squad to surround the house and there is no doubt that they were able to get within metres of it before they were accidentally noticed. Patrick Higgins was in the cottage and described what happened:

> Tea was being made about 3 p.m.; we were packing up preparing to leave and the guards were withdrawn, as the Clonmult Company were to take over outpost duty (that is, as I understood the position to be). Two of our lads, John Joe Joyce and Michael Desmond, had gone to a well nearby for water. These latter two were unarmed, so far as I know. At this point someone looked out a window of the house and said that the military were surrounding the place. Shots rang out. It was the soldiers firing on Joyce and Desmond. We did not see the latter again.

Jack O'Connell now decided that we should make a rush from the house and fight it out in the open. He led the way, carrying a rifle and fixed bayonet, and got safely across the yard under heavy fire from the military. Michael Hallinan [*sic*], who followed him, was shot dead immediately outside the door, and Richard Hegarty a few yards from the door. (He was Captain of the Ballymacoda Company). James Aherne, the third man to go out, was shot and killed after getting about fifty yards away. The door of the house was then closed and we decided to continue the fight from inside, hoping that some help might come.

I was now the next senior officer in charge and I directed the lads to positions at the windows, where a steady fire was kept up on any soldiers who came into view. We made an effort to bore a hole in the gable end wall of the house, through which we might be able to get out, and also in the back wall, but this was not a success. The enemy spotted our intention and directed heavy fire on these places, wounding one of our lads who tried to get through.

It was now about 4.30 p.m. The military still kept up continuous heavy fire and threw bombs on to the roof. These bombs fell off the thatch. Eventually the roof was set on fire by the enemy and our position became a hopeless one. Our ammunition was getting scarce; we had no hope of getting out into the open country and the place would soon be an inferno, which meant we had to surrender or be burned alive. We hung on for another while, as we knew that the North East Cork Column was not many miles away and there was always the hope that they might have got word of our plight and would come to our help.

The military repeatedly called on us to come out and surrender. I discussed it with the boys and said I would do as the majority wished. The majority were in favour of surrender, as further resistance seemed useless and the house was now well on fire. Three of us were in favour of fighting it out, viz. Liam Aherne of Midleton, myself, and the youngest member of the column, a lad by the name of Jimmy Glavin from Cobh (the bravest little lad I ever met; he was no more than seventeen years of age). We shouted out we would surrender, and then threw our guns into the burning house. We were told to come out with hands up. We did so.

We were lined up alongside an outhouse with our hands up. The Tans came along and shot every man, with the exception of three, namely Paddy

O'Sullivan, Maurice Moore, both from Cobh, and 'Sonny' O'Leary, who had been wounded in the fight in the house. These three were saved from the Tans by the officer in charge of the military party.

A Tan put his revolver to my mouth and fired. I felt as if I was falling through a bottomless pit. Then I thought I heard a voice saying, 'This fellow is not dead, we will finish him off.' Only for the military officer coming along, I, too, would be gone.[3]

This, from all the reports, is an accurate description of what happened. A party of Auxiliaries (not Black and Tans, as Higgins said), who were raiding Dungourney and Clonmult, had followed the sound of firing to the site and it seems that they did much of the shooting of the prisoners. It is possible that if the Auxiliaries had not reinforced the Hampshire Regiment some of the flying column could have escaped. Without the intervention of the Hampshire officer Higgins would also have died.

# 28 FEBRUARY 1921

On the morning of 28 January 1921, halfway between the villages of Coachford and Dripsey, the IRA set up an ambush for a convoy of British troops that regularly took this route between Ballincollig and Macroom. Mary Lindsay, a woman with strong loyalist convictions, became aware that the IRA was there and went to the local priest, Fr Shinnick. They agreed that the priest would warn off the IRA and Mrs Lindsay would warn the British Army at Ballincollig. She went to the RIC barracks at Ballincollig (the military camp was next door) and informed the British authorities of what she knew. However, the priest's attempt to inform the IRA was rebuffed by the IRA vice-commandant, Frank Busteed, who thought he was only trying to mislead them.

Troops from the 1st Battalion of the Manchester Regiment left the barracks for Dripsey village at 3.30 p.m. Once there, the troops dismounted from their lorries, divided into five groups and set out to surround the ambush party. The planned encirclement was spotted by an IRA scout, who alerted his comrades, and firing soon broke out. Eight IRA men and two civilians were captured.

On 8 February the trial of John Lyons, Timothy McCarthy, Thomas O'Brien, Jeremiah O'Callaghan, Daniel O'Callaghan, Patrick O'Mahony, Eugene Langtry (civilian) and Denis Sheehan (civilian) opened in the gymnasium of Victoria Barracks in Cork. The proceedings lasted two days. Jeremiah O'Callaghan, Langtry and Sheehan were found not guilty and released. The remaining defendants were sentenced to death. Of the two remaining men, Captain James Barrett was too ill to stand trial and died on 22 March 1921. Denis Murphy was tried separately, in Victoria Barracks on 9 March, and was also sentenced to death, but his sentence was later commuted to twenty-five years' imprisonment.

The IRA 'persuaded' Fr Shinnick to reveal that Mary Lindsay had supplied the information to the military authorities. On 17 February a group of IRA men arrived at Leemont House and abducted Mrs Lindsay. They also took James Clarke, her chauffeur. On 26 February Michael Ingerton cycled past Victoria Barracks and dropped an envelope from his pocket. One of the two sentries retrieved it. It was addressed to 'General Strickland, Victoria Barracks'. In the envelope was a letter from Mrs Lindsay, which read:

Dear Sir Peter,

I have just heard that some of the prisoners taken at Dripsey are to be executed on Monday and I write to get you to use your influence to prevent this taking place and try and reprieve them – I am a prisoner as I am sure you will know and I have been told that it will be a very serious matter for me if these men are executed. I have been told that my life will be forfeited for theirs as they believe that I was the direct cause of their capture. I implore you to spare these men for my sake.

Yours very truly,

M. Lindsay.[1]

With it was a covering letter, which stated:

We are holding Mrs Mary Lindsay and her Chauffeur, James Clarke as hostages. They have been convicted of spying and are under sentence of death. If the five of our men taken at Dripsey are executed on Monday morning as announced by your office, the two hostages will be shot.

Irish Republican Army

General Strickland, who was a personal friend of Mrs Lindsay and a regular visitor for tea (according to his diary), discussed the situation with Nevil Macready, the British commander-in-chief in Ireland. While Strickland was worried, both men doubted that the IRA would shoot a woman, so the executions went ahead.

Early on the morning of 28 February large crowds gathered outside the gates of the military detention barracks and at eight o'clock shots were heard. More firing was heard at eight-fifteen and again at eight-thirty. Shortly afterwards a note was posted on the gate officially announcing the executions. A sixth man was also executed that day along with the Dripsey prisoners, although he had not been involved in the ambush. Seán Allen, from Bank Place, Tipperary, was a member of the Tipperary No. 3 Brigade.

That evening Signaller Bowden of the Royal Signal Corps met his girlfriend at Summerhill and they went up nearby Leycester's Lane. They had been 'talking there for a while' when two men approached them and told Bowden to 'put your hands up'. His girlfriend thought it was a joke 'but both men fired at point blank range and Bowen [sic] fell dead'. She ran up the lane towards Montenotte and heard more shots. The two men came back down the lane past her and disappeared. At the top of the lane Private Whitear, a bandsman of the Hampshire Regiment, who had also been talking to his girlfriend of fifteen months, had also been shot dead.[2] The time was 8 p.m. When the local priest was informed of the shooting, he telephoned for an ambulance. This did not arrive until 10.20 p.m. as 'all [the] ambulances were out'.[3]

On the other side of the city, on the Douglas Road, Corporal Hodnett walked out with his fiancée at 8.15 p.m. They had walked a few yards when a woman warned Hodnett that he was likely to be shot if he went any further.[4] At that moment men approached him and told him to put his hands up. Despite efforts by his fiancée to save him, he was shot by five men and died around 9.40 p.m. in the home of a local doctor. Incredibly, another soldier, who was going to visit a Miss Murphy, had passed the men and seen one of them draw an automatic weapon from his pocket only minutes before the shooting, but appears to have done nothing.[5]

Not far away, outside the Victoria Hospital, Lance Corporal Beattie was shot and the porter informed the soldier who was trying to bring the body into the hospital that 'the matron was uneasy having a soldier brought in'.[6] Similarly, Private Wise was talking to a young woman on St Patrick Street when two men approached them and shot him.[7] Wise died near the ruins of Cash's department store. Further down the street Private Gill was taken out of a music shop along with Private Bettersworth and shot dead.[8] Bettersworth was injured, as was Private Hill on the South Mall in a separate incident. Finally, at the bottom of St Patrick's Hill three soldiers were shot coming out of a pub by four men. One, Private Price, was shot in the head while lying on the ground and was lucky to survive to tell the story at the inquest.[9]

The calculation of Strickland and Macready at the start of March that, as a woman, Mrs Lindsay would not be shot initially proved correct. However, on 3 March Strickland recorded that he had received another letter from Mrs Lindsay. He wrote 'Letter from Mrs. L. saying she would get away if the next lot of Dripsey men got off'.[10] This is probably referring to the approaching trial of Denis Murphy on 9 March. On 11 March Mrs Lindsay and James Clarke were shot dead.[11]

# THE CROSSBARRY AMBUSH

On 15 February 1921, shortly after 10.30 a.m., the westbound Cork and Bandon train pulled into tiny Upton Station. Without warning, an improvised IRA ambush party of fourteen men under Brigade Commandant Charlie Hurley opened fire on the two central carriages, where they believed twenty members of the Essex Regiment were seated. As there was no love lost between both sides, an attack of this sort had a particular appeal for the Cork No. 3 (West Cork) Brigade. The planned attack was relatively low risk,

Charlie Hurley
(*Courtesy of Mercier Press*)

as the heavily wooded glen provided plenty of escape routes for the attackers if anything went wrong. Unfortunately, another fifty soldiers had boarded the train at Kinsale Junction, less than three kilometres to the east. While Hurley had posted scouts at the junction and they tried to warn him, there was little chance that a bicycle was ever going to out-run a train.

The ambush turned into a rout with three IRA dead and Hurley badly injured. Ten civilians, who were mostly commercial travellers but included one woman (May Hall), were killed in the crossfire. One IRA man was captured and under interrogation revealed the location of the brigade headquarters at Ballymurphy.[1]

One month later the British mounted an impressive swoop on the area.[2] There is no doubt that the ultimate intention of the British was to capture the headquarters, which moved between Ballymurphy and its two neighbouring townlands, Belrose and Ballyhandle, as an annotated map survives in General

Strickland's papers outlining the plan, with these locations shaded.[3] Major Percival was to lead a column of the Kinsale-based Essex Regiment from the south-east, while a second column was to approach from Bandon in the south-west. The Strickland map shows that the British columns were first to converge on Crossbarry, where field kitchens would serve breakfast, before continuing uphill towards the Belrose and Ballyhandle townlands. Another column was to come from Cork city via Waterfall to encircle the IRA headquarters from the north-east, while the Auxiliaries from Macroom were to cut off any escape to the west. However, a sympathetic RIC officer had made the IRA aware that the location of headquarters had been revealed, so it appears that some sort of an attack by the British was expected.[4]

The first indication that the British forces were on the move was when the lights of the lorries coming from Bandon were spotted around 2.30 a.m. A hasty IRA council of war decided that they should wait and see what happened, but when it became clear that the British were heading their way, and without any knowledge that there were soldiers to the north of them, Tom Barry moved the small flying column force of 104 men that was in the vicinity downhill to Crossbarry. Barry had elected to ambush one of the approaching columns before trying to escape north-west and it was clear that the British column coming from the south-west was well ahead of the others.

The IRA men were in position on the Bandon to Crossbarry road by around 4.30 a.m. One group of approximately fourteen men was based at Crossbarry Bridge, protecting the left flank of the column. Another group of thirteen was on a low hill to the west, protecting the right flank. Seven sections of varying size lined the road between these two groups, on either side of Beazley's and Harold's houses, with some men inside the houses. These sections were led by Seán Hales, O/C, 1st Battalion; John Lordan, vice-O/C, 1st Battalion; Column Adjutant Michael Crowley; Quartermaster Denis Lordan; Peter Kearney; Tom Kelleher and Jack Corkery. Tom Barry and Liam Deasy were in overall command. After discussions between Barry

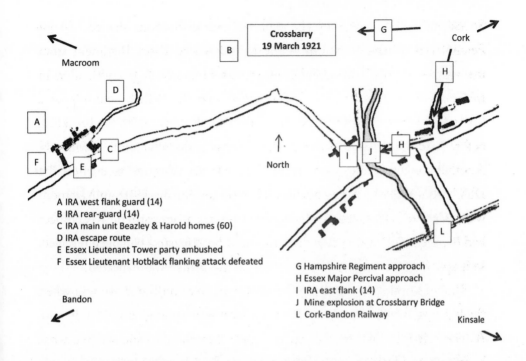

A IRA west flank guard (14)
B IRA rear-guard (14)
C IRA main unit Beazley & Harold homes (60)
D IRA escape route
E Essex Lieutenant Tower party ambushed
F Essex Lieutenant Hotblack flanking attack defeated

G Hampshire Regiment approach
H Essex Major Percival approach
I IRA east flank (14)
J Mine explosion at Crossbarry Bridge
L Cork-Bandon Railway

and Deasy, Kelleher's section was then moved 300 metres uphill to the rear, to prevent a flanking movement or an attack from the rear, as shots had been heard in that direction. They then waited for events to unfold.

The shots that the column had heard were the result of the first action of the morning, which took place at Ballymurphy, to the north-east of where the column was waiting. The Strickland map shows the route to be taken by the British column coming from Cork, but it appears that they turned off the main road one road too soon during their search and had to backtrack. As a result they were late getting to Humphrey Forde's house in Ballymurphy, arriving around 6.30 a.m. The Cork No. 3 Brigade headquarters had recently moved there and Brigade O/C Charlie Hurley was inside recovering from wounds suffered in the ambush at Upton five weeks earlier. When Major Hallinan knocked on the door, Hurley ran down the stairs. He fired through the door, wounding the major, before escaping out the back. He was shot in the head by a soldier who was guarding the escape route. This was the shooting that alerted the column leadership to the likelihood of complete

71

encirclement and caused the repositioning of Kelleher's group.[5] There is no doubt that if the British had coordinated their encirclement more effectively, then the West Cork flying column would have been wiped out as a fighting unit.

Back at Crossbarry, around 8 a.m., Lieutenant Tower, who was in charge of eight empty lorries (the troops had been dropped off four miles behind to conduct a house-to-house search), approached the crossroads from the south-west, where he was to wait for the 'chuck lorries' to arrive from Bandon with breakfast. The search party appears to have been no more than twenty minutes behind Tower's party. This was led by Lieutenant Geoffrey Hotblack, a close colleague of Major Percival in the Essex Regiment. Unfortunately for Tower and the approximately twenty troops who were still with him, the IRA column was already waiting. In the ensuing attack Lieutenant Tower and his men took significant casualties.

Michael O'Driscoll provides a good account of what happened to his section at Crossbarry, which was based in the farmhouses of the Harold and Beazley families:

> When we got to Crossbarry, the Column O/C told us that the British were trying to surround us and we would fight them at Crossbarry. The column was in sections of fourteen men, and every section had a job to do.
>
> We went into position on the Bandon–Cork road (old) at Harold's and Beasley's [sic] farmhouses … the lorries were sighted coming on the Bandon–Crossbarry road. We knew that the British were also coming from other directions.
>
> When the first lorry was opposite our position, there was a shout and the lorries stopped. Some soldiers started to get out of the lorries. We got orders to open fire and we gave it to them point blank. We had three lorries in easy reach of our rifles, and another four were stretched back along the road. The British had jumped from their lorries and any who were not hit ran some way into the open country. During all this, Flor Begley, the Assistant Brigade Adjutant, had being playing the pipes in Harold's yard …

When the firing ceased at our front, we were ordered out on the road to collect arms and prepare the lorries for burning. The driver of one lorry was jammed in his seat. He had been wounded in the leg and could not move. We had to leave his lorry unharmed. When the lorries were being prepared for burning, firing broke out on our left flank and we were ordered back to our position. The firing was short and sharp but soon died away. Next firing commenced on our right flank. This too died away. We were just moving back to the high ground at our rear when firing started in that direction. A large party of British troops attempted to come in behind us but they were met by a section under Tom Kelleher. There was some tough fighting before the British took flight. We continued to move back from Crossbarry up the high ground. We were told off as rear guard and, as we moved, a party of British were observed reforming. The O/C ordered the whole Column to line the fence, gave us a range and ordered three rounds rapid. That finished the British reforming …

I would say the whole action lasted over an hour.[6]

During the ambush the British lost at least nine soldiers and one RIC man was also killed. Significant among the casualties was Lieutenant Hotblack, who had raced with his men to the aid of Lieutenant Tower's party. He lost his life when trying to rally his men after they had run into the ambush at Beazley's. The IRA also lost three men.[7] They included Peter Monaghan, who was a British deserter in charge of mining the road.[8] Lieutenant Tower died in 1923, probably from the wounds he received at Crossbarry.

The catalyst for the IRA's retreat from the ambush was an attack by a British column from the south-east led by Major Percival, and the eventual arrival of further troops from the north-east to the rear of the IRA.[9] The retreating IRA column fired on these troops, who retreated. The rearguard then joined the rest of the column and escaped west along the ridge to the north of Beazley's house. The Auxiliaries from Macroom, who were supposed to deliver the *coup de grâce* and block this escape route, had gone to the wrong place (Kilbarry) and so failed to close the trap, though according to Peter Kearney it was a close-run thing.[10]

This is the standard history of the battle and there is no substantial difference between this and what was presented by Major Percival to the Staff College in his lectures based on what happened in the Irish war, except for the usual dispute about how many people were involved on both sides.[11]

It is worth reproducing here a much-neglected source which gives a very different viewpoint on the battle. On 26 March William Beazley gave his much more colourful description of the ambush. His daughter was also an eyewitness to the horror of the event. The *Connacht Tribune* was one of a number of newspapers that carried their story:

The immediate scene of the ambush is a few yards west of Crossbarry on the main road to Bandon, and on a section of the road with 300 yards straight with sharp bends at either end. To the north are the farm buildings of Mr. Beasley [*sic*] and Mr. Harold. Opposite Beasley's on the side of the road is a long cowshed with a tin roof and on the left, looking towards Crossbarry road is a long cowshed with a zinc roof which afforded admirable cover. Inside the low ditch, which commanded a clear view of the road, a strong barricade of stones and thick sods was erected. About 30 yards above this the road was mined with what must have been powerful explosives. Mr Beasley says that about 1 a.m. on Saturday a knock came to the door, and looking out he saw a large party of men. He told his son to go down, that it was no use making any resistance and open the door. The son, before opening the door, asked who was there and the reply was 'The IRA'. He opened the door and a large body of young men, all armed [with rifles and revolvers] entered. They were a fine, jolly lot of fellows and made themselves quite at home. They cooked some meals and then they played cards, and some went into the front room, played the piano and sang. After a while 8 or 9 of them went to bed. I wanted to go out, but one of the men, who was evidently on guard held up his gun and told me I could not go out … About 5 o'clock another large party arrived, and then most of the men were called out into the yard. There was great activity. It was like a scene on a barracks square … The fight began at 8 o'clock … Miss Beasley said 'when the lorries turned the bend of the road above Harolds' fire was opened on them. She saw nothing as she lay down in the corner of the room. There were several explosions like bombs, and one bigger than the others shook the house ... After about 16 minutes there was a lull, and it began again and lasted about 20 minutes. When the firing ceased the IRA who were upstairs came down and went out by the back door, and all the men retreated up the hill.' Mr. Beasley's house was not much damaged ... while in Harold's only one window was [smashed] by a bullet. Continuing her narrative Miss Beasley said that when she ventured out on the road a horrifying sight met her eyes. One lorry which ran into a wall was burning and a man ... was lying dead in the middle of the road. Further up outside Harolds' there were two other lorries and one was blazing. In the centre of the road 3 soldiers were lying; one was dead, and the other two were almost dying. Mr. Healy [a neighbour] had a third soldier in his arms, he asked for a priest and someone put a rosary beads into his hands: he too called piteously for his mother. He lived on 15 minutes ...[12]

Crossbarry is presented as a famous victory for the West Cork Brigade, but it was (like Waterloo) a very close-run thing. Through a combination of luck, opportunism, local knowledge and experience, the column had been extracted from a seemingly impossible position. Once again, the passengers on the Cork to Bandon train were treated to a ringside seat, as the train passed within 100 metres of the battle at its height and the passengers 'had a most thrilling experience'.[13]

As always with this war there was a postscript. On 23 April 1921 *The Irish Times* reported that the houses of William Beazley and Charles Harold were burned down.[14]

# THE DESTRUCTION OF ROSSCARBERY POLICE BARRACKS

By the end of 1920 the IRA had created safe zones in much of the Beara peninsula and along the ridge north of Bandon and Dunmanway. After an attack the IRA flying column would retreat to this ridge, where they could rest in relative safety, while the Beara area was used for more general 'rest and relaxation' by members of the 5,000-strong West Cork Brigade. These safe zones had been created by the destruction of small RIC barracks in the area and the retreat of the police from others to the larger towns. Another safe area could be created if the large RIC garrison at Rosscarbery could be removed, so this became a prime target for the IRA and was the subject of repeated attacks.

## 2 February 1921

On 2 February 1921 the flying column arrived at the home of Thomas Kingston, justice of the peace, at Burgatia House just outside Rosscarbery. Their purpose was twofold. First, Kingston was suspected of providing information to the British forces. Given Kingston's known unionist politics and his position as a local magistrate, this was hardly a robust deduction by the IRA. Second, the IRA needed a safe base close to the village to wait out the day before a planned attack on the barracks and nobody would expect them in Burgatia.

For Kingston the stakes were enormous. On the previous evening Thomas Bradfield had been shot for giving information about the IRA to Tom Barry, mistakenly believing him to be an Auxiliary.[1] James 'Spud' Murphy gave a detailed description of what happened at Burgatia:

> This house was occupied by a loyalist family named Kingston. It was about one mile from the R.I.C. barracks at Rosscarbery which we were to attack the

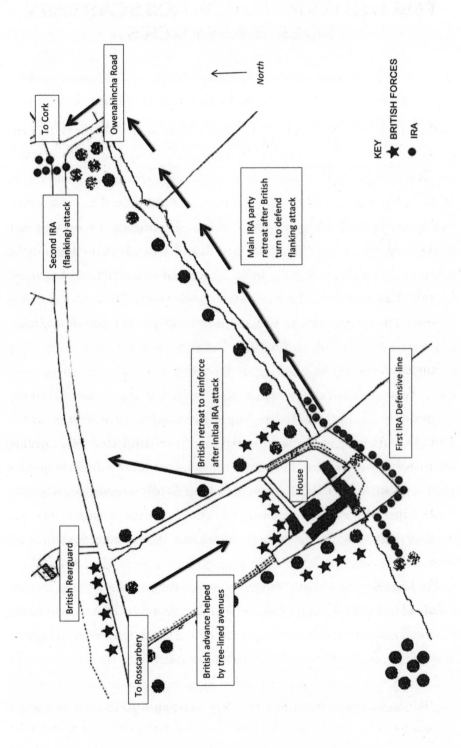

Owenahincha Road

To Cork

North

KEY

★ BRITISH FORCES

● IRA

Second IRA (flanking) attack

Main IRA party retreat after British turn to defend flanking attack

British retreat to reinforce after initial IRA attack

First IRA Defensive line

House

British Rearguard

To Rosscarbery

British advance helped by tree-lined avenues

following night. We arrived at Burgatia about 3 a.m. and placed the members of the household under arrest. Sentries were now posted, a meal was prepared and, having eaten, we settled down to rest for the remainder of the night.

On the following morning, the owner of the house – Kingston was tried on the charge of carrying messages to the enemy. He admitted doing so, but pleaded that it was because he wished to save the lives of the soldiers and to avoid ambushes. He was found guilty, but was not sentenced to death. He was ordered, instead, to leave the country and his property was confiscated.[2]

Just as the trial of Kingston was ending, the postman arrived and was dragged into the house. This presented Tom Barry with a problem. If he held on to the postman this would be noticed and he would be looked for; if he let him go it was probable that he would inform the RIC. After a hurried conference it was decided to swear him to secrecy under threat of his life. In a time when an oath on the Bible was taken very seriously, there was a possibility this might have worked. It did not. As soon as he was out of sight, the postman pedalled straight to the RIC barracks and told them about the column at Burgatia. According to Murphy it was around 12.30 p.m.

Shortly after 4 p.m. the sentries reported that 'Black and Tans carrying rifles were moving around in front of the house and that lorries of military were in the district'.[3] The IRA men took up defensive positions but soon realised that with military reinforcements flooding into the area it was only a matter of time before they were overwhelmed. The British closed in, firing as they came, but the IRA did not respond until they reached point-blank range. Murphy recalls that a 'sudden burst of rifle fire sent the enemy rushing for cover'. He led his section, while under fire, east to the Owenahincha road and crossed to the northern side of the main road from where he opened fire on the attacking forces on their flank. When the British turned to face this new threat, the rest of the column were able to escape from the trap by heading east. After half an hour, Murphy and his men also withdrew safely.[4]

## 31 March 1921

The failure in February meant another attempt had to be made. The problem was how to get close without letting the RIC know. As there was a strong loyalist community in the area, the West Cork Brigade found it difficult to avoid being seen and this being reported. However, on 31 March they tried again. There are many versions of the story but that of Michael Coleman is used here:

> We moved in for the attack at midnight after removing our boots. Not a sound was heard in the village. The mine was lofted on the shoulders of four officers, who walked at a steady pace through the wicket gate and laid the mine at the barrack door. They crept back. Suddenly there was a large explosion. The house across the street from the barracks was blasted [by the force of the explosion at the barracks]. We opened up and the assault party moved to rush the opening. There was a cry of 'we surrender' from the barracks and everything halted. Then there was another shout 'we hold the barracks'. Orders were given to resume the attack. The Column O/C went in under cover of our fire and lobbed in some bombs, while the R.I.C. lobbed out some bombs also. This went on for some time until the R.I.C. and Tans were forced upstairs. Then paraffin was thrown in and the barracks took fire. The garrison threw their arms into the flames and came out through a window after lowering their wounded. Eight or nine of the garrison were wounded. Two were killed and their bodies burned in the barracks and twelve unwounded surrendered. We had no losses either killed or wounded.[5]

This matter-of-fact description does not describe the full horror of the events that night. The attack went on for more than four hours and the fire in the barracks was so intense that everything inside the building was consumed, including the bodies of Constable Charles Bowles and Sergeant Ambrose O'Shea.

The IRA left the town at 5 a.m. and six hours later Auxiliaries from 'O' Company in Dunmanway reached the beleaguered garrison, who had been left in the local hotel, where their wounds were being treated by the local doctor. All that was left of the barracks was a pile of rubble and three outer walls. A search of the rubble was organised by Lieutenant Faraday, which quickly found the charred remains of Bowles. Of Sergeant O'Shea no trace was ever found. While they were working their way through the rubble a crowd of locals gathered and some of these were helping with the search, including a fourteen-year-old girl who found a grenade and handed it to one of the Auxiliaries, Constable Doyle. Unsurprisingly, he threw it as far away as possible. Unfortunately, it landed among the spectators and local men George Wilson and Patrick Collins, along with four-year-old Frank Fitzpatrick, were killed by shrapnel. Eight other civilians were injured. At an enormous cost the IRA had achieved its aim of driving the RIC out of the area between Clonakilty and Skibbereen.[6]

# TOM BARRY'S TRENCH COAT

Some tales are apocryphal and this one has always been regarded as one of the taller tales in a war that generated an enormous literature. Despite Tom Barry dining out on it for years and including it in his narrative of the war, *Guerilla Days in Ireland*, to show his favourable view of the King's Liverpool Regiment in Skibbereen and Bantry, it was met with scepticism by many historians.[1] However, Stephen O'Brien, who was guarding the house where the incident occurred, gives a detailed description of what happened:

The Column had arrived at Maultrahane and there was to be a Battalion Council there which was to be attended by Brigade Headquarters staff who were part of the Column. They were put up at the house of the teacher, Charles O'Sullivan, and a bed-sittingroom was fitted up for Liam Deasy, O.C. Brigade, Tom Barry, O.C. Column, Tadgh O'Sullivan, Brigade Quartermaster, Denis Lordan and Seán Buckley. The meeting lasted the whole day. That night Barry put me on sentry duty on the boreen running from the house to the main road. I was armed with a rifle. About 3 a.m. just at dawn I heard lorries on my left and bicycles on my right – about 200 yards away. Luckily they took another road and I ran back to the house and gave the alarm and the Brigade Staff got out and crossed the road and remained inside the fence while the house was being raided. All the Brigade papers, Barry's coat, waistcoat and watch were taken. The day after he wrote a letter to Colonel Hudson in Skibbereen, demanding them back. The Brigade Staff was then at Gurteenduig. Decently enough Colonel Hudson handed them over to Richard Connelly, Manager of 'The Southern Star' and brother of Neilus Connolly, O.C. Battalion. An account of this, written by Seán Buckley, now T.D., was published in 'The Southern Star' for 12th December, 1936. Had the British come directly my way that night I should have had to stand and try to delay them and at the same time give the alarm by using my rifle, but, however, when I found that the cycle party had taken another road I felt that the best action on my part was to get back to the house and quietly warn the Brigade Staff, which was what I had done and which had resulted in their getting away that morning.

Colonel Hudson, O.C. King's (Liverpool) Regiment, stationed in Skibbereen, was a gentleman and was regarded as such by the I.R.A. His Second-in-Command – Major Wyatt – was a gentleman, also. They did not care for their work and never wanted any trouble. They were very different to Major Percival and his Column from the Essex Regiment ...[2]

Extraordinarily, in Tom Barry's papers in the CCCA is a letter from Hudson enquiring of Barry if he had got his coat back and a note from Barry saying that he had. The letter was written from the Curragh at the end of July 1921; Hudson also noted his regret that he had not met up with Barry while he was in Cork.[3]

Another example of Barry's relatively cordial relationship with Colonel Hudson comes from Denis Lordan. In his BMH witness statement he recalled how earlier in the year (9 February) Barry wrote to Hudson to excuse two soldiers whom his column had captured for being absent without leave. Some weeks later Barry again wrote to Hudson, this time in high dudgeon (Barry did high dudgeon better than most), when he learned that the soldiers had submitted compensation claims for injuries received. He stated:

The O.C. of the Flying Column ... addressed a letter to the Officer Commanding the British troops in Skibbereen (Colonel Hudson) reminding him that the two soldiers in question had been allowed to return to their barracks uninjured and had not been deprived of any equipment as they had none when captured. Their Column O.C. further expressed the hope that Colonel Hudson, as a soldier and a gentleman, being aware of the facts of the case would take the necessary steps to prevent this unjust claim being pressed any further. No written reply was received to the communication but the claim for compensation was dropped.[4]

But this, apparently, was not the whole story of the relationship between Hudson and the IRA. Hudson, like many of the senior officers in the British Army, was an avid fisherman and, according to Tom Barry, was allowed to fish on any of the rivers and lakes across West Cork without hindrance. The only requirement was that an IRA man was his gillie. Whether this was actually the case is not known, but more than one source mentions Hudson's fishing trips, so there appears to have been an attitude of live and let live.[5] Certainly, if an IRA member was captured by the Liverpools, they were imprisoned but were treated well by their captors.[6]

There seems to have been an often overlooked, yet extraordinary sophistication in the way the war was managed by both sides. Florence J. Crowley, who was the IRA spy inside the Auxiliaries' barracks in Dunmanway Workhouse, tells another seemingly incredible story.[7] He was asked to go to the IRA headquarters at Togher (north of the town) to meet with Liam Deasy and Seán Buckley among others in June 1921. Crowley was thought to be 'sound' by the Auxiliaries and was never searched on his many fishing trips, even though this was how he got information out. As he was leaving the workhouse, Brownie, the intelligence officer, asked if he could accompany Crowley on this particular fishing trip. Crowley could not refuse but delayed his arrival at Togher by pointing out all the beauty spots along the way. He was not sure if Brownie was suspicious of him, but when they arrived at the village the Auxiliary announced he would be on duty in a few minutes and dashed off. Much relieved, Crowley made his report, only to be told by Seán Murphy that Brownie had been shot on the return journey. This would have put Crowley in an impossible position, as it would be assumed that he had led Brownie into a trap. As it turned out this was 'a joke in bad taste', but it seems incredible that Brownie should have taken such a risk to go into the heart of enemy territory in pursuit of intelligence or, for that matter, fish.[8]

In many ways the story of Crowley and Brownie goes to the heart of the nature of the war in West Cork. While Brownie was willing to put his life on the line, the IRA was willing to allow a chief target to walk within yards of its headquarters without shooting him. Either Crowley is exaggerating or they realised that such a shooting would endanger their operations and be counter-productive.[9]

This sophistication is equally reflected in the quantified difference in attitude of the King's Liverpool Regiment stationed in Skibbereen and Bantry and the Essex Regiment stationed in Bandon and Kinsale, and the IRA's reaction to them. It must be remembered that while the war was conducted with savagery in Cork city and around Bandon, this was notably absent elsewhere in West Cork.[10]

# MASSACRE IN WEST CORK

Less sophistication and more savagery would be the hallmarks of the conflict in West Cork in the months leading up to and during the Civil War, as fully evidenced by the events in Ovens and Dunmanway in April 1922.

Around 1.30 a.m. on 26 April 1922 Acting Commandant of the Cork No. 3 Brigade Michael O'Neill was shot by Captain Herbert Woods, MC MM, on the stairs of Ballygroman House in Ovens, Co. Cork, and died a short while later. The following morning IRA reinforcements captured Woods and his relations Thomas Henry Hornibrook and Samuel Hornibrook. They were taken to Newcestown, where all three were shot. A number of years later the bodies were retrieved from a bog-hole and quietly buried in a nearby Protestant churchyard.[1]

Herbert Woods, seated centre. *(Courtesy of Donal O'Flynn)*

Over the next four nights (26–29 April 1922) there were widespread attacks on loyalists across West Cork. The motive for these attacks has generated huge debate within Irish history regarding the interpretation of evidence, and the actual evidence tends to get lost in the debate. In total, nine Protestants were killed between the towns of Dunmanway and Bandon in West Cork, one in Clonakilty and another was shot and badly injured in Murragh, on the main road between Bandon and Ballineen. If the Ballygroman killings are included, as well as those of four British soldiers who were kidnapped and executed while on intelligence work at Macroom, twenty-five kilometres north of Dunmanway, this brings the total dead to seventeen. If those who were targeted but not killed are included, the figure rises to at least thirty. In Dunmanway, for example, the house of William Jagoe, who lived next door to James Buttimer, one of the victims, was attacked and if he had been at home it is probable that he, too, would have been shot. George 'Appy' Bryan had a gun placed to his head but the gun jammed and he fled. Local schoolteacher William Morrison also escaped from an attack, as did John McCarthy and Tom Sullivan. This level of attack on defenceless civilians was unheard of in the Irish War of Independence, and as virtually all the victims were Protestant, it raised fears that the killings were sectarian.

Specifically, on the night of 26–27 April three men were shot and killed in Dunmanway: local solicitor Francis Fitzmaurice was killed at 12.15 a.m., chemist David Grey at 1 a.m. and retired draper James Buttimer at 1.20 a.m. All were shot on their doorsteps. According to David Grey's wife, his killers called him a Free Stater a number of times while they were shooting him. All this took place within 100 metres of the police station in Dunmanway, which was controlled by the anti-Treaty IRA under Peter Kearney, who failed to stop the shootings. The killers probably arrived in the town from the east on the Bandon road and then worked their way around the corner onto Sackville Street, killing as they went, until they reached the Methodist manse next door to James Buttimer.

During the second night of violence, 27–28 April, John Chinnery and Robert Howe were shot in Castletown-Kinneigh to the north of Ballineen, at around 10.30 p.m. on 27 April for Howe according to *The Irish Times* of 2 May, or 1.30 a.m. on 28 April for both according to *The Skibbereen Eagle* of

6 May. Chinnery and Howe were next-door neighbours. The pattern was the same in both cases. Howe's wife, Catherine, gave evidence to his inquest that he was attacked in the bedroom of his house at around 10.30 p.m., having refused to harness a horse. When he refused a second time he was shot and killed. John Chinnery was shot while harnessing a horse for the raiders.

On the same night Alexander Gerald McKinley (the son of an RIC constable also named Alexander), who was sick in bed, was shot in Ballineen after 1.30 a.m. His aunt was put out of the house and he was shot in the back of the head. At Caher, three kilometres west of Ballineen, John Buttimer and his farm servant James Greenfield were shot at 2 a.m.:

> Frances Buttimer (John's wife) stated that she heard noise and shots – Her son said 'we are being attacked', and jumped out of bed. She became weak, but recovered quickly. She met her husband on the landing, and said 'for God's sake get out', and he said 'shure I can't'. Greenfield called on her to stay with him. She came down stairs, and met a man and said 'Where are you going?' He replied 'Where are the men?' She said 'I do not know. What do you want them for?' He said 'only very little'. She said to him 'Take my house, my money, or myself and spare the men'. She put her hand to his chest to keep him back, and he pushed past her, and went upstairs calling on her husband in a blasphemous manner to come down. She went away from the house and returned after a while and met a man and said 'You have killed them, but you cannot kill their souls'. She went into the house and found her husband dead in a sitting position in Greenfield's room, and Greenfield was dead in bed.[2]

Church of Ireland curate Rev. Ralph Harbord was shot (but survived) in Murragh on the same night. Robert Nagle was killed in Clonakilty after 11 p.m. Two men called to the house and, having questioned Robert about his age, doused the light in his bedroom and shot him. His mother, who was in the house and witnessed the events, said one of the killers was drunk. He was shot in place of his father, Tom, the caretaker of the Masonic Hall, and on the same night the Masonic Hall was burned.

The final victim was John Bradfield of Killowen Cottage at Carhue, four kilometres west of Bandon. He was killed at 11 p.m. on the night of 29–30 April in place of his brother William:

> Elizabeth Shorten (his sister) … stated that at 11 p.m. on Saturday a group of men called to the door to get a horse and car. Her brother got out of bed, but did not answer. They knocked on the door and broke the windows. On entering the dining room, they asked for her brother William. They entered John's room and she heard a shot. John was unable to walk without sticks.[3]

More than thirty men of both religions were targeted, shot at or forced to flee over the same three days, but all those killed were Protestant. When the killings continued into a third night, the officer in charge of the Royal Navy based at Queenstown (Cobh) began putting contingency plans in place to evacuate loyalists and Protestants from southern Irish ports. He even suggested that this might well be the start of a pogrom.

The IRA commandant at Bandon, Tom Hales, rushed back from Dublin and ordered all guns to be handed in. He had been negotiating a truce between pro- and anti-Treaty forces, with Michael Collins among others, when he heard of the murders. At this stage there is little doubt that the anti-Treaty IRA carried out these attacks or that they were a co-ordinated reprisal for the death of Michael O'Neill. While most people assumed that these events were in response to the Belfast 'pogroms', this was probably at most a secondary motive in the killings.

As the culprits remained silent, there is no way of knowing the actual motive and historians can only speculate. However, the apparent reason for targeting those shot has become clearer in recent years.[4] Francis Fitzmaurice provided information to the British during the War of Independence.[5] David Grey was originally from Cavan and, it is claimed, was suspected of trying to extract information from local children.[6] James Buttimer was the uncle of both a named spy living in Clonakilty and an identified spy who lived at

Manch, also called James Buttimer. John Chinnery was identified as a spy by Kate Nyhan of Castletown-Kinneigh in her Military Service Pensions application. She also identifies a Howe and a Buttimer as spies, although she does not specify which of the family members.[7] However, it is probable that the home of John Buttimer at Manch, loyalist certainly, was attacked simply because it was next to Sunlodge House where James Buttimer lived. James Greenfield was shot because he was living with the Buttimers at Manch, and the son, William J. Buttimer, would have been shot if he had not escaped through the skylight, the scar of which he bore on his leg until he passed away many years later. Robert Nagle was shot in place of his father, Tom, who was hiding behind a cupboard in the kitchen when the house was attacked. Tom had been on a list of 'enemy agents' submitted by the 3rd Brigade in July 1921 and by the 1st Southern Division in February (approximate) 1922. John Bradfield was shot in place of his brother William, who had been in the British Army and who had been providing information to the British. Alexander Gerald McKinley was related to Thomas Nagle, but there is no evidence that he was passing information to the British. His name did appear (misspelled) on the February 1922 IRA Southern Command list of 'hostile' suspects and was possibly linked to the murder of the Coffey brothers in nearby Desertserges.[8] The survivors had all admitted they were providing information to the British, were all former members of the British Army or, like R. J. Helen, had been previously identified as 'enemy agents'.[9] George 'Appy' Bryan, in an interview in 1923, admitted that he gave information. William Jagoe stated in his claim to the post-war compensation commission that he and Francis Fitzmaurice provided information to the British.[10]

However, confessions aside, there is little other documentary evidence to show that these men were what they were claimed to be by the IRA. As I have written previously, these murders had the mark of unfettered military power at their centre. The rule of law was very far from the minds of the men who meted out 'justice' to those who had been their 'enemies' during the War of Independence for a crime they had no involvement in.

# MICHAEL COLLINS: 'THE MAN WHO COULDN'T BE KILLED'[1]

Everyone who has watched the 1996 film *Michael Collins* knows what happened to Michael Collins at Béal na Bláth on 22 August 1922. At approximately 8 p.m. he was shot in the head during an improvised ambush and died at the scene. He was thirty-one. However, the attack that day was neither unusual in the year leading up to his death nor should it have been surprising. Shocking certainly, but surprising no.

Collins had spent the time since the Easter Rising in prison in Stafford and in north Wales at Frongoch, then on the run, breaking various Sinn Féin leaders out of jails in England and Ireland, running the Department of Finance in the Sinn Féin government, leading the secretive IRB, managing the intelligence war against the British state and courting Katherine Kiernan. He did all this successfully while cycling around Dublin under the noses of the British military. Frank Thornton, who would know, commented afterwards 'that he never carried a gun during these journeys, neither was he accompanied by a bodyguard'.[2]

Michael Collins
(*Courtesy of Mercier Press*)

Béal na Bláth was not the first time Collins was attacked in Cork. On 19 July 1921 he had taken the train from Dublin to Clonakilty. On the way he had applied for a permit to visit his brother Johnny, who was interned on Spike Island in the middle of Cork Harbour. Unsurprisingly, this was refused by a British military still smarting from the Truce.[3] According to *The Southern Star* he was accompanied on his trip by Liam Deasy, Tom Barry, Gearóid O'Sullivan and Timothy O'Sullivan.[4] When Collins arrived in Clonakilty he was immediately recognised by his neighbours and friends and inevitably the news of this favoured son's return reached the British military in the town. One of them decided to deal with their most hated enemy. Armed with a rifle he approached the hotel where Collins was and started shouting for him to come out. In response Collins' bodyguards came out onto the street armed with revolvers. The incident was diffused when a senior British officer arrived and ordered the soldier back to barracks.[5] While Collins did not mention this incident in his letters to Kitty Kiernan, he did note that the military were being 'arrogant and provocative'.[6] On the trip he also visited the ruins of his family home at Woodfield, which had been burned a few weeks earlier by soldiers from the Essex Regiment.[7]

On 17 September 1921 another incident occurred in Clonakilty when a senior IRA officer was recognised by local people, who mobbed the car. This attracted the attention of a group of drunken Auxiliaries, who came over to see who the visitor was. The incident involved much swearing and abuse, but when the Auxiliaries tried to take photographs they were warned off by the men in the car. Sadly, no names were used so it is impossible identify this famous Irish republican who excited so much attention and abuse.[8]

In October Collins was sent to London, at Éamon de Valera's suggestion, as one of the Irish delegates to negotiate with the British at Downing Street, arriving a day after the others, on 9 October 1921. Seven weeks later, between 2 and 2.30 a.m. on 6 December 1921, a treaty between the British state and the Irish revolutionaries, granting dominion status with full fiscal autonomy to three-quarters of Ireland, was signed. The granting of fiscal autonomy had been the final card in Lloyd George's deck of concessions and a previous attempt at a settlement in November 1920 had been blocked by him because, as a former chancellor of the exchequer, he understood that if 'this were done Ireland could not remain an integral part of the United Kingdom. The scheme put forward was not compatible with her so remaining. She could either support us or not, as she chose.'[9]

This was as far as the British prime minister and his government were willing to go in 1920: to do otherwise could fuel demands throughout the British Empire for similar concessions. So for Collins and Griffith to extract full fiscal autonomy in December 1921 was an Empire-shattering event, but as the concession was to delete references to a free trade area it went almost unnoticed by commentators at the time.[10] In contrast, on 10 November 1921 Egypt had been offered (and rejected) independence in nothing but name.[11] At the same time Lord Curzon was fighting a rearguard action against Secretary of State for India Edwin Montagu's plans for 'self-government' in India.[12]

The main concession on the Irish side was that they had to concede faithfulness to the crown. Another problem with the Treaty was that they had failed to break off negotiations over the essential unity of Ireland (which they had said in advance would be their tactic) and instead accepted a Boundary Commission that they believed would return large parts of Northern Ireland to the south.[13] The price to be paid for 'real' independence was that Ireland would simply have to swallow the imperial pill, although it had been made as sweet as possible.

The terms of the Treaty caused a split among Irish nationalists, chiefly over whether it was worth restarting the War of Independence because the oath of loyalty was to an Irish Free State and faithfulness to the crown, instead of an oath of allegiance to a republic. In January 1922 the Dáil decided by a narrow majority to accept the Treaty. Although its opponents eventually accepted, worked with and amended the settlement, Collins prophetically commented that he was 'signing his actual death warrant'.[14]

Three months later Collins arrived in Cork to address a pro-Treaty monster meeting in the city scheduled for 12 March. Two platforms had been erected on Grand Parade and many of the most senior supporters of the Treaty were to speak. These included Collins, Seán Milroy, Liam de Róiste, J. J. Walsh, Fionán Lynch, Joseph McGrath, Seán Hayes, Seán Hales, Piaras Béaslaí, Patrick O'Keeffe and Seán MacEoin.[15] The night before the speeches both platforms were dumped in the River Lee and white flags were erected along the street by anti-Treaty supporters, but by the time of the meeting the platforms had been fished out of the river and the flags removed. An enormous crowd filled the street, including some anti-Treaty supporters armed with revolvers, which they fired when any of the pro-Treaty speakers tried to speak. The event was on the verge of collapse until Collins took to the main stage and his bodyguards appeared in the crowd. He addressed the meeting through 'a fusillade of shots', but his speech was a success and he carried the crowd.[16]

In an era when manhole covers are routinely welded shut every time the United States president visits a city, it seems incredible that opponents with guns could have been let so close to Collins during a period of high tension. However, this was not the most serious incident that happened in the city that weekend. On the previous day Collins had gone to St Finbarr's Cemetery to visit the graves of the Republican dead, including Terence MacSwiney and Tomás MacCurtain. As he approached the gates he was confronted by armed men, who ringed the plot and warned him that if he took another step forward he would be shot. After a brief stand-off, Collins and his party left. There is no doubt that he was upset by the events of the morning, as is clear from a photograph taken outside the cemetery immediately after the stand-off. That evening, as he approached the home of his sister Mary Collins Powell in Sunday's Well on the north side of the city, a gunman stepped from the shadows saying, 'Collins, I have you now.' Before he could open fire Seán MacEoin set upon him and wrestled him to the ground.[17]

Cork was not the only place where Collins faced violence. On 16 April 1922 he exited his car outside Vaughan's Hotel at 29 Parnell Square in Dublin and began walking down the street. Suddenly ten members of the 'unofficial IRA' rushed out of their headquarters around 100 metres away at No. 44 and opened fire on the car. Some were armed with rifles. Collins, who had been heading towards No. 44 with fellow IRB member Seán Ó Muirthile, returned fire. Gearóid O'Sullivan, who had been in the hotel, rushed out and joined the battle. The gunfight, which lasted about three minutes, resulted in the capture of one of the 'unofficials' by Collins. On being searched at nearby Mountjoy Prison, he was found to be carrying a grenade.[18]

The fundamental political problem remained: how to make the dominion of the Treaty into the republic the anti-Treaty IRA wanted. Collins had organised the writing of a republican Free State constitution which was presented to the British Treaty signatories for approval. The draft constitution resulted in tense negotiations between the two sides, with Lloyd George describing it as 'a Republic with a thin veneer'.[19] As a holding operation to stop outright war between the pro- and anti-Treaty IRA, de Valera and Collins had agreed a pact which stated that, however the Free State elections went on 16 June, seats would be allocated in cabinet between the pro- and anti-Treaty sides of Sinn Féin in what would be in effect a coalition government. This was never going to last once the Irish side in the London negotiations conceded to redrafting the constitution to suit British requirements in the face of a threat of war.

This failure to secure a republican constitution led, in turn, to one of the more controversial moments of that summer. On 14 June, two days before the election, Collins and J. J. Walsh returned to Cork (Walsh was a candidate for the city and Collins for the combined constituency of Cork North, Mid and West Cork). Speaking from a hotel window 'while a downpour drenched his audience', and as he was 'not hampered now by being on a platform where there are Coalitionists', Collins urged the voters to 'vote for the candidate they thought best'. This is often claimed to have been a planned attempt to repudiate the 'coalition' pact between pro- and anti-Treaty Sinn Féin, but given the context of the speech this is probably overstating the position.[20] Whatever its importance or intentions, the speech did Collins no harm. He swept the boards at the election for a constituency where the anti-Treaty IRA believed it would take a majority.[21]

Events quickly cascaded out of control once the election was over. On 28 June, two days after Deputy Chief of Staff of the National Army J. J. 'Ginger' O'Connell was kidnapped by anti-Treaty forces, Rory O'Connor rejected a call for his forces to evacuate the occupied Four Courts and the building was attacked by the National Army. The Irish Civil War had commenced. The conventional phase of the war lasted from the attack on the Four Courts in Dublin to the arrival of Free State troops in Cork city on 10 August, when, after a sharp battle to the east of the city in Rochestown in which approximately fifteen soldiers were killed, the anti-Treaty forces abandoned the city. As a parting shot, the main city police barracks and Victoria Army Barracks were both burned.[22]

A couple of days later Michael Collins, who had become commander-in-chief of the Free State forces, set out on a tour of inspection of the newly captured territory, but had to return to Dublin almost immediately when he received the news that the president of Dáil Éireann, Arthur Griffith, had died. Collins attended the funeral and delivered the oration at the graveside before heading south again. Collins' tour is often seen as reckless, but an extraordinary document in the Desmond FitzGerald Papers suggests his trip to West Cork may have been to recover gold bullion he had buried in a child's coffin and money bags.[23]

At Kingstown (Dún Laoghaire) on 19 August Collins' car was involved in a collision with a Crossley tender driven by National Army troops coming from the harbour and a replacement car had to be found. Late the following night he arrived at General Emmet Dalton's headquarters in the Imperial Hotel in Cork. Suffering from a heavy cold and a kidney infection, he visited some local banks in an effort to trace £100,000 in customs revenue collected by anti-Treaty troops during their occupation of the city. On returning to the hotel he found the guards asleep. He banged their heads together before going to bed.

Florrie O'Donoghue
*(Courtesy of Mercier Press)*

Shortly after 6 a.m. the following morning he headed west to inspect garrisons and visit the smouldering ruins of Macroom Castle, which had been burned by anti-Treaty forces when they abandoned the town. While in Macroom he met Florrie O'Donoghue, who was neutral in the war, to discuss the situation. He then motored on to Bandon via Béal na Bláth, where he was recognised by anti-Treaty forces who were holding a staff meeting in the area on the same day. De Valera had been staying nearby the previous evening and actually arrived in Béal na Bláth just minutes after Collins had left. De Valera was accompanied by local IRA commander Liam Deasy, who decided to organise an ambush in the likely event of the Free State convoy returning.

They would have a long wait. The Collins party proceeded to Skibbereen before returning to his home place at Sam's Cross, just to the west of Clonakilty. Collins' biographer T. Ryle Dwyer takes up the story:

On reaching Sam's Cross, the convoy stopped off at the pub of Collins' cousin, Jeremiah. The Big Fellow bought two pints of Clonakilty Wrastler for each of his crew. While there he met his brother Johnny, and two of Johnny's daughters – Mary and Kitty – as well as his first cousin Michael O'Brien. He told them that his main goal was to end the Civil War and then he would be re-dedicating himself to the task of securing full national freedom. He was not about to be content with the Treaty settlement but would get further concessions from the British government once peace was restored. He seemed in good form, according to Johnny, but this was probably because his spirits were lifted in the midst of his family and friends, not to mention that he had consumed a fair bit of alcohol that day.

'I hope you are travelling in the armoured car, Mick, because there is still danger around,' Johnny said.

'Not at all, this is my bus,' Michael replied motioning towards the open touring car.

He crossed the road for a brief visit to his aunt and some other people in the neighbourhood. 'Take care Michael,' one of them said to him, according to Johnny, 'take good care of yourself.'

'They will never shoot me in my own country,' he replied.[24]

The party left Sam's Cross and returned to Bandon, where they were in-formed that the main road to Cork was not secure, so it was decided to return via Béal na Bláth. The touring car left Lee's Hotel (now the Munster Arms) at around 6.45 p.m. Ryle Dwyer continues the story:

With the light failing, around 7.15 [p.m.] the Free State convoy approached the ambush site. It was surrounded by hills and when the first shot was fired [Emmet] Dalton realised it was an ideal spot for an ambush. 'Drive like hell!' Dalton shouted, but Collins put a hand on the driver's shoulder.

'Stop!' he ordered. 'We'll fight them.'

Collins got to his feet and went over behind the armoured car to use it for cover as he fired some shots. 'Come on boys!' Collins shouted, apparently believing the ambushers were on the run. He left the protection of the car and moved about fifteen yards up the road. He dropped into the prone fir-ing position and opened up on the retreating republicans. A few minutes had elapsed when Commandant O'Connell came running up the road under fire and threw himself down beside Dalton asking, 'Where is the Big Fellow?'

'He's round the corner,' Dalton replied. They could hear Collins shooting. At one point he was standing up on the road firing as if he was daring some-body to shoot him ...

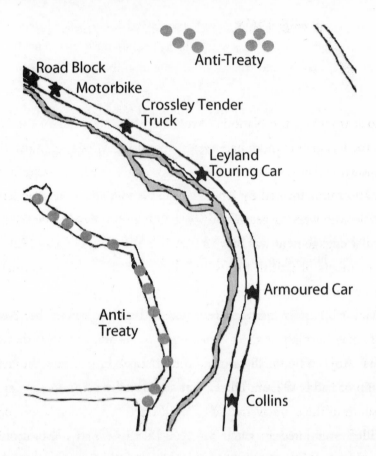

'Next moment,' Dalton said later, 'I caught a faint cry: "Emmet I'm hit."'

Dalton and O'Connell found Collins lying on the road, still clutching his rifle. He had a gaping wound at the base of the skull behind his right ear. 'It was quite obvious to me with the experience I had of a ricochet bullet, it could only have been a ricochet or a "dum-dum",' Dalton recalled.

O'Connell dragged Collins behind the armoured car. 'I bandaged the wound and O'Connell said an "Act of Contrition" to him,' Dalton said. 'He was dying if not already dead.' The body was placed in the armoured car and moved down the road out of danger and it was then transferred to the touring car. They asked a local man, Ted Murphy, to guide them to the nearest priest. He got into the tender.

'This is a night that will be remembered,' one of the soldiers remarked.

'Why?' Murphy asked.

'The night Michael Collins was killed.'[25]

# THE DOOR TO MADNESS

The shock troops of the National Army were the members of the Dublin Guard, the leaders of whom had been members of Michael Collins' 'Squad' (also known as the 'twelve apostles'). This was a special intelligence and assassination unit formed by Collins during the War of Independence to kill people who were suspected British agents in Dublin. The Squad's most spectacular engagement was on the morning of Bloody Sunday 1920 when fifteen members of British forces and some civilians (killed in error) were shot in a counter-intelligence operation directed by Collins.

In May 1921, after many of their members were captured and interned following the burning of the Customs House, the Squad and the Dublin Brigade's ASU were amalgamated into the Dublin Guard, under the leadership of Paddy O'Daly. During the Civil War the Guard was deployed in the south of the country and had a very rough time. Many senior officers were killed or injured in the fighting with anti-Treaty IRA forces. For example, Hugh Thornton, who had been sent to West Cork and trained the Volunteers after the 1916 Rising, died in Clonakilty on 29 August 1922. The unit also suffered severe casualties when it was ambushed by a machine-gun unit of the anti-Treaty IRA as they fought their way into Tralee. On 18 August, outside Barraduff, between Killarney and Rathmore, Colonel James McGuinness had been hit in the head and severely wounded by republican fire and, of course, Michael Collins was killed in Béal na Bláth on 22 August.

On 16 September Colonel Commandant Tom Keogh led a small patrol from Macroom to clear a mine barring the road to the anti-Treaty stronghold in Ballyvourney. Keogh's main column of 230 troops had already successfully cleared Wexford of the anti-Treaty IRA. The road-clearing operation was designed to allow his men to link up with Paddy O'Daly's forces coming from Killarney. Keogh's men reached Carrigaphooka Bridge without incident and set about removing the mine. However, a booby-trap bomb exploded (also setting off the mine), blowing the soldiers to pieces. 'The head and shoulders of one man were found five fields away,' reported *The Irish Times*.[1] Tom Keogh's legs were shattered and one of his feet severed. He died the following day in the Mercy Hospital in Cork. Eight men were killed (see page 308 for their names) and the explosion blew a massive crater in the road. One victim was so badly mangled he still remains unidentified.

Tom Keogh (23) had led the 'twelve apostles'. In January 1920 he had assassinated the new head of the Dublin Metropolitan Police, William Charles Forbes Redmond, who been brought in from Belfast to reorganise the police intelligence service after a slew of resignations.[2] On Bloody Sunday he shot Lieutenant James Angliss. Keogh had been captured at the Customs House in May 1921 during the IRA's destruction of the building and was incarcerated in Ballykinlar Internment Camp in Co. Down until January 1922. His death was as profound a shock as that of Collins three weeks earlier. Paddy O'Daly, writing to Tom's sister, stated 'we have lost the dearest and bravest comrade we ever knew'.[3]

Two days later the newspapers reported that the body of local anti-Treaty soldier James Buckley had been found in the hole left by the landmine. He had been shot through the head. Nobody was in any doubt about who had done the shooting. National Army Commandant Conlon in Macroom wrote immediately to General Dalton in Cork. He was outraged:

> The shooting of this prisoner here in the operations has caused considerable contempt amongst the Garrison here. They have paraded before me and have given me to understand that they will not go out on to the hills anymore. Therefore you will want to tell these officers from Dublin that they will want to stop that kind of work or they will corrupt the Army. But at the same time that does not clear me here, and the situation here is at present very critical, I may tell you among the men. If I was taken prisoner I would want to be treated as one. Therefore, we must do the same. I oppose that policy in the strongest way.'[4]

Dalton, bemused that the troops were unfazed by the deaths from the mine but outraged by the shooting of Buckley, reported the incident to Commander-in-Chief Richard Mulcahy, stating that the killers were members of 'the Squad'. Mulcahy invited Dalton to return to Dublin anyone he thought was unfit to serve. Nothing happened.[5]

While arresting members of 'the Squad' would have been deeply embarrassing for the government, Mulcahy's failure to take action opened the door for similar atrocities in Kerry six months later. After five National Army soldiers were killed by a trap-mine in Knocknagoshel (an atrocity in its own right) on 6 March 1923, nine anti-Treaty IRA prisoners were tied to a mine at Ballyseedy the following day, which was then detonated. Eight of them were killed. On the same day at Countess Road, Killarney, four prisoners were bombed and machine-gunned. A week later at Caherciveen a further five anti-Treaty IRA were 'accidentally' blown up by a mine which they had been forced to clear.[6] When Mulcahy supported his troops in the Dáil, the moral authority of the Free State suffered enormously because he failed to understand that nobody is above the law.[7]

# PART 2

## THE DEAD

**2 May 1916**

**Head Constable William Rowe**

**3 May 1916**

**Volunteer Richard Kent**

**9 May 1916**

**Volunteer Thomas Kent**

At 4.30 a.m. on 2 May 1916 RIC under Head Constable William Rowe surrounded Bawnard House in Castlelyons to arrest Thomas, David, William and Richard Kent for republican activities.

According to Frank King, who was part of the raiding party, 'It was daylight by this time as it was now 4.30 a.m. When we heard the shot we decided that standing in the open near these windows was very dangerous so we retreated back in the direction of some shrubbery to take up position where we would have some cover from any fire. There were several more shots as we moved back. When I got back some distance from the house I could see the Head Constable [Rowe] crouching behind a low wall on the far side of the house. Several shots rang out and I saw him fall back on the ground. His head was almost completely blown off by a shotgun blast.'[1]

The Kents surrendered after a three-hour firefight involving more than 100 British reinforcements, who came from Moore Park Officer Cadet Training School in nearby Fermoy. Richard, a renowned athlete, made an escape attempt but was shot in the side. He died a day later in Fermoy Military Hospital according to his death certificate. William and Thomas were court-martialled on 4 May 1916. William was acquitted thanks to testimony given by King, but Thomas was convicted.[2] He was executed on 9 May 1916 at Cork Military (Victoria) Barracks and buried in the yard. David Kent was also sentenced to death but his sentence was subsequently commuted as he had been too badly injured to be certified fit for execution.

The body of Thomas Kent was found in the grounds of Cork Prison in May 2015 and he was reinterred after a state funeral at Castlelyons, near his home at Bawnard House.[3]

**25 June 1917**

**Abraham Allen**

The final 1916 prisoners had been released and Sinn Féin was determined to celebrate the event with welcome home parades. Several of the prisoners reached a very disturbed Cork on the evening of 24 June. The celebrations turned into a riot. Unable to contain the situation, the RIC called for military assistance. The RIC and military then charged the 5,000-strong Sinn Féin demonstration outside the British recruitment office on St Patrick's Street with fixed bayonets. In the course of the mêlée, Abraham Allen (25) received a bayonet wound in the thigh, which led to his death, and thirty others were injured. Constable John Brown was shot at and injured, and District Inspector Oswald Swanzy was also injured. The recruitment office was destroyed.[4]

**14 May 1918**

**Volunteer Denis Quinlan**

'In the month of May in this year we lost a very fine officer in Denis Quinlan, O/C of the Inchigeela Company. While on his way to attend a Battalion Council Meeting at The Turrett, Macroom, he was accidentally shot through the brain while examining an old pin fire revolver. This early demise of a promising soldier was deeply regretted.'[5]

An article in *Cumann Staire* states, 'On that night the O.C. did not return to Inchigeela. He stayed with some friends near Teralton [*sic*] and the following day went to attend a 7th Batt. meeting in Macroom. He was carrying his revolver and on his way home that evening he was accidentally shot.' He is buried at Newcestown.[6]

**24 July 1918**

**Na Fianna Seamus Courtney**

P. J. Murphy, company commander of Na Fianna Éireann in Cork city said: 'As the result of imprisonment and poor health, our Commandant, Seamus

Courtney, died. He was buried in Passage West.' He was in jail for illegal drilling.[7] James Allan Busby wrote: 'My brother, Jerome, and I joined up in company with about fifty other boys, including two lads named Seán Healy and Seumas [*sic*] Courtney. Both these two were later officers in the Fianna, and while prisoners in Cork Gaol they took part in the big hunger-strike of political prisoners which took place in that gaol in 1917. Seumas Courtney died sometime later in Kerry. A firing party of Fianna rendered military honours when he was buried at Monkstown, Co. Cork.'[8]

## 23 November 1918
### Na Fianna Joseph Reid

'Joe Reid, a Cobh Na Fianna boy, died from wounds received when a revolver he was cleaning, in preparation for Courtney's funeral, was accidentally discharged.'[9] This version of Joe's death is the standard one, but it is incorrect. *The Cork Examiner* reported his shooting on 25 November (calling him Reed). At the inquest a US naval officer failed to recall a statement he had given earlier to the police, that Reid had apparently said 'the B___ shot me'. The coroner advised Joe's brother that if he gave evidence he might incriminate himself, so he declined to do so. If Joe was shot by his younger brother, the boy could have been prosecuted for murder or manslaughter, so it appears that Reid had said before his death that the bullet wound was self-inflicted to avoid this. As the bullet passed through the abdomen it was no surprise that the young man died a few days later of peritonitis.[10]

## 14 December 1918
### Volunteer William Murphy

*The Cork Examiner* records the death of William Murphy but gives no details of location. Peter Hart states that he was killed accidentally at Clogheen. On 11 December Murphy had been examining his old revolver when it went off. He was operated on but died of peritonitis on 14 December at the North Infirmary. Murphy was with Volunteer Michael Bowles at the time of the shooting and although the RIC claimed that Bowles was on the run, he turned up at the inquest.[11]

## 24 December 1918
### Volunteer Con O'Dwyer

'Early in August, 1918, Sergt. O'Connell and Constable Cummins of the R.I.C. attempted to arrest Con O'Dwyer, who was accompanied by Michael Foley and Peter Harrington. Christy O'Connell arrived on the scene and, although unarmed, attacked the R.I.C. Constable Cummins, who was armed, fired a few shots and Sergt. O'Connell used his baton, but they were forced to retire to their barracks without carrying out the arrest. However, within a short time Christy O'Connell, Michael Foley, Peter Harrington and John Driscoll were arrested in connection with this incident by a strong enemy party. They were later sentenced to varying terms of imprisonment. Con [O']Dwyer escaped on this occasion and went "on the run". He was moving round the area [Castletownbere] until he got the 'flu towards the end of the year 1918 and died just prior to Christmas. He was buried with full military honours on Christmas Day, 1918.'[12] Con O'Dwyer, Eyeries Company, 6th Battalion, 3rd Cork Brigade is buried in Foildarrig (Lower) Cemetery, Castletownbere.

On 12 April 1919 a brief report in *The Skibbereen Eagle* stated that both Sergeant O'Connell and Constable Cummins had been shot and wounded in Castletownbere.[13]

## 20 May 1919
### Volunteer Miceál Tobin

Seán O'Connell recorded: 'In the month of May, 1918, [*sic*] when I held the rank of Company Quartermaster, I, and others of "G" Company, were involved in an explosion on the premises of Andy Hearne's boot shop in Grattan Street, Cork ... On the night in question, Dick Murphy our Company Captain, Miceál Tobin and myself, went into Hearne's and proceeded to empty the tins of powder into linen bags outside of which was a coarser type of bag. Dick and Miceál were holding a bag and I was emptying one of the tins into it when all of a sudden a terrific explosion occurred. … Dick Murphy was removed to the North Infirmary where he was treated and subsequently recovered. Miceál Tobin and I were taken to the hospital of the Sisters of Mercy where poor Tobin died.' The date of this explosion was actually 28 April 1919. Tobin was wounded and eventually died on 20 May at the Mercy Hospital from heart failure as a result of burns and blood poisoning. As well as the Volunteers, Mrs Hegarty, the owner of the building, and two innocent passers-by were injured.[14]

## 7 September 1919
### Private William Jones

Approximately fifteen British soldiers marched with their rifles each Sunday from their barracks on the north side of Fermoy to the Methodist Church next to the courthouse on the south side of the town. The rifles were stacked outside the church during the service. On 7 September 1919, as they were entering the church, the soldiers were rushed by members of the local IRA. Private William Jones attempted to prevent them stealing the rifles and was shot and killed. A number of other soldiers were also shot. The minister's wife later recalled that she heard at least a dozen shots. The six-strong IRA party, led by Liam Lynch, Liam Tobin and George Power, sped off eastwards with the weapons, quickly followed by the military, who commandeered any available cars. However, a short distance out of the town the way was blocked by a fallen tree. The telephone wires had also been cut, indicating a well-planned operation. Three planes that searched the area failed to find any trace of the attackers.

Following the attack, a number of local men were arrested. Eight were released without charge, while the rest remained in custody. On the night after the killing almost sixty shops in the town were wrecked and looted by members of the Shropshire Regiment. At a public meeting the following day Colonel Dobbs, the commander of the forces, complained bitterly that nobody in the town had helped the injured. When the chairman of the Urban District Council (UDC) criticised the damage to the town, he responded, 'you have no industry: you are simply living on the army', which was entirely correct. Neither Tobin nor Power, whose father was a member of Fermoy UDC, was arrested.[15]

## 9 September 1919
### Volunteer Bryan Crowley

Bryan Crowley (27) from Glanmire was knocked down by a British Army truck which was bringing prisoners from Fermoy, possibly the men who had been arrested after the death of Private Jones. As he was coming out of Cook Street onto St Patrick's Street the lorry hit him and he fell forward under the wheels, which rolled over him. His 'neck and face were crushed in a terrible manner' and he died from his wounds. There is no further information about what happened. However, it has been confirmed by his family that he is buried in St Finbarr's Cemetery. The funeral cortège was led by a Volunteer band and the coffin was covered with a tricolour.[16]

## 14 December 1919
### Constable Edward Bolger

Constable Edward Bolger of the RIC was shot and killed in the middle of Kilbrittain, Bandon, as he made his way from his home to the barracks. According to the IRA he had been aggressively pursuing them and needed to be stopped. Seven members of the local Volunteers had been imprisoned after he had identified them.[17] He was shot on the night they returned to the village. His widow and four young children were awarded £3,000 compensation at Bandon Quarter Sessions, where Justice Bird said, 'Constable Bolger was a quiet, inoffensive man, doing his ordinary duty as a peace officer in the protection of life and property of the people in his district. About six o'clock he went to his home for his supper ... About 6.30

p.m. he started to return to the barracks and almost immediately after he left his own door shots rang out.' His daughter Annie found him dead in the street.[18]

## 27 December 1919
### Corporal Harry Corless

Corporal Corless was having a few drinks in Victoria Barracks, Cork, when he sat down on the window sill. He apparently overbalanced and fell, smashing his skull on the barracks square two storeys below.[19]

## 13 February 1920
### Constable Michael Neenan

Constable Michael Neenan was killed during an attack on Allihies RIC Barracks. 'The attack opened at about 3.45 a.m. with the explosion, which blew in a large portion of the brick wall of the barrack, throwing some of the police out of bed, and continued until about 5 o'clock. The deceased constable volunteered to go to the room where the rifles and ammunition were, to procure them and was shot by a bullet in the back, which penetrated through the abdomen, while passing the breach in the wall, through which a heavy fire was poured and maintained after the explosion had made an opening.'[20] Despite the building being on fire, the RIC refused to surrender and the IRA retreated. About twenty IRA men, led by Seán Hales, destroyed the building the following day, after it had been evacuated by the RIC, who withdrew to Castletownbere never to return. The barracks was the property of the Bantry Estate and was rebuilt by the Free State before being occupied by An Garda Síochána.[21]

## 18 February 1920
### Timothy Quinlisk

Timothy Quinlisk was shot as a spy on the orders of Michael Collins and Florence O'Donoghue at Pouladuff, Cork. He had been a member of Roger

Casement's Irish Brigade. Richard Walsh gives an enormously detailed account of Quinlisk's activities in Michael Collins' headquarters at 44 Mountjoy Street, Dublin, where most senior members of the IRA slept when in Dublin. Once Collins stopped paying for Quinlisk's lodgings he was apparently persuaded by his father, who was a member of the RIC, to join the British side. Collins was warned of a raid on his headquarters by his spies in Dublin Castle and the source of the information was confirmed as Quinlisk. He was persuaded to 'follow' Collins to Cork. While there Florrie O'Donoghue confirmed his double role and he was executed. Two weeks later his father arrived to exhume the body from a pauper's grave (where unidentified bodies were buried) and return it to Waterford.[22]

## 28 February 1920
### Private William Newman
Private William Newman died when the IRA attempted to capture arms in Queenstown (Cobh). Five soldiers were held up outside Rushbrooke Docks, and Private Newman was shot when he tried to escape. The rest were deprived of their rifles but unhurt. Michael Burke stated: 'Cobh Volunteers attacked and disarmed a party of four [sic] soldiers at Bunker's Hill, Cobh, in the forenoon. One soldier was killed in the affair. The O/C of the Volunteers engaged was Captain Jack O'Connell of the Cobh Company, who had eight men with him, all armed with revolvers. Some of these revolvers were procured from a dump located at my home in Cobh. The night of the Bunker Hill attack, with some other Volunteers I helped to remove the captured rifles from their place of concealment (temporary) to a safer dump at Cushkenny, Cobh.'[23]

## 12 March 1920
### Constable Timothy Scully
Joseph Cashman explained the events surrounding the death of Timothy Scully: 'Our nearest RIC barracks was located at Glanmire and it had a

garrison of a sergeant and six men. In March 1920, it was decided by our company – Riverstown – to try and capture it. As a rule, about three of the garrison went on patrol together in the area. Our plan was to try and hold up this patrol of three men, disarm them and march them to the barracks and make them give their usual password to the man in charge within so that we could rush in and seize whatever arms were inside. With a number of the local Volunteers I had been placed near the barracks to take part in the rush on the door when it opened, while the company captain and a few of the men proceeded to hold up the three R.I.C. men who were sheltering under a hedge during a shower. Our men were armed with a revolver or two and some shotguns. When the R.I.C. got the order "Hands up", one of them – a Constable Scully – resisted and was shot dead. This put an end to our attempted seizure as, after the shooting, we returned to our homes for the time being.'[24]

### 19/20 March 1920
### Constable Joseph Murtagh
### Lord Mayor and IRA 1st Cork Brigade Commandant Tomás MacCurtain

For details of these deaths, see Part 1: The Murder of Lord Mayor Tomás MacCurtain and the 'Stolen' Jury.

### 12 April 1920
### Volunteer Patrick Morrissey

On 9 April *The Cork Examiner* reported that three Morrissey brothers had been arrested at Youghal on the previous night. On the following night a man was admitted to the emergency room at the North Infirmary with gunshot wounds to the buttocks. The wounds were made by pellets from a shotgun, fired at close range. Morrissey died of septicaemia a couple of days later. His name was initially given as John Walsh from Carrigtwohill but *The Cork Examiner* of 13 April reported that he had been identified as Patrick Morrissey of Gortroe, Youghal.[25]

**22 April 1920**

**Constable Michael McCarthy**

Constable McCarthy, a member of the Dublin Metropolitan Police, went home to Clonakilty on leave to help out on the family farm. He was working in a field when two men approached him and shot him, asking 'if he had had enough' as he lay on the ground. He died shortly afterwards.[26]

**26 April 1920**

**Sergeant Cornelius Crean**

**Constable Patrick McGoldrick**

Sergeant Crean and Constable McGoldrick were shot dead at Innishannon. On that fateful day they were part of a three-man foot patrol that was ambushed by members of the West Cork Brigade. The third member of the patrol, Constable Power, told the inquest that McGoldrick had stopped to light his pipe when he was shot dead. Crean told Power to run, but they were fired upon, so Crean decided to fight. As he turned, he was hit in the chest with six rounds and fell to the ground. He died a short time later.[27]

**10 May 1920**

**Sergeant John Flynn**

**Constable Edward Dunne**

**Constable William Brick**

Sergeant Flynn and Constables Dunne and Brick were shot in Butlerstown, Timoleague. The policemen were part of a four-man patrol, which left the barracks in the village and had travelled about a mile when they were attacked by a large group of men with rifles and shotguns. The local IRA had lain in wait for the patrol on at least four occasions in the weeks before the shooting. After the event the local coroner's jury was 'persuaded' to change their verdict of 'wilful murder' to 'Shot by persons unknown' by IRA member Tadhg Sullivan.[28]

**12 May 1920**

**Sergeant Denis Garvey**

**Constable Daniel Harrington**

Sergeant Garvey and Constable Harrington were shot dead on the Lower Glanmire Road, Cork, near the railway station. Their companion, Constable Doyle, was badly wounded. Daniel Healy recalled: 'We received instructions early in May, 1920, that Sergeant Garvey of the R.I.C., stationed at Lower Road Police Barracks, Cork, was to be shot at sight. I have a suspicion that Garvey was to be shot for his part in the murder of Tomás McCurtain [*sic*], Lord Mayor of Cork, in the early hours of the 20 March 1920 …

'It was known that, at a certain hour each night, three R.I.C. men left barracks and Garvey was one of the three. The police then boarded a tram for the City at a tram stop on the opposite side of the road to the barracks. Our plans were that some of our men would take the tram to Tivoli, returning on the same tram with the intention of meeting the R.I.C. men as the latter boarded the tram at the Lower Road. Two more of our men, pretending to be lovers, stood at a blank wall opposite the barracks. These latter would join in the attack when the firing commenced … The tram duly came along and, as the policemen made to board it, revolver fire was opened on them by our party. Garvey and Harrington fell dead. Doyle was severely wounded.

'The following members of "C" Company took part in the affair:– "Pa" Murray, Jerry Dennehy, Martin Donovan, Leo Aherne, Garret Murphy, Dom Sullivan, Mick Bowles, Willie Deasy, Billy Lynch and myself.'[29]

**12 June 1920**

**Constable Thomas King**

Constable King was shot and killed outside Bantry by members of the IRA: 'On 12th June, 1920, R.I.C. man – Constable King – was shot at Ardna-gashel by a party under the Battalion O/C'.[30] According to Ted O'Sullivan: 'on Saturday morning, one R.I.C. man passed through in the direction of Bantry. As we were expecting some others to follow, we allowed him to proceed. Although we remained in our position until about 4 p.m. there was no appearance by the enemy. We then decided to move on towards Bantry to meet the R.I.C. man, Constable King – who had passed in the morning. We met him in the vicinity of Snave and duly executed him, as it was reported that he had taken part in the murder of I.R.A. men at The Ragg, Co. Tipperary. Amongst those who took part were: Dan O'Mahoney, John J. O'Sullivan, John Wrynne, Michael O'Driscoll, Denis O'Sullivan.'[31]

Attorney-General Denis Henry informed the House of Commons on 17 June that 'Constable King was murdered near Bantry on Saturday evening last, when returning in plain clothes on a bicycle to the barracks at Glengariff [*sic*]. He was fired at and wounded, he then escaped and hid in a farmer's house, but was followed, dragged outside and shot dead. He was on leave of absence at the time. He had served four years in the Navy, and took part in the battle of Jutland.'[32]

## 21 June 1920
### Constable James Brett

A cycle patrol regularly travelled between Glengarriff and Bantry along the main road. The Bantry IRA waited in ambush for more than a month for the right opportunity to attack this patrol, and on 22 June the attack took place. The *Evening Herald* observed that a 'week since the shooting of Constable King took place, and now another policeman has met his death. Last night at 7 p.m. five policemen returning off duty were ambushed in a district named Clonee, about three miles from Bantry by between 20 and thirty [*sic*] armed and masked men … At Clonee Sergeant Driscoll was leading, followed by Constable Brett and the three others, all unconscious of the danger when a shot rang out. Constable Brett was seen to fall, mortally wounded, and roll into the ditch.' A firefight developed and Sergeant Driscoll was also hit (not fatally) in the back of the head. The attack resulted two days later in the 'Sack of Bantry'.[33]

**24 June 1920**

**Cornelius Crowley**

John Annan Bryce was a former Liberal MP who had bought the Eccles
Hotel, Glengarriff, in 1916 as a convalescent home for wounded soldiers.
In September 1920 he wrote to *The Times*: 'The only damage to loyalists'
premises has been done by the police. In July they burned the stores of Mr.
G. W. Biggs, the principal merchant in Bantry, a man highly respected, a
Protestant, and a lifelong Unionist, with a damage of over £25,000, and the
estate office of the late Mr. Leigh-White, also a Unionist. Subsequently, in
August, the police fired into Mr. Biggs's office, while his residence has since
been commandeered for police barracks. He has had to send his family to
Dublin and to live himself in a hotel. Only two reasons can be assigned for
the outrages on Mr. Biggs, one that he employed Sinn Feiners – he could
not work his large business without them, there being no Unionist work-
men in Bantry – the other a recently published statement of his protesting
– on his own 40 years' experience – against Orange allegations of Catholic
intolerance.

'The July burning was part of a general pogrom, in which a cripple, named
[Cornelius] Crowley, was deliberately shot by the police while in bed and
several houses were set on fire while the people were asleep. A report was
made to Dublin Castle by Mr. Hynes, the County Court Judge, who happened to be on the spot for quarter sessions. Questioned in the House of
Commons, the Government refused to produce this report on the ground
that production would not be in the public interest, which means – as Parliamentary experience teaches one – that it was damning to Government.'[34]

Ted O'Sullivan observed that Crowley was a member of Sinn Féin and
that none of the IRA was in the town at the time of his death.[35] However,
David O'Mahony's shop and John Lehane's home were burned, while the
homes of Ralph Keyes and John Cotter were also attacked and wrecked. All
were IRA men. The home of John Downey of Glengarriff (Chairman of the
Bantry Guardians and a member of Sinn Féin) was also burned.[36]

**17 July 1920**

**Colonel Gerald B. F. Smyth**

For details of Smyth's death, see Part 1: The Death of Colonel Smyth.

**18–25 July 1920**

**James Bourke**

**Volunteer John O'Brien**

**William McGrath**

The *Irish Independent* stated that after a soldier tried to arrest a man who had held him up previously, the man fired a shot and hit a private who was helping him, after which a 'fracas developed' and the three men were killed. However, given the locations where the men were wounded and the large number of other non-fatal casualties around the city, this version of events is unlikely to be correct.[37]

In fact, these three shootings were typical of the nature of the war in Cork. John O'Brien, aged eighteen, was actually shot on 18 July while helping an old lady (Miss Donovan), who was wounded at the bottom of Shandon Street. He died the next day in the North Infirmary. He had been part of an IRA picket blocking access to the city where the British were firing indiscriminately. His funeral was recorded in *The Cork Examiner* with a large photograph and an account of the failed inquest. The *Examiner* noted that it was attended by a large body of IRA men.

In the case of James Bourke (sometimes called Burke in the sources) the newspaper report is blunt: 'Murdered by police at the base of Shandon Street Cork, [he was] bayoneted in the stomach by military while halted with his hands above his head.' Bourke had been walking down Shandon Street from his home off Blarney Street when he was stopped by soldiers. They were apparently trying to arrest a suspect who had tried to disarm one of them on North Main Street. As a former member of the Royal Field Artillery, who had no political affiliations, *The Cork Examiner* was justifiably outraged at his death, and his inquest and funeral were covered in minute detail.[38]

The irishmedals.org website says of this incident: 'On the morning of Sunday the 18th of July 1920 James Bourke aged 42 was killed by a military patrol near North Gate Bridge Cork. Bourke was an ex-British soldier and was admitted to the North Infirmary at 3am on Sunday morning; he was suffering from a large gaping wound through which the liver protruded on the lower right side of the chest. Dr D. Fennell told the inquest the wounds were inflicted by a bayonet or other sharp instrument used with great force.'[39]

William McGrath was shot on North Main Street by a passing armoured car: 'William McGrath, an ex-soldier of Cork, mortally wounded during promiscuous firing by soldiers and police on unarmed civilians in the streets.'[40] He had walked down North Main Street with his brother Thomas. Seeing a young child in the middle of the street in the path of an approaching military convoy he picked him up and retreated down Coleman's Lane near Adelaide Street. As the convoy passed the lane a shot was fired at point-blank range into it. The McGrath brothers stepped out of the lane to see what was happening and William was shot in the chest by firing from the back of the lorry. He died the following Sunday, 25 July.

Photographs of all the dead and seriously wounded appeared in the *Irish Independent* between 20 July and 6 August.[41]

**21/22 July 1920**
**Volunteer Daniel McGrath**
**Volunteer Thomas McDonnell**

Daniel McGrath was at a social gathering at Coracunna Cross, Mitchelstown, Co. Cork when a shot was fired from a passing lorry. 'McGrath was shot dead while running for cover. Thomas McDonnell was shot in similar circumstances and the rest of the party fled in terror.'[42] McGrath was seventeen and McDonnell twenty-five. *The Cork Examiner* noted that the inquests and the medical evidence showed that Daniel McGrath had been shot in the head and had died instantly. Patrick Luddy recalled: 'On July 22nd, 1920, two Volunteers (Dan McGrath and Thomas McDonnell) were shot by a party of British Military at Corracunna [*sic*] Cross about 1½ miles from Mitchelstown on the road to Cahir. They were standing with a crowd of civilians at the crossroads. I arrived at the crossroads shortly after the shooting and had to send other Volunteers who had been with me on parade to search the fields to ascertain if any others had been shot. At the inquest held on these Volunteers the jury brought in a verdict of murder against the Crown Forces and I think that this was one of the last inquests held. The Crown Solicitor representing the British Forces involved asked the jury not to bring in a verdict of murder or they would all be shot.'[43]

There seems to be some doubt over the actual day of the shootings, as the memorial at the crossroads states that they took place on 21 July.

**21 July 1920**
**Captain James O. Airy**
**1 August 1920**
**Private Ernest F. Barlow**

On 21 July 1920 a Manchester Regiment patrol was sent to re-supply Ballyvourney, and Captain Airy (35), who had just arrived in Ballincollig, went along for the journey. He was to be stationed at Mount Massey in Macroom. Private Barlow, from Crompton, Manchester (where he is buried), was also on the patrol. He was twenty-six according to his death certificate when he died of septicaemia on 1 August. The patrol was attacked to the east of Ballymakeera, at a narrow twisting section of the road called Geata Bán, which was a favourite place for IRA ambushes.[44] The Coolavokig ambush on 25 February 1921 took place a short distance to the east of this.

Patrick Lynch, captain of the IRA's Ballyvourney Company recalled: 'on the 17th July [*sic*], our expected lorry came along. It was full of soldiers armed with rifles. As it came into the ambush position a private car taking a patient to hospital also drove into the ambush position. The private car had been signalled to stop but the driver ignored the signal. The private car was going towards Macroom. We waited until the private car got past the lorry before we opened fire. In the first volley the driver of the lorry was wounded in the cheek. The lorry for the moment went out of control and mounted the fence on the side of the road. After travelling a couple of yards with its two left wheels on the fence, the driver managed to get it back on the road after which it disappeared from our view around a bend … In this encounter a Captain Eyrie [Airy] was shot dead and most of the soldiers were wounded by the buckshot used in our shotguns …

'We learned later that Captain Eyrie, who was stationed in Fermoy, had only come to Macroom the morning he was killed and had only come for the drive to Ballyvourney. A short time previous he had criminally assaulted a young girl in Fermoy as she was returning from school and apparently the authorities were of the opinion that he had been killed by members of the Fermoy I.R.A. for the offence.'[45]

### 24 July 1920 (date uncertain)
### John Crowley

In a matter of fact way Frank Neville reported, 'Another job which did not come off was a prepared ambush for a military cycle party in Ballinadee one Sunday. This was just for the purpose of disarming the party. Word came out from Cork at this time that there was an ex-British soldier named Crowley in the Company Area who had informed on members of the party which had ambushed the R.I.C. at Upton. For this he had got an award of £20 (Twenty Pounds) and had been promised another like sum. He was arrested and executed.' This was John Crowley of Lissagroom near Upton, who was reported missing on 10 July 1920, according to a newspaper notice placed by his brother Michael. A letter from his sister in the Collins Papers in the Military Archives disowns him.[46]

### 25 July 1920
### Detective Sergeant William Mulherin

If any of the killings up to this point had failed to impress on people the seriousness of the war, then the killing of Detective Mulherin (Mulhern in some of the newspaper reports) inside St Patrick's Catholic church in Bandon certainly did so. As he walked into church for early Mass at 8 a.m., he paused for a few seconds to give money to the collector. Two men walked up behind him and shot him. He fell forward on top of the collector and was dead before he hit the ground. Mulherin was a prime target for the IRA as he was the chief intelligence officer for the RIC in West Cork. According to the news reports, he had been expecting to be shot as he had received numerous warnings about his activities, but the location of this shooting sent a message to all and sundry that nowhere was safe. The killing was immediately condemned by Roman Catholic Bishop of Cork Dr Daniel Cohalan, who excommunicated the unknown killers and refused to allow further services in the town until the church was re-consecrated. Michael Collins also complained bitterly about the shooting inside the church. Originally from Mayo, and a married man, Sergeant Mulherin was thirty-eight when he died, and he left a wife and young family behind.[47]

### 27 July 1920
### Corporal Thomas Maddox

Two nights after the killing of William Mulherin, Major Arthur Percival, intelligence officer of the Essex Regiment, decided to raid the home of Seán Buckley. Buckley was chairman of the Bandon Town Commissioners, a prominent Sinn Féiner and, more importantly, intelligence officer of the IRA's 3rd (West Cork) Brigade.[48] He lived 500 metres from the regiment's headquarters in Bandon Barracks. Percival and Maddox (a Scotsman) made their way cautiously through the gardens to the back of the house. Maddox was about 30 yards ahead of Percival when he was shot in the head by a shotgun blast. Percival fled. Maddox was found the following day with a rifle next to him and his pistol across his body.

Michael Riordan stated: 'When Sergt. Mulherin, RIC Intelligence Officer, was shot in Bandon on July 25th 1920, it was anticipated that enemy forces would take reprisal action. The home of the Brigade Intelligence Officer (Seán Buckley) was one of those likely to be attacked and arrangements were made to provide a guard in the vicinity of the house. With Jim Doyle of our company (Kilpatrick) I went to Frank Hurley's, Lauragh – Tinker's Cross Company area. Accompanied by two or three men from the latter company, we moved on to the vicinity of Seán Buckley's where we remained for some time. There was no sign of any enemy activity, so we withdrew to our home areas. We were all armed with shotguns. This was on the night of July 25th. Similar procedure was followed by other members of the same companies (Tinker's Cross and Kilpatrick) on the following night, with like results. On the night of July 27th the representatives from Kilpatrick were: Michael Doyle and John Coveney. They had only just taken up their positions when two soldiers made their appearance. The leading man was about 30 yards in front of the second. When the leader was within about 10 yards of our guard, fire was opened on him and he was killed. The second soldier then dashed away and escaped. Our men withdrew without delay as they were within 100 yards of Bandon military post. The soldier who had been shot was later reported to be Lance Corporal Maddox, Essex Regiment.'[49]

## 28 July 1920
### Constable James Murray

James Murphy stated: 'Towards the end of June 1920, the first batch of British Black and Tans (consisting of three) arrived in Clonakilty. Amongst the party was Constable Murray, who made himself unpopular by his activities within a short time. About 25th July 1920, he fired at a number of unarmed civilians and it was decided that he should be dealt with at the first available opportunity. About 8.30 p.m. on 27th July, it was reported that he was alone on the Western Road and a party of four obtained revolvers from a dump at O'Donoghue's of McCurtain Hill. The party consisted of "Flyer" Nyhan, Stephen O'Neill, Michael Crowley and myself. We divided up into two sections. I accompanied "Flyer" to the Munster and Leinster Bank corner where we were informed that Murray had proceeded down Kent St. to Rossa St. We just caught up with him as he was entering Fitzgerald's green-grocer shop in Rossa St. We opened fire. He was shot through the head as the result of which he died at 2 a.m. on the morning of July 28th, without regaining consciousness. The other two (Ml. Crowley and Stephen O'Neill) had proceeded out the Western Road in search of Murray, but failed to find him as he had returned to town. Following this incident "Flyer" Nyhan and myself left the town for a couple of days after which we returned to work.'[50]

## 31 July 1920
### John Ahern

John Ahern (sometimes Aherne in the sources) was shot at Ballynoe four miles north-east of Cork city during an ambush on the mail lorry travelling between Fermoy Barracks and Victoria Barracks. As the mail truck passed through White's Cross just south of the village, it was attacked by an IRA ambush party. There was much confusion about what happened.

The *Weekly Irish Independent* reported on 7 August: 'Telegraphing on Sunday night, our Cork correspondent states – In the attempt to ambush the military lorry yesterday morning, which was conveying mails from Cork Barracks to Fermoy garrison, a civilian, John Aherne, of Coole East, was killed, and other civilians were wounded. A number of persons arrested by troops afterwards in the vicinity of the outrage have been set at liberty, as they satisfied the military authorities that they had taken no part in the affray. The civilian who was picked up dead was wearing, it is said, the uniform of an officer of the Republican Army.' There is no evidence that Ahern was involved in the IRA and no memorial to him.

The inquest into Ahern's death was held on Tuesday 3 August, but had to be abandoned according to the *Weekly Irish Independent*: 'Coroner McCabe attended at the Cork military barracks yesterday evening to inquire into the death of John Aherne, of Coole East, White's Cross, whose dead body was picked up by the military on Saturday afternoon at the scene of the desperate attack on a military mail van, when five soldiers were wounded by a bomb hurled amongst them. District Inspector Heggert represented the authorities. Only six jurors attended, and the police said that it was impossible to empanel a jury. At the same inquest District Inspector Heggert confirmed that Private Ernest Barlow, of the Manchester Regiment, had died on Sunday.'[51]

## 7 August 1920
## Constable Ernest Watkins

Constable Watkins was a Black and Tan stationed in Fermoy. Each week a police cycle patrol left Fermoy and travelled through Kildorrery. On 4 August the IRA were lying in wait. Edward Tobin of the East Limerick Brigade, who took part in the ambush on this patrol, recalled what happened next: 'We left Ahern's farmhouse early on the morning of the 4th August, 1920, and took up positions about 300 yards from the town. The Column men numbered twelve or fourteen and were reinforced by three or four men from Ballinlough who were attached to Glanworth Company. ...

'We were not an hour in position when we heard the Tans coming. They were talking and laughing. Looking at Howard we saw him rubbing his gun as they passed him – he was great fun. When they came in a line with my position we opened fire with a roar of "Surrender" – no surrender – instead they got down on one knee and opened a rapid fire on our positions. It cut the top of the fence very near O'Donnell sending a shower of small stones and earth into his face. We fired back as true as we knew how ... When their magazines were empty they surrendered. ...

'One Tan was badly wounded in the leg very near the body and was lying on the road. She [a nurse who lived nearby] ordered one of his comrades to take his coat off and put it under his head. She was not long stopping the flow of blood. When she had this done she advised his comrades not to leave him until he was attended by a Doctor. We heard later that when they reached the barracks they left him and went out drinking while he tore off the bandages and died.'[52]

This last bit of the story is untrue – according to his death certificate Watkins actually died in Fermoy Military Hospital on 7 August. The IRA captured six rifles and a quantity of ammunition during the attack.

## 14 August 1920 (date uncertain)
### John Coughlan

For details of Coughlan's death, see Part 1: The Disappearance of John Coughlan.

## 14 August 1920
### Private Albert Edward Nunn

Little is written about the death of Private Nunn in the newspapers. *The Cork Examiner* had a vague reference to it on Monday 16 August and his name is mentioned in the *Irish Independent* a week later. It is recorded in a joint statement made in BMH WS 744: 'On August 14th, 1920, a military plane made a forced landing in Drominagh locality, and a detachment of troops from the Kanturk garrison was despatched to guard the plane. In conjunction with the Millstreet Battalion we decided to attack the party of about fifteen or twenty soldiers guarding the plane and capture whatever arms they had and destroy the plane. …

'On our arrival it was noticed that the Guard, less a sentry on duty, had made a fire and were sitting around it with their rifles stacked near them. Our intention was to fire a volley into them and then rush the position and which ruse would in all probability have proved successful. Unfortunately, however, an incident occurred which upset all our plans, for before we were actually in position one of our men, Con Cunningham, who had a Mauser rifle with one round loaded, in the excitement of the moment fired at the sentry shooting him dead.'[53]

**16 August 1920**
**Volunteer John O'Connell**
**Volunteer Patrick Clancy**

Inevitably the shooting of Private Nunn brought about a response. BMH WS 744 continues: 'Following the shooting of the sentry mentioned above, the Kanturk Company remained on the alert on the nights of the 14th and 15th August as we anticipated reprisals. Nothing untoward happened, however, on these two nights. On the night of the 14th August, Paddy Clancy, who had been home on annual holidays in East Limerick, returned to Kanturk. He was employed as a Creamery Manager in Allen's Bridge, near Newmarket. Paddy knew nothing, of course, of the proposed attack on the aeroplane party and it was later that night he returned.

'At this time, Paddy Clancy held the appointment of Vice Brigadier of the old Cork No. II Brigade. On the morning of August 16th Paddy Clancy and Jack O'Connell went back to O'Connell's home in Derrygallon for a rest as both of them had been on vigil for the previous two nights. Jack O'Connell was a draper's assistant in town and on that day he was commencing his annual holidays.

'The two of them moved across a high field overlooking the town on their way to O'Connell's home and must have been seen by some enemy agent, for the information was conveyed to the R.I.C. and military. It was rumoured that a daughter of an ex-soldier and friendly with the troops saw them and gave the game away, but this rumour could not be definitely verified.

'However, late that morning a detachment of military with Sergeant Dennehy, R.I.C. as a guide, surrounded O'Connell's home. A sister of Jackie, who saw the military surrounding the house, immediately ran into the house and awakened the two lads who were asleep in bed. The two lads got up and only put on their trousers, decided to make a run for it and try and fight their way through. (The farmhouse had no back entrance). Immediately they were observed at the door, the military opened fire and Paddy Clancy, who was getting over a fairly high wire fence from farmyard into a copse, was fatally wounded. Jack O'Connell succeeded in getting about 50 yards away into a clump of trees before being killed. When the troops found his body some of them used their bayonets on it. Both the bodies were badly ripped up and from the proceedings of an enquiry held subsequently at the old Kanturk Workhouse, the details of which were published later in the "Cork Examiner", it was stated that dum-dum ammunition had been used by the enemy that morning.'

This is a substantially accurate report of the inquest and there is no doubt that the killing dealt a severe blow to the IRA in North Cork.[54]

## 18 August 1920
### Lieutenant Frederick Sharman

Lieutenant Sharman from the Manchester Regiment was leading a cycle patrol from Macroom to Ballyvourney. The patrol was ambushed at the top of a hill just outside Ballyvourney. An IRA man called on them to halt but they attempted to ride through the ambush. Four were injured and Sharman died at the scene. His body was returned to England and a year later his wife was awarded £2,000 compensation.[55]

## 20 August 1920
### James Herlihy

Patrick Collins stated: 'The presence of enemy spies in our districts was a constant menace to our activities. Many of these spies (apart from those already referred to) came from the ex-British army class. One such was a man named James Herlihy who lived in G/Company district. He, and some other civilians, were known to our Intelligence Service to be in touch with the British military and to have supplied to them the names of prominent IRA men in our district. We also learned that these spies had been supplied with revolvers (by the British) for their protection in case of attack by the I.R.A.

'As the result of military raids on houses of prominent I.R.A. men in our area, it became known that Herlihy was one of those who had given information and we were instructed by the Brigade to pick him up. One morning, he was taken into custody by men from G/Company and removed to the Pouladuff district south of the city, where he was executed by a firing squad from the company, on instructions from the Brigade.'[56]

## 20 August 1920
### Volunteer Timothy Fitzgerald

An account of the ambush where Fitzgerald was killed is given by Liam Deasy in *Towards Ireland Free*. Essentially, Deasy said that the IRA had set up an ambush for the Essex Regiment at Brinny. There is a very narrow humpback bridge followed by a sharp bend, which would require any lorries to slow to a crawl, giving the ambushers a chance of annihilating the patrol before it could fire back. The planned ambush was surprised by British forces that attacked from the south. The IRA managed to extricate themselves with great difficulty, but Volunteer Tim Fitzgerald was killed. He was the first member of the Cork No. 3 Brigade to be killed.

Michael Riordain gave a slightly different version of events: 'During the last week in August, 1920, about thirty men drawn from Kilpatrick, Crosspound, Kilbrittain, Timoleague, and Tinker's Cross Companies took up positions at daybreak at both sides of Brinny Bridge and on both sides – east and west – of the road. There were a few rifles amongst the party. We were armed mainly with shotguns. We were awaiting a military cycle patrol which normally travelled from Bandon via Innishannon and Brinny back to Bandon.

'We were still in our positions when about 4 p.m. we were surprised by a party of military which came on us across country from the south on the western flank of our position. The leader of the military party (Lieut. Heartblack) [*sic*; Hotblack] crept to within about 40 yards of one of our men before opening fire. His fire struck the stock of our man's shotgun

(John Crowley's). Crowley returned the fire, and while Lieut. Heartblack was trying to find fresh cover Crowley crossed the road and escaped. All the men on the southern side of Brinny Bridge – both east and west of the road – now left their positions and retired towards Bandon. During this withdrawal Lieut. Tim Fitzgerald (Tinker's Cross Company) was killed. As it was obvious that the enemy were aware of our positions and were trying to surround us, the men on the north side of the bridge decided to withdraw northward in the direction of Crosspound. I was one of a party of five or six which was in position at the north side of the bridge and west of the road. Seán Hales was, I think, in charge on this occasion.'[57]

## 21 August 1920
### Sergeant Daniel Maunsell

Inchigeela Barracks was a prime target for the IRA as its destruction would create a 'safe zone' free of enemy forces. A determined attempt to destroy it in February 1920 had not been a success and the barracks had been heavily reinforced. On Saturday 21 August Sergeant Daniel Maunsell (49), originally from Kerry, was killed in an ambush at Inchigeela. He had attended Mass with his family in the local Roman Catholic church and they were walking back to the barracks in the village. He was holding his daughter Cis by the hand. As they neared the hotel (Creedon's) three members of the IRA shot him. He was carried into the barracks but died shortly afterwards from three bullet wounds. He was buried in St Finbarr's Cemetery, Cork, beside his young son Thomas, who had died six months previously.[58]

## 22 August 1920
### Volunteer Michael Galvin

After the killing of Sergeant Maunsell at Inchigeela, a lorry load of police drove to the town from Bandon the next morning to investigate the incident. They passed through Lissarda on the way and a group of local IRA made preparations to ambush them on their return journey. As the police returned through Lissarda they were forced to stop by a cart blocking the road. They were ordered to surrender but opened fire on the ambushers. As they had managed to get into good cover, the RIC (who had better weapons and far more ammunition) were impossible to dislodge. Michael Galvin was shot and fatally wounded during an operation to outflank them, and another IRA member was injured when a homemade grenade went off in his hand. In the ensuing gun battle a number of the RIC were wounded, with Sergeant Runane being the most serious.[59]

## 24 August 1920
### Private Joseph Evans

Private Evans was accidentally shot in the commandeered barracks on the Main Street of Charleville by another soldier. According to news reports some of the machine gun corps were 'playing with revolvers' when one 'accidentally went off'. Private Evans was shot 'above the mouth' with the bullet exiting through the back of his skull. It seems that the soldiers may have been playing Russian roulette, with the inevitable consequences.[60]

## 25 August 1920
### Constable Matthew Haugh

The newspapers of the time barely mention the killing of Matthew Haugh, which seems odd. However, Maurice Donegan, O/C of the Bantry Battalion, gave a detailed account of the shooting in his witness statement: 'At my first Battalion Council meeting I arranged for several jobs to be carried out. One was to be at Glengarriff and I was going in charge of this myself; another at Drimoleague and another in Bantry. The latter job I detailed to Ralph Keyes, O.C. Bantry Company. It was the elimination of two obnoxious young R.I.C. men named Haugh and Power who, by their overbearing manner and brutal conduct, had the town of Bantry terrorised. It was said that Haugh it was who had shot the cripple – young Crowley – in bed ... At all events, I ordered Keyes to have them wiped out before I came back from the Glengarriff job and he did it, actually on the same date, August 26th [*sic*].

'Four of his Company, including himself, armed with revolvers and shotguns, posted themselves behind a wall running along a high flight of steps leading up to the police barracks ... The job was particularly dangerous for Keyes and his three men as the position they took up was practically overlooked from the military barracks. They got into their places in the darkness of the night and when morning came waited while certain of the R.I.C. including the notorious Haugh and Power passed down the steps and on into the town. On their return they were fired on as they came up the steps. Haugh was killed instantly, a shotgun accounting for him, but Power escaped. However, this daring operation had its effect and while Haugh was definitely cut short in his career, no more trouble was given to the townspeople after that day by Power.'

On 28 January 1921 Haugh's family claimed compensation at the crown court in Bantry and were awarded £2,000.[61]

## 26 August 1920
### Private John Kelly

While on patrol in Millstreet, Private Wardell of the Manchester Regiment, who was attempting to load his rifle, accidentally discharged it. The discharged bullet passed through Private Dodd's neck and went on to strike Private Kelly in the left forearm and the chest. Kelly was taken by ambulance to Cork, but died on the way. The court of inquiry stated that Wardell should not have had a round in the chamber, perhaps suggesting that they felt he was inexperienced.[62]

## 26 August 1920
### Constable John McNamara

Clearly by this stage of the war the death of a policeman was becoming unremarkable, so the *Irish Independent* of 26 August carried only a brief report of these shootings. Michael O'Driscoll later recorded the details of the shooting of RIC men in Glengarriff: 'Ted [Sullivan] called me to him and asked me if I could use an automatic. I said I could. He picked myself, William Dillon and Michael Lucey and told us that there were three R.I.C. men drinking in O'Shea's public house in Glengarriff and we were to go in and shoot them. ... There was no sign of the R.I.C. men at the bar, but I found that they were in a small snug at the end of the shop ... a man came to the door and saluted one of my party. They spoke for a while and, while they were speaking, the three R.I.C. men came out of the snug and walked between us out of the shop.

'I called to the others to come on. By this time, the R.I.C. were on the street. We each picked one and opened fire. William Dillon's gun misfired, and the R.I.C. man he was facing pulled the trigger and his gun also missed fire. Before the R.I.C. man could fire again, he was hit and went down.' The day following the shooting, the barracks was evacuated.[63]

## 26 August 1920
### Private Charles Edward Hall

The Irish newspapers reported on 28 August that a soldier was shot dead in Castlemartyr. The *Derbyshire Courier* of 4 September 1920 identified the dead man as a local, Charles Hall (19). The *Irish Independent* correctly identified the location of the attack on a joint police/army patrol as Cahirmore, two miles outside Midleton, but got the victim's name wrong, calling him Private Hill. It further stated that during the attack Lieutenant Beggs had been shot in the kidney and was most unlikely to survive. As Lieutenant Beggs was awarded an MBE in 1921, clearly the paper was wrong. Another member of the patrol was shot in the leg. Michael Kearney later recalled that the ambush took place at Whiterock just outside Midleton on the morning before the Buckley brothers were arrested and subsequently shot. The ambush had largely been a failure as the tree that had been meant to block the road was toppled too late and it was only a 'lucky' shot that killed Hall.[64]

**27 August 1920**

**Volunteer John (Seán) Buckley**

According to Pat Barry, 'two brothers named Buckley, from Ballyedmond, about a mile north of Midleton, were arrested at their father's house and, while being conveyed in a military lorry to Cork on the following day, one, John, was shot dead and the other wounded. The official explanation of the shootings was that both prisoners "tried to escape". [This explanation became painfully frequent in the later stages of the struggle.] John Buckley was an active volunteer and secretary of the local Sinn Féin Club. His funeral cortège from Cork to Midleton was huge, described at the time as one of the largest in living memory in that district.'

Seamus Fitzgerald tells a similar story: 'In the case of the Buckley brothers, who were shot by Crown Forces when bringing them in a lorry to Cork from Midleton on the 25th [*sic*] August, the Crown Forces felt that Seán Buckley and Batt Buckley were both dead. Batt Buckley, however, lived to tell his story, despite his bullet-riddled body.'[65]

**28 August 1920**

**George Walker**

*The Struggle of the Irish People* recorded that, 'George Walker, Queenstown, County Cork, a wounded and crippled ex-soldier unable to raise his hands rapidly enough when called upon by [the] military, was promptly shot and after falling, was bayoneted.' Walker lived at 27 Cottrell's Row in Cobh/Queenstown, and he was originally from Liverpool. He was a member of the Church of England and had married a local girl, Julia Donovan, in 1907. By the time of his shooting they had six children. The military failed to attend his inquest and the jury stated that he died of shock from wounds inflicted by a patrol of Cameron Highlanders, who, it was declared, had the night before 'wrecked the town' in reprisal for the death of Private Hall and for an IRA arms raid on troops in the town. The *Ulster Herald* stated that Walker had been wounded twice in the war and was a veteran of the Boer War.

Quoting the Press Association it stated: 'The soldiers ... entered the town armed with rifles and heavy pieces of metal and commenced to wreck the business houses in the principal streets. About 100 plate-glass windows were smashed, and looting took place, much valuable property being lost. Some private houses were also attacked, and the residents were kept in a state of terror until daybreak.' The paper also noted that the 'shops of Unionists, and even the Royal Soldiers' Home, according to our correspondent's account, did not escape from the "25 to 30" rioters'.[66]

## 5 September 1920
## Volunteer Patrick/Liam Hegarty
## Michael Lynch

According to *The Struggle of the Irish People*, Patrick Hegarty of Ballyvourney was 'shot dead when machine-gun fire was opened from an apparently deserted military motor lorry which was being viewed on the roadside by a crowd of young people'. On the same day, Michael Lynch of Ballyvourney was also 'shot dead when cycling past an apparently deserted military motor lorry from which machine-gun fire was opened on a crowd of young people who were viewing it by the roadside'.[67]

In his lectures to the Staff College after the war, General Arthur Percival spoke approvingly of this tactic, despite the fact that it was clearly illegal in a 'police action' as the British legally construed the war. Other sources point to this incident as marking a profound change in the nature of the war in North and West Cork. Manus O'Riordan says of the incident: 'Within a few weeks, however, the character of warfare in the area dramatically altered, and it was Britain itself that brought about such a transformation. On Sunday, September 5, 1920, as people emerged from mid-day Mass at Ballyvourney Church, a covered British army lorry seemed to break down and apparently could not be repaired either by its own crew, or by the soldiers from an accompanying open lorry. Having finally said to "let it there to hell", all of these soldiers mounted the open lorry and drove away.

Sometime later a number of unarmed Volunteers were brought over by the local children and lifted a corner of the lorry's body covering to investigate.' Micheál Ó Súilleabháin, a member of the local IRA, said of that day: 'From within came a fusillade of rifle shots. Liam Hegarty, whether hit or not, managed to cross a low bank which served as the road fence on his side. Then turning left he travelled in its small shelter for a short distance before he fell. The other Volunteers and the children all escaped injury. A young man, Michael Lynch, lived a few hundred yards down the road to Macroom. Hearing the shooting he ran onto the roadway. He was mortally wounded by a rifle bullet. Whether the killers in the lorry aimed at him or not is not certain. But it is certain that one of the miscreants crossed the fence and shot Liam Hegarty again as he lay wounded.'[68]

## 14 September 1920
### Constable William Carroll

Constable Carroll was killed in a traffic accident near the workhouse in Douglas on 14 September 1920 after he and two other members of the police commandeered the van of a Cork timber and iron company.[69]

## 15 September 1920 (date uncertain)
### John O'Callaghan

Patrick Collins recalled the story of O'Callaghan in his witness statement: 'Another civilian spy dealt with by G/Company was a man named Callaghan [*sic*]. The Brigade had ample evidence that this man was conveying information to the enemy and I received instructions to get in contact with him and take him into custody ... he came with us to the Thomas Ashe Hall, Father Mathew Quay, Cork, where he was placed under guard. Later that evening he was taken by car outside the city and executed.' Nothing else definite is known about what happened, but O'Callaghan's name appears on the register of cases being dealt with by the Compensation Commission after the war.[70]

**29 September 1920**
**Sergeant William George Gibbs**

The IRA raided Mallow Military Barracks on Sunday 29 September, while the troops were exercising their horses. Matt Flood explained: 'There was a Sergeant Gibbs there and he was [the] only Catholic in the garrison, this is the queer part of it now. The Officer had gone out and he was the senior N.C.O. He was supervising the shoeing of a horse just on the left as we came through the gate ... and when he got the word "Hands up" he made a dash for the guard room. He knew the machine guns and rifles were there. He was told to stop and there was a shot fired at him ... your man dived for cover and was hit in the wrong place anyway. He lived only about fifteen minutes. The rest surrendered then and it was only a case of walking in and collecting all we could take, ammunition, lances, rifles, machine-guns. It was a terror to see motor-cars going out of town with those long lances sticking out of them ... But that night we saw flames over Mallow. They brought in troops from Cork and Fermoy and left them run amok.'[71] Among the items taken were two Hotchkiss machine-guns, and Flood gave the column training in how to use these. Gibbs was a member of the 17th Lancers and is buried in Bedford.

**September 1920 (date uncertain)**
**(Unknown) Brady**

The details of this death are sketchy, with neither a first name nor a date to go on, other than that it took place in or after September 1920. As a result the information must be treated with caution. In his witness statement Charles Browne recalled: 'An instance of co-operative effort on the part of the public may be instanced here. A man named Brady, a native of Dublin, who was employed as a printer in Macroom, had been under suspicion as an enemy agent. On a night in September he was drinking with Auxiliaries at the Market Bar and was overheard by the proprietor, Mr. Shields, and two recently resigned R.I.C. men, brothers, named Vaughan, giving information that Barret's house in the South Square was being used by the I.R.A. as a billet. Word was conveyed to our men by Shields and the Volunteers using the house were alerted and when the raid took place no one was found on the premises. Brady was arrested by us, convicted after a trial and deported from the country. He returned after some weeks and again made contact with the enemy, this time at Union Quay Barracks, Cork. He was shadowed one night as he left this post and was shot dead at Torytop Lane.'[72]

## 1 October 1920
### Volunteer John Connolly

John Connolly of Bandon was 'found buried near the military barracks where he had been a prisoner in custody for fifteen [*sic*] days'.[73] According to John Desmond, who has recorded the Connolly family grave, 'John Connolly was a Lieutenant in the Bandon Battalion of the local IRA. Lieut. John Connolly was arrested at his cousins' farm house, Fitzgerald's of Maulnaskimlehane, on the 23rd September 1920. Lieut. Connolly was taken into the barracks at Allen Square, where he was brutally tortured and interrogated for a full week. On the 1st of October he was forcefully taken to the Bandon Park and executed without trial or charge. A steel cross still marks the spot in the Park where he was murdered.'[74] According to Martin O'Reilly: 'Two ladies collecting firewood found his body. He had etched his name on the dungeon walls of Castle Bernard which still remains to this day. I have often wondered did this brave man know the fate that was to befall him!'[75]

## 3 October 1920
### Constable Clarence Victor Chave

RIC Constable Clarence Victor Chave (24), who was born in Sheerness, England, was fatally wounded when his police patrol came under attack at 12.35 a.m. on 3 October. Two other policemen were wounded when they were fired upon from Blackthorn House opposite Woodford Bourne on St Patrick's Street in Cork city. Chave was taken to the nearby military hospital, where he died two hours later. He was stationed at Empress Place (Summerhill), which suggests that he was an Auxiliary, as that was their headquarters. Some reports state his name was Shade, but Shade was actually one of those injured in the same attack.[76]

## 5 October 1920
### Volunteer Jeremiah Herlihy

When the Essex Regiment surrounded an IRA ambush at the Chetwynd Viaduct just outside Cork city, Michael O'Regan, the local IRA battalion commander, along with Leo Murphy, Jack Herlihy and John Horgan fought a 30-minute rearguard action to let the main body of sixty Volunteers escape. O'Regan stated: 'One of the main body, a man named Jeremiah Herlihy, signaller, was captured by the military and told to run. He turned and just walked away and was shot in the neck as he did so. He was found, a few hours later, taken to a hospital in Cork city where he died the next day. He was later buried at Cloundrohid [*sic*] with military honours.'[77]

Equally disturbing is the record of this incident in BMH WS 810, which draws attention to the actions of the Auxiliaries, who seemed bereft of any sense of the rule of law: 'Among the British forces who attempted to surround the 3rd Battalion at the Viaduct, October 5th, 1920, was a squad of Auxiliaries. Capturing a number of civilians on the Cork–Bandon road they carried them to Lynch's outhouse, situated half a mile from Waterfall, 2½ miles from the Viaduct. This outhouse was divided into two compartments, one for cattle, the other containing old damp hay. The "Auxies" thrust their prisoners into the cattle compartment, padlocking the door. They then set fire to the old hay and stood some distance away to enjoy the sport. The hay was slow to fire but dense smoke rose up in the sky. Apparently seeing the smoke, a military officer rushed his men for the house and, after a bitter show-down with the "Auxies", the Officer, to his credit, released the smothering prisoners.'[78]

## 8 October 1920

### Private John Gordon Squibbs

The *Irish Independent* reported the death of Private Squibbs of the Hampshire Regiment but was confused about the actual details of the attack. He was, in fact, killed by a grenade thrown into a military lorry. *The Freeman's Journal* had a report of the military inquiry on 9 October, which establishes the facts. At 8.40 a.m. a military lorry drove through Cove Street on its way to Elizabeth Fort. Workers going into the city and children heading to nearby Sullivan's Quay Boys School filled the street. As the lorry made the right turn onto Barrack Street it was attacked with rifles and grenades. One of the grenades landed in the back of the lorry. Squibbs (17) attempted to throw it back but it exploded, blowing his arm off. He died from his wounds later that day.[79] After the attack 'Revenge tonight' was scrawled on the wall at the South Gate Bridge. That night the first attempt to burn Cork City Hall occurred.

## 9 October 1920

### Lieutenant Robert Robertson

## 13 October

### Lieutenant Gurth Richardson

The Essex Regiment, under the command of Major Percival, was on patrol in the heart of the IRA 'safe zone' at Newcestown when the IRA attacked the patrol in an impromptu ambush. The patrol arrived in the village shortly before 11 p.m. and decided to raid the pub, which they suspected was an IRA safe house. They were not wrong. Apparently IRA Commandant Seán Hales was in the pub when they arrived and slipped out the back. He dashed down the road and joined his twenty troops stationed about a mile away. William Desmond stated: 'I was in the middle of my preparations when Seán Hales O.C. Battalion rushed in and said "The military are in Newcestown. Come on and we'll attack them." All of us who were there ... went off at the double in the direction of Newcestown, a good mile away.' They attacked the lorries just outside the village and a ludicrous firefight in the dark ensued. British aim was not helped by the fact that the IRA was in a field of hay ricks, but they eventually managed to outflank their attackers, who withdrew. During the fight, Lieutenant Robertson was killed and Lieutenant Richardson wounded. Richardson died in Cork Military Hospital a few days later. There were no casualties on the Irish side. Afterwards, Major Percival, Sgt Benton and Private Wotton were all awarded medals for this engagement.[80]

## 11 October 1920
### Private Edward Cowin

On this day a ration lorry was ambushed at Ballydrohane, halfway between Kanturk and Newmarket. Private Edward Wade Cowin, the driver, died and four soldiers, including an NCO, were wounded when the provisions lorry was attacked by the IRA. The Hotchkiss captured in Mallow got its first use according to Matt Flood: 'Lynch saw that I was disappointed that all my training on the machine gun might come to naught. "Never mind Matt, we'll have a tune out of the gun next Monday for we are going to fix one up". He meant Ballydrochane [*sic*]. … the next minute came the signal. Only one lorry turned up so we opened fire and shot the driver. The lorry went out of control and ran into the back shafts of the cart [blocking the road]. … every soldier in the lorry was wounded, and the driver killed. You see when I fired that was the signal for them all to open up. After it was all over Lynch told our lads to dress all the wounded men and British Tommies. Moylan got the credit for this and when he was later captured, it saved his life. You see Moylan was captured by the British and they would have plugged him only for the Tommies and the Officer telling about the incident.'[81]

## 11 October 1920
### Maurice Griffin

The newspapers reported that Maurice Griffin was shot in the back during a police search in Cork city on 10 October. He died the following day according to his death certificate. There is little other information but *The Struggle of the Irish People* stated: 'Griffin (aged 60), Cork city, being deaf and not hearing a challenge to halt in the street at 2.40 p.m., was fired upon and mortally wounded by military.'[82] He was, in fact, fifty-two.

## 13 October 1920
### Samuel Shannon

Despite claims by the late Peter Hart that Sam Shannon of Lissaclarig was executed for helping his father resist an arms raid, this is not true.[83] According to *The Skibbereen Eagle* armed men had broken into the Shannon household and the father, Philip, had fought them off with a blackthorn stick. This was despite having a revolver pointed at him. The armed men retreated. The following morning when the Shannons came out of the house 'a fellow ran in the gate and fired point blank at Samuel Richard who was shot in the side'. He died on 13 October without recovering. Philip claimed £10,000 for his death and judgement was reserved.[84]

## 15 October 1920
### James Lehane

There are many versions of this story, but the one from Daniel Harrington is probably the most accurate: 'In the month of November a convoy of eight lorries of military, R.I.C. and Tans arrived in the village of Ballyvourney and rounded up every man in the village, shooting at random all the time. In the meantime they placed tins of petrol along the village street preparatory to burning down the village. While this was happening, a group of Tans called to the house of the local blacksmith, whose name was Sullivan. Here they arrested a man named Lehane, a civilian. When the Tans had ascertained his name, they took him into a by-road where they riddled his body with bullets. Lehane was found later with his pipe in one hand and a penknife in the other. He had been in the act of filling his pipe when they arrested him. We had a very good I.R.A. man of the same name in the local company.

The military officer in charge, hearing the shots in the by-road, immediately ordered the tins of petrol to be collected, after which the raiding lorries hurriedly left.'[85]

## 16 October 1920
### Volunteer Patrick McNestry

Anyone who visits the Republican Plot at St Finbarr's Cemetery is surprised by some anomalies. The leader of Cork No. 3 Brigade is not buried in the plot, but nearby, while the Civil War Free State Minister J. J. Walsh is buried just in front of it. The plot itself contains many graves with names that would not come readily to mind for historians of the period or the general public. Patrick McNestry is one of these forgotten victims. Described as 'an outstanding character', he took part in the fierce fighting in the streets on the north side of the Four Courts in Dublin in 1916. His fellow officers included nationalist 'royalty' such as Piaras Béaslaí, Liam Archer and Diarmuid O'Hegarty. Dubliner McNestry was a silversmith in Egan's Jewellers on St Patrick's Street. Its owner, Barry Egan, was a Sinn Féin member of Cork Corporation. Patrick died in Cork Fever Hospital of typhoid. His family claimed for a pension on three separate occasions, but this was not awarded as it could not be proven that his death had occurred due to his military service. This was despite the fact that he was awarded the highest medal awards, had been sentenced to death in 1916 and was in solitary confinement until early 1917 in Portland Prison in Dorset. At the time of his death he was staff officer with 'C' Company, 1st Battalion, Cork Brigade IRA.[86]

## 17 October 1920
### Volunteer Michael Fitzgerald

Following the September 1919 attack on a British armed party outside the Wesleyan church at Fermoy in which one soldier was killed, a number of local IRA men were arrested and detained. However, despite the threat of heavy penalties, no jury could be empanelled to try the prisoners and many remained in custody at Cork Gaol (now University College Cork). Among them was Michael Fitzgerald, O/C 1st Battalion, Cork No. 2 Brigade. An attempt was made on 9 June 1920 to send him for trial in Derry, but this was refused by the judiciary on the grounds that he was unlikely to get a fair trial. George Power takes up the story: 'the brigade decided to capture the most senior of the British officers in Fermoy and to hold him as a hostage for Fitzgerald'.[87] The officer captured, on 26 June, was General Lucas, who caused so much trouble for his captors that he was later allowed to escape.[88] On 9 August Fitzgerald sent a letter to the governor of Cork Prison demanding unconditional release after almost a year on remand. On 11 August Fitzgerald, together with a number of other untried prisoners, began a hunger strike for release, which ended in his death sixty-seven days later. He is buried at Kilcrumper Cemetery, Fermoy.[89]

## 22 October 1920
## Captain William Alfred Dixon
## Private Charles Reid
## Private Thomas Bennett

The Toureen ambush was the first attempt by the new West Cork Flying Column to mount a significant attack against the Essex Regiment, which had two companies stationed in Bandon. These had been raiding constantly, aggressively and successfully to take the war to the IRA. The column needed good intelligence before mounting the attack, as senior officers, including Battalion O/C Mick O'Neill, were being moved to Cork along this route, having been captured. The location chosen was a farmhouse at a bend in the road halfway between Cork and Bandon. Having taken possession of Forde's house and yard during the night, the column planted a mine in the road and split into three groups to await their quarry. Two lorries swept into the ambush shortly after 8 a.m. As the lead lorry drove over the mine it failed to explode, so some of the ambushers opened fire. The lorry sped on towards Cork, abandoning their comrades 50 metres behind. The second ambush party opened fire on the rear lorry at point-blank range, hitting the driver and bringing the lorry to a halt. Captain Dixon led the fightback from the lorry until a second IRA volley killed him and the two privates. The remaining soldiers, some of whom were wounded, surrendered. Those wounded were Woodward, Walding, Decker, Dowse, Taylor and Briggs.[90]

**23 October 1920**

**Constable Bertie Rippengale**

**8 November**

**Constable Albert E. Rundle**

In an ambush at Leap three members of the RIC were injured. The local IRA unit which carried out the ambush was unaware of any fatalities, even as late as 1949, as neither of the two BMH witness statements that mention this ambush record any deaths. Initial reports in *The Cork Examiner* suggested that the men were wounded and that Glandore came under sustained attack at 4 a.m. from guns and bombs in reprisal. However, *The Skibbereen Eagle* confirmed Rippengale's death on Saturday 23 October. Rippengale (25) was from Shanway, Essex. Rundle (26) died in Cork on 8 November, after developing a bowel obstruction resulting from his shooting.[91]

**25 October 1920**

**Edward Meade**

Edward Meade was shot dead in Victoria Barracks, Cork. He was shot accidentally by one of the soldiers. He was a civilian clerk working in the barracks. Like many of the clerks working there he was an ex-soldier, and had been injured in the Great War. He left no family.[92]

**25 October 1920**

**Lord Mayor and IRA Cork No. 1 Brigade Commandant Terence MacSwiney**

**Volunteer Joseph Murphy**

For details of these deaths, see Part 1: The Funeral of Terence MacSwiney.

## 30 October 1920
## Lieutenant Bernard Brown
## Lieutenant David Rutherford

The two men were motorcycling from Fermoy to Killarney and are usually believed to have been captured just outside Cork city, near Killeens, where their motorcycle was found. However, Charlie Browne of Macroom Company stated: 'In November, 1920, two enemy Intelligence Officers – Lieutenants Rutherford and Browne – were captured at Fargus [*sic*] by members of Coachford Company. They were dressed in civilian clothes, were armed, and were travelling in a motor-cycle with sidecar attachment. They were transferred to "E" Company for interrogation and Brigade H.Q. were notified. They were subsequently shot as enemy spies and were buried at Laharn, Rusheen [Coachford, near Leades Cross].' Given the detail and Charlie Browne's usual accuracy, his report is likely to be true. Their bodies have never been recovered.[93]

## 4 November 1920
## John (James) Hawkes/Mahony

*The Southern Star* reported on 18 September 1920 that Dunmanway had been raided by British troops led by John Hawkes. Hawkes had previously been arrested by the IRP for theft. Following his release he had been staying in the army barracks in Bantry. However, having left Bantry, he had gone to the police barracks in Skibbereen on 3 November in a state of panic, telling them that the IRA was after him. He was shot the following morning as he left the workhouse where the RIC had put him for the night. Although named as Hawkes in the paper, it appears from the evidence of the inquest into his death that his real second name was Mahony. As a suspected spy, he had spent the previous weeks under police protection. The military confirmed that he had been working for them. On 2 July 1921 *The Southern Star* reported that his mother was awarded compensation of £300 for his death. She had claimed £3,000.[94]

## 5 November 1920
### Private William King

A company of the Hampshire Regiment was stationed in Youghal but was effectively besieged by the IRA, who had the run of the town except when the regiment carried out the occasional raid. During one such raid, on Bransfield's Barbershop, one of the local IRA fired on Private King as he entered the yard at the back of the shop. He was shot in the heart and died. Later that night members of his regiment, armed with canes, attacked a number of shops in the town and were driven back into their barracks by the local people. On the way they severely beat a local man called Casey. Shortly afterwards they reappeared on the street fully armed and fired indiscriminately into houses and tenements throughout the night.[95]

## 6 November 1920
### Constable T. J. Walsh

Walsh was listed as missing in the official British list of 22 August 1921. Seán Healy recalled: 'In November 1920, a Black and Tan Inspector named Walsh, who was one of those Irishmen in the British forces, was removed from a train at Blarney and given the reward he deserved. A member of the Parcels Office staff at Cork Railway station, named M. Kelly, reported that an armed Black and Tan officer in mufti had entered the Parcels Office and carefully examined the place, at the same time scrutinising all members of the staff. ... Inquiries revealed that he intended travelling to Dublin by the night mail train on a special mission. I contacted Lieutenant D. Duggan and Volunteer Val Ivers, two members of our Active Service Unit. The three of us then decided to travel on the same train and alight at Blarney and deal with this man, as instructed.

'When we alighted at Blarney station, we entered the compartment in which the Black and Tan was travelling. We told him we were I.R.A. men and disarmed him and removed him from the train, at the same time informing him that he was to be brought before a courtmartial and that if he attempted to escape he would be shot. ...

'A Drumhead Courtmartial took place. He was found guilty of being a traitor to his country and he paid the supreme penalty.'[96]

## 8 November 1920
## William (John) Mulcahy

Yet another victim of British shooting at individuals for failing to halt, William Mulcahy was shot dead on Kyrls Quay in Cork city centre around 10 p.m. on his way home. He received a 'gunshot wound on the right shoulder, which penetrated the chest, and he died while he was being conveyed to the military hospital'. There is little further information.[97]

## 8 November 1920
## Private Percy Starling

Three marines were badly injured by the accidental discharge of a rifle at the Coastguard Station in Union Hall on Friday 5 November. All three were taken to Haulbowline, where Private Starling (23) died on 8 November. He was a gunner in the Royal Marine Artillery and had been married three weeks earlier.[98]

## 10 November 1920
## Volunteer Christopher Lucey

On 10 November 'C' Company of the Auxiliaries raided Ballingeary. They were spotted by Lucey as they arrived in the village and he attempted to make his escape, but died in a hail of bullets. A BMH witness statement by officers of 'B' Company, 1st Cork Brigade, stated: 'Christopher Lucey (formerly a Section Commander of the Company) while on the run in the Ballingeary district took part in the hold up of two military lorries and having disarmed the soldiers burnt the lorries. Several rifles and equipment were secured. He was killed by Auxiliaries on the 10th November, 1920. His remains were brought to the City and interred in the Republican Plot at St. Finbarr's Cemetery, the firing party at the graveside being provided by the

Company.' Lucey had been on the run from his home in Pembroke Street due to increased pressure on the IRA in the city, which had led to most of the senior IRA officers in the city retreating westwards.[99]

## 12 November 1920
### Constable Daniel O'Brien

Because there was no inquiry, little is known about the death of Daniel O'Brien other than that he fell out of a truck and struck his head. He was pronounced dead at the Cork Military Hospital.[100]

## 15 November 1920
### Captain Stewart Chambers
### Captain Montague Green
### Lieutenant William Watts

These three officers were taken off the Cork to Bandon train along with a Lieutenant Goode. Goode was released and was the chief witness at the subsequent inquiry. The three men were taken over the bridge crossing the railway and shot in a nearby field. It seems on balance that this was a case of mistaken identity and that the real target was an intelligence officer named Green who was implicated in the torture of West Cork IRA leaders Tom Hales and Pat Harte. Laurence Nugent seemed certain in his BMH witness statement that they had captured Hales' torturer, and 1st Brigade Commander Mick Murphy also mentions the incident although he doesn't mention Hales.[101]

## 16 November 1920
### Auxiliary Bertram Agnew
### Auxiliary Lionel Mitchell

There is much confusion about the deaths of these two men and they are often mixed up with Brown and Rutherford who were captured two weeks earlier. The date commonly given is 6 November, but the newspaper reports all refer to 15 November. The men left Macroom and travelled to Cork on weekend leave. They checked into the Imperial Hotel on 15 November and left the following morning at 9 a.m. to collect a car from the Johnson and Perrott garage in Nelson (Emmet) Place. It appears that they were captured there, then taken into the country and shot.[102] Their bodies were never found, but according to *The Cork Examiner* of 5 November 1921 their deaths were confirmed by Tom Barry after the Truce.

## 17 November 1920
### Sergeant James O'Donoghue
### Na Fianna Patrick Hanley
### Eugene O'Connell
### James Coleman

Sergeant James O'Donoghue, RIC, was shot dead by the IRA in White Street, Cork, on the evening of 17 November. That night three men were shot dead in Cork by men in military uniform; they were Patrick Hanley of 2 Broad Street; Eugene O'Connell of 17 Broad Lane and James Coleman of 15 North Mall. Two others – Charlie O'Brien of 17 Broad Lane and Stephen Coleman of 2 Broad Street – were wounded. There is little doubt that the later killings were part of a reprisal for O'Donoghue and, in the case of Coleman, for his refusal to serve rowdy members of the 'new police' in his bar.[103]

## 21 November 1920
### Constable Henry Clement Jays

Constable Jays was killed at Leap shortly after leaving the hotel in the village to walk the very short distance to the barracks. *The Cork Examiner* on 23 November 1920 reported that on the previous Sunday night, 'between 8 and 9 o'clock, as Constables Jays and Mills were passing through the village volleys were fired at them from behind a hoarding near the Cross turning to Glandore. Jays was mortally wounded and died almost instantaneously.'[104]

**22 November 1920**

**Volunteer Patrick McCarthy**

Patrick McCarthy was shot during a gun battle with Auxiliaries stationed in Millstreet. The local community website states: 'The late Paddy McCarthy was born in Meelin and reared in Freemount, not far from Millstreet. He became an active member of Óglaigh na hÉireann following the 1916 Easter Rising. On May 8, 1918 he was charged with a gun offence and imprisoned for 18 months. He was held in Belfast and in Manchester where he managed to escape in October 1919. He took part in the capture of Mallow Barracks in September 1920, which was the only military barracks to be taken over in the war. Captain McCarthy met his fate on Mill Lane on the night of the 22nd November 1920, when his Flying Column took on the British Forces in Millstreet.'[105]

**23 November 1920**

**Captain Joseph Thompson**

Tim Herlihy related: 'There was a Captain Thompson, I.O. Manchester Regiment, who used to go into shops and houses in Ballincollig village, brandishing a revolver and saying that if anything happened to him the village would go up but he was caught at Carrigrohane on his motor bike and shot dead, his arms and bike being taken. No reprisals took place but there was tension for a while. This was in November, 1920. Captain Thompson was shot dead by Leo Murphy and two other Volunteers on the Model Farm Road. Thompson had previously raided Leo Murphy's mother's house. He was drunk at the time and boasted that he was out to get all IRA leaders as he had got the leaders in Egypt. He treated Rose Murphy very roughly and this helped to cause her early death. When captured he tried to save himself by informing his captors that a cease fire was coming and that Ireland was getting Dominion Home Rule. He said he had this from Dublin Castle. This special pleading didn't work, however, and he was shot out of hand.'[106]

**23 November 1920**

**Volunteer Denis Ring**

*The Cork Examiner* reports the funeral of Denis Ring in Midleton but makes no mention of him being shot. He is recorded in the Cork IRA Roll of Honour but no details survive other than that he died of 'traumatic pneumonia' and was buried in the Republican Plot in Midleton.[107]

**23 November 1920**

**Volunteer Patrick O'Donoghue**

**Volunteer Patrick Trahy**

**Volunteer James Meihigan**

Three members of the IRA were standing on St Patrick's Street at the junction of Princes Street when a grenade exploded between them. All three were mortally wounded. Michael V. O'Donoghue was nearby when the incident occurred: 'What happened that night at Prince's St. corner is still much of mystery. At first the rumour was circulated that the Tans had thrown a bomb among a group of young "Shinners" and some eye-witnesses actually "saw" a uniformed figure silhouetted on the palisaded roof of the newly-built Pavilion Cinema as he threw the missile – this was the generally accepted story. But I and those with me are positive that no uniformed police or military were in the immediate vicinity then or even subsequently. Later, I ascertained from their comrades and a fellow officer of the victims that they had had a Battalion Staff Volunteer Conference and afterwards had dispersed. These Blackrock Volunteers had dallied for a final chat before parting on reaching Patrick St. One of them had a percussion bomb in his possession and, through some mischance which will never now be explained, it must have dropped on the pavement causing the frightful tragedy.'[108]

**24 November 1920**

**Denis O'Donnell**

This shooting occurred in Kildorrery, which was the scene of a low-level war of attrition between the police and the IRA. O'Donnell was taken from his bed, according to the various newspaper reports, and shot nine times in front of his family by the police, including twice in the head and twice in the heart.[109]

**26 November 1920**
**Volunteer Christopher Morrissey**
**Volunteer Liam Mulcahy**

Maurice Forde and others mentioned these deaths: 'Later in the year, however, – in November – Christy Morrissey and Liam Mulcahy were killed outright when in their inexperience they tampered with a bomb in an upper room of O'Leary's Undertaking Establishment at Blackpool. They had belonged to "E" Company and so did Donal Kelleher who, coming up the stairs at the time, stopped outside the room to light a cigarette just as the bomb exploded. He escaped with injuries.' The local and national newspapers gave detailed coverage of the events (calling Morrissey Denis rather than Christopher) but this is the most succinct account.[110]

**26 November 1920**
**Private Walter Gammon**
**Private Ernest Hall**

Two days after the shooting of Denis O'Donnell, two lorry loads of the Buffs Regiment escorted the crown solicitor from Fermoy to his inquest. They were observed passing through Glanworth and, as they would almost inevitably have to return by the same route, the North Cork Brigade flying column was assembled. The aim was to ambush the staff officers and crown solicitor, who were in a staff car. Around 5 p.m., with the IRA lining the road, the convoy began the ascent of Labbacallee Hill, just to the west of Glanworth. The staff car pulled in to let the first lorry up the hill before it made the climb. One of the IRA column opened fire and the rest joined in. After a grenade landed in the body of the truck, the two soldiers inside stood no chance. Four others were injured, including Lieutenant Millow, who was blown out of the truck. The staff car was abandoned and the crown solicitor made an ignominious return to Fermoy across country in the second truck.[111]

## 27 November 1920
## Volunteer William (Liam) Heffernan
## Constable Timothy Quinn

Though thousands pass it every day, few stop to look at the fine monument in the centre of Castlemartyr. The inscription reads: 'In lasting memory of Vol. Willie Heffernan of Conna 4th Batt. B Coy., 1st Brigade I.R.A who was shot in action at Castlemartyr 27-11-1920 and who is interred at Knockmourne Conna. Ar dheis Dé go raibh a anam.' Heffernan was sitting in his car outside a shop in the middle of the village waiting for an IRA officer when he was spotted by Sergeant Curley and Constable Timothy Quinn, who walked up to him. The company commander of Midleton, Joseph Aherne, was spotted in the back seat and both men drew their weapons. Shots rang out and Heffernan was mortally wounded. He had to be pulled from the driver's seat and Aherne drove off.[112] Quinn had been shot through the arm and into the lung. He died the following day in the Cork Military Hospital.[113]

## 28 November 1920
## Thomas Downey

Thomas Downey (sometimes called Downing) was kidnapped on 23 November and was shot as a spy according to Cork IRA spymaster Florence O'Donoghue. It is probable that Downey was taken to the Cork No. 1 Brigade 'prison' in Knockraha and executed.[114] On 27 November *The Cork Examiner* published a copy of a notice circulating in the city from the Black and Tans stating, 'If Mr. Downey is not returned to his home within 56 hours citizens prepare, especially Sinn Feiners', which shows they were particularly concerned about his disappearance.[115]

**28 November 1920**

**Lieutenant Colonel Francis Crake**

**Auxiliary William T. Barnes**

**Auxiliary Cecil James Bayley**

**Auxiliary Leonard Bradshaw**

**Auxiliary James Gleave**

**Auxiliary Cecil Guthrie**

**Auxiliary Philip Graham**

**Auxiliary Stanley Hooper-Jones**

**Auxiliary Frederick Hugo**

**Auxiliary Albert Jones**

**Auxiliary Ernest Lucas**

**Auxiliary William Pallester**

**Auxiliary Horace Pearson**

**Auxiliary Arthur Poole**

**Auxiliary Francis Taylor**

**Auxiliary Christopher Wainwright**

**Auxiliary Benjamin Webster**

**3rd Brigade IRA Column Vice-Commandant Michael McCarthy**

**Volunteer Patrick Deasy**

**Volunteer Jim O'Sullivan**

For details of these deaths, see Part 1: The Kilmichael Ambush.


**29 November 1920**

**Volunteer Denis (Din-Din) O'Riordan**

For details of O'Riordan's death, see Part 1: Cascading Death.


**29 November 1920 (date uncertain)**

**Frederick Blemens**

**James Blemens Snr**

For details of the Blemens' deaths, see Part 1: Cascading Death.

## 29 November 1920
### Denis (Denny) O'Sullivan

Denny O'Sullivan's death does not appear in the official records, but *The Lee Valley Outlook* reported that he 'was killed by the Auxiliaries during reprisals for Kilmichael Ambush, Sunday, November 28 [*sic*] 1920. Denny, who worked for Cronins, Cooldaniel, had gone by horse and cart on Monday to collect provisions from Cronins Provision Stores and Bar at Dromleigh ... He was having a drink, a reward for giving a lift to Mrs Cotter, Johnstown Bar, when three truckloads of Auxiliaries, bent on revenge for the deaths of their comrades, arrived. Denny, who was not involved in any organisation, couldn't answer their questions satisfactorily and he was taken out and shot. The soldiers went on to burn O'Mahony's house across from Dromleigh School ... At the ambush site the Auxiliaries burned the Kelly and O'Donoghue houses. It was a frightening sequel to the ambush for the people of Kilmichael.' *Cumann Staire* (Ballingeary) suggests that a Denny Mahony was killed in Kilmichael on 30 November but it seems that this is incorrect.[116]

## November 1920 (date uncertain)
### Constable James Gordon

James Gordon of Leitrim was captured while drunk some time at the end of November, according to BMH 719. He had just resigned from the RIC and was heading home. He was linked by the IRA to the killing of a number of nationalists in Tipperary and other stations. According to the Irish Military Pensions application of Edward Maloney of Knockraha it is possible that Gordon was the Black and Tan held in 'Sing Sing' vault for three weeks before being shot by a group that included Maloney. He stated that four British officers were held there at the same time. The only difficulty with the information provided in BMH WS 719 is that no newspaper record of a James Gordon has been found and the only mention of him is the record of a payout on the Compensation Commission Register.[117]

## 1 December 1920
## Carl Johansen (Jolinsin)

Carl Johansen (25), a Norwegian sailor on the SS *Tonjar*, was mortally wounded by Auxiliaries. The shooting took place at 4 a.m. as he was returning to the ship on Customs House Quay. Johansen was shot in the back and the bullet perforated his gut in two places. He died some hours later. According to his death certificate, he was unmarried.[118]

## 2 December 1920
## Volunteer Joseph Begley
## Volunteer James Donoghue
## Volunteer John Galvin

Percy Taylor, an Essex Regiment deserter who had been captured by the IRA along with another deserter called Thomas Charles Watling around 1 November and held prisoner, had a brother in Bandon Barracks. While prisoners, their duties included setting the table for the flying column. Taylor told Tom Barry that he could get information for an attack on the barracks. Taylor wrote a letter arranging a meeting with Barry at Laurel Walk on the west side of Bandon on Thursday 2 December. Joe Begley (24), John Galvin (18) and Jimmy Donoghue (18) met, as arranged, in the vicinity of Bridge Street and headed west to meet Barry and to provide protection for the meeting. However, just before he left for the meeting Barry suffered a heart attack. As the others approached the rendezvous on the main Bandon to Dunmanway road, Joe Begley was first over the fence. He landed in the middle of an Essex Regiment ambush. He was shot dead immediately. John Galvin tried to help Jimmy Donoghue, who was shot in the hip. Both were then shot in the head. The soldiers then retreated, leaving the three bodies behind. They were buried together on Sunday 5 December in the new Republican Plot at Bandon.[119]

## 3 December 1920

### Nicholas de Sales Prendergast

The compensation claim reports of November 1921 pulled no punches, stating that the killing of Prendergast was 'a singularly cowardly and atrocious murder'. Members of 'K' Company of the Auxiliaries, en route to their new posting in Cork, stopped at Prendergast's Royal Hotel looking for rooms as their lorry had broken down. The Auxiliaries named by the papers were Watson, Jackson, Redford and Courtney; the fifth, 'Jock', appears to have been Scottish. Later in the night 'Jock' took out his revolver 'looking for drink'. Prendergast refused and was attacked by the other Auxiliaries, who had been playing billiards. They dragged him across the square, forced his false teeth down his windpipe and threw him into the flooded Blackwater. This was witnessed and testified to by a British Army officer, Lieutenant Hogue, who was congratulated for his honesty by Mrs Prendergast's counsel, Mr Tim Healy, the former MP and future governor general of the Irish Free State. Prendergast's decomposed body was found a month later two miles downriver, stuck in Clondualane Weir. The date of death is taken from the compensation claim.[120]

## 3 December 1920

### Constable Maurice Prenderville

Once every month a patrol of six RIC crossed to the Waterford side of the Blackwater to deliver his pension to an ex-policeman. On this Saturday the party of six was led by Sergeant McMorrogh. The West Waterford IRA Brigade ambushed them and Constable Prenderville was wounded in the abdomen. While he was lying wounded, Lady Edward Browne drove across the bridge and helped him into her cart, before picking up the military chaplain and bringing both to Youghal, where Prenderville died at 6.30 p.m. surrounded by his family. His body was returned to Listowel accompanied by his brothers, two of whom were also in the police, for burial.[121]

**4 December 1920 (date uncertain)**

**Private Percy Taylor**

**Private Thomas Watling**

Inevitably, suspicion fell upon Percy Taylor and Thomas Watling after the death of the three Bandon Volunteers on 2 December. These men appear in many BMH witness statements and there is little doubt that Frank O'Connor's short story *Guests of the Nation* was written about what happened to them. Their fate was sealed and a couple of days later they were shot in Kilbree, Clonakilty, by the local company. Senior IRA officer John L. Sullivan, in whose house they had stayed, poignantly recalled the events in 1973 and even then he was visibly upset about what happened.[122]

**7 December 1920**

**Volunteer Denis Regan**

On 7 December a body was found on the road between Clonakilty and Timoleague with a bullet wound in the back of the head. The newspapers had confirmed his identity by the following Saturday. The *Irish Independent* recorded: 'The dead body found near Clonakilty on Tuesday has been identified as that of Denis Regan, 21. It is stated, On Tues. deceased and his employer, Mr. D. Flynn, Gaggin, were arrested by military from Bandon, and taken to Clonakilty. Afterwards, it is stated, Regan was taken in a lorry to Bandon, where he was released, and nothing was heard of him afterwards until the discovery of his body that evening.' It also noted that, 'In Bandon and Tipperary more notices have been posted up declaring that prominent Sinn Feiners will be shot if members of the Crown forces are molested' and that a military lorry had been heard in the area shortly before Regan's body was found.[123]

**8 December 1920**

**Volunteer Michael McLean**

Tom Barry developed heart trouble after the exertions of Kilmichael and spent three weeks in safe houses and a Cork hospital. While he was absent, Seán Lehane from Schull was placed in charge of the flying column and organised an ambush at Gaggin, outside Bandon.[124] Ned Young gave a detailed account of what happened: 'All sections were in position at Gaggin about 8 a.m. The main body was placed south of the road. I was a member of a section which was in position at the eastern end of the ambush site north of the road ... About noon, scouts signalled the approach of an enemy lorry from the west (Clonakilty). Just as the lorry was about to enter the ambush, a shot was discharged accidentally by a member of the main body. This alerted the enemy who put on speed and drove madly through the ambush position. Some shots were fired at the enemy party, but it got through. The lorry was halted some distance nearer to Bandon. The occupants detrucked and entered the fields south of the road – moving back towards the position occupied by the main body of the column – with the apparent intention of taking the column in the rear. However, the column had already begun to withdraw from their position and so made contact with this enemy party before it had carried out an encircling movement. The retiring column was fired upon and returned the fire driving off the enemy. The whole column then withdrew safely to the mountain area ...

'Following this engagement, Michael McLean – a member of the column who had injured his foot and had been instructed to stay in a house in the vicinity until the engagement was over – was shot by enemy reinforcements which came out from Bandon.'[125]

## 8 December 1920
## Michael Francis Murphy

Murphy's death has the distinction of being the subject of the first military court of inquiry under the newly proclaimed martial law. Thus for the most intense period of the war, from December 1920 to July 1921, we have far greater detail about each individual than we have either earlier or later. The difficulty is that these inquests provide only one side of the story, which is often violently in conflict with the IRA version. However, in Murphy's case there is no conflict about what happened. On that day, the Feast of the Immaculate Conception, the traditional Christmas shopping day for country people and a religious festival, Murphy was attending evening Mass. As he was leaving Ss Peter and Paul's church, just off St Patrick's Street, around 9 p.m., he was hit by a bullet just over the heart. This was curfew time in the city and it appears that large groups of Auxiliaries were 'clearing the streets' when Murphy was shot. Some witnesses suggested that they were firing their revolvers to 'hurry things along'. He was pronounced dead by Dr Denis Fennell at the North Infirmary at 9.25 p.m. The court of inquiry found that he was shot by 'persons unknown'.[126]

## 9 December 1920
### John Fleming

John Fleming of Cattle Market Avenue, Cork city, died in agony as a result of wounds received when fire was suddenly opened from a passing police lorry on himself, two brothers and a friend as they were walking along Low Road at 4.30 p.m. Fleming's wounds proved that he had been shot from above and the right. The wounds were extensive in both his large and small intestines and an operation to save his life failed. He died from shock at 8 p.m.[127]

## 9 December 1920
### Harriet K. Meara

A fatal accident occurred on the Grand Parade outside St Augustine's church at noon. Harriet Meara stepped off the pavement just as four lorry-loads of Macroom Auxiliaries rounded the corner from Washington Street. She was knocked down by one of the lorries and killed. Other than a scalp wound she had no other visible injuries. Her body was taken to the nearby Mercy Hospital where she was pronounced dead. She was identified by Dean Babington of St Fin Barre's Cathedral as one of his congregation and was from 1 Wellington Avenue, College Road.[128]

**9 December 1920**

**George Horgan**

There is no doubt that George Horgan was shot for spying on the IRA and that his disappearance was the subject of a threat made by loyalist forces, which was copied on the wires and published in *The Mail* in Adelaide, South Australia. The threat, later denied, was to the point: 'LONDON, To-day – If Horgan is not returned by 4 p.m. on Friday, rebels of Cork, beware, as one man and one shop will disappear for every hour after the given time.'[129] The Auxiliaries were the most likely source for the notice.

George was born in Killarney in 1889 to a mixed marriage. His father had died by 1911 and the family had moved to Ballintemple in Cork city.[130] According to some commentators his body was removed from Lakelands on the Douglas Road and returned to his family after the War of Independence.[131]

**10 December 1920**

**Private Robert Cambridge**

James Brennock describes what happened: 'We assembled about 7 a.m. on the morning of the 10th and set out to move across the country to Waterpark (10 miles) where we were to pick up the O/C, Con Leddy. On our way we sighted an enemy lorry on the Rathcormac–Aghern road. We were at the time about three-quarters of a mile distant from its position. The lorry was approaching Leary's Cross which was actually the junction of five crossroads, and we had to decide to get into position to ambush the party should they travel on any of the two roads going west.' Once the ambush started the soldiers left the lorry and ran for cover. The ambushing party decided they were now too far away (300 yards) to do any damage so they moved forward to be able to fire directly on the soldiers, who were hiding behind a wall. When they got into position they called on the soldiers to surrender. In reply, Cambridge opened fire and was shot dead. The rest surrendered.[132]

**10 December 1920**
**Sarah Medaile**

During the night before the burning of Cork, Auxiliaries raided the buildings surrounding Tuckey Street police station. In one of the tenements they burst through the rooms, ransacking them during their 'search' operation. A room on the second floor was occupied by the Medaile family and Sarah, who was over sixty, had a heart attack and died. It seems likely that the shock of the search contributed to her attack.[133]

**11 December 1920**
**John O'Brien**

The Cameron Highlanders raided Cloyne and managed to trap the East Cork flying column in a large house in the centre of the village. Under fire, 'Paddy Whelan and Jack Ahern rushed from Walsh's house across the street to a gateway and opened fire down the street. Under cover of this fire the men all got across safely from Walsh's and were able to move out of the village without suffering any casualties.'[134] However, as the Camerons left the village they opened fire on a young man, John O'Brien, and shot him dead. It appears that Sergeant Major Mackintosh used a Lewis gun on what he thought was the flying column, according to the Camerons' records, and the use of the gun is confirmed by Whelan.[135]

**12 December 1920**
**Auxiliary Spencer R. Chapman**

For details of Chapman's death, see Part 1: The Burning of Cork.

**12–18 December 1920**
**Volunteer Jeremiah Delaney**
**Volunteer Cornelius Delaney**

For details of the Delaneys' deaths, see Part 1: The Burning of Cork.

**15 December 1920**
**Canon Thomas Magner**
**Volunteer Tadhg (Timothy) Crowley**

On that day Canon Thomas Magner of Dunmanway, out on his daily walk, came to the assistance of the Bantry resident magistrate, R. S. Brady, whose car had broken down just to the east of Dunmanway at Ballyhalwick. Tadhg Crowley was already there, helping him. Two lorry-loads of 'K' Company were on their way to Cork for the funeral of Cadet Chapman. Travelling in the second lorry Cadet Hart, a section leader, ordered it stopped. Leaving the lorry, he pistol-whipped and then shot Crowley. He then forced Canon Magner to the ground and shot him in cold blood.[136] His comrades made no serious attempt to intervene until after the priest was shot. Brady testified at the trial that after Canon Magner was shot, he ran away through the fields back into Dunmanway, a mile to the west. He said that the Auxiliaries fired after him. They certainly tried to hide the victims by throwing them over a fence. At Hart's trial it was said that he had been drinking all day because Chapman had died from wounds suffered during the Dillon's Cross ambush, and that when examined he was on the brink of Delirium Tremens.[137] Hart and Chapman's friendship was confirmed by Sir Hamar Greenwood during a tetchy exchange in the House of Commons on 17 February 1921: 'Yes, Cadet Hart was a chum and companion of Cadet Chapman, who was massacred in an ambush a few days before in Cork, and undoubtedly that had an effect on his mind.'[138]

**21 December 1920**
**Volunteer Patrick Tarrant**
**Timothy Donovan**

This is yet another episode that is virtually ignored in the public record. On 21 December an IRA unit raided the Cork General Post Office on the newly renamed Oliver Plunkett Street. Patrick Tarrant jumped over the counter in the parcels office and made a dash for the main door, where he turned and warned the people in the office that he would shoot unless they put their hands up. Unfortunately for him, two undercover police were in the office. According to the inquest they challenged him and he fired three shots at them. One of the constables returned fire, hitting Tarrant in the face and chest. They then foiled the raid in progress but failed to arrest anyone. It took a few days to identify the body but at the inquest his father (from Ballintemple) stated that he was nineteen and associated with the Volunteers. Timothy Donovan (31), working as a labourer, had been posting parcels for his employer when he was shot in the crossfire. According to his brother he had been a member of the Royal Munster Fusiliers and had no connection with any political organisation.[139]

## 28 December 1920
### Constable Martin Mullen
### Constable Ernest Dray
### Constable Arthur Thorp(e)

Patrick Whelan was a member of the East Cork flying column and he told the BMH: 'The whole column, including Jack Aherne and myself, moved into Midleton under cover or [sic] darkness, and assembled at a saw-mills in Charles Street [now Connolly Street]. ... From the saw-mills, Jack and I continued on to the main street. We arranged that I would take up position at the corner of Charles Street which is situated about midway in the main street, and at right-angles to it. Jack posted himself further down the main street, in the vicinity of the Midleton Arms Hotel. We were armed with .45 Webley revolvers and wore trench coats and capes.

'I was only about five minutes at my post when I saw a patrol of Black and Tans, marching slowly towards me. They moved in pairs, about six paces apart and on both sides of the street, four pairs on my side and two pairs on the opposite side, together with an old R.I.C. man named Mullins [sic]. All were armed with rifles and revolvers, with the rifles slung on their shoulders ...

'We were only about five minutes in position when the patrol returned

– still in the same order as I had seen it earlier. Hurley judged his shot to perfection, and at once all of us opened fire. The patrol was taken completely by surprise and, in comparatively short time, the attack was over. Some of the Tans did fire back at us, and there were a few narrow escapes on our side … Constable Mullins [*sic*] was shot dead, and about six other Tans wounded, some of whom died later from their wounds. Some of the patrol threw their rifles on the street and ran away … Two of the Black and Tans were lying on the footpath near me, bleeding profusely.'[140]

## 31 December 1920
### Private George Lockyer

According to *The Skibbereen Eagle* of 8 January 1921, Lockyer (22), a member of the King's Liverpool Regiment was accidentally shot through the head during a raid on Patrick Driscoll's home at Mohanagh, outside Skibbereen.

## December 1920 (date uncertain)
### Not named

Denis Dwyer recalls: 'Sometime late in 1920, or early in 1921, a British soldier in uniform without badges was caught in the locality [of Grenagh]: he stated he was a deserter. As far as I can recollect, he gave no name or regiment. He was held in arrest for some short time while enquiries were being made. We were very suspicious of him for about this time many of the alleged deserters were British spies. It was eventually decided to execute him and I was one of the party detailed for the job. He died very bravely without the slightest flinching, which convinced us that he was a British Intelligence Officer. He was only in our custody for less than two (2) days, during which he was kept in an unoccupied cottage on the farm of a Matt Donovan of Ballyvalloon, situated about 1½ miles from the village of Grenagh. His remains were buried on the farm, roughly about 300 yards from the cottage mentioned above, and as far as I know, the remains are still there.' This may be a soldier named Belchamber who went missing from Buttevant.[141]

**1 January 1921**
**Constable Francis Shortall**
**21 January 1921**
**Constable Thomas Johnston**

On 1 January, shortly before 8 p.m., a party of nine RIC left their Union Quay Barracks to take dispatches to the Auxiliaries' headquarters at Empress Place on Summerhill North. They did this every evening after 7 p.m., which turned out to be a fatal mistake. They managed to get 100 metres before they were ambushed by the 2nd Battalion of the city IRA, who were 'armed with revolvers, grenades and a Lewis gun … those not killed or wounded ran helter-skelter back to Union Quay Barracks firing wildly from rifles as they ran. Some took cover and replied to our fire. They were machine-gunned all the way up Union Quay by a Volunteer named Healy who operated our Lewis gun on the occasion and who was, incidentally, an ex-British army gunner.' Inevitably, the chief witness on the police side, Constable Cook, gave a very different version of events in which the RIC chased after their attackers pursing them across the bridge and down the South Mall before returning to help Frank Shortall (35), who had been shot in the thigh and died shortly after. Shortall had married three months previously in the city. Three weeks later Constable Thomas Johnston (19) from Co. Cavan died from injuries inflicted by a grenade according to his death certificate.[142]

**3 January 1921**
**Jeremiah Casey**

District Inspector (DI) Fleming of the Macroom-based 'C' Company Auxiliaries led a raid to Derryfineen on the road from Halfway to Ballingeary and arrived around 12.30 p.m. They raided Denis Riordan's home and Fleming sent the raiding party, including Cadets Wilson and Owen, in pursuit of some runaways from the house. After twenty minutes Wilson reported that a man had been shot and this turned out to be Jeremiah Casey, who was 'between sixteen and seventeen years old' according to his mother.

Cadet H. W. Owen said he had inflicted the fatal wounds, having called on the man to halt several times. In a statement of exceptional similarity, Cadet E. R. Wilson confirmed this version of events. The court of inquiry blamed Jeremiah for not halting when ordered. He was unarmed.[143]

## 5 January 1921
### Brother Finbarr D'Arcy

The basic facts of this case could not be simpler. The Hampshires raided the Imperial Hotel; Brother D'Arcy escaped through a window, was recaptured and later shot dead. However, the *dramatis personae* on the British side were individually, and as a unit, despised by their opponents and notorious for their mistreatment of prisoners. Robert C. Ahern, the intelligence officer of Cork No. 1 Brigade, recalled: '[Captain Kelly] specialised in the torturing of I.R.A. prisoners and was head of a group of British intelligence officers in Cork barracks who were notorious for their barbarous treatment of prisoners. The names of some of the latter were Hammond, Keogh [*sic*], and Cusack.' Lieutenant Koe, who interrogated D'Arcy, was assisted in the arrest and search of D'Arcy by 'K' Company Auxiliaries Wilson and Wakefield, who happened to be staying in the hotel. Koe's version of the interrogation is textbook and entirely proper, suggesting it is fabricated. There is no doubt that D'Arcy was forced to strip naked and in this condition escaped through the window of room 5 before being recaptured. According to the three main witnesses, he was insane or drunk, so he was put in a lorry and warned by Lieutenant Koe that he would be shot if he tried to escape. This he apparently did and was shot by two members of the Hampshire Regiment who were guarding him. Lieutenant Koe and the Hampshire Regiment seem to have been particularly unlucky with prisoners and this sequence of events was repeated regularly over the next six months. It appears from Eoin 'Pope' O'Mahony's BMH witness statement that D'Arcy had just robbed the GPO (which could be accessed from room 5) along with two others.[144]

**6 January 1921**

**John MacSweeney**

The death of John MacSweeney (15) is recorded in *The Struggle of the Irish People*. According to it, the military raided Allenstown just south of Kanturk and on the approach of the lorries John ran away. In a tragedy repeated again and again over the following months, he was shot in the back. He died of peritonitis.[145]

**15 January 1921**

**Gerald Oswald Pring**

After the shooting of two detectives, Jack Maliff and Thomas Ryan, on the Western Road in Cork city around 4.30 p.m. on this day, tension in the city was high. So when the Pring family were walking home through the city centre, they decided to stay off the main streets, but to no avail. Shortly after 8 p.m. Gerald Pring (30), a customs and excise officer in Midleton, was shot dead. The evidence given to the court of inquiry could not be more graphic. Gerald's brother Harold described what happened: 'We came on to the Western Road just by the Courthouse, where Western Road joins Washington Street. About 50 yards from the Courthouse we parted company from Dalton, and went on. I, in the middle, with my sister on the outside, and my brother on the inside. Just as we were passing Fernhurst Avenue [O'Donovan's Road] two lorries of the Crossley Tender type passed us, meeting us. Time was between 2010 and 2020 hours. They had no lights. The men in the cars were dressed as policemen. I saw this by the light of a gas lamp close to which the lorries passed us. They were going about 30 miles an hour. When there was about 60 yards between us I heard a shot and felt the wind of a bullet pass close by my neck, and I saw my brother pitch forward. He was about two paces in front of me and a little to the left. My sister went into the road and shouted after the lorry, and I bent down and picked up my brother. There was a big piece hanging down from the back of his skull. A crowd came round and pulled me away. I went home with my sister.'[146]

## 16 January 1921

### Volunteer Patrick Donovan

Patrick was shot at Ballincollop, Timoleague by the military on 16 January according to *The Struggle of the Irish People*. According to John O'Driscoll, captain of the Timoleague Company of the IRA, the company were going to a parade when the military conducted a round-up in the village. The IRA members were fired on but all made good their escape with the exception of Richard Collins, who was arrested, and Donovan, who was shot dead. There are sparse details of Patrick's death in the British court of inquiry other than that he ran away and was shot.[147]

## 19 January 1921

### Volunteer Denis Hegarty

Denis Hegarty (30) worked for John Good of Barryshall, Timoleague. He slept in a house in the yard. Good told the court of inquiry that he heard movement in the yard during the night and in the morning the young man's body was found at the end of the lane. It is probable that he was shot by loyalist forces but, as there was never an admission of guilt and there were no eyewitnesses, there is no way of knowing.[148]

## 20 January 1921 (date uncertain)

### Daniel Lucey

'About this time, we laid a trap for a suspected spy in the area, in conjunction with some men from Ballinagree company. The unfortunate fellow fell for it, so he did not spy any more. Our spy was visited by two men from [the] Donoughmore area, disguised as British officers. He was asked if he had seen any of "the Boys" – meaning IRA men – lately. He gave his questioners all the information he had, while, with some other men from Rusheen company, I waited outside the door. He was taken prisoner on the spot, and was held prisoner for about a fortnight, during which time he was tried by the Brigade Staff, and sentenced to death. He was executed after a fair trial in Kilcorney area, Millstreet Battalion, Cork II Brigade. His name was Dan Lucey.'[149]

## 20 January 1921
### Michael (Denis) Dwyer/O'Dwyer

Michael Dwyer was waiting on the roadside at Carhue when members of the 3rd Brigade flying column, including Tom Barry, came along. He started to give information about local IRA members, clearly believing that they were members of the Essex Regiment or Auxiliaries. Once they had questioned him, he was shot and his body was left on the roadway to lure out British forces. However, they ignored reports about the body as they suspected the trap. William Desmond recalled: 'Two nights before this when Barry and John Lordan went to inspect the ambush position they found a suspicious character on the side of the road. He apparently took them for British military and made it obvious he was a friend. They took him prisoner and after interrogation discovered he was a spy. He was given a trial, found guilty and was executed the next morning. His name was O'Dwyer of Castletown-Kenneigh [sic] and he was an ex-British soldier ...

'As I already stated, the spy had been executed and was lying on the road a short distance away from us at Farnalough Cross Roads and we expected the military would come out to remove the body. Comdt. Barry had made sure that they were made aware that the man was dead on the road. They didn't come, however, until sometime after we had left the position.'

In early 1920 Dwyer had been taken from his bed and tried in an out-house over 'something he said'. His mother and father received compensation of £1,000.[150]

## 21 January 1921
### Constable Henry Bloxham

One IRA tactic was to fire randomly at RIC barracks or other targets in the hope of drawing the police out to investigate. Once this happened an ambush was arranged. This is precisely what happened in this case. Two police set out on their bicycles from Ballincollig to investigate shootings at Waterfall Railway Station. As they approached the station, fire was opened on them and both men increased their speed. After 60 yards Bloxham collapsed, while Larkin cycled into the station and caught the train to Cork. He returned with an ambulance to find his colleague still where he had fallen. He was dead. Bloxham (40) was married with an eight-month-old child.[151]

## 22 January 1921 (date uncertain)
## Patrick Rea

While the surname was wrong in the *Irish Independent* missing list in August 1922 (Ray), there is no doubt that this man was killed. He lived in Church Hill, Passage West. *The Freeman's Journal* states on 14 January 1922 that 'Patrick Rea of Passage West, an ex-soldier who worked in Passage [West] Docks was removed while going to the P.O. on 22 January 1921, and he had not been heard of yet.' His wife was awarded £1,200 and each of the four children £200.[152]

## 23 January 1921
## Richard Morey

The competent military authority (Colonel Willis) issued new curfew orders for Cork commencing Saturday 22 January stipulating that people had to be off the streets between the hours of 5 p.m. and 3 a.m. on Saturdays and Sundays. On this day a crowd had gathered around 8 p.m. at the junction of Shandon Street and Wolfe Tone Street and shots were fired into it by a military patrol. One ten-year-old boy, Richard Morey, was shot above the heart, while another, George Raymond, was injured. Both were rushed to the North Infirmary 200 metres away and Richard, whose condition was regarded as hopeless from the outset, died shortly after admittance.[153]

**23 January 1921**

**Thomas J. Bradfield**

More has been written about the killing of Thomas J. Bradfield than most of the victims of the revolution. Anna Hurley O'Mahony provides the best description of what happened: 'This was where we parted and we went our own road after getting our bicycles. When some distance away, we heard a single shot back in the direction we had come from, but no further sound after that.

'The next day we heard that the body of a loyalist named Bradfield was found stretched at the crossroads where we had parted from the Column the night before. What had happened was this. When the Column came into the area it dispersed to different houses to secure food and shelter and some of its Officers entered Bradfield's home and asked for a meal. Contrary to the reception they expected they were welcomed heartily by the owner and invited to partake of whiskey. For some little time they were puzzled and then discovered that due to their appearance – trench coats and bandoliers and semi-uniform look, and also to the accent of Peter Monahan, an Irish Scot, they were mistaken for Auxiliaries. Bradfield unbosomed himself to them and gave all the information he could of rebels and rebel houses in the district. He asked them why they did not get Frank Hurley (my brother). He was told they had him already and one of the "Auxiliaries" stepped outside and arranged for Frank to be brought along. He was duly escorted in without trench coat, arms or equipment and, to all appearances, a prisoner. The delighted Bradfield immediately identified him as an important rebel, deserving of all he obviously hoped was coming to him. It was not long, however, till he was undeceived as to whom his guests were and was told of what his fate was to be. When later on I was in the field where the Column had re-assembled, the informer must have been there too, and when I accompanied the marching Column part of the way Bradfield must have been in its midst walking to his death.'[154]

## 24 January 1921
### Volunteer Daniel O'Reilly

Daniel Canty stated: 'On the following night – January 23rd I think – the column took up positions in different parts of the town of Bandon about 9.30 p.m. They remained in these positions until about 2 a.m., when they opened fire on the enemy military posts. This fire was returned and intermittent shooting by the enemy continued for about half an hour. One of our men – Dan O'Reilly, Kilbrittain Company – was killed. Enemy casualties were unknown. The column now retired to billets in the surrounding area.' Denis O'Brien seemed to believe that O'Reilly had not heard the three whistle blasts which signalled the withdrawal and refused to retreat. He was found shot dead later.[155]

## 25 January 1921
### Francis Barnane

Constable Murphy was driving a Crossley tender from Bandon to Union Quay in Cork and turned on to St Patrick's Street from Lavitt's Quay. Barnane (73), who lived on Cathedral Walk, was crossing the road and according to the inquest, despite his attempts to avoid being run over, he was hit by the mudguard. According to Constable Murphy he was not able to stop in time as the road was muddy and slippery from the rain. Given the sharpness of the turn it is unlikely that he was travelling faster than the 10 miles per hour he claimed. Barnane had severe injuries and passed away at 3 a.m. in the North Infirmary.[156]

## 28 January 1921
### Constable John Moyles (Miles)
## 29 January 1921
### RIC District Commissioner Philip Armstrong Holmes

Constable Andrews reported: 'On 28th Jan. I drove Major Holmes in a touring car from Listowel to Tralee. Sgt Charman was in the car and we were escorted by about 28 men in a touring car and two Crossley tenders. There was a second touring car as Major Holmes' permanent escort. We left Tralee in the touring car with the permanent escort i.e. a driver and three constables, about 11.30 a.m. About 11.55 we were going up a winding piece of road on a hillside when I had to pull up because of a trench dug across the road. There was a burst of rifle and machine-gun fire all around us. No one was hit at the first burst. We all left the cars, and spread out. I was hit leaving the car. Major Holmes was close to me. He fired one shot and then was hit in the head. He said to me "One, two, three, four Andrews" and rolled on his back: from which I concluded that he was hit four times. There was no cover but the cars.' The entire escort party was injured. Sergeant A. Charman had a fractured arm; Constable J. H. Andrews was wounded in the face, right arm and leg. Constables J. Hoare and F. D. Calder were slightly wounded. They were given first aid by the flying column that had attacked them, led by Seán Moylan, and were transported to Tralee before returning to Cork on the train the following day. Major Holmes barely made it into Cork Military Hospital before he died at 10.15 a.m. Constable Moyles (21) died at the scene.[157]

## 1 February 1921
## Constable Patrick O'Connor

A party of four police were returning to their barracks in Drimoleague around 8.45 p.m. It was dark. Constable Patrick Carroll gave evidence that when they got within 50 yards of the barracks he heard a voice say 'fire, let them have it boys' and fire was opened from the left. Constable O'Connor (22) was shot over the heart and died instantly. Constable Griffin was injured and the others escaped.[158]

## 1 February 1921
## Volunteer Cornelius Murphy

Once martial law was declared, the stakes on both sides increased dramatically.

If an IRA member was caught in possession of a rifle, or worse, captured during an ambush, then he would be executed. On 4 January Cornelius Murphy (23) of Ballydaly, Millstreet was arrested after a short chase and found to be in possession of a revolver and ammunition. At his trial on 17–18 January he was convicted of the charge and informed that the sentence of the court would be promulgated. However, the county was shocked when, on 1 February, the young man was shot at 8.10 a.m without prior notice in Victoria Barracks. Murphy had been interned in Frongoch after the 1916 rebellion and at the time of his execution was a Sinn Féin member of Millstreet Rural District Council.[159]

**1 February 1921**
**Mrs Alice King**
**Denis Bennett**
**Patrick Devitt**
**Daniel Mullane**
**Joseph Greensmyth**
For details of these deaths, see Part 1: The Incident at Mallow Station.

**1 February 1921**
**Thomas Bradfield**
On 1 February, a week after they executed Thomas J. Bradfield, the IRA called to the house of his cousin, also called Thomas Bradfield. There was suspicion that he was providing information to the Essex Regiment. Having accidently tricked Thomas J. Bradfield, they tried the same strategy on his cousin, dressing like Auxiliaries. James 'Spud' Murphy recalled what happened next: 'The remainder of the column, under Tom Barry, moved into Clonakilty battalion area. We were in the Ahiohill district on the night of 31st January 1921, when the column O/C asked Dan Corcoran and myself to accompany him to the house of Thomas Bradfield, Desertserges. We were driven there in a horse and trap by Tim Coffey, Breaghanna,

Enniskeane. Tom Barry approached the house and asked the maid whether Mr. Bradfield was at home. She said that he was out in the fields. Dan Corcoran accompanied the maid to the field to call Bradfield and to inform him that the officer wanted him. We were all wearing Sam Browne belts outside our trench coats and Bradfield assumed that we were members of the British forces. When Bradfield came in he welcomed us and invited us into the sitting-room where he gave us some refreshments. He sat down and began to talk to Tom Barry about the activities of the I.R.A in the area, giving a number of names of prominent officers. At this stage I had taken up position at the front door and Dan Corcoran was likewise at the back door. When Bradfield had given sufficient information, Tom Barry disclosed his identity and Bradfield was certainly shocked. We immediately placed him under arrest and removed him on foot to the Ahiohill area. He was tried that night and when we were moving from Ahiohill to Burgatia House on the night of 1st Feb. 1921, Bradfield was executed. His body was labelled as that of a spy and was left on the roadside.'[160]

This account is corroborated by Denis Lordan who also notes the execution took place on Tuesday 1 February, presumably while the column was marching to take over Burgatia House in Rosscarbery.[161] The unionist *Cork Constitution* blamed General Strickland's new order that loyalists had to hand up information on pain of arrest and punishment. It asked, 'In short, is it an offence to remain neutral?' Given its stridently loyal position since its foundation ninety years before, this statement is most remarkable.[162]

**3 February 1921**
**Constable Edward Lionel Carter**
**Constable William Henry Taylor**
Constables Carter (19) and Taylor (23) were shot at Ballinhassig. According to the *Lancashire Evening Post* Constable Carter is buried in Blackpool, where his father was a police inspector. He had joined the police two months previously. Taylor was married and his wife was living in Leeds. Edward Sisk

recalled: 'On the 1st February, 1921, Richard O'Mahony, in charge of about sixteen members of Ballinhassig Company, took up ambush positions to attack an R.I.C. patrol of six or seven men near the village. After waiting for two days for the patrol to appear O'Mahony had to leave the attacking party. On the third day while the party were in charge of their Company Captain, Michael Walsh, the patrol came along and walked into the ambush position. Walsh and his party opened fire killing two R.I.C. and wounding one. The remainder of the patrol made good their escape along the River Onabhuide. The attacking party were armed with rifles and shotguns. Military from Ballincollig and Kinsale and R.I.C. and Tans from Ballinhassig and Cork City subsequently raided the countryside, threatening everyone and shooting indiscriminately.'[163]

## 4 February 1921
### Volunteer Patrick Crowley

Mary Walsh (née O'Neill) describes the death of Patrick Crowley in graphic detail: 'Volunteer P. Crowley remained at this time in our district. He was awaiting an appendix operation. A dump was prepared by us for him. (He had his meals in our house after being told there was no raiding). Unfortunately, the place was surrounded this morning by military in single formation which closed in on the suspected houses. When word came, Paddy and my brother [Daniel] ran by a fence to cover, only to run in to Percival himself. They retraced their steps, Percival following and firing. My sister and I ran after the two boys hoping to save them from the firing as we felt sure he would not fire on us. My brother then gave up hoping that Paddy could get out as he had to be held prisoner, but another soldier was called on to cover him. Then my sister caught Percival by the legs (he was on a gate) and held him fast, even though he beat her knuckles with a gun. When he could not release himself he pointed the gun at our brother, and said he would shoot him dead if she did not let him go. We had hoped by this time that Paddy had got well away. He was followed by Percival and was found stretched dead about a quarter of a mile from our home by a Cumann na mBan girl that was crossing to let us know of the raid.'[164] This was all part of an Essex Regiment raid on Kilbrittain in reprisal for an attack on the barracks in the village two weeks previously. At the time of Paddy Crowley's shooting, the Crowley house in Kilbrittain was burned down and their shop dismantled by a forced work gang; Simon McCarthy's pub was also burned. According to *The Skibbereen Eagle* a sense of dread hung over the village. Paddy Crowley was the brother of Con and Michael J. Crowley, who were both prominent in the West Cork Brigade and the flying column before and after his death.[165]

## 5 February 1921
### Alfred Kidney

The *Derry Journal* of 9 February 1921 reports that Alfred Kidney of Youghal had died in the Workhouse Hospital on 5 February 1921 after being shot by civilians on Thursday 3 February. In fact, he was shot in the back by a member of the IRA when walking down the street in Youghal. He died shortly after 8 p.m. Two soldiers and an RIC officer were in Fitzgerald's shop, opposite the shooting on North Main Street, and rushed out 'to see a very tall man running away'. According to the report he had nearly been kidnapped the previous 20 October on suspicion of giving information to the police.[166]

## 6 February 1921
### Daniel Maloney

Daniel Maloney was shot dead by troops of the Essex Regiment during the raids in Timoleague and Kilbrittain in which Patrick Crowley was also shot. He was seventy and, beyond the death records and a single line in the *Irish Independent*, his death was forgotten by history.[167]

## 6 February 1921
### Michael John Kelleher

The soldiers' evidence to the subsequent military inquiry was that they were searching for a party of armed men who had been reported to them by a local loyalist. Their sworn evidence was that one of the party of twelve to eighteen men turned and fired on them at around 4 p.m. The lieutenant in charge was asked by the Lewis machine gunner if he should open fire and he replied: 'If you have a target fine.' As the troops advanced, their 'targets' turned out to be three local boys aged fourteen, twelve and eleven, who had been playing hurling in the field where the firing was directed. No armed men or guns were found. Michael John was shot and killed. The troops' version of events was completely rejected by the locals and a letter outlining their version of what happened, written by the local schoolteacher, was published in the *Irish Independent* on 12 February 1920. It stated that just five or six local men had been watching the hurling match and they ran away as soon as they heard gunfire from the military. Realising the propaganda damage such a letter could do (especially after a version was also published in the widely circulated English *News of the World*), the senior British Commander Colonel Cummings demanded the teacher's prosecution, but wiser heads suggested that this would only draw further attention.[168]

## 7 February 1921
### Patrick O'Sullivan

Patrick O'Sullivan's fate was sealed when two men fell out of a pub on Patrick's Quay and began fighting in the street. One stated, 'I don't care much for the Black and Tans.' Two other men approached from the direction of Brian Boru Street and one pulled a revolver and fired six shots. Patrick (17), his brother Cornelius and Thomas Long, innocent passers-by, all ran around the corner into Scott Lane by the side of the Metropole Hotel. As they ran down the lane Patrick was shot in the head and, although he was taken to the North Infirmary, he died without regaining consciousness just after midnight. He was unemployed and unmarried. Peter Shea, from Blackpool, was seriously wounded in the same incident but survived.[169]

**8 February 1921**

**Volunteer Patrick O'Driscoll**

Denis Lordan explained what happened to Patrick O'Driscoll: 'On Sunday night the Column marched from Revouler to Mohana district, close to Skibbereen, where they rested in billets for a few hours. It was intended to take up position on Monday from which to ambush British troops from Skibbereen. Unfortunately, an accident occurred in which a member of the local Company named Patrick O'Driscoll was accidentally shot by a comrade.' BMH WS 1481 confirms the date was 8 February.[170]

**8 February 1921**

**William Johnston**

The *Cork Constitution* of 9 February reports: 'At 2pm yesterday a young man named William Johnston was shot in Kilbrittain. He was the son of an ex-RIC man and a protestant. He resided in the town with his mother, brother and sister.' According to the family, William had been warned not to go out on the night he was shot but stepped out to say goodbye to friends before joining the RIC. He was then shot by a neighbour who had only recently joined the IRA. However, according to the compensation claim of his mother in April 1921, he was shot at 2 p.m. while hunting rabbits. Helped by Constable William Fenton, William's mother and the remaining five children cycled away from Kilbrittain during the night of 4 November 1921, having received threats from the local IRA. They arrived in Dublin two days later, before fleeing to Northern Ireland in April 1922, where Fenton joined the RUC. He married Amelia Arabella Johnston. One sister, who had married in 1920, remained in Cork.[171]

**9 February 1921**

**Alfred Charles Reilly**

At around 5.30 p.m. Alfred Reilly's pony and trap arrived without him at the front door of his home in Douglas. A search quickly found his body and he was pronounced dead by the local doctor, Lynch. He had been shot four times and a note left on the body which read: 'Spys Beware: Penalty for all: IRA'. There is absolutely no doubt about what happened as William Barry told the BMH that he had killed Reilly: 'four of us, armed with revolvers, got into the trap and drove him to his home at Rochestown. We shot him outside the gate of his house and affixed a card to the body with the words "Spies and Informers Beware" written on it'. A Methodist, Reilly was appointed a trustee of the church in 1915 when it was incorporated by parliament. Though most of Cork's 'merchant princes' were Church of Ireland, he was a member of this tiny, close-knit, mostly Protestant South Mall business community, who worked and socialised together. According to *The Cork Examiner*, when his case came before the courts his family were awarded £9,000, split equally between his second wife, Agnes, and his daughter. His first wife, Louisa, had died of pneumonia in 1910. He was killed despite being a Home Ruler, refusing jury duty in 1920 (for which he was fined) and organising a petition to save the life of Terence MacSwiney. As he appears in the Compensation Commission Register as a British liability, this suggests that they regarded him as being on their 'side'.[172]

**11 February 1921**
**Sergeant Frederick Boxold**
**13 February 1921**
**Private John Holyome**
In early 1921 the North Cork IRA decided to capture arms from a troop train. Two ambushes were arranged: one at Millstreet for eastbound trains and the other three kilometres to the east at Drishane for trains heading west. Fifteen members of various regiments were spotted aboard a west-bound train and two members of the IRA (Jack O'Keeffe and Dan Coakley) took control of the engine and forced the driver to stop it at the ambush position. It was night-time. The British troops had made the fatal mistake of congregating in one carriage but still responded to a surrender call by open-

ing fire. A ten-minute firefight resulted in severe casualties on the British side and they surrendered. Sergeant Boxold was already dead and Private Holyome died a short time later. Fourteen rifles were captured, 500 rounds of .303 rifle ammunition and fourteen sets of military equipment. There were no IRA casualties. Sergeant Boxold (24) from Arundel was a member of the Royal Fusiliers. He is buried in Killarney. John Holyome (23) from Tower Hamlets in London was also in the Royal Fusiliers.[173]

## 11 February 1921
## Daniel O'Mahony

One of the few mentions of Daniel O'Mahony's death was by Ballingeary men John P. and James D. Cronin in 1933: 'Before dawn next morning, Feb. 11th (St Abbeys Day) we took up ambush positions on the Gortnabinna side of the Mouth of the Glen three miles north of Ballingeary on the road to Renaniree. We waited until nightfall and returned to camp. On that day the Tans raided Clondrohid and shot 16 year old Daniel O'Mahony.' Daniel was, in fact, fifteen. The court of inquiry convened at Macroom gave the details only from the British side and said that as the Auxiliaries approached the village they were forced to stop by a destroyed bridge. Some civilians were standing around and when they saw the Auxiliaries they began to run. They were fired on and Daniel was shot through the back of the head and died instantly. The shooting took place just before sunset. The court of inquiry (comprising Captain Martin and Lieutenants Yolland and Vining of the Manchester Regiment) found that the blame for being shot in the back of the head rested entirely on the civilian's failure to halt.[174]

## 12 February 1921
## Constable Patrick Walsh

The *Connacht Tribune* reported the death of a native son: 'Constable Patrick J. Walsh was shot dead in the village of Churchtown, near Charleville, on Sunday night. Deceased, who was only 24, was a native of County Galway.

The official report states that Constable Walsh was shot dead within 100 yards of the police barracks at 9.45 p.m. Churchtown is about five miles from Charleville. Constable Walsh had been only recently transferred to Churchtown, and on Saturday he had been to Buttevant on leave. He was returning to the barracks after leaving a public-house in Churchtown on Saturday night when he was attacked as he passed a gateway near Mrs. O'Keeffe's. Eight shots were fired, one of which penetrated the brain, blowing away part of the head. Death was instantaneous. The body was found shortly afterwards in a pool of blood and medical and spiritual aid were at once summoned by Mrs. O'Keeffe but the unfortunate man was beyond aid. After the tragedy a number of shots were fired and some pellets entered the house of Const. Rigney but no damage was caused. Deceased was a native of Rossmuck [*sic*], Connemara. He was the son of an ex-head-constable, and had over four years' service in the R.I.C. He was a man of splendid physique, being over six feet tall.'[175]

## 12 February 1921
### Robert Eady

The shooting of Robert Eady (sometimes spelled Eedy in the newspapers) has been examined by many commentators and, despite attempts by the local RIC to suggest that his reason for entering the barracks late at night was entirely innocent, the reason for his shooting is agreed by all. Ted Hayes of the West Cork Brigade recalled: 'During the months of December, 1920, and January, 1921, I was engaged with the members of the intelligence staff in covering the activities of a suspected spy in the area. Eventually we succeeded in confirming that he was supplying information to the R.I.C. He actually visited the R.I.C. barracks dressed up as a woman in a hooded cloak. He was arrested in February, 1921, tried by court-martial, found guilty and executed as a spy. This man's name was Robert Eady. He resided at Clogheen, Clonakilty.' The evidence given by RIC Inspector Keany at his widow's claim for compensation agreed that he had entered the barracks in a hooded cloak to 'obtain a permit to travel to England'. However, no such permit was required. Reporting his death, the *Cork Constitution* stated 'he had dashed out to meet some men who called for him, and they abducted him and took him half a mile from the house where they shot him three times in the back of the head'. The *Cork Constitution* suggests that the shots were heard at his home, but that the body was not located until the following morning.[176]

## 14 February 1921
## William O'Sullivan

The *Irish Independent* reported: 'About 8.15 last night the Cork Fire Brigade were called on the telephone and directed to send the ambulance to Tory Top Lane, a by-way situated at the outskirts of the city. The caller did not disclose his identity. On reaching the spot the driver of the ambulance noticed the figure of a man lying on the ground at the intersection of Tory Top Lane and Curragh Rd. It was found to be the dead body of a young man with a bullet wound in the head. Pinned to the clothes of the deceased was a paper with the following inscription: "A convicted spy. Penalty: Death. Let all spies and traitors beware." The body was taken to the South Infirmary, where it lies at present. It is stated that the deceased's name was William Sullivan, but of this there is no confirmation.' In this case we know exactly what happened from Jerome Coughlan: 'In the month of February, 1921, I, with five others of our company, were warned by the Battalion O/C to keep a sharp look-out for a man named William O'Sullivan who was known to be acting as a spy for the enemy. This man, O'Sullivan, had been seen leaving the R.I.C. barracks at Empress Place, Cork, on several occasions after curfew. He had been told that, if he continued his association with the enemy, the consequences for him would be serious. He ignored these warnings and, as a result, we were instructed by the Battalion O/C to pick him up and execute him. It was difficult to locate O'Sullivan, as he seldom came home except during curfew.

'On 15th [*sic*] February, 1921, we received information that the man for whom we were searching was in a public house on Sullivan's Quay, Cork. A party of six of us, with William Barry, Company Captain, in charge, picked him up in the public house and took him by car to a spot on the Curragh Road, where he was shot.'[177]

**14 February 1921**

**Volunteer James Coffey**

**Volunteer Timothy Coffey**

On 15 February the *Cork Constitution* noted the murder of brothers Timothy and James Coffey in Breaghna, Desertsergus (Enniskeane). It noted that Thomas Bradfield had been shot in the same locality two weeks previously and suggested that the brothers were shot in response to his murder. *The Skibbereen Eagle* is not so coy. It gives many more details in its report of the family's compensation claim in April. According to their parents: 'The head was nearly shot off one of them, and the other was shot in the neck. On a card on one body was written "Revenge". On the other body was *Convicted Vide Bradfield – Anti Sinn Féin – of murder.*'[178] It is possible that Tim Coffey had been recognised driving Tom Barry and the others to the Bradfield House, as they were neighbours. At the court of inquiry into Bradfield's killing, his brother had specifically mentioned the Coffeys, and this may have led to their murder.[179]

**15 February 1921**

**John O'Leary**

John O'Leary had joined the Leinster Regiment in 1916. He had been captured by the Germans in early 1918 and held prisoner until November. With the end of the First World War, he returned to Ireland and left the army, but took a job in the records section of Victoria Barracks. He was shot outside his home at 9 p.m. on 14 February 1921 by men who stopped him and asked if he had any documents. He replied that he had not, but when they found his pass for Victoria Barracks they shot him. He was wounded in the abdomen and hand. Taken to the North Infirmary, his wife, Annie, asked him several times if he knew any reason why anyone would shoot him, but he could think of none. It appears that he suddenly took a turn for the worse on the morning of 15 February and died. There is no doubt about who ordered the killing as Michael Murphy, the IRA ASU commander stated: 'On 14th February 1921, a civilian employee in the office of the British Military Intelligence Officer (Captain Kelly) in Cork military barracks, named O'Leary, was shot in Nicholas St. Cork. He was known to be bringing information to the enemy.'[180]

**15 February 1921**
**Volunteer Patrick Flynn**
**Volunteer Patrick Dorgan**
**Volunteer Eamon Creedon**
**Volunteer Michael Looney**
The Mallow IRA flying column decided to ambush senior British officers who would be returning from a major strategy conference with the other commanders in the region. The officers would be travelling to and from Cork city by road and the location chosen for the ambush was near Mourneabbey. By early morning on 15 February the IRA unit, augmented by local companies, lined both sides of the road waiting for any British convoy. Just after sunrise they heard firing to the north-east of their position and it soon became clear that the ambushers had become the ambushed. Supported by machine gunners and armoured cars, the British were closing in on three sides. Unsurprisingly, the column retreated. Those on the western side of the road were lucky, as the British troops failed to cut them off, but on the eastern side of the road three members of the ambush party – Patrick Flynn (25), Patrick Dorgan (22) and Eamon Creedon (20) – were shot dead in the initial engagement, while Michael Looney died subsequently. Thomas Mulcahy and Patrick Roynane were captured and taken to Victoria Barracks for trial.[181]

**15 February 1921**

**Richard Arthur**

**James Byrne**

**William Donoghue**

**William Finn**

**Mary Hall**

**Sean Hegarty**

**Charles Penrose Johnston**

**Thomas Perrott**

**John Sisk**

**John Spiers**

**Volunteer Batt Falvey**

**Volunteer Patrick O'Sullivan**

**Volunteer John Phelan**

On 15 February a group of Cork No. 3 Brigade, led by Charlie Hurley, decided to ambush a train carrying British military when it arrived in Upton Station. The website irishmedals.org provides the simplest account of the deaths that ensued: 'Accounts of what happened differ; the Military stated that no civilians were allowed in carriages occupied by the Military while the IRA claimed that civilians and Military were dispersed throughout the train. Intense fire was opened on the entire length of the train the moment it stopped in Upton Station, Cork. The Military Court held in lieu of an inquest found that William Donoghue and Sean Hegarty died from wounds inflicted by the Military in the lawful execution of their duty and the other victims were wilfully murdered by John Buckley alias Patrick Coakley and other persons unknown. Three IRA men were killed in the ambush.' There were no British casualties and the ambush was an unmitigated disaster for the No. 3 Brigade, both in the men killed and injured, and in the propaganda war. Richard Arthur was the ticket checker at Upton Station and was from St Luke's in Cork. The *Irish Independent* mistakenly claimed 'James Barrett the station master died subsequently in the Cork Military Hospital' on 24 March.[182]

**16 February 1921**

**Volunteer Timothy Connolly**

**Volunteer Jeremiah O'Neill**

**Volunteer Cornelius McCarthy**

**Volunteer John McGrath**

More often than not the medical evidence of how people actually died conflicts with the claims made by one side or the other about incidents. This is a case in point. Four members of the Kilbrittain IRA Company were trenching a road to block passage for British convoys and raiding parties. Apparently, the two guards left their posts and decided to help, meaning that their enemy could creep up on them. Major Arthur Percival, who was leading a raid on Kilbrittain, gave evidence that when the four men were fired on they ran towards his party and he fired at them. The four men doubled back and when Percival saw three of them running across a field he fired again and they fell. The medical evidence, however, states that one of the victims was shot in the back of the head and a second was shot at the base of the skull, both shots being fired at close range. Major Percival's testimony conflicts categorically with the medical evidence and could be construed as covering up a war crime under the Geneva Convention.[183]

**16 February 1921**

**Charles Beale**

For details of Beale's death, see Part 1: Cascading Death.

**18 February 1921**

**Michael Walsh**

**Unnamed infant (date uncertain)**

On Friday 18 February 1921 Michael Walsh was taken from a ward in the Workhouse Hospital South Infirmary, Cork and shot dead. Walsh (43), an ex-soldier, was married and lived at Kearney's Lane, Cork. He worked as a labourer at the Ford Works. His sister told a court of inquiry that he had been suffering from dropsy (oedema) and she had taken him to the hospital on Monday 14 February. He had not worked in Ford's for more than six months as he had been arrested there previously by the IRA. He had been deported, but returned thinking he was safe. A month earlier fourteen shots had been fired into his sister's house and he had been pursued into the building. A child she had been nursing had been trampled during the incident and died. Michael had escaped over the back wall of her cottage. On the night he was killed he had been taken to the back gate of the Workhouse and shot at least four times.[184]

**19 February 1921**
**William Connell**
**Mathew Sweetman**[185]

Two Skibbereen Protestants, Sweetman and Connell, were murdered on 19 February for having 'given evidence against a man who had been levying subscriptions for the IRA'. *The Skibbereen Eagle* reported the killings on 26 February and stated that Sweetman was shot at 8.45 and Connell a short time later. The district commissioner of the RIC for Cork West Riding said they had given evidence to a 'court martial' in his monthly report. Connell's wife stated in her compensation claim in April that he had been arrested on the morning he was shot and forced to give evidence to the trial about IRA arms levy collectors. The presence of the IRA column around their homes had been noticed by locals and brought to the attention of magistrates, who decided there was no threat and failed to inform either of the two men or the local military barracks. Both men were unionists and visibly pro-government. Refusing to pay the IRA arms levy and then identifying the collectors to a military tribunal sealed their fate.[186]

**19 February 1921**
**George Tilson**

For details of Tilson's death, see Part 1: Cascading Death.

## 20 February 1921
## William Mohally

While witnesses were waiting at the South Infirmary for inquests into the deaths of Richard Arthur (killed in the crossfire at Upton) and Michael Walsh (shot at the back gates of the workhouse) yet another ambulance drew up carrying a seriously wounded man. This was William Mohally and his 'face was a mass of blood, and the hair on the left side was thrown over the forehead and the left eye was clotted with blood. His breathing was not perceptible and the only indication of life was a trickling of blood from a wound near the left eye.' He was examined and it was discovered that he had been shot. He was placed in a surgical ward on the ground floor but was not expected to survive the night. He did. However, at 9 a.m. the following morning three armed men forced an entrance and ordered the staff to carry him from the building on a stretcher. He was carried up a laneway 60 metres from the main gate and shot twice, dying instantly. The unfortunate stretcher-bearers were told by the house surgeon to return, collect the body and take it to the morgue in the hospital. Mohally had fought in the Boer War and had been a recruiting agent for the army during the Great War but that was not what identified him for death. Pinned to the body was a note: 'For a spy there is no escape: IRA'.[187]

## 20 February 1921 (date uncertain)
## Michael Finbarr O'Sullivan

The initial reports of this death were sketchy. The *Irish Independent* reported on 28 February that an 'Un-named man well-dressed aged about 40, blindfolded and five bullets in body' had been found. It is highly likely that the body was that of O'Sullivan. William Barry, a senior member of the Cork IRA, had captured and, along with others, shot O'Sullivan in the vicinity of the Douglas river.[188] The body was dragged from the estuary a couple of weeks later. The man had been shot four times. The IRA believed O'Sullivan was a spy. This is confirmed by *The Skibbereen Eagle*, where it was reported that his mother, Mrs Kate O'Sullivan, sought compensation for Michael's murder. The report said his body was pulled from the Douglas River on 20 February 1921 at the brickyard, and, according to her claim, he was blindfolded with a handkerchief. His mother also stated that his father had died three days after the funeral such was the shock of his son's murder. She claimed Michael had decided to join the Royal Army Service Corps on 31 January and was kidnapped and shot. She was awarded £2,000; an enormous sum given that his Disability Pension from the Great War was £62 per year.[189]

**20 February 1921**
**Volunteer James Aherne (Ahern)**
**Volunteer Jeremiah Aherne**
**Volunteer Liam Aherne**
**Volunteer Donal Dennehy**
**Volunteer David Desmond**
**Volunteer Michael Desmond**
**Volunteer James Galvin**
**Volunteer Michael Hallahan**
**Volunteer Richard Hegarty**
**Volunteer John Joe Joyce**
**Volunteer Joseph Morrisey**
**Volunteer Christopher Sullivan**
For details of their deaths, see Part 1: The Clonmult Shootout.

**22 February 1921**
**George Fletcher**
George Fletcher (17) lived at 21 Kyle Street. He was working as a messenger boy in Union Quay RIC Barracks when Constable Joseph Prendergast accidently discharged his rifle, hitting Fletcher. The boy was shot through the groin and died shortly afterwards. Constable Prendergast had been

checking his rifle before going on duty and had pulled the trigger not realising that there was a bullet in the chamber. Prendergast was charged with manslaughter but acquitted at the end of March. The court stressed the need for the new police to be fully trained in the use of firearms.[190]

## 23 February 1921
## Private James Knight
## Lance Corporal Herbert Stubbs
## Constable Frederick Perrier

The two soldiers were walking with two girls at the Laurel Walk in Bandon town when they were captured by a group of the IRA who had come into the town specifically to shoot any Essex Regiment soldiers they found, in reprisal for a series of shootings of unarmed and surrendered IRA members over the previous month. Two wireless operators from the Royal Navy had also been captured and released with a letter for Major Percival, informing him that any of the regiment found out of barracks (armed or otherwise) would be shot on sight.

Tom Barry also came close to being shot that night in Bandon, but by his own side. Daniel Canty recalled: 'One party, under Tom Barry (Column O/C) took up [ambush] positions at the junction of Cork road and Watergate St. Tom Barry crossed the bridge towards the post office, and in his absence Pete Kearney was in charge of the section. At this stage a party of Black and Tans was observed coming down North Main St. and Pete Kearney's section opened fire, killing at least two of the enemy and wounding some others. On hearing the shooting, Tom Barry returned towards his section to find that he was between two fires. Some of the section recognised him and ceased fire. He (Tom Barry) then followed one Black and Tan [Perrier] in[to] John Marshall's house in North Main St. and shot him there.' Surprisingly, when Barry ran into the shop after Perrier (who was armed), the man did not do the obvious thing and shoot him. Canty, who was not part of the ambush, is clearly mistaken in claiming that Black and Tans were killed by Kearney's section.[191]

**25 February 1921**
**Major James Seafield Grant MC**
**Auxiliary William Arthur Cane**
**1 March 1921**
**Auxiliary Clive Soady**

Many of the leading members of the Cork City IRA retreated west into the mountains surrounding Ballyvourney for respite from the intense urban warfare of February 1921. Many were also unemployed after the burning of the city. Not wanting to be idle, Seán Hegarty and Dan 'Sandow' Donovan arranged an ambush at Coolavokig just to the east of Ballyvourney. They intended to draw the Auxiliaries and military into a trap where they could use their newly acquired Hotchkiss machine gun. Despite waiting for a week no British appeared, until at last Major Grant, the district commissioner of the police, decided to investigate reports of their presence. Grant was in the lead car of a convoy of eight, which, extraordinarily, even though they knew where the ambush was, still drove straight into the middle of it. Grant began to organise his forces to fight back, seemingly impervious to the bullets flying. Inevitably, he was shot dead and the British retreated to a cottage from where they continued to fight. Auxiliary Soady of 'J' Company was firing out the window when he was hit in the jaw. He died a few days later from septicaemia. Auxiliary Arthur Cane was shot 'most likely by a machine gun' inside the house during the four-hour firefight, which only ceased when British reinforcements arrived and the IRA retreated.[192]

**27 February 1921**
**Alfred Cotter**

The *Irish Independent* carried the briefest of reports, 'Aged 35, shot at 9.15 p.m. at his mother's home in Ballineen. No reason given, Master Baker.' A week before he was shot he was observed by the local postman and IRA intelligence officer Patrick Carroll pointing out houses to be searched by the Black and Tans in Ballineen. He and his brother Pierce were supplying the

Essex Regiment with bread, and both were suspected informants. Senior IRA member Jack Hennessy stated that the Cotter case was under constant review by the brigade from early 1920 up to the time of his shooting, which was ordered by the brigade in February.[193]

**28 February 1921**
**Volunteer Seán Allen (Tipperary)**
**Volunteer Daniel O'Callaghan**
**Volunteer Thomas O'Brien**
**Volunteer John Lyons**
**Volunteer Timothy McCarthy**
**Volunteer Patrick O'Mahony**
**Private Alfred Edward Whitear**
**Private George Stokes Bowden**
**Private Thomas Wise (Wyse)**
**Private William Alfred Gill**
**Lance Corporal John Edward Lawrence George Beattie**
**Lance Corporal Leonard Douglas Hodnett**
For details of their deaths, see Part 1: 28 February 1921.

**28 February 1921**
**Volunteer Michael John O'Mahony**
Michael John O'Mahony (18) died in his father's home on Railway Street, Passage West, of septicaemia. He told anyone who asked him that he had been shot in the thigh by a rivet while at work in the local dockyard. The investigation showed that he was not at work on the night he was shot and that the metal object removed from his leg in the South Infirmary was flattened. He had discharged himself from hospital fearing arrest by the military, who had interviewed him twice. Little was reported in the newspapers. At Passage West a roadside memorial erected by Daniel Spillane records O'Mahony's death and says he died of wounds received in action

against the crown forces. The event which led to his shooting has not been identified but it must have occurred before 21 February, when he was taken to hospital.[194]

### 28 February 1921
### Charles (Charlie) Daly

On 28 February 1921 three armed and masked men entered the Great Southern and Western Railway station at Cork and took away Charles Daly. His dead body was found some hours later in the railway tunnel next to the entrance of the station; he had been shot dead. It is often believed that this was a random reprisal for the mayhem earlier in the evening, but the evidence of Patrick Crowe suggests otherwise: 'During the early period, when Officers of the British Army came on furlough they generally possessed a brown double-strapped holdall. I found that they generally contained macs, puttees, short knee trousers, revolvers in holsters, Sam Brown[e]s and, at times, the latest in field glasses. Only the revolvers in holsters appealed to me and, after abstracting them, I had the holdall placed in the cloak-room and not kept in the parcel office, so as to throw off all suspicion. This generally happened on night duty. Quite a number were got in this way until one night I was replaced in my old job. A plank was laid for my successor to see if in this case the revolver would disappear and it did.

'Empress Place [Auxiliary Headquarters] then struck. We had got an excerpt from Domie Sullivan of a despatch to Dublin Castle, which stated the offices at Glanmire Station were honeycombed with I.R.A. or accomplices. A few of the murder gang came down about 1.30 a.m., [and]took out Charlie Daly who replaced me in the parcel office on a Monday night. He was taken to the tunnel, shot in the heart and his chest placed on the rail so that his body would be mangled by the down night mail and thus destroy evidence of his murder. But Charlie was found. (He lived in the Lough, I think). He was sympathetic to the cause, not actually in it. Still he was buried with full honours. Thereafter the large gates outside the station were closed at night and a sentry put on the roof to watch any incursions by the mob in Empress Place. This happened the first night Daly went on (Monday) about 3rd March, 1921 [*sic*], and so I was back on the job on Tuesday night, a worried and a scared man. It was tough to be working solo and at night in an office, not knowing when the call would come to the door.'[195]

## 1 March 1921

### Lieutenant Victor B. Murray

'Officer Wounded at Spike Island. Lieut. V. B. Murray, Cameron Highlanders, was found suffering from severe shot wounds at Spike Island yesterday. The cause of his injuries has not been officially disclosed.'[196] His death certificate records his death nineteen hours after the shooting, which, it states, was from a self-inflicted wound.

## 1 March 1921

### Constable Alfred V. G. Brock

Alfred Brock (31) was fatally wounded when his patrol was fired on near their barracks by the IRA at Rosscarbery. The *Irish Independent* reported on 2 March that a patrol on mess duty was fired at by men concealed on the public road. Constable Brock was shot in the stomach and died of his wounds. James 'Spud' Murphy stated: 'On March 1st, 1921, accompanied by Jim Hurley, Battalion O/C., and Tim Donoghue, Vice O/C., I went into Rosscarbery to attack a patrol of R.I.C. We were standing at the junction of Tan Yard Lane and the Square in Rosscarbery about 9 p.m. when we saw about four Tans in uniform. We opened fire on the party and killed one – Constable Brock. Suddenly, shooting broke out behind us and we found that we were under fire from two Tans who had passed just as we took up our positions and whom we thought were civilians. I was wounded in the right hand in the crossfire.'[197]

## 1 March 1921
### Volunteer James Foley

Michael O'Regan explained: 'For about a fortnight, we had an intensive course in the use and handling of the rifle. When the course was over we proceeded towards Ballincollig in extended formation with Leo Murphy in charge. On the way we halted at a farmhouse for tea. We were more dry than hungry. As I took out a bucket of tea to the column who were waiting around outside, one of the column, who was examining his rifle, accidentally discharged a shot which shot the vice O/C. James Foley through the stomach. He died next morning and was later buried with military honours. I was then appointed battalion vice O/C. in his place. ... Leo Murphy had intended to attack an RIC patrol in the neighbourhood of Ballincollig, but had to abandon the idea for the time being, as the death of James Foley had upset his plans.'[198]

## 1 March 1921
### Seán O'Brien

In the public domain virtually nothing is remembered about the death of Seán O'Brien, something which made him one of the catalysts for me to write this book. On 5 March *The Freeman's Journal* reported O'Brien's death in one sentence. However, Richard Smith gives a graphic account of the events of the night: 'On that night the Tans came into the town mad looking for blood. They went to the home of Seán O'Brien, who was a well-known Gaelic Leaguer and Irish Irelander – he had never served with the Volunteers. The Tans knocked at his door and Seán, without opening the door, enquired what they wanted, and the Tans' reply was to fire several volleys through the door and also threw [*sic*] some grenades through the fan-light. Poor Seán died almost immediately. Seán was Chairman of the U.D.C., and also President of the Gaelic League Branch.'

Extraordinarily, the individuals responsible were identified. On 16 April 1921 'the two Tans who had murdered Seán O'Brien had travelled to Buttevant. Mick Geary contacted immediately some reliable members of the Company and decided to capture or shoot those Tans on their return by the evening train at 6.20 p.m. ...

'Were it not that the military arrived at the station at the critical moment, the two Tans – Spain and Spellman – would have received their just deserts.'[199]

## 1 March 1921
### Daniel Casey

Around 4 p.m. Intelligence Officer Lieutenant Hammond was searching people outside the GPO in Cork city when he saw five men run up Caroline Street. He pursued them and got onto the roof of one of the shops overlooking 13 Caroline Street. From his vantage point he saw the five men hiding in the back yard of No. 13 and he opened fire. They fired back and ran into the house. Seeing a man on the stairs, he fired at him through the window. Later he discovered that this was, in fact, a resident of the house, who had come out onto the stairs when he heard the firing. Daniel Casey (30) was boarding in the house and his death was recorded as misadventure.[200]

## 1 March 1921
### Thomas Cotter

Around 9.30 p.m. on Sunday 1 March Thomas Cotter was taken from his home at Curraghclough, Kilmurray, Co. Cork and shot dead. A note was pinned to his body stating 'Convicted Spy, IRA'. He had been shot about 3 yards from the front door. Cotter was Church of Ireland and had been involved in a long running 'land-grabbing' dispute involving his next-door neighbour. The dispute had been mentioned in the House of Commons throughout the period 1891 to 1914 and both men were boycotted on several occasions. Whether this had anything to do with his killing is unproven, but his name has been tenuously linked to the killing of the Coffey brothers in Ballineen earlier in the year.[201]

**2 March 1921**

**Denis O'Brien**

O'Brien was shot on Castle Street, Cork when he failed to respond to the challenge of a British Army patrol to halt. He was buried as a pauper. O'Brien was positively identified at the subsequent court of inquiry and his death on 2 March was discussed in the House of Commons on 2 June. According to Sir Hamar Greenwood, Chief Secretary for Ireland: 'This occurred in the martial law area, and I am informed by the Commander-in-Chief that the court of inquiry in this case found that the deceased man, Denis O'Brien, was out in a street in Cork City during curfew hours, that he was challenged several times by the curfew patrol, and failing to answer or to stop, was shot. It is most unfortunate that this man should have been exposed to the risk incurred in disregarding the curfew restrictions, but no blame for the unhappy result can attach to the man who fired.' The soldiers were 130 yards away when they shot Denis O'Brien, who was seventy and undoubtedly couldn't hear them.[202]

**4 March 1921**

**Bridget Noble**

Bridget Neill had married Alexander Noble from Scotland and returned to live in the family cottage in Ardgroom by 1911. On 22 August 1921 she was recorded in the official list of the missing from the War of Independence as published by the British. On 28 January 1922 *The Skibbereen Eagle* reported her husband's compensation claim, which stated that she had gone to visit her father who was eighty and had disappeared. Her husband believed that the reason for her disappearance was that she had visited the police barracks on a number of occasions and this was confirmed by DI Oates. The judge had been handed a letter that her husband had received from the IRA, which stated she was dead. DI Oates stated that he had received similar information and he had 'certain authority' for saying she was murdered. Judge Hynes awarded her husband £1,500.[203]

**5 March 1921**

**Volunteer Jeremiah O'Mahony**

Philip Chambers stated: 'On the 5/3/1921 I was detailed, under Section Leader Denis Hickey, to commandeer men and tools for road cutting operations in our Company area. The Company O.C. (Jeremiah O'Mahony) was to meet us with some arms. We waited at the appointed place until well after midnight but he failed to turn up. Eventually his brother, Dan, arrived with the sad news that Jeremiah had been accidentally shot dead by a comrade Volunteer. We dismissed the commandeered party and proceeded at once to the scene of the accident. I got the late Canon O'Connell of Enniskeane to administer the last rites and, on the suggestion of Canon O'Connell, we buried him temporarily in a rifle dump on his own farm. The following night we produced a rough coffin and removed his remains to the graveyard at Castlwtown-Kenneigh [sic] where we buried him in the Republican Plot alongside the three Volunteers who had been shot in the Kilmichael ambush some months before.'[204]

**5 March 1921**

**Brigadier General Hanway Cumming**

**Lieutenant Harold Maligny**

**Private Harold Turner**

**Private William Walker**

William Reardon of the Millstreet IRA gave an exceptionally detailed account of the Clonbanin ambush to the BMH. Large forces of the IRA lay in wait for Brigadier General Cumming, whom they knew was conducting a tour of inspection. Various groups drove through the ambush site, including two British Army lorries heading west. Reardon stated: 'They were allowed to go on their way and there was no further activity until about 2 p.m. when the approach of an enemy convoy from the west was signalled. This convoy consisted of two lorries, a touring car followed by an armoured car and a lorry. It drove into the ambush position and as the leading lorry reached our position the signal to open fire was given. This lorry managed to get through the position and got under cover of a farmhouse beyond the eastern end. The touring car was crippled by a burst of machine-gun fire and the armoured car, in an endeavour to avoid the touring car, got ditched. The crew were, however, in a position to continue to use their machine-guns effectively. The remainder of the enemy party left their transport at the opening blast and took cover behind the roadside fences. The fighting went on for about 2 hours, but as we were unable to silence the machine-guns in the armoured car the engagement had to be broken off. The members of the Millstreet Column withdrew with the Kerry 2 Brigade Column to Cullen area and the other columns withdrew towards their home areas. The I.R.A. had no casualties but the enemy lost General Cumming and a number of others as well as several wounded.'[205]

Cumming (53), Maligny (40) and Turner (25) were all married. Walker (18) was single. Both privates were members of the East Lancashire Regiment escort.

## 6 March 1921
## Volunteer Cornelius Foley

Charles (Charlie) Browne recorded what happened to Foley: 'On Saturday, March 5th, the Column was divided into four Sections of six to seven each and distributed to "C", "D", "J" and "G" Companies and a programme of training, where extra men from these Companies could be given a short course, was outlined. The Section which moved into "J" Company had a narrow escape from capture on the night of the 6th of March when the Auxiliaries in force made a surprise raid on Toames and, though the members of the Column escaped under fire, a Volunteer from "J" Company, named Cornelius Foley, was killed.' Major W. P. Gill of the Auxiliaries gave evidence that the shooting took place at 4 p.m. and that Foley (27) had died two hours later in Macroom Castle.[206]

**8 March 1921**

**Constable Nicholas Somers**

The evidence of what happened is clear: 'On the 8th March, 1921, the Battalion Column went into position at Fr. Murphy's bridge, Banteer (Shronebeha). After waiting some time a patrol of four R.I.C. consisting of a Sergt. George and Constables McCarthy, Moran and Summers [*sic*], made its appearance and was fired on. Constable Summers was killed and Constable McCarthy was wounded. Sergt. George and Constable Moran, who were unwounded, were allowed to go free, on giving a promise to resign. It is not known if they kept this promise. Four (4) revolvers were obtained from this ambush.'[207]

**10 March 1921**

**Volunteer Edward Waters**

**Volunteer Michael (Timothy) Kiely**

**Volunteer David Herlihy**

**Volunteer Edward Twomey**

Leo O'Callaghan recalled: 'As this was obviously a case in which there was a leakage of information, Liam Lynch (Brigade O/C.) held an investigation into the happenings [Mourneabbey ambush] some days later. At the time there was no proof as to how the information concerning this ambush reached the enemy but, following the incidents in the round-up at Nadd early in the following month, it became the general opinion amongst the column that the information was passed on by Shiels.

'Shiels was an ex-British soldier who joined the Kanturk Battalion some time in 1920. He worked as a farm labourer in the Kanturk locality. Something of a braggart, he was very fond of drink and, generally, was not popular with the unit. While he participated in the training activities of the battalion column he was always absent, on some pretext, when an engagement was due. ...

'In March of 1921, Shiels was with the Kanturk Battalion Column at the brigade headquarters at Nadd. He went into Kanturk to draw his British army pension. The I.O. of the Kanturk Battalion (Michael Moore) noted that Shiels was drinking in the Kanturk public-houses, and then became aware of the fact that Shiels had called at the Kanturk R.I.C. Bks. Moore sent a dispatch with all haste to Nadd. The dispatch never arrived. Next morning there was a huge dawn concentration of British military on Nadd and convoys of troops from Kanturk, Ballincollig, Fermoy, Buttevant and Tralee encircled the mountain. General Liam Lynch and his staff got through the one gap in the khaki ring, but Volunteers Kiely, Herlihy and Twomey of the Kanturk Battalion were surprised asleep in Herlihy's house with Joe Morgan, Lieut. Ned Waters and Volunteer John Moloney of the Mallow Battalion.

'As they were being lined up in their stockinged feet to be executed at the rere [*sic*] of the cottage, Morgan and Moloney made a daring break for liberty. Both were wounded, but succeeded in escaping into the mist. Both are still alive. The others were shot where they stood.

'Shiels was at Nadd that morning with the British. He was in Black and Tan uniform and was recognised and saluted by Tom Bride of Nadd, the proprietor of the pub there. He disappeared and was never traced.'

All this was substantially accurate.[208]


## 10 March 1921
## John Good

Good's son James described what happened to the court of inquiry. Around 8.30 p.m. John went to the back door for a smoke before he let the dogs out for the night. James heard him open the door and then heard three shots. He rushed to the kitchen, where he found his father, clearly in shock, still standing in the doorway. When he turned around it was obvious he had been shot. James went to the doctor in Timoleague, who refused to attend in fear of his life. James returned with Reverend Flannery, who stayed with John until he died. James stated that his father was sixty-six and a farmer. The word Protestant was inserted in the record of inquiry as an afterthought. There seems little doubt that this killing is directly linked to that of Good's brother-in-law, Thomas Bradfield, outside Ballineen six weeks previously. Indeed, on the day that he was shot Good had assisted his sister in attempting to sell her farm, the sale of which had been stopped by a warning notice that anyone who tried to help spies or their families would be shot. The killing is unique as no justification is given in any of the witness statements for the killing other than that he was a spy.[209]

## 11 March 1921 (date uncertain)
## Mrs Mary Lindsay
## James Clarke
For details of their deaths, see Part 1: 28 February 1921.

## 13 March 1921
## Timothy Hourihan
Hourihan was shot during a police round-up in Castletown-Kinneigh. He was apparently looking after some goats. The local IRA captain, Philip Chambers, confirmed that he was shot by the Auxiliaries: 'On Sunday, the 13/3/1921, I received a despatch – I think it was from Tom Barry – to the effect that the dumped rifles and equipment held in the Company area were to be moved to Galvins of Gurtaleen as the Column was mobilising again … I then left for home and was carrying the despatch on me and I also had an empty revolver which I had got that day from a comrade Volunteer. Some short distance away I met a man whom I knew well – Tim Hourihane [sic], a labourer. I had a brief conversation with him and then we parted. I crossed into my own farm and about 150 yards away I saw an Auxie on high ground, armed with a rifle, and apparently scanning the countryside. … A short time later the shadow of the armed Auxie showed right in front of me and I was convinced that I was nabbed but obviously he had missed seeing me. About the same time, Tim Hourihane, to whom I had been speaking a short time before, appeared about 20 yards away. I beckoned to him to move off and just

as I did the Auxie, who had seen him, came along and searched him. I remained under cover. After the search Hourihane was allowed to proceed and as he moved along the high ground I heard a shot and saw poor Hourihane fall to the ground. In a short space of time about twenty Auxies were gathered around him. They secured a door from a nearby farmhouse and brought the remains on a door to his own home which was only a few yards away.' DI Peglar gave evidence to the court of inquiry that he fired a warning shot at a man 200 yards away running towards him, before firing the fatal shot when Hourihan then ran away. British Commander Colonel Higginson was unimpressed by this evidence and made this very clear to the court.[210]

## 14 March 1921
### Richard Newman

Richard Newman (23), who was wounded by the military in Allihies, died at 2 a.m. on Monday 14 March.[211] He was shot around 2 p.m. the previous Sunday by Private J. Reid in the vicinity of the village. According to the court of inquiry he had been arrested and tried to escape. He was a local.[212]

## 14 March 1921
### Thomas Hennessy

Thomas Hennessy opened a door into the yard of Sisk's farmhouse and was confronted by an armed man who told him to put up his hands. When he failed to do so, he was shot dead. A plain-clothes British Army and police patrol had come across from Queenstown (Cobh) to Crosshaven to search the farm where Hennessy was working. The incident caused great worry to General Strickland at general headquarters in Cork, as he had decided that his main duty was 'to keep the name of the British Army unsullied'.[213]

## 15 March 1921
### Michael Joseph Murray

According to the evidence of Miss Margaret O'Sullivan, 8 Victoria Street,

Michael Murray attacked her while she was walking up Alexandria Road towards her home. She had screamed for help and a military officer (unidentified) stated that as he was going to help, he had met an NCO. The NCO stated that, thinking Murray had a gun, he fired at the man. No gun was found. Murray was shot in the chest and died of his wounds four doors from his own house at 'Cahillville' (probably Charleville), St Luke's Cross. His family flatly contradicted the evidence, stating that he was returning from work in the nearby railway station when he was shot. The court did not pursue this conflict of evidence, even though Miss O'Sullivan appears to have been in a relationship with the NCO.[214]

## 15 March 1921
### Volunteer Charles O'Reilly

Charles O'Reilly was shot near Newmarket: 'One evening in March 1921 Charlie "Cha" Reilly [*sic*] was travelling with two companions in a pony and trap on the Line Road, North Cork, when they were challenged by a party of Military. The three men abandoned the cart and fled across country on foot under a hail of bullets. Cha Reilly was mortally wounded but managed to crawl to a nearby cottage where he spent the night. The next day he was taken to his home in Newmarket where he died from his wounds a few days later.'[215]

## 18 March 1921
### Miss Nellie Carey

Alice Mellrick of Mills Road, Fermoy, heard a knocking at her door around 5.15 p.m. When she opened it a young girl, Nellie Carey (19), collapsed into her arms. She tried to support her, but the dead weight of the girl was too much for her. The police, who were across the road, picked Nellie up, only to discover that she had been shot in the abdomen. She had been with her fiancé, Private William Price of the Royal Field Artillery, in the Mart and they were standing next to a wall. Price told the court of inquiry what happened next. Nellie obviously heard a noise because she suddenly spun around and fire was opened on them from behind the wall. Both were hit and when the firing stopped Price found her lying on the ground next to him. He ran to get help and when he returned she had gone. She died the following day, around 5.30 p.m., in the Military Hospital. Nellie was from Redmond Street.[216]

## 19 March 1921
### Constable William Elton

On 18 March, about 50 yards north of the RIC barracks in Castletown-roche, a patrol of RIC, under Sergeant Gillen, was ambushed by the local IRA. Constable Elton was in front and was seriously wounded. While his colleagues returned fire he made his way back to the barracks. After 10 minutes the attackers were driven off and when the patrol returned to the barracks they found Constable Elton slumped in the door. His wounds and those of Constable Crowley were dressed by the local doctor around 11 p.m. At 6 a.m. Elton (25) collapsed. He was dead. He was unmarried and from Hounslow.[217]

## 19 March 1921
### Private Harold Baker
### Private Sidney Cawley
### Private Joseph Crafer
### Private Alfred Gray
### Lieutenant Geoffrey Hotblack
### Constable Arthur Kenward
### Private Cyril Martin
### Private Stanley Steward
### Private Edward Watts
### Private William Wilkins
### Volunteer Peter Monaghan

**Volunteer Jeremiah O'Leary**

**Commandant Charlie Hurley**

**Volunteer Con Daly**

For details of their deaths, see Part 1: The Crossbarry Ambush.

**19 March 1921**

**Cornelius (Long Con) Sheehan**

At approximately 8.30 p.m. there was an abrupt knocking at the door of 198 Blarney Street. Mrs Sheehan went to the door to ask who was there and was told to open the door. While this was going on Cornelius Sheehan tried to escape out the back door. Six shots were fired at him when he stepped into the yard and he died instantly. The killers jumped over the wall and escaped through the Walsh home two doors away. There is no doubt that he was targeted by the IRA – a couple of months earlier he had been shot while in the company of a policeman. He had recently resigned as an attendant at the Lunatic Asylum, where a number of arrests of IRA members (including Alderman Tadhg Barry who was later shot in Ballykinlar Internment Camp) had occurred.[218]

**20 March 1921**

**David Nagle**

The various BMH reports of David Nagle's death are confused about the date, but not about the fact that he was shot as a spy. According to the *Irish Independent* Nagle, the postman from Waterfall, was passing information to a spy called O'Sullivan in Cork. O'Sullivan was also shot by the IRA according to Michael O'Regan, and according to Patrick Cronin he was the person who informed on Leo Murphy. On 14 January 1922 the *Irish Independent* reported that Nagle, ex-RIC, had been taken from his home near Waterfall on 20 March 1921 and never returned. His wife was awarded £500 and his six children £1,400 in compensation.[219]

**20 March 1921**

**Jeremiah Mullane**

There is much confusion about this shooting, not least because a man of the same name was shot two nights later in Clogheen. Both *The Skibbereen Eagle* and the *Irish Independent* (which were usually accurate) reported that he had been shot by the military. However, the military evidence given to the court of inquiry was that he had been shot by three unknown civilians. Yet in the BMH witness statements there is no mention of a shooting around this time on North Main Street. Jeremiah (22) was living on St Paul's Avenue with his parents when he died.[220]

**20 March 1921**

**John Sheehan**

John Sheehan was sitting at home with his mother on 22 February 1921 around 9 p.m. There was a knock on the door and he told his mother, Kate, not to answer it as it was the Sinn Féiners looking for him. His mother opened the door and a man asked John who he was. When he confirmed his name he was taken away. On 20 March his body was found in a field in Archdeacon's farm at Dromalour, Kanturk. Around 8 a.m. the following morning Lieutenant McKerron of the Machine-Gun Corps recovered the body. Sheehan had been shot in the head. On the body was a notice warning spies, traitors and informers to beware. Lieutenant McKerron confirmed that he had known Sheehan before he was shot, but denied that he had ever given any information to the police.[221]

**22 March 1921**

**Arthur Mulcahy**

William Buckley recalled: 'This party [flying column] now returned across country to Ballynoe and next night moved on to Kilcronat where Dan Breen arrived the same night. As a result of a report received that an ex-British soldier from Tallow had been seen in the area it was suspected that he would report our position to the enemy and it was decided to move the column to Ballyard, Castlelyons. It was lucky that we had moved as the Kilcronat area was surrounded by the enemy that night (38 lorries and eight armoured cars) but the column was outside the ring. This was the night of March 22nd when Arthur Mulcahy (a native of Currabeha, Conna) was shot.' The *Irish Independent* noted that on Tuesday 22 March, in the course of some searches in the Conna district, a civilian, Arthur Mulcahy, was shot dead. He was apparently 'attempting to escape'.[222]

## 22 March 1921
### Volunteer James Barrett
For details of Barrett's death see Part 1: 28 February 1921.

## 23 March 1921
### John O'Shea, Chairman Midleton Urban District Council
John O'Shea died in Cork on 23 March 1921 and although not killed in action, his name is inscribed on both the National Monument and the Republican Plot in Midleton as having died on 23 March. He spent six months in Belfast Jail and, three months before his death, his house, along with six others, was burned in the first official reprisal of the war.[223]

## 23 March 1921
### Volunteer Daniel Crowley
### Volunteer William Deasy
### Volunteer Thomas Dennehy
### Volunteer Daniel Murphy
### Volunteer Jeremiah O'Mullane
### Volunteer Michael O'Sullivan
Morgan O'Flaherty, a witness to the events of that morning at Clogheen, stated in an affidavit: 'I remember the morning of the 23rd March, 1921. About 4.30 a.m. ... I was awakened by my brother, who told me that

somebody was firing over in O'Keeffe's farm. I said he was dreaming about it. He replied that he was not; that he had heard shots. I then got up and came to the window with him. We were standing at the window about 10 minutes or a quarter of an hour, and I was just going to go to bed again when a volley of shots rang out in the field near O'Keeffe's farm. I thought it was some of the Volunteers practising. It was a fairly bright night and I could see about 30 or 40 men in O'Keeffe's field. After another quarter of an hour I heard a voice saying "Run for it" or words to that effect, and someone screamed. I then heard another volley fired in the same place. I went back to bed for safety, and 2 or 3 volleys were fired between that time and 5.30 a.m., when my brother called me again and told me to come out of bed and have a look at the people coming down the field, as they looked very much like police. I then saw 3 policemen coming down the field, and afterwards saw 4 more policemen carrying something in a white blanket. Another lot of policemen then came along with something wrapped in a blanket, which I saw, when they were putting them into motor lorries, were dead bodies. They went back again and brought down more bodies. About six motor lorries came at 6.30 a.m and the bodies were put into one of these. As the lorries were coming the police on the road who had been at O'Keeffe's farm, started cheering.' It seems that six Volunteers had been caught asleep in a barn on O'Keeffe's farm and were shot by members of the RIC and Black and Tans.[224]

## 25 March 1921
### John Cathcart

At 3.30 a.m. on the night of 25 March, Minnie Foley, who worked for John Cathcart (52), heard a noise and saw a man in the backyard. She went upstairs to Mr Cathcart and told him that there were men downstairs. He said not to worry as it was probably only a raid. Cathcart shouted at the men, who told him they were looking for arms. When he replied, they ran upstairs and shot him four times. He worked in the grocery trade and was a managing director according to Miss Foley. Originally from Glasgow he was managing the Pasley and Co. bakery. He was widowed and left three children. According to his grandson he had been supplying information to the British, which was discovered when a plane carrying dispatches had crashed. A note on the body stated that he was a convicted spy and was signed 'IRA'. *The Skibbereen Eagle* of 26 March reported that Auxiliaries posted a notice on the house which simply bore the inscription 'Revenge' and this was condemned at his funeral service in the Methodist Church.[225]

## 27 March 1921
### Volunteer Timothy Whooley

While members of the West Cork Brigade were demolishing a bridge at Shannonvale, Clonakilty, on 27 March 1921, Lieutenant Timothy Whooley was shot. While there was a suggestion by Daniel Burke in evidence given to the office of the adjutant general that Whooley had been shot by the military, who came upon the scene as they were attempting to destroy the bridge, it seems probable that the local view – that he was accidentally shot – is correct.[226]

## 28 March 1921
### William Good

When William returned from Trinity College, Dublin to settle his father John's affairs he was bludgeoned to death as a spy. The court of inquiry heard that he had been killed by a blunt instrument at Ballyconeen, Timoleague between 4 p.m. and 6.30 p.m. shortly before he reached home. A second wound to the skull could have been a second blow to the head or as a result of a fall from his horse and trap. As an ex-soldier and a member of the army reserve, there is no doubt that he took an enormous risk driving alone into the heart of 'enemy territory'.[227]

## 30 March 1921
### Frederick Stenning

Originally from England, Fred Stenning (55) was the estate sub-agent for the Frewen Estate and was responsible for collecting rents in Innishannon. He was shot on 30 March 1921. His son, also called Frederick, was killed in the Great War on 30 September 1918 in France. Richard Russell stated: 'At the end of March, 1921, it had been established that Fred C. Stennings [*sic*] … was acting as a spy. A party under the Battalion Vice O/C (John Lordan) was assembled to arrest him on the night of March 30th 1921. I was a member of this party and took up a position at the rear of the house. The front door was approached by the Battalion Vice O/C (John Lordan) and another man. They knocked and the door was partly opened by Stennings, who tried to close it again but was prevented from doing so by John Lordan. Stennings then dashed along the hallway, pursued by Lordan and his companion. As Stennings dashed away, he drew a revolver and opened fire on his pursuers, who, replying to the fire, shot him dead.' Both Stenning and Warren Peacocke were fishing conservators (water bailiffs) and Stenning appears on a list of loyalists in the British Archives.[228]

## 30 March 1921
### Denis Donovan

Denis Donovan (40) was shot on 28 March 1921 at his front door on Watergate Street in Bandon. Shortly after 7 p.m. (curfew) two men called to the door and asked for him, saying they were enquiring about insurance. When he came out they closed the door behind them and shot him twice in the head. The RIC Auxiliary barracks was less than 100 metres away but the attackers escaped. He was taken to the military barracks rather than the workhouse, which was the usual for civilians, and appears to have died early on 30 March. Donovan did twenty-three years service in the Royal Navy and had retired in 1919. On the following morning the military ordered all businesses to close as a result of his death. He left a wife and three children.[229]

**31 March 1921**

**Constable Charles Bowles**

**Sergeant Ambrose O'Shea**

**Patrick Collins**

**George Wilson**

**Frank Fitzpatrick**

For details of their deaths, see Part 1: The Destruction of Rosscarbery Police Barracks.

**March 1921 (date uncertain)**

**Unnamed**

BMH WS 744 states: 'During March, 1921, a spy was found guilty of giving information to the enemy and was executed by members of the Kanturk Battalion. In view of the fact that relatives of this man are still resident in the locality and will probably continue to live in the district for many years to come, it is not considered desirable to elaborate on the details of this shooting.'[230]

**8 April 1921**

**Constable Frederick Lord**

The one-sentence newspaper descriptions of the incident in which Constable Lord (31) lost his life do no justice to the dramatic story told by his colleague Constable Lawrence at the court of inquiry. The two men had gone into Macroom early in the morning to buy supplies for the isolated barracks in Carrigadrohid. Around 3.30 p.m., as they passed Coolacareen Wood, a volley of shots was fired from the left and Constable Lord fell back into the cart with blood flowing from his mouth. According to Lawrence the horse bolted and he jumped off to grab the reins. He counted six men in pursuit after the ambush. He ran along with the horse. Two men jumped out on the road in front of him and he fired six shots at them before they jumped out of the way. He reached Carrigadrohid and organised a rescue for Lord who had fallen off the cart during the pursuit. When they reached him the local doctor was attending to him and confirmed that he was dead.[231]

## 8 April 1921
### Major Gerald Barry

Major Gerald Barry had been with the South Wales Borderers in the Great War and had lost a leg. As an invalid he was placed in charge of the detention centre in Victoria Barracks. He was shot and killed at the main barracks gate by one of the sentries. He was the son of Colonel John Barry of Inver and had been born in Queenstown (Cobh).[232]

## 8 April 1921
### Volunteer Liam (William) Hoare

A two-car police patrol arrived in the village of Ballymacoda on 8 April. According to Constable Connaughton, William Hoare was on a bicycle when he spotted them, and apparently jumped off and ran away. He was called on to halt by Constable Thompson and when he failed to do so he was shot. When the policemen searched the body they found two revolvers and subsequently, when the body was taken to Midleton, ammunition and IRA documents were found on it. When Hoare was examined at Belmont it was confirmed that he had died of the gunshot wound.[233]

However, the IRA version of events was violently different. Kevin Murphy recalled: 'I was arrested and taken to the military camp at The Hutments, Belmont, Cobh, where I was put into the guardroom. Here two soldiers stood in front of me, loading and unloading their rifles and all the time threatening to shoot me if I failed to give information regarding the I.R.A. After half an hour or so of this sort of business, and failing to make me give them any information, I was put into a cell adjoining the guardroom and left there for the night without a bed of any kind on which I could lie. In the morning I noticed what appeared to be clotted blood on the floor of the cell, and after a while the soldiers brought me a bucket of water, a scrubbing brush and cloths to clean up the floor. I refused point blank to do this. I learned later that an I.R.A. prisoner named Hoare from East Cork who had been shot by the Cameron Highlanders, tied with ropes to a military lorry and dragged for miles along the road, had been thrown into the cell which I now occupied. This accounted for the clotted blood on the floor which I was ordered to wash.'[234]

## 9 April 1921 (date uncertain)
## Denis 'Din Din' Finbarr Donovan

Denis Donovan was shot as a spy in Ballygarvan on brigade instructions and a label 'spies and informers beware' was placed on his chest. Cork No. 1 Brigade Intelligence Officer Leo Buckley later told the BMH why suspicions had been aroused. In November 1920, after the shooting of Sergeant O'Donoghue, four men were shot in retaliation. 'These shootings gave food for thought. The ex-soldier who was shot lived in the home of Willie Joe O'Brien and was his brother-in-law. When O'Brien, Healy and myself met next night, we came to the conclusion that the R.I.C. had got information from some source in relation to the shooting of the R.I.C. Sergeant. Hanley had been shot in mistake for Healy, while the shooting of O'Brien's brother-in-law and brother clearly had significance. We proceeded to worry out who the police spy could be. Only four people knew who participated in the shooting of the R.I.C. Sergeant, viz. Healy, O'Brien, the Company Captain (Dick Murphy), and myself. At the time, Dick Murphy was on very intimate terms with a man named Denis Donovan, Barrack St., Cork. Barrack St. was in the 2nd Battalion area, while we were in the 1st Battalion, Cork No. 1. We had all got to know Donovan well, and we had a nickname on him – "Din Din" for the reason that he was ever and always suggesting ways and means of shooting up the military and R.I.C. I remember asking Dick Murphy whether he had mentioned the R.I.C. shooting to "Din Din". He pooh-poohed any suggestion that anything was wrong with "Din Din", and we allowed the matter to rest.' Later he confirmed that Donovan was shot as a spy in Ballygarvan.[235]

**10 April 1921**

**Constable Joseph Boynes**

**Constable George Woodward**

Yet another non-descript ambush in the long-running, low-level guerrilla war in Kildorrery. For reasons known only to themselves the two constables went for a walk and were ambushed about a mile and a half from the village by the Castletownroche Company of the IRA. Both were shot dead. An official reprisal was ordered and six houses were destroyed in the locality on 13 April.[236]

**11 April 1921**

**Private Michael O'Brien**

On 14 March 1922 the Irish Department of Defence informed O'Brien's mother that 'your son was arrested on a charge of espionage, court-martialled … found guilty, and executed on 11th April 1921'. He had been a member of the Royal Army Service Corps until January 1921. No body was ever found.[237]

**13 April 1921**

**William Kenefick**

Early on the morning of 13 April William Kenefick died at the Mercy Hospital from shrapnel wounds he had received the previous day on Washington Street. Two police lorries were heading back to barracks when a bomb was thrown at them. However, it bounced off the side of the truck and landed among civilians, where it exploded. Initial reports suggested that Kenefick had been shot by the police but the medical evidence showed that this was not the case. Mr Kenefick (48), who lived on Blarney Street, was married. Four other civilians were wounded, including a two-year-old girl.[238]

**20 April 1921**

**Volunteer Tadhg O'Sullivan**

Michael Murphy stated: 'On 20th April 1921, one of my best company captains named Tadhg Sullivan was held up in Douglas St. by two British intelligence officers in mufti. He made a dash to escape and got into a house – No. 80 Douglas St. He ran upstairs and got out on the roof through a landing window, closely followed by the two British officers. Sullivan got on to the roof of the adjoining house when the officers appeared at the landing window and shot him dead. He was unarmed.' DI Patrick O'Riordain and Sergeant Patrick Hollywood gave evidence of the shooting and the medical evidence stated that a bullet wound which pierced an artery in the neck was the cause of death. O'Sullivan had four other bullet wounds. He was originally from Rathmore, Co. Kerry, and was a member of 'C' Company. He had been a juror at the inquest into Lord Mayor Tomás MacCurtain's murder.[239]

## 21 April 1921
### Patrick Goggin

At 4 p.m. on 21 April Patrick Goggin (7) was returning from counting the cows at Carrigthomas, Ballinagree. His father was in the yard when he heard two shots. His son called out for help and when his father found him he said that he had been shot by a soldier from a lorry which was 'bogged down half a mile away. Two soldiers came running up … an officer said that the boy would not have been fired at only they thought he was bigger.'[240] Patrick died at the scene.

## 22 April 1921
### Constable John Cyril McDonnell

On 17 April Kathleen Murphy, who had been walking with Constable McDonnell around 9.45 p.m. on Cove Street, stated that two civilians came up behind them and grabbed him by the arms before removing his revolver. He unsuccessfully ducked to avoid being shot and while he was on the ground four or five other shots were fired into his head. The gunmen and the other civilians ran away and Kathleen dragged him into a house. She ran around the corner to get the Fire Brigade ambulance, but extraordinarily when they returned they met McDonnell walking towards them. On admission to the military hospital it was discovered that bullets had fractured his jaw and his spine at the neck. On 22 April at 7 p.m. he died from asphyxia.[241]

## 23 April 1921
### Private John Marquis

During a search operation in Banteer, Private Marquis (25) of the Gloucester Regiment was shot in the head as the result of an accidental discharge of a rifle by a colleague. He was born in Guernsey and single. He died in Buttevant Military Hospital.[242]

## 26 April 1921
### Private Norman Fielding

In the intense propaganda war no incident was beyond use. Private Fielding was walking alone near Churchtown in North Cork when he was captured by the local IRA and shot as a spy. Denny Mullane of the Charleville IRA stated: 'On the 25th April, 1921, a British soldier, who gave his name as Private Fielding, and who posed as a deserter from Buttevant Barracks, was captured by Denny Noonan, who was in charge of a party of three, namely, Mick Collins, Con Browne and Jack Sheahan. He was tried by courtmartial and executed as a spy in the Charleville Battalion area. Later, I learned from the regiment's official "Lily White Magazine" that he was a high ranking, highly efficient Intelligence Officer. No more would-be deserters visited the area.' Fielding's body was photographed where it was found and kept in a scrapbook of photographs included in the Strickland Papers for later use.[243] Just nineteen years of age, it is highly unlikely that Fielding was a senior intelligence officer.

## 28 April 1921
### Volunteer Patrick Roynane
### Volunteer Thomas Mulcahy

**Volunteer Patrick Sullivan**

**Volunteer Maurice Moore**

The men captured at the Clonmult and Mourneabbey ambushes were tried by military court and on 31 March Roynane and Mulcahy were sentenced to death. Previously, three of the eight Clonmult prisoners, Sullivan, Moore and Sonny O'Leary, had been sentenced to death (O'Leary's sentence was commuted), while a fourth, Patrick Higgins, was too ill to stand trial. The executions were delayed as the men's lawyers appealed to the High Court in Dublin. The case submitted was that as no proper state of war existed, then martial law could not be declared and military courts (with their power to order immediate execution) were illegal. The case was argued between 25 and 27 April but the judges found that 'a state of war exists' and there was nothing they could do to stop the military courts.

The executions were immediately scheduled for the morning of 28 April. At 8 a.m. two of the prisoners were taken to the prison yard accompanied by two priests and shot dead. Their bodies were anointed and the procedure was repeated at 8.15 a.m. A final attempt to overturn the High Court's decision in the cases of Roynane and Mulcahy, by serving a writ on General Macready in Dublin, came to nothing as the executions had already taken place.[244]

**29 April 1921**

**Constable John Edward Bunce**

On yet another raid at the home of William and Kathleen Keyes McDonnell at Castlelack, the Auxiliaries found the road trenched. Under DI H. F. Smith they stopped to fill it in and placed the spare rifles against the fence. As they were completing the job Smith ordered Constable Bunce (29) to join the covering party. As Bunce was getting up on the fence his leg touched one of the rifles and it went off. He was shot through both thighs and both femurs were broken. He was taken initially to Bandon, before being moved to Cork, where he died from shock and haemorrhage around 10 p.m. He was married and from Windsor.[245]

## 30 April 1921
## Major Geoffrey Compton Smith

The number of senior British officers who 'took a day off the war' and were captured is remarkable. The most famous case is that of General Lucas, who was captured while fishing on the Blackwater. Undoubtedly the most tragic is that of Compton Smith. He was captured at Blarney Railway Station by senior IRA officer Frank Busteed. Compton Smith wrote: 'While away sketching yesterday, I had the misfortune to get held up by the IRA. I am now a prisoner, but being very well treated and going strong.' In early May a letter he had written to his wife was discovered in a raid and she later received some personal effects:

My own darling little wife

I am to be shot in an hour's time. Dearest your hubby will die with your name on his lips, your face before his eyes, and he will die like an Englishman and a Soldier. I cannot tell you sweetheart how much it is to me to leave you alone – nor how little to me personally to die – I have no fear, only the utmost, greatest and tenderest love to you, and my sweet little Anne. I leave my cigarette case to the Regiment, my miniature medals to my father – whom I have implored to befriend you in everything – and my watch to the officer who is executing me because I believe him to be a gentleman and to mark the fact that I bear him no malice for carrying out what he sincerely believes to be his duty. Goodbye, my darling, my own. Choose from among my things some object which you would particularly keep in memory of me, and I believe that my spirit will be in it to love and comfort you.

Tender, tender farewells and kisses – your own
Geof

Many efforts were made to recover his body after the war, including by Michael Collins, but it was not until 1926 that the location was revealed and he was given a military funeral before being interred in Fort Carlisle Military Cemetery.[246]

## 30 April 1921
## Michael O'Keeffe

On Saturday 30 April 1921 Michael O'Keeffe of Main Street, Carrigtwohill, Co. Cork was shot dead. An inquest into his death heard evidence from his wife, who told the court that 'her husband had been woken by a knock at the door. He went down and opened the door; she saw or heard no more of him until his dead body was found 200 yards from his home early the following morning. A card attached to O'Keeffe's sleeve when the body was found read "Spies and informers beware, I.R.A." The dead man [left] one child and was in receipt of a British Army disability pension.' In file PR6/32 in the CCCA, Thomas Cotter states that he and others from the Carrigtwohill Company shot Michael O'Keeffe on orders from the brigade. Francis Healy stated that the men responsible called to his house twenty minutes before the shooting.[247]

## 30 April 1921
## Constable Arthur Joseph Harrison

*The Cork Examiner* recorded: 'COACHFORD MYSTERY. Disappearance of a Constable (Press Association Message). Constable Arthur W. Harrison, RIC who left Carrigadrohid for Coachford Railway Station, Co. Cork district, at 2 p.m. on April 30th on completion of his service with the RIC has not yet reached home says the official report. He was travelling to the station in a motor bread van and has not since been seen. It is reported that he was kidnapped at Coachford and afterwards shot.' There was not another word about the fate of Constable Harrison until his wife Ellen sought compensation in October 1921, when she gave evidence that he had been dragged from a train at Coachford and disappeared. She was awarded £500 and their infant child £250. His fate was confirmed in a response from Captain D. J. Collins, assistant intelligence officer of the Southern Command, on 9 July 1923, to a request for information about Harrison, which stated that he was shot outside Coachford.[248]

**30 April 1921**
**Volunteer James Horan**
**Volunteer Patrick Starr**
**1 May 1921**
**Volunteer Patrick Casey**
**19 May 1921**
**Volunteer Timothy Hennessy**

These deaths all resulted from the same incident on the Cork/Limerick border. The Green Howard Regiment became embroiled in an all-day fight with the East and Mid-Limerick IRA Brigades. The plan had been for the East Limerick Brigade to ambush the Howards, but they were unaware that the Mid-Limerick Brigade was already in the tiny village of Shraharla. As the Green Howards approached the planned ambush, they happened upon the Mid-Limerick Brigade and a firefight broke out. The East Limerick Brigade tried to help and fought a series of gun battles with the superior British forces to draw fire away from the Mid-Limerick Brigade. A running fight developed as the IRA men tried to retreat uphill to safety. As they approached the churchyard they were surprised by another party of eight British soldiers who had outflanked them, and Starr and Horan were killed. Hennessy was mortally wounded (he died three weeks later) and Casey was captured. Later in the day Tim Howard and Willie O'Riordain were involved in a second firefight with the Green Howards at Lackelly, Co. Limerick, and they were also killed. Patrick Casey (28) was taken to Victoria Barracks where he was tried and executed within twenty-four hours, presumably to avoid the possibility of an appeal. He was convicted of having a rifle, revolver and fifty rounds of ammunition. With exquisite military attention to detail, the time of death was noted on the file as 6.31 p.m., one minute after the appointed time. The stakes in the war had been raised to the highest level.[249]

**1 May 1921**

**Volunteer Joseph Coughlan**

According to the men who killed him, about 2 a.m. on 1 May six members of the IRA were walking along the road at Sunfort, Churchtown, when they were fired on by a party of military. A challenge had been issued according to the unidentified members of the British party. Joseph Coughlan (14) was shot and died at the scene. He had been trenching the road to Liscarroll and the 'six men' included a horse and cart. According to the MSPC he was riddled down the right side, which seems surprisingly accurate fire when the military claimed at the court of inquiry to have fired only twenty bullets at six men in the dark.[250]

**1 May 1921**

**Constable William Smith**

**2 May 1921**

**Constable John Webb**

Four policemen, unarmed, left the police barracks to go fishing in the nearby demesne of Castlemartyr House. Smith and Webb went for a walk along the riverbank and both were shot. Smith (28) died instantly. British Commander-in-Chief General Sir Nevil Macready was incensed: 'There is no excuse for this man losing his life. Here are four constables going unarmed to fish in one of the worst areas. The sooner police understand that restrictions which have been observed by the military should be equally observed by them, the better. In my opinion, the police officer responsible for this police constable is to blame for his death.' It is hard not to agree. Webb died the next day in the Military Hospital in Cork.[251]

**4 May 1921**

**Volunteer John Stokes**

The death of Joseph Coughlan a few days earlier had, in fact, heralded a change of tactics by the British. Copying Major Percival's 'flying column' in

West Cork, they were now camping on the roadside and waiting to ambush the IRA. This time they stopped midway between Liscarroll and Freemount. The North Cork Brigade flying column, which was nearby, was informed and as a second party of British reinforcements had arrived in Charleville, they decamped to Tullylease. The ten-strong column arrived at 11.30 p.m. and went into billets. At daybreak John Stokes and Michael O'Regan went to wake the O/C, Seán Moylan, who was sleeping 300 yards away. They were called on to halt and Stokes was shot dead. O'Regan was captured. A party of thirty soldiers had arrived in the night. Moylan heard nothing and was woken only when an aeroplane flew close overhead. He made a run for it with Patrick O'Brien just as four soldiers came around the other gable of the house, and the two men hid in a drain waist-deep in water for two hours.[252]

## 6 May 1921
### James Lynch

On 5 May 1921 Brigid Lynch heard a knock shortly before midnight and went to the door. A man, who held the door of the house closed, asked for her husband, James. He got dressed and according to Brigid left with the men, apprehensively. She stated that 'six or seven weeks previously two men had come to the door and accused him of giving information to the military, which he denied. They said they would not give him another warning.' At 8.30 a.m. the following morning Robert Dawkins found the body of James Lynch (50) lying on the road in the middle of Whitegate, about 2 yards from his own house. He had been shot in the head and chest. According to his NAK file he had no connection with the military; the only possible motive was that he was friendly with a family 'now under military protection'.[253]

## 7 May 1921
### Private Thomas Collins

Fanny and Elsie Sheehan had literally danced all night in the military barracks in Youghal and were returning home at 5 a.m. (during curfew) with

Paddy Lynass, Thomas Collins and Jack McCarthy. Fanny spotted two men behind a low wall at Fair Green on North Main Street. The men opened fire, wounding Lynass. A third man stepped from the shadows and fired at Collins and Elsie Sheehan. Both were wounded. Fanny Sheehan had been warned three weeks previously by masked men about attending military dances. Thomas (25), who was married, died later that morning in the work-house hospital. According to the NAK file he was a private in the Cheshire Regiment, but he is also described as a civilian. That night more than 100 houses and shops were wrecked and looted by 'marauding bands'. A few days later Thomas was buried and a party of Cameron Highlanders joined the cortège.[254]

### 7 May 1921
### William (James/John) Purcell

According to Michael Murphy, IRA commander in Cork: 'On 9th [sic] May 1921, a civilian named Purcell was shot for spying. He was traced through letters captured by our lads in the mails.' Originally from Tipperary, Purcell was identified as a spy, taken from his lodgings on South Main Street to Tory Top Lane and shot. The post-mortem examination, which took place on 8 May, showed that the body had nine bullet wounds. He was eventually identified by his landlady as William B. Purcell (45), unmarried, of 7 Charlotte Quay. He was unemployed at the time of his death.[255]

### 8 May 1921
### Constable Frederick Sterland

Constable Frederick Sterland (28) from Birmingham was married with two children when he was shot on a Sunday afternoon in Cook Street in the centre of Cork. He was rushed to the South Infirmary where he was pronounced dead at 6.15 p.m. According to the court of inquiry, he was shot by persons unknown. Nothing could be further from the truth. Robert Ahern told the BMH exactly what happened: 'I got in touch with "Sailor"

Barry, Captain of "D" Company, 2nd Battalion, Lar Neville and Jeremiah Coughlan. The latter two were also officers in "D" Company. The four of us, armed with revolvers, called to Barrett's as arranged, and not finding our lads there we went in to the city to the Rob Roy Hotel. …

'Arriving at the hotel, we went upstairs to the lounge and saw Mahony, Cogan and Sterland drinking at the bar. I nodded to Mahony. I then left the lounge with my three men, went downstairs to the hall and closed the door leading to Cook St. Shortly afterwards Mahony, Cogan and Sterland came down to the hall. We drew our revolvers and ordered the three of them to put up their hands. They did so, Mahony and Cogan pretending to be taken by surprise. …

'We then searched Sterland and took his papers and his revolver. I left the Rob Roy and went up to the South Mall (about sixty yards distant) to see if there were any military patrols near us. I then returned to the hotel.

'In Cook St. there happened to be a car from which milk was being delivered, and we considered the idea of putting Sterland in the car and taking him out of town. We decided, however, that the prospects of taking him away alive were practically nil. We were surrounded on all sides by enemy forces, who kept a special watch on all bridges leading out of the city. If we got through the patrols safely (which was indeed most unlikely), we could scarcely hope to have the same good luck crossing any of the bridges with our prisoner. As time was against us, we took Sterland out on to Cook St., where he was shot and killed. We then ran up Cook St., crossed The Mall safely, and seeing a side-car parked outside South Chapel we climbed on it and drove the horse furiously to the Evergreen Road district, where I took possession of the guns and dumped them safely.'[256]

## 8 May 1921

### John Hodnett

The war was fought on many fronts. One of the most important was at parliamentary questions in the House of Commons, where the tiny opposition tried to hold Chief Secretary for Ireland Hamar Greenwood to account. In many ways the prevarication and excuses provided by Greenwood made him increasingly a figure of ridicule and profoundly changed public opinion in England on the war. The chief inquisitor for Cork was Liberal Lieutenant Commander Kenworthy, while Greenwood often planted questions via Lieutenant Colonel Archer-Shee. Sometimes it was not always clear that everyone was working from the same script. 'Lieut.-Colonel Archer-Shee asked the Chief Secretary whether he can give the House any further information as to the murders of John Hodnett, of Courtmacsherry, County Cork, who was murdered on his way to mass on Sunday, the 8th May; of William Bransfield, of Carrighwohill [sic], County Cork, who was murdered on Sunday, 8th May, outside his house; of Head-constable Storey, when leaving mass on Sunday, 8th May, at Castleisland, County Kerry; of Martin Scanlon and John M'Gawley, who were murdered on Sunday, 8th May, at Kilrooskey, County Roscommon; of William Simpson, an old-age pensioner, murdered at Enniskillen on 8th May; and of Constable Thon [sic] Hopkins, murdered at Dromore, County Tyrone, on Sunday, 8th May; and whether he is aware that, in the case of the attempted murder of Sergeant Butler, Royal Irish Constabulary, at Castleisland, his life was saved by the heroic action of Mrs. Butler?' The reply in the case of John Hodnett could not have been more bereft of emotion, 'The facts of these cases as reported by the police are as follows: John Hodnett, a farmer of Lislee, Courtmacsherry, County Cork, was shot by a party of Crown forces owing to his failure to halt when challenged, and he died the same day from the effects of his wounds.' Hodnett (35) had been on his way to Mass when he was shot dead. He was unmarried.[257]

## 8 May 1921
### Volunteer William Bransfield

Between 2 a.m. and 3 a.m. in Carrigtwohill Volunteer William Bransfield was taken out of his mother's house and shot 20 yards away. Given the rough and ready nature of courts of inquiry, the one into Bransfield's death was surprisingly meticulous. The court had discovered that Bransfield's late wife was the sister of Michael O'Keeffe's wife. O'Keeffe had been shot as a spy on 30 April. According to local gossip there was 'bad blood' between the two families, besides the fact that 'O'Keeffe was a loyalist ex-soldier and Bransfield a Sinn Feiner'. They also discovered that 'O'Keeffe, at one time had given Richard Masterson a beating'. None of this evidence was sworn. Masterson worked for Edward Keegan, who had stated that his house had been burned down by masked men around midnight the same night that Bransfield was killed and that while he was trying to put out the flames he had heard the shooting. The men who burned his house 'did not have south of Ireland accents'. According to Masterson, who witnessed Bransfield try-ing to escape and being shot, the men also 'did not have Cork accents'. The original findings of the court agreed the fatal shot was to the face while Bransfield was lying on the ground after he was wounded. On the fol-lowing day the intelligence officer of the 2nd Battalion of the Cameron Highlanders stated that 'Bransfield was known as a member of the Irish Republican Army' and was 'known to have carried arms'. Bransfield was widowed with one child.

Local IRA member Frank Healy also recorded the events of that night: 'At 1 a.m., 9th May, 1921, I was awakened by the sound of revolver shots being discharged in the vicinity. A short while after, I heard loud knocking on the front door and then the door was forced open. I could hear men speaking in pronounced Scotch accents in the living-room underneath my bedroom. As luck would have it, the house where I resided was old-fashioned and the stairs was concealed in a kind of a wardrobe partition. ... I was only in suspense for a few seconds when I heard the strangers again leaving the house. I was fully satisfied by this time that the party were members of the murder gang drawn from the Cameron Regiment stationed at Cobh, Co. Cork, who were known to be frequently engaged on night raids and shootings in East Cork.'[258]

**9 May 1921**

**Constable James Cullen**

James 'Spud' Murphy stated: 'About the first week in May, Tom Lane, Jim Lane and myself came into Clonakilty to search for any Tans that might be moving around the town. We searched a number of public-houses and got some scouts to search others. We were eventually informed that there were three Tans in Kingston's public-house in McCurtain Hill, and two in a public-house next door. Tom Lane was left to cover the public-house next door while Jim and I moved to Kingston's where I threw a bomb into the shop. The bomb blew out all the glass in the front of the shop, killed one of the Tans and seriously wounded another. I was struck in the buttock by a splinter of the bomb and seriously wounded.' Constable Cullen was removed to Cork where he died on 9 May.[259]

**9 May 1921**

**Volunteer Godfrey (Geoffrey) Canty**

**Volunteer Frank Hurley**

Godfrey Canty (26) and Captain Frank Hurley were shot during a general round-up by the Essex Regiment. Canty was shot and wounded while trying to escape the net at Newcestown. He was taken prisoner but local people later came across his body on the roadside near Murragh.[260] Surprisingly, there is no other record of his death, and it appears no court of inquiry took place. However, his death certificate, not issued until 1933, recorded that his dead body was found in a wood in 1921 and that he had died from gunshot wounds after an encounter with British military forces.

The capture of Frank Hurley was a major achievement for the regiment. Charlie O'Donoghue provided the basic details: 'With two other Volunteers, O'Leary and Donovan, he ran into a British column patrol in Scott's farmyard at Carhoo.' His sister Anna Hurley recalled: 'My brother, Frank, was an active Volunteer and participated in the Glandore Camp [1919], returning early one morning to tell me of its break up by the British. He was O.C. Mount

Pleasant Company and also a member of the Brigade Column, taking part in many fights, notably Crossbarry. He was killed on the 9th May, 1921, being captured while in possession of a revolver. When crossing a small bridge in Castle Bernard Park he made a run for it and might have got away had not one foot got caught in a rabbit hole and he stumbled and so lost his life, being shot down. The story of his end was told by another Volunteer captured at the same time, but unarmed. My brother would have been shot anyway, no doubt, following a Drumhead Courtmartial, for having a gun.'[261]

## 11 May 1921

### Volunteer Cornelius Murphy

Two days after their success around Bandon, the Essex Regiment scored another success. IRA Lieutenant Con Murphy was shot dead by soldiers from the regiment at Cloundreen, Kilbrittain. He was from Clachfluck, Timoleague in Co. Cork. John O'Connor stated: 'On 11th May, a Battalion Council meeting had been held and the captain of Timoleague Company – Cornelius Murphy – ran into a column of military when returning from the meeting and was shot dead. We buried him at midnight in Clogagh with full military honours.' Michael Coleman witnessed what happened: 'On the 9th [*sic*] May, 1921, a meeting of the 1st Battalion Council was held at Kilbrittain for the purpose of arranging details of an operation which was to take place on the 14th. The brigade had ordered an attack on all enemy posts and personnel on that date. I was ordered to arrange to attack Courtmacsherry. I left Neill's of Kilbrittain along with David Sullivan and Con Murphy and called to Mahoney's of Cloundirreen. We entered the gateway at Mahoneys and went to the door to enquire of Mrs. Mahoney whether there was any news of Percival's column who had billeted at Clogagh school the previous night. ... Suddenly, members of Percival's column came from the side of Mahoney's opposite and started to surround the yard in which we were standing. Sullivan and Murphy rushed from the yard and made for the open country. I stepped unobserved into an open-fronted cowshed, got down beside a butt (cart) and bent up my knees so that I wouldn't be noticed. Percival's men crowded into the yard. Some of them had chased Sullivan and Murphy, firing as they went. ... After some time an officer blew a whistle and all the troops moved out of the yard ... About 150 yards from the house I found the body of Con Murphy.'[262]

## 14 May 1921
### Private Roland Madell

A long-awaited general shoot-up of British forces across Cork was planned for 14 May 1921. Writing in 1953 Seán Moylan was somewhat dismissive: 'G.H.Q. decided to issue a general order to all Brigades for an attack everywhere on the British on the 14th May, 1921. The order was doubtless the outcome of political exigencies which must on occasion over-ride military considerations. From a military point of view it was not well conceived. Opportunities may be grasped. It is seldom possible to create them. It may be said that the result of the order did not produce any more effective activity on that day that would distinguish it from other days.'

William McCarthy described the incident in which Madell died in detail: 'The British had been executing I.R.A. men taken under arms and, as a reply, we had been ordered to arrange to shoot up all British forces at 12 noon on the 14th May. I was picked for Courtmacsherry, and on the day before all arms needed for the job were brought to a spot near Courtmacsherry. The plan for the day was that five would enter the village to shoot up any troops in sight, while six riflemen would open fire on the military post as cover ... One soldier was killed and two wounded in the village.' The fatality was Madell.[263]

## 14 May 1921
### Sergeant Joseph Coleman
### Constable Thomas Cormyn
### Constable Harold Thompson

Sergeant Coleman was having a drink in a public house on the main street near the RIC barracks in Midleton around 3 p.m. when he was shot. He was taken back to the barracks and around 4.30 p.m. it became obvious that he needed a priest. A number of constables headed off towards the Roman Catholic church at the far end of the town. John Kelleher recalled what happened: 'Saturday 14th May, 1921, saw another attack made on the R.I.C. in Midleton. So far as I can remember orders were received from Brigade Headquarters in Cork that an R.I.C. man should be shot in every town in the battalion area. Early on that day, Sergeant Coleman of the R.I.C. was shot dead in a public-house in Midleton. At about 2 p.m. [*sic*] two Black and Tans were proceeding down the town when they were ambushed by three IRA men, Jackeen Ahern and Tom Buckley from the Midleton Company and Tom Riordan from the Lisgould Company. The three lads lay in ambush behind a low wall at the end of the town. They had rifles which were brought in by Mick Murnane of Coppingerstown. Fire was opened on the "Tans" at about 150 yards range, both of whom were killed and their guns captured. Another policeman named Sergeant Gleeson narrowly escaped, although fire was brought to bear on him too. Gleeson, subsequently, got back safely to the barracks.'[264]

## 14 May 1921
### Royal Marine Bernard Francis
### Royal Marine Coastguard William Parker

According to David Cashman: 'In the middle of May, 1921, an order was received from Brigade Headquarters that all British military personnel in uniform should be shot at sight whether they were armed or unarmed. The date, so far as I can recollect was 14th May, 1921. In compliance with this order, Phil Hyde and I met with two British Marines in the neighbourhood of Ramhill, Ballinacurra. We fired on them, killing both.' The bodies were dumped in the nearby gravel quarry. The two men had gone for a walk from their post at East Ferry about three miles away and were unarmed. Francis was from Lewes in Sussex and Parker was from Manchester. They had both fought on battleships during the war, and Parker was aboard the HMS *Malaya* during the Battle of Jutland, when it was heavily damaged. Both were in their early twenties. Despite the local paper reporting the death of Francis under a headline 'We shall not forget', the truth is they did.[265]

**14 May 1921**
**Constable Peter Coughlan**
**15 May 1921**
**Constable John Ryle**
**23 May 1921**
**Constable Patrick Hayes**

The details of this attack are horrific. A patrol of seven RIC was walking along Watercourse Road from their barracks at Shandon Street. Given the mayhem over the rest of the weekend it was unfortunate that they were all close together. As they reached the junction with O'Connell Street, two men who had been having a chat dropped two grenades among the policemen, which exploded, causing havoc. Constable Coughlan had severe injuries and Constables Ryle, Rothwell and Hayes had their lower limbs badly lacerated and shattered by bomb fragments. All were taken to the North Infirmary 200 metres away but Coughlan, a long-serving policeman with a wife and large family, was dead on arrival. The survivors were then taken to the Military Hospital, where Constable Ryle died on 15 May. He was also of long service and had arrested Peter O'Keeffe in December 1916 for attempting to purchase weapons from a Private Davis. There is no doubt about who was involved in this attack, as Patrick 'Pa' Murray (later Lord Mayor of Cork) told the BMH: 'Late in the evening, the men on duty at the north side of the city were informed that an R.I.C. patrol had gone down O'Connell Street, Blackpool. They immediately ran to the attack and threw some bombs, killing one and wounding three policemen.' In fact, three policemen died as a result of the explosions.[266] According to Hayes's death certificate he died on 23 May.

**14 May 1921**
**Private John Alexander Hunter**
**Private Robert McMillan**
**Private Donald Chalmers**

Christopher O'Connell accounts for the shooting dead of these three unarmed soldiers: 'When the general order to shoot up enemy forces as a reprisal for the execution of I.R.A. prisoners was received, arrangements were made to visit Castletownbere for this operation. A party of eight or nine men moved into position at Toormore, about a quarter of a mile from Castletownbere, on the road to Eyries, about noon on May 14th, 1921. They sent scouts into the town to see if any Tans or R.I.C. were moving round. Before the scouts returned, another messenger arrived to tell us that the enemy were aware of our presence and that the military at Furious pier were moving out to cut off our retreat at Bealnalappa on the main Eyries coast road. Six or seven of the party under the battalion O/C (Peter O'Neill) withdrew after exchanging shots with some Tans who had moved outside the town (Castletownbere) while, with Liam O'Dwyer, I moved towards Bealnalappa to intercept the military from Furious pier. This latter force did not put in an appearance, so we had no engagement. ...

'While we were endeavouring to engage the Castletownbere garrison on this occasion, the men from Rossmacowen company under Micheál Óg O'Sullivan attacked a patrol of military at Furious pier where they killed three and wounded two of the patrol.' Hunter and McMillan were from Glasgow, and Chalmers was from London.[267]


**14 May 1921**
**Private Francis Shepard (Sheppard)**
**Cornelius Looney**

Tom Barry decided that Cork No. 3 Brigade would organise a 'spectacular' to attack the British in the centre of Bandon as part of the general shoot-up. Peter Kearney provides the most detailed account of the incident, which is slightly less heroic than Barry's account in *Guerilla Days*. Kearney recalled: 'On the 14th May I took part in the attack on the enemy in Bandon town with Tom Barry, Sean Lehane, Mick Crowley and Billy O'Sullivan. We had our one machine-gun, two rifles and several revolvers, while Sean Lehane drove the motor car in which we travelled. We emerged on the main Dunmanway–Bandon road about three miles from the latter town and then headed for Bandon. The hood of the car was down, the Lewis gun rested on the framework of the windscreen and we proceeded at a reasonable pace, very much on the alert. Close to the town of Bandon we passed an enemy sentry and, as it appeared that they were very much on guard, we decided to open fire on a group of the enemy who were playing football in a field adjoining the barrack. After staying in the town for ten minutes we retreated back the same road, but the enemy outposts were, apparently, too terrified even to fire at us. We endeavoured to take the car off the main Dunmanway road a few miles outside the town of Bandon, but as the incline was too sharp, the car would not travel forward due to a small supply of petrol, consequently, we had to put the car in reverse and back up the hill. On reaching the top of the hill, we set the car on fire and proceeded across country.' Private Shepard of the Essex Regiment, who had been guarding the match, was killed in the first burst of machine-gun fire.[268]

On the same night Cornelius Looney and Patrick Walsh were making their way home to Boyle Street through a field near Warner's Lane where there was a footbridge over the Bandon river. They were both hit by bullets and Looney died shortly before 11 p.m. in the workhouse hospital. His children received £500 compensation the following October.[269]

## 14 May 1921

### Constable John Kenna

Con Flynn informed the BMH about the shooting of Constable Kenna: 'When the order for the general "shoot up" of enemy forces as a reprisal for the execution of I.R.A. prisoners was received, arrangements were made for a party consisting of Jack Corkery, Bill Hales and Tim McCarthy – all from Ballinadee Company – in co-operation with some men from Innishannon unit to ambush a patrol of R.I.C. at Innishannon on May 14th 1921. The Battalion Adjutant (Jim O'Mahoney) was in charge of this operation, in which one member of the enemy patrol was killed. The IRA had no casualties.'[270]

## 14–15 May 1921
**Volunteer Richard Barry**
**Michael Ahern**
**Richard Flynn**
**Edward MacNamara**
**Volunteer John Ryan**

As has been previously stated, the Irish War of Independence was as much a propaganda war as anything else. Attorney-General for Ireland Denis Henry told the House of Commons in June 1921 that 'The Court of Inquiry found that these men were shot by Crown forces in the exercise of their duty and that no blame attached to any member of the Crown forces concerned. Ryan and Ahern were shot in an attempt to escape from military escort after being warned that in the event of any such attempt they would be fired on. In the case of Richard Flynn a military party which had been sent to arrest him was fired on from the house and Flynn himself was shot while running out from the back door. His son Timothy Flynn who attempted to escape with Ryan and Ahern was wounded.'[271] This was a reasonable explanation for these three deaths.

However, according to John Kelleher, there were five shootings and they didn't happen quite as Henry had said: 'On Saturday night, 14th May, 1921, a large party of Cameron Highlanders came into Midleton and commenced raiding houses. Some of the soldiers went in the direction of the local Golf Links where they chanced to meet a youth named MacNamara who was walking to his home along the railway line. The military shot and killed

MacNamara. Later that night some others of the party called to the house of a Volunteer named Richard Barry who lived about a mile outside Midleton. Barry was arrested by the Cameron Highlanders. Next day his dead body was found on the railway line about a mile on the Midleton side of Carrigtwohill. Seemingly this same force of Camerons then went to the home of Jackeen Ahern at Ballyrichard and, not finding him at home, arrested his brother Michael. On the following day Michael's dead body was found inside a fence about three hundred yards west of Carrigtwohill near where the main road to Cork branches off to Cobh. Another I.R.A. man named Ryan from Woodstock, a short distance north of Carrigtwohill, was taken from his home that night and shot dead by the same party of Cameron Highlanders. Two [*sic*] other Carrigtwohill men not members of the IRA were murdered the same night by the Cameron Highlanders' raiding party.'[272]

## 15 May 1921
### Patrick Sheehan

Around 2.30 a.m. on Sunday morning, Miss Crowley, the landlady of 9 Langford Row, was awakened by a loud hammering on her front door. When she answered, four men brushed past her and ran up the stairs to the room occupied by newly married Patrick Sheehan (41) and his wife, Catherine. They asked through the locked door if he was Patrick Sheehan and when he said yes they fired through the door and killed him. He was a native of Newcestown and is buried in Templemartin.[273]

## 15 May 1921
### Constable Hugh McLean

*The Skibbereen Eagle* is the only source to discuss this ambush in any detail: 'A sensational affair took place on the Inches road, Hollybrook, within a couple of yards of Ballyhilty Bridge, at 3.45 p.m. on Sunday evening, when Constables Cooper, an Englishman, and Constable McLean, a Scotchman, were ambushed from a grove, by, it is stated, 15 armed civilians. Some sixteen shots were discharged by the ambushers while the police were taken so completely by surprise that they were unable to return the fire. Constable McLean received a wound in the spine, the bullet passing right through his body, as he was apparently about to fire his revolver, which fell out of his hand. Constable Cooper, who was unarmed, stooped to pick up the weapon, and while in the act of doing so received a bullet in the lower part of the back, the wound being slight. He immediately ran to Skibbereen by the Marsh road and reported the affair. A lorry of armed police then hastened to the scene and found Constable McLean lying on the road, in a critical condition with his undischarged revolver a couple of yards from him. Dr. Burke attended to the wounded man and had him removed to Skibbereen hospital, where he died about 7 p.m. Constable Cooper meanwhile was attended by Dr. O'Meara and removed by train to Cork Military Hospital on Tuesday morning; the dead body of his comrade being conveyed by the same train for interment in Scotland.' Constable McLean was twenty-one. *The Skibbereen Eagle* also records a compensation claim the following October in which McLean's father, Hugh, claimed £5,000 for the loss of his son. The father (44), who had also been in the police, along with his two sons, was awarded £1,200.[274]

## 15 May 1921
### Reverend James O'Callaghan

'The tragedy took place at Upper Janemount, Sunday's Well, at the residence of Alderman Liam de Roiste, who has been an M.P. for the city for the past few years ... de Roiste was not in his house on Saturday night, but Rev. Fr James O'Callaghan, who is attached to the North Chapel, and who is chaplain to the Good Shepherd's Convent resided in the house. About 4 a.m. ... a party of men in civilian dress arrived at the house, and knocked loudly at the door. As there was some delay in responding to the knock, the men are reported to have smashed in the glass panels, with the weapons which they carried in their hands. Fr O'Callaghan, hearing the noise and commotion, came on to the landing. By this time some of the men had come up the stairs and immediately a volley of bullets were [*sic*] fired at him from a distance of a few yards. One bullet passed clean through his body and the priest collapsed on the landing, blood pouring copiously from the terrible wound. The raiding party then retired as quickly as possible. Mrs de Roiste and her servant, who were terribly shocked, rushed to the priest's assistance. The Corporation ambulance was summoned at 4.15 a.m., and at once proceeded to the spot. They found Fr. O'Callaghan lying on the landing, very badly wounded. Owing to the very steep, hilly nature of the place, they had to wrap him in a blanket, put him on a stretcher and carry him some distance down, until they got to the ambulance. They then drove with all speed to the North Infirmary, where the Rev. gentleman was attended to by the skilled medical and nursing staff of the institution.' He died from his wounds at 6 p.m. that day and is buried in Clogheen, just outside the city.[275]

## 16 May 1921
### Volunteer Daniel O'Brien

Daniel O'Brien had been surprised along with other members of the North Cork IRA in the O'Donnell household at Aughrim two miles north of Liscarroll on 9 May. It was the third 'surprise' in a few weeks for the North Cork IRA. In the same incident newly appointed battalion quartermaster, John O'Regan, was badly wounded. Both men were arrested and taken to Victoria Barracks in Cork. John O'Regan was too badly injured, but Daniel O'Brien was tried by court martial, convicted of being in possession of a revolver and executed on 16 May. The execution took place at 8 a.m.[276]

## 16 May 1921
### David Walsh

Though dismissed by British sources and questioned by some historians, it seems Walsh was the informant who gave the army information about the IRA men billeted at Clonmult. The BMH witness statement of James Coss provides the following evidence: 'Amongst the information received by me from my intelligence officers in the military barracks was a copy of a file which gave particulars of the individual who gave the information to the enemy forces which led to the massacre of a number of I.R.A. men. – they were, I think, Midleton Battalion Column – at Clonmult, near Midleton, in February 1921. Within 24 hours of receiving the information the spy in question had been arrested, tried and executed. His name was David Walsh.'

William Buckley confirmed what happened: 'It was about this time also that David Walshe [sic], Shanagarry, was arrested by members of the Glenville Company on suspicion of having given information to the British which led to the massacre of I.R.A. forces at Clonmult on February 20th. He was held prisoner for about a week when he eventually admitted his guilt. He was tried by members of the battalion staff and sentenced to death. The sentence was confirmed by the Brigade staff. He was executed at Doon, Glenville.'[277]

## 18 May 1921
### Lance Corporal Arthur Wilfred (Wilfrid) Hill

Lance Corporal Hill (21) went off duty at 5.30 p.m. from Glanmire Road Railway Station in Cork city. He then visited a lady friend, leaving at 9 p.m. The curfew patrol found his body face down in a pool of blood not far from the level crossing on the road by Tivoli. He had been shot twice in the head. He was from Farnham in Hampshire. According to 'The Cairo Gang' website, the IRA believed he was an intelligence officer.[278]

## 20 May 1921
### Edward Hawkins

An old quarry at Mount Desert on the western outskirts of Cork city was the scene of another shooting. Three men – Daniel Hawkins (52), his son Edward (29) and John Sherlock (35) – were picked up at 8 a.m. by the IRA on Shears Street, near their homes in Broad Street and Devonshire Lane, while they were on their way to work. All three were shot. Edward Hawkins was shot through the skull and the arm and died half an hour after admission to the Mercy Hospital. John Sherlock had also been shot through the head and was removed to the Military Hospital, where he was not expected to live, but did. Daniel Hawkins was not seriously injured, having used the leg of a chair he was carrying to protect his head. Both Edward Hawkins and John Sherlock were ex-soldiers. Edward was employed by the military, the father of three young children and had been on his way to load stores on the Bandon railway. John Sherlock was a train driver. Both families claimed compensation and the British government accepted liability, which meant that these men were considered supporters of the government.[279]

## 20 May 1921
### Francis Leo McMahon

There is little mention of Francis McMahon in the newspapers. The *Irish Independent* quoted an official notice: 'Francis L. McMahon who was employed as a clerk in the War Pensions Office at Cork was kidnapped on Thursday by unknown men as he was going to his office, and has not been seen or heard of since.' Daniel Healy stated: 'It was, so far as I can remember, in June [*sic*], 1921, when we received instructions from the Brigade to arrest and execute a civilian spy by the name of McMahon. We picked him up as he was going to work and took him out to the country in a two-wheeled cab. He was shot by members of the Active Service Unit.'[280]

## 21 May 1921
### William Bourke

Mr Bourke was shot dead in Ballyhooley: 'At Ballyhooley a farmer's son named William Bourke was shot dead by the military because he "refused to halt when called upon."' According to some of the reports he was in failing health, which probably meant that he was suffering from tuberculosis. There is no record of a court of inquiry.[281]

**23 May 1921**

**Volunteer Stephen Dorman**

Stephen Dorman worked in the readers and compositors' department of *The Cork Examiner*. Alan Ellard wrote: 'Stephen had been on the night shift and left the offices about 3 a.m. on May 23 with Chris Walsh, Fred Murphy and a man called Collins, who I did not know. They were walking home and had passed the top of Nicholas Street to walk down Douglas Street when a bomb was thrown and they came under revolver fire. Stephen took the main impact of the blast. Chris was badly wounded while the other two escaped with minor cuts and bruises.' Stephen was a member of the IRA and was buried in the Republican Plot of St Finbarr's Cemetery.[282]

**23 May 1921**

**Two Machine Gun Corps Soldiers (names unknown)**

BMH WS 754 recorded: 'Two British soldiers, in uniform, were captured on the Newmarket road just outside Charleville – they had a map of the district in their possession. At their trial they admitted they were on intelligence duties. They were executed and died very bravely. Their one request was, if they were to be shot, to have the job done quickly.'[283]

**23 May 1921**

**William McCarthy**

A small advertisement on page 2 of *The Cork Examiner* of 21 July 1921 stated: 'William McCarthy has been missing from his home, 17 Barrack Street Mallow since 23rd May. He proceeded to Mourneabbey that day and was seen passing the Railway Station at 4 o'clock p.m. Age about 49, dark hair turning grey, height 5'11", dressed in grey tweed coat and trousers, blue vest, was an army pensioner, was employed in the coal mines at Wales and was home owing to the coal strike. Any information would be gratefully received by his wife and family.' McCarthy had been a colour sergeant in the Royal Irish Regiment. According to *The Freeman's Journal* of 14 January

1922, his wife informed the probate court that she had received a letter from the IRA in September saying that her husband had been shot as a spy.[284]

### 24 May 1921
### Lieutenant Seymour Vincent

Lieutenant Vincent was captured while carrying out intelligence work according to the chief IRA spymaster in Cork, Florence O'Donoghue, and the senior IRA officer in Fermoy, George Power. It appears from the evidence that he was probably on intelligence duty, possibly working for the British chief spymaster, Basil Thompson. Power recalled: 'The enemy appeared to depend on information supplied by loyalists who were organised in some area[s] with a view to reporting movements of armed or well-known wanted men. For instance, in January 1921, a number of houses in the area south-west of Fermoy were raided by small enemy parties on the day following that on which the brigade O/C. had stayed in a particular house.

'The manner in which these loyalists were organised came to light early in 1921, when a British officer from the Fermoy garrison was captured near Watergrasshill disguised as an ordinary tramp. In his possession was found a notebook containing a list of known loyalists in the area that it was proposed to contact. The capture of this officer, whose name was Lieutenant Vincent, was reported to the brigade, and I left immediately for the Fermoy battalion area to interview him. On arrival, however, I found that the British officer had been killed. He had made a desperate attempt to escape during an enemy round-up in the Glenville area on the morning following his capture.'[285]

### 24 May 1921
### Patrick Hickey

Hickey was cutting turf with two other men at Lavoltoura, Enniskeane, when he was shot and killed around 3.30 p.m. An Essex Regiment patrol appeared and challenged them to halt. From the evidence it appears that the noise from a nearby stream meant that Hickey, who was elderly and hard of hearing, may not have heard the challenge. One of his companions, Patrick Murray, heard the shouting but 'did not think he was shouting at us'. The soldiers opened fire and all three men made a run for cover but Hickey was shot in the chest. He died fifteen minutes later. The British government later admitted responsibility for the killing, which they mistakenly said had taken place on 25 May. The court of inquiry was chaired by Percival and, despite the evidence, concluded that the shooting had occurred 'during a conflict with rebels'. Colonel Higginson, one of the senior British officers in Cork, who answered queries from the Dublin Castle administration where all court of inquiry files were sent for review, changed this to 'shooting at rebels', which was equally incorrect. *Nemo judex in sua causa* (no man shall be the judge in his own case) does not seem to apply in the case of the Essex Regiment dealing with the Essex Regiment.[286]

## 25 May 1921
## Patrick Keating

On the previous Sunday (22 May), around 8.30 p.m., Patrick Keating was shot in the abdomen on Shandon Street. This was thirty minutes after curfew. The shooting mystified the newspapers but the first witness to the court of inquiry – Lieutenant F. S. Grey of the Hampshire Regiment, who was in charge of the curfew patrol – stated that he had shot Keating after he had failed to respond to a challenge to halt: 'I saw a civilian. He was about 50 yards distance from us. He was walking away from us. I called on him to halt. He turned around and looked at me and then continued on. I again challenged him several times. When he had increased his distance to about 75 yards he broke into a run. I myself fired one shot at the civilian who fell.' Patrick (24) had fought for the Munster Fusiliers in the Great War and was suffering from shell-shock. He died in the North Infirmary. He lived with Thomas, his brother, in St Patrick's Square.[287]

## 27 May 1921

### Christopher O'Sullivan

O'Sullivan was shot as a spy. The *Irish Independent* reported that he was taken away on 27 May and riddled with bullets. The source for this was a police report.[288] A subsequent report in the same paper on Tuesday 18 October 1921 stated: 'Mrs. Madeline O'Sullivan, widow, and Mrs. Kate O'Sullivan, mother, applied for compensation for the death of Christopher William O'Sullivan, who was killed on the 27th May near Dennehy's Cross. O'Sullivan was an ex-soldier, and shortly before his death he worked in the Cork Military Barracks as a motor-driver. He earned £3 10s 0d a week, and was in receipt of a pension of £1 per week. He married on the 23rd December last, and had a young widow and his mother, who were dependent on him.'

## 28 May 1921

### Daniel McCarthy

Daniel McCarthy left Ballincollig Barracks, where he had come under suspicion of trying to get information from detainees being held there. McCarthy, who was from Bantry, was later picked up by members of the local IRA, who were waiting for him, and shot at Ovens: 'Another spy named McCarthy, where from we don't know, was with the I.R.A. prisoners in Ballincollig Barracks. He was there about three weeks when we heard from a prisoner to look out for him. We reported the matter to Leo Murphy, who said to arrest him. So one evening he came out of the Barracks and as there was no one around but J. Ahern he had to follow him to the city, on account of having no arms, where he met a Volunteer in Washington Street, Frank O'Donoghue, 1st Battalion, who came with him. They captured the spy in Patrick Street near the Lee Cinema. We walked him to Clarke's Bridge where we got a side car and took him to the old Carrigrohane road. There we met J. Murphy, T. O'Keeffe, D. O'Sullivan and F. O'Sullivan. We sent O'Donoghue back on the side car and we took the spy in a horse and trap to Killumney and handed him over to Leo Murphy and others and in a few weeks after, he was shot by Leo Murphy, Dick Murphy (1st Battalion) and others and was afterwards taken to Ballincollig Barracks and was buried at Carr's Hole, Douglas Road, Cork City. He never spoke a word while a prisoner.' *The Skibbereen Eagle* reported that the body of Daniel McCarthy was found on 28 May next to the post office in Ovens.[289]

## 28 May 1921
### Volunteer Diarmuid (Jeremiah) O'Hurley

Patrick 'Pa' Whelan described what happened: 'On the night of 27th May 1921, Diarmuid [O']Hurley, Jacko O'Connell, Joe Aherne, Tom Buckley (Midleton) and myself were billeted in the townland of Bloomfield, about a mile from Midleton and three miles from Carrigtwohill. Diarmuid, Jos. and I slept in the same bed that night. On the morning of 28th May, Diarmuid learned that an enemy cycle patrol from Cobh had raided several houses in the Carrigtwohill area, and were permitted to return to Cobh unmolested. He was very annoyed at this, particularly as instructions had been issued by him to all company commanders that they should arrange to have Volunteers on duty at all hours, to take any steps in their power to harass the enemy; even if only, in this instance, the roads had been sprinkled with broken glass, to puncture the bikes of the military – anything to keep the nerves of the enemy on edge. Diarmuid considered it more important for himself to go into Carrigtwohill and enquire into this matter rather than keep his appointment with Con Leddy. He, therefore, instructed Tom Buckley and me to go to the meeting at Conna, and he would go into Carrigtwohill.

'On his way to Carrigtwohill, about a mile from Midleton, there is a road junction, one road leading to Carrigtwohill, the other to Lisgould. When in the vicinity of this junction, Diarmuid had the misfortune to run into a foot patrol of R.I.C. and Black and Tans from Midleton. He was armed with a revolver and a Mills grenade. He was recognised by some members of the patrol and called upon to halt. Hurley opened fire on the patrol, threw his grenade, and made a dash for cover alongside a low fence. When he was a few yards from the corner of the fence, he was fatally wounded by a bullet which entered his back, and came out through his stomach. He died where he fell, and, for some reasons best known to themselves, the patrol left his body there and returned to their barracks at Midleton.'[290]

## 28–29 May 1921
## Thomas Fitzgerald
## Henry Fitzgerald

A report from October 1921 reported: 'Brigid Fitzgerald said she was the mother of Thomas and Henry, and lived with them at the railway crossing between Mallow and Killavullen. Thomas, who was married, was gatekeeper, employed by the G. S. and W. Railway Co., and since Henry was demobilised from the army he lived in the house. On the night of the 28th May a knock came to the door. Thomas, thinking he was wanted in connection with the opening of the railway gates, went out. She heard men talking to him, and she asked what they wanted, but got no answer. Tom came upstairs then and said to Henry, who was in bed, "There is a chap here who wants to see you." Henry dressed and went out, and she followed both of them to the door, Tom having gone out before Henry. She heard talking outside, and they then went up the road towards Mallow. She listened as long as she could hear the tramp of feet and she then called Thomas's wife. She got up and they called after Thomas and Henry, but got no answer. They listened then for some time and after a lapse of ten or twelve minutes she heard shots going as quick as possible. "When I heard the shots," she continued, "I got the signal lamp and went up the road, and I found Tom alone in the middle of the high-road, quite dead. The other boy was down the road near Crowe's avenue; he was alive, and lived until three o'clock next day. I asked him who did it and he said they were Sinn Feiners. I asked him what he had done that they had put him there, and he said: "I never did a wrong turn to any man, nor never drank a shilling but my own." Henry was 40 years of age and Thomas 30, and shortly before his death the Government gave Henry £75 to buy a horse and car.' Her solicitor, Mr Carroll, said, 'I am not at all sure that that was not the cause of his death – a wrong impression about what the money came for.'[291]

## 29 May 1921
### John Sullivan Lynch

On 29 May John Sullivan Lynch, who was a parcel clerk for the Great Southern and Western Railway, was 'kidnapped' from his home at Castle Cottage according to his wife, Johanna. On 9 June she was ordered to leave the country. In September she had asked Tom Barry for information about her husband and for permission to return to Ireland, but this was refused. Her solicitor, John Travers Wolfe, was equally unsuccessful that November, but by the time of the probate case in January 1922 she had received a letter from Dáil Éireann 'informing her that it was now pretty definite that John Sullivan Lynch had been tried and executed for spying'. She was also informed that there was no objection to her returning to Cork.

There is equally no doubt about what exactly happened as Tim O'Keeffe told the BMH: 'About the same time a spy named Lynch living on the Carrigrohane road in a house which was also occupied by Patrick O'Sullivan (a brother of Joe, who was executed for the shooting of Sir Henry Wilson) had to go on the run. This man was an Englishman; so J. Ahern and T. O'Keeffe watched his movements and saw him entering the Orderly Room of the Military Barracks on several occasions and reported to Leo Murphy, who informed the Brigade. He was arrested shortly afterwards and shot by "H" Company, 1st Battalion, whose area he was living in. He was buried about 20 yards from the Republican Plot.'[292]

## 29 May 1921
### John O'Connell

Michael Leahy told the BMH: 'On 25th August 1920, the Cobh Company, in charge of Michael Burke, Cobh, brought off a coup at a place known as

"The Quarry" on the eastern outskirts of Cobh. There was a large hut on a piece of waste land near which was a disused quarry. The hut was used by ex-British servicemen and was being dismantled by a military party of about a dozen soldiers. Some Cobh Volunteers noticed what was happening and decided to attack and disarm the soldiers. ...

'Mick Burke got six or eight men together, armed with revolvers. They approached the quarry. A few ... entered a forge which was there. ... Burke and his men suddenly emerged from the forge and ordered the soldiers nearest them to put up their hands. ... A few of the Tommies were inclined to resist. These were fired on and wounded. ... All the Cobh men got back to their homes without harm and none were arrested following the incident.

'A tragic feature of the matter was that, about a year following the event, the owner of the forge in the quarry, a man named O'Connell – well over 60 years of age, was walking along the seafront at Cobh when a patrol of the Cameron Highlanders came along. Gordon Duff, the captain ... drew his revolver and shot dead poor O'Connell. The man (O'Connell) had no part at all in the attack on the Camerons at the quarry.'[293]

### 31 May 1921
### Volunteer Patrick White

At around 6 p.m. prisoner Patrick White reached through the barbed wire surrounding the internment camp at Spike Island to get a ball which had landed just inside it. He was seen by Private H. W. Whitehead of the King's Own Scottish Borders, who occupied No. 2 sentry post. Whitehead fired without warning as were his orders. The court of inquiry file was discussed at the highest levels of the British government in Ireland before General Nevil Macready finally decided that while a more experienced sentry might not have fired without warning, they had been given strict orders to do so. A few weeks earlier a number of IRA members had escaped from the island, so the guards were probably on a hair trigger. Pádraig Óg Ó Ruairc records Thomas Ringrose's recollection of events that day: "'The circumstances were the hurling ball went near the wire and the players shouted to hit back the ball into play as he was nearest to it. The sentinel, a Scottish soldier, was evidently out to have a go and let him have it." Republican prisoners, who had taken part in the game with White, claimed that he had called out to the sentry to return the ball. The British sentry replied, "Come here and get it" and shot White dead when he followed this order. White was buried at the republican plot in his native parish. Thirty-six years after his death, in June 1957, a plaque was unveiled at Spike Island, Cork to mark the spot where Patrick White had been killed.'[294]

## 31 May 1921
**Private Louis Whichlow**
**Private Francis Burke**
**Private Reginald McCall**
**Private Frederick Washington**
**Private Frederick Evans**
**Private George Simmons**
**Private Frederick Hesterman**

Seven members of the Hampshire Regiment were blown up by a new IRA tactic, the remote detonated mine, around 8.20 a.m. The attack took place on Youghal golf course, where the Hampshires had set up a temporary firing range. A further nineteen men were injured.[295] Patrick Whelan provides the details: 'Prior to Sunday, 20th February 1921 – the date of the Clonmult tragedy – Paddy O'Reilly arrived at column headquarters in Clonmult, bringing an empty shell case which he had received from Tom Hyde. He planned to explode a mine under a party of soldiers who regularly went from their barracks in Youghal to a rifle range, about one and a half miles outside the town. Diarmuid Hurley, the column O/C and then O/C of the battalion, agreed to the proposal, and told me to fill the shell case with explosives and instruct Paddy O'Reilly in the use of the exploder. Paddy and I moved to a field, about 100 yards from the column headquarters. I filled the shell with three or four different explosives, including gelignite, and inserted the detonator which, incidentally, had a short lead. The exploder was of the box type, about nine inches square, and electrically controlled by a switch, the 'off' and 'on' positions being indicated. Paddy had a lead of about 150 yards …

'On their way to range practice, the soldiers in Youghal travelled on foot by either of two routes. One was through the Main Street of the town, the other, at the rere [*sic*] of the town (known as the lower and upper route respectively). Tommy and Paddy selected suitable positions to explode the mine on each route, but, on the first three occasions they lay in wait, the military used the other route. On the fourth occasion, the soldiers passed over the route where the mine was concealed. Paddy pressed the switch to "on", when he judged that the main body of troops was marching over, or close to the mine. Several tommies were killed and wounded in the explosion, including some of the regimental band. It appears that Paddy pressed the switch too soon. Had he waited a second or two longer, the effects would surely have been more disastrous, as the troops proper would be in more dense formation than the band. Paddy and Tommy got safely away after the occurrence.'[296] Private Hesterman was just fourteen years old when he was killed.

## 31 May 1921
### John (Patrick) Kenure

John Kenure was a jarvey driver living at Powers Lane, Youghal. At 7.30 a.m. he was asked to take Father Roche to visit a parishioner after first Mass on Sunday. Around 8.45 a.m. he was fired on by a party of the Hampshire Regiment who had shouted at him to stop. He died within a few minutes. Father Roche was injured in the foot. As the military party were more than 500 yards away it is probable that Kenure did not hear the shouts. After what had just happened to their regimental comrades, it is hardly surprising that the Hampshires were firing at anything that moved, no matter how illegal their actions might have been.[297]

**May 1921 (date uncertain)**

**James Saunders**

Tim Sexton recalled: 'In May, 1921, a Volunteer named Davy Flynn, who was a carter, met a man named Saunders on the road, who inquired for the names of farmers likely to give him employment. Flynn sent him to me, telling him that I would be able to direct him. While in conversation with the stranger – Saunders – being a shoemaker, the first thing I observed about him was that he was wearing a pair of British army boots which were new. As I was much taller than he was, I observed a tab on the collar of his shirt which showed that it was also issued by the army authorities. After delaying him for some time, I had him arrested by Volunteers James McKeown, Tim Owens and Denis Leahy, who took him to John Murphy's of Bohard. A day or so later he was court-martialled by members of the Brigade Staff. He confessed to having an appointment with the military a day or two after his arrival in our area. He also confessed to having informed the enemy of the Mourneabbey ambush and was responsible for the arrest of a number of Volunteers at Killeens. He was sentenced to death, executed and buried in a nearby bog. The body was subsequently disinterred and buried elsewhere.'[298]

**1 June 1921**

**Lieutenant Colonel (retired) Warren John Peacocke**

Warren Peacocke's death was discussed in the House of Commons on 2 June 1921 and Hamar Greenwood suggested: 'The only motive that I know is that this gallant officer was a loyalist and an ex-officer of His Majesty's Army.' When questioned by Lieutenant Colonel Willoughby, who asked if 'this officer was known to have ever given any information to the Government as to any action of the Sinn Féin party?', Greenwood replied, 'He had no connection whatever with the Government or any public office, or with any political movement in the county in which he lived.'[299]

Once again a BMH witness statement provides exceptional detail from one of the men who actually carried out the shooting as to why Peacocke was targeted and how he was killed: 'I think it was on June 1st 1921 that Lieut-Colonel Peacocke a "retired" British army officer who resided at Innishannon, was shot. He had been operating in the area as an intelligence agent and had guided raiding parties of military in the area. His identity had been established some time prior to Xmas 1920, when during the course of a raid the mask which he always wore on such occasions slipped. From the date of this incident, Peacocke lived in Bandon military barracks and only visited his home in Innishannon on odd occasions. Information was received on May 31st (I think) that he had been seen at his home. Tom Kelleher and Jim Ryan – two members of the Column – were sent to Innishannon to shoot Peacocke. They were scouted by Jack Murphy, Ml. McCarthy and Tom O'Sullivan of the local company (Innishannon). The men detailed to carry out the shooting (Tom Kelleher and Jim Ryan) hid in the laurels outside the house, and when Peacocke came to the hall door he was approached by them. He attempted to draw his gun but was shot by our men, who were fired on by Peacocke's guard of Black and Tans. Our men, including scouts, withdrew without casualties and returned to their H.Q. in Crosspound area.'[300]

## 1 June 1921

### Constable Joseph Holman

Constable Holman (21) was shot at Kilworth. He was walking with his girlfriend near the village when a single shot was fired at them from trees at the side. He was obviously shot by a shotgun as he was wounded in the face, neck and chest. His girlfriend, who was closer to the gunman than Holman, was only slightly injured as the gunman had fired over her head. Holman had just enough time to draw his revolver before he died. He was from Sussex.[301]

## 5 June 1921

### Edwin (Eugene) Swanton

The *Irish Independent* of 8 June quoted a Dublin Castle announcement that Eugene Swanton had been taken from his home at Ballinacurra, Midleton at 1 a.m. on the previous Sunday and 'had not been seen or heard of since'.[302] His body has never been recovered.

**5 June 1921**
**Bandsman Matthew Carson**
**Bandsman Charles Chapman**
**Bandsman John Cooper**

There is no doubt about what happened to these three soldiers of the Manchester Regiment. All three were members of the military band and had gone for a walk. Tim O'Keeffe told the BMH: 'In June, 1921, with a squad from Srelane Company I captured three British soldiers of the Essex Regiment after a chase from Ovens. We found them hiding in Kilcrea Abbey. They surrendered without a fight. They had been detailed from a special branch [this is incorrect] organised by the infamous Major Percival, who had committed many wanton murders in West Cork. Our Brigade H.Q. had the three Essex Regiment men shot.' They were shot as suspected spies. In August 1923 Matthew Carson's father found the three bodies in a disused house south of Aherla. He had the remains coffined and taken to Bandon, where they were buried. In September 1924 the remains were taken back to England and buried together in Ashton under Lyne.[303]

**5 June 1921**
**Daniel O'Riordan**
**8 June 1921**
**Seán Jeremiah Kelleher**

O'Riordan was shot at Carrigaphooca by British forces and Kelleher was shot in Ballyvourney according to Jamie Moynihan. The court of inquiry was told by the Cameron Highlanders that they had challenged O'Riordan, who was watching them, but 'failed to get any intelligent reply from him'. They were repairing Carrigaphooca Bridge on the way to Ballyvourney. From the report it appears that Lieutenant J. F. McIntyre was only yards away when he shouted at O'Riordan, who began to walk off. McIntyre opened fire and ordered his men to do likewise. O'Riordan's body was riddled with bullets and he died instantly. There was no further inquiry but on a 'blue form' it was stated that he was a captain in the IRA, which was incorrect. Locals described him as an 'innocent', meaning he could not have understood the danger he was in.

The *Irish Independent* of 14 June reported the death of John [*sic*] Kelleher (65), Shanacloon, Ballyvourney on 9 [*sic*] June in the Mercy Hospital, Cork. He had been wounded on 5 June by crown forces. The court of inquiry in his case heard evidence from the same party of Cameron Highlanders, who stated they arrived in the village of Ballymakeera around 6.30 p.m. According to them they saw two lines of men drawn up in formation. They advanced and the men ran away. They fired after them and were fired on. When they reached the spot they found Seán Kelleher shot in the abdomen. The court found that he had been shot in crossfire. The only problem is that there are no BMH, newspaper or Irish military records of this supposed incident, beyond a mention of the shooting and death of Kelleher.[304]

## 8 June 1921
### Volunteer Daniel Buckley

Major Halahan of the Essex Regiment was leading a raiding party from Percival's flying column through Toames, Macroom. His troops were on their way home from an unsuccessful round-up when they saw a man near a farmhouse. Halahan heard a shot and saw the man running towards the farmhouse through his binoculars. About 20 yards from the farm he fell to the ground, dead. Buckley's father stated that he had sent him out to get water, although the military suggested that the bucket found 20 yards from his body on the other side of a fence was in fact being used by his sister to milk a cow. However, Charles Browne presented a very different picture of these events: 'On June 4th the Brigade O.C., Seán Hegarty, moved into "J" Company area and contacted Battalion H.Q. at Delaneys, Toames. He remained there until the night of June 8th. On this evening the raiding parties to the West returned to their bases and among them was Major Percival's Flying Column of 140 men of the Essex Regiment stationed at Bandon. This Column operated with field kitchens and travelled on foot, often crossing country with one platoon of forty men mounted on cycles. These acted as flankers, using parallel roads to the main body. They arrived at Toames about 6 p.m. on the 8th and opened fire at Sonny Buckley, a Volunteer of "J" Company, who was running to warn Battalion H.Q. of their proximity. He was killed and the firing being heard by the Brigade O.C., the Battalion O.C. and the writer, we had to gather up our papers and beat a hasty retreat.' Buckley was almost nineteen.[305]

## 8 June 1921
### Private Henry Woods
Private Woods of the Royal Fusiliers was guarding a train at Blarney Railway Station when his rifle accidentally discharged and he was shot through the heart. He died shortly afterwards. There is no other information and he has not been traced in British military records.[306]

## 8 June 1921
### Daniel Crowley
Around twenty members of 'O' Company of the Auxiliaries stationed in Dunmanway launched a night-time raid on the farm of J. P. Crowley at Behagullane a few miles outside the town. His son Tim was a member of the IRA and the raid was to capture him. Daniel (30), another son, who was living in the family home, rushed around a corner of the house and was shot six times in the head, body and shins.[307]

## 9 June 1921
### David Fitzgibbon
The local curate heard a rumour that the body of David Fitzgibbon was on

the road at Killinane just to the west of Liscarroll. He went to investigate and quickly found the body, which was then wrapped in a white sheet and taken to the house of Fitzgibbon's aunt, where he had lived. Fitzgibbon was a widower with five children, the eldest of whom was twelve or thirteen. He had been blindfolded and his legs and hands tied. A note on the body stated 'Spies beware this body must not be touched'. It was signed 'IRA'. This killing provoked an angry reaction from Lieutenant F. C. Sherwood, the Kerry Brigade's intelligence officer, who stated that Fitzgibbon was 'the only member of his family (which are all rank Sinn Feiners) who refused to have anything to do with the IRA and for that reason alone he was considered "in the way"'. Sherwood continued that he was absolutely certain that the death was 'engineered by the IRA' and that the IRA was shooting innocent people to advertise the success of its 'intelligence' service and to cover up the fact that it had failed to locate any spies or informers.[308]

## 9 June 1921
## Thomas O'Keeffe

At 5.15 p.m. on Tuesday 9 June two young men left Blackpool in Cork city and walked up Spring Lane. They were sitting on the grass in a field by Victoria Barracks when they were ordered away. As they were moving off a rifle was discharged and Thomas O'Keeffe of 8 Corporation Buildings, Blackpool, was shot. Father Tierney of St Joseph's, Mayfield, was sent for and anointed the dying man, who died where he fell. There is no record of an inquiry.[309]

## 11 June 1921
## John Lucey

One of the difficulties with imposing martial law on a civilian population is that inevitably many either do not take it seriously or do not understand what is required. Imposing an 8 p.m. curfew in a country where the sun does not set until 10 p.m. in June was ridiculous. It was also clearly counter-productive, as it drove the population into the arms of the insurgency. John Lucey was playing with a mouse on a street corner for the entertainment of a group of young men. They were fired on by the curfew patrol and Lucey was shot in the chest. He was rushed on the shoulders of his comrades to the nearby North Infirmary, but was dead on arrival.[310]

## 12 June 1921
### Volunteer Matt O'Donovan

Charles Browne of the Macroom IRA was captured by Major Percival's flying column shortly after the near capture of the Cork No. 1 Brigade headquarters and O/C Seán O'Hegarty at Toames. He recalled: 'We were held by the Column for two days at Sweeney's farmhouse, Gurranereagh, and then we marched via Newcestown and Quarry Cross to Bandon which we reached on Friday, 12th. When passing by Quarry Cross one of Percival's officers interrogated a cottier named Mat Donovan [*sic*] and shot him dead.' According to Charlie O'Donoghue, O'Donovan was a member of the Quarries Cross Company. In March the following year Matt O'Donovan's wife sought compensation of £2,000 for the 'murder of her husband'. It was stated at the time of the shooting that he had failed to obey an order to halt.[311]

## 13 June 1921
### Michael Driscoll

*The Cork Examiner* reported that Driscoll was found with a bullet wound in the thigh. He had bled to death. His body was found at Waterlands about a mile from Kinsale. He was almost nude when found and the report stated that he was 'weak minded'. On the same day Major Halahan of the Essex Regiment organised a court of inquiry to discover what had happened. It transpired that Lieutenant Bowen of the Essex Regiment was in charge of a patrol near Charles Fort when he was told that two civilians had been spotted by troops on the left flank (near the military playing fields). When he went to investigate he heard a shot behind him and found Driscoll had been shot in the thigh. According to the soldier who shot him, Driscoll had attacked him with a stick, so he shot him in self-defence. The medical evidence stated that he was shot while running or lying on the ground. According to the evidence he had 'spent two years in a lunatic asylum'. The body was found the following morning propped up against a hedge even though the front gate of the Essex headquarters at Charles Fort was only across the road.[312]

## 14 June 1921
## Leo Corby

On 11 March 1922 the *Irish Independent* reported: 'Today, in the Probate Division Mr. Justice Dodd, in the case of the goods of Corby, deceased, Mr Philip O'Donoghue applied on behalf of Dr. Henry Corby, of Queen Street, Cork, to presume the death of his son, Leo Corby, dentist, and for a grant of administration. Counsel said the deceased was a bachelor and died intestate. He had had dental chambers at 2, Queen Street, Cork, where he practiced. It was his custom to go to Cashel as he had a branch practice on Thursdays, on his motor bicycle, returning on the following Sunday. On Thursday, 11th June last he left Cork for Cashel. Dr. Corby was informed, and believed, that he arrived at his place of business in Cashel, and left afterwards for Cork again on Sunday. He was last seen to pass through Mitchelstown, but no motor bicycle passed through Kilworth that day. On the 11th July, 1921, Dr. Corby received a letter from "Headquarters, First Southern Division" and signed "Commandant." which set out that his son had been observed passing through a certain area and it was decided that he should be "halted" and examined. He failed to respond to the order to halt and was fired at. A permit and a photograph from the military authorities were found in his pocket. The letter added the remains were afterwards "buried in a good coffin and shroud in a Roman Catholic cemetery." Subsequently, Dr. Corby was conducted to the Ballyhooly graveyard, where his son was buried. The application was granted.'[313]

## 15 June 1921 (date uncertain)
## Private F. Roughley

Approximately ten days after the shooting of the Manchester Regiment bandsmen captured at Kilcrea Friary, another member of the regiment went missing. A number of years later the intelligence officer of the new Irish Army in Cork reported that they had found a body and that he was trying to confirm that it was Roughley, which apparently it was. Little else is known.[314]

## 16 June 1921
## Auxiliary William Boyd
## Auxiliary Frederick Shorter

According to Millstreet.ie: 'The railway line between Banteer and Millstreet had been cut in several places so the Auxiliary forces based at Millstreet had to travel to Banteer by road for their supplies a couple of times every week. Therefore, a combined force of 130 men were mobilised to attack the Auxiliaries as they returned from Banteer. The volunteers were from the Millstreet, Kanturk, Newmarket, Charleville and Mallow battalion columns in the second division area and were under the command of Paddy O'Brien from Liscarroll.

'On the night before the ambush the I.R.A. volunteers slept at Rathcoole Wood, which overlooked the planned ambush position. Shortly after sunrise the following morning, Captain Dan Vaughan laid six landmines on the untarred road and covered them with dust. After a wait of several hours a convoy of four armour-plated lorries, each mounted with a machine gun and carrying ten men, was observed heading for Banteer. The volunteers prepared and at 6.20 in the evening, as the lorries passed through the ambush area on their return journey, three of the landmines which had been placed on the road exploded with devastating results. One mine detonated as the last of the four lorries drove over it, another exploded under the leading lorry in the convoy. Both vehicles were out of action with the two other lorries were [*sic*] trapped between them. A third mine exploded amid a party of Auxiliaries as they attempted to outflank the position. A bitter firefight developed. Each time Auxiliaries tried to outflank the I.R.A. they were driven back, suffering losses of more than twenty dead and over a dozen wounded.'

In fact, the only deaths were the two members of 'L' Company, Shorter and Boyd, both from Sussex, both twenty-one and both unmarried. Both had been shot in the head and died instantly.[315]

## 18 June 1921
### Josie Scannell

The incident that led to the death of Josie Scannell began when Patrick 'Pa' Murray decided to attack the police: '... our intelligence officers were constantly engaged in trying to find out the movements of the police. We noticed that they congregated outside the different barracks for a short time in the evenings, and decided to attack them in Tuckey Street and Shandon Street barracks. To do this, we got two motor cars. Members of the A.S.U. drove the cars and were accompanied by three men in each car. We decided to concentrate on Tuckey Street. The operation was timed so that the barracks would be attacked simultaneously. A number of Volunteers were organised to try and rush Tuckey Street after the bombs had been thrown by the men from the motor cars. Unfortunately, however, the driver of the car attacking Tuckey Street had some trouble with the motor, and drove the car to the attack about two minutes before the agreed time. As a result of this, some thirty or forty Volunteers, who were leaving their own points to converge on Tuckey Street, heard the bombs before they were in a position to attack. I was in charge of these particular bodies and withdrew them. The men in the car threw some three or four bombs, and wounded several of the Tans.'[316]

Josie Scannell was killed by a bullet which came through her window and hit her in the chest on French's Quay, where she worked as a seamstress. The Auxiliaries and military denied responsibility but admitted to firing after a car which had thrown a grenade at nearby Tuckey Street police station. Also injured were Mrs O'Connor and her children May (13 months) and

Molly (12). Hugh Murray, May Murray, Denis Lenihan and Railway Guard Sheehy were also wounded following firing that went on for thirty minutes after the attack.[317]

## 21 June 1921
### Daniel O'Callaghan

*The Freeman's Journal* of 23 June 1921 reported that O'Callaghan 'had been taken from his house on Tuesday night by two men who shot him outside. He died the following morning in Cove [*sic*] Hospital.' Although he cannot remember the exact date, Thomas Cotter stated that he and other members of the local IRA company shot Dan O'Callaghan (30) as a spy in Carrigtwohill. O'Callaghan's cousin Kate Foley told the court of inquiry that minutes before his death he had told her that he was wanted 'as a spy and he was intending to seek protection from the military'. A couple of minutes later two men went to his house and dragged him out to a waiting horse and trap. As they drove off he managed to punch one of the men and escape. They followed him down the laneway beside his house, firing as they went and he collapsed. They shot him in the head, but according to the medical evidence they only grazed his chin. He died at 6.30 a.m. in the military hospital in Cobh the following morning from a gunshot wound in the abdomen. He was single and had recently worked in Haulbowline. A note on the file by the Hampshire Regiment stated that for compensation purposes the man was loyal.[318]

## 22 June 1921
### Volunteer John Murphy

Seán Hales was a senior commander of the IRA from Ballinadee. His brother Tom had been O/C of No. 3 (West Cork) Brigade before his capture and torture in June 1921. The Hales family had a long involvement in 'advanced nationalist' politics and Terence MacSwiney had been arrested in their home after the 1916 rebellion. John Murphy (22) was working on their farm when it was raided by the military. There was no court of inquiry, but initial newspaper reports stated that he had been shot in the neck. However, *The Southern Star* reported that he had actually been bayonetted to death and such was the condition of the body that his friends had buried him immediately.[319]

## 22 June 1921
### Auxiliary George Duckham

George Duckham was returning to Macroom from leave when he was shot at Carriganima and buried in the bog. Daniel Corkery was a little put out: 'A lone Black and Tan was shot by some members of the local company on the Macroom–Millstreet road about the end of June, 1921, and his arms were taken. His body was left on the roadside in the neighbourhood of Carriganima in the hope that his colleagues would come to collect it, while I lay in ambush with the Battalion Column close by. The body was, however, removed by some local people and buried.'[320]

Tim Buckley provides the essential details: 'About mid June I was one of a section of five or six who spent five or six days in ambush positions about 1½ miles from Macroom waiting to attack an officer of the Auxiliaries stationed in Macroom Castle. While I was engaged on this job, I got a report from Macroom that a Black and Tan – a member of Millstreet garrison – was to travel by horse and side-car back to his base next morning. As I could not withdraw from the position we held near the town, I got four or five members of the company (Clondrohid) to hold him up. They were armed with shotguns and when the Tan came along they held him up and took him prisoner. As he had a bad record, he was shot that night. Amongst the men who captured this Tan were:– Jim Twohig, Lackaduv, who was in charge; John Riordan, Jerh. Dineen; Tim Murphy and Paddy Carroll acted as scouts. When this prisoner was searched, a list of names of the members of the Millstreet Battalion Column, who were to be shot at sight, was found on him. He is buried in Clashmaguire Bog.' On 4 July 1921 *The Freeman's Journal* reported that Constable Duckham's father had received a letter saying that his kidnapped son had been tried and executed. Duckham's body was never found.[321]

## 24 June 1921
## Michael Dineen

Two days after the 'disappearance' of Constable Duckham there was another shooting in the locality. The British had changed tactics again and were now using massive forces to 'sweep' areas, question every male and arrest anyone who could not fully satisfy them about their identity or movements. This policy led to a dramatic increase in internments but often the people captured were civilians. About 7 a.m. on Friday 24 June Michael Dineen of Ivale, Kilcorney, Millstreet, was accused by a group of Auxiliaries raiding his home of being an IRA officer and being involved in the Rathcoole ambush a week before. He was taken out of his home, beaten and shot. According to his brother's statement, he had no involvement with the IRA. Notably, there is no record of this murder in official reports or any of the newspapers, though there is no doubt about the guilty parties and there is a death certificate.[322]

## 26 June 1921
## Mary Parnell

Mary Parnell was a war widow. The *Irish Independent* suggested she was shot but not killed, but this was not true. When John Twomey of North Main Street Cork was being removed from Cork Bridewell to the military barracks he attempted to escape. He ran in the direction of Kyle Street and shots were fired after him. He ran into Bradley's public house. Constable Joseph Strange followed him and he was recaptured inside the pub. He had been wounded in several places. Mrs Parnell (30) was killed when hit by a bullet fired at Twomey. She had fallen into the doorway of the pub. The shooting took place around 8.15 p.m., after curfew, and according to the court of inquiry it was therefore her fault that she was shot accidentally.[323]

## 26 June 1921
## Constable Thomas Shanley

Shanley was one of two RIC constables shot at point-blank range in Kildorrery (not Kilbrittain as the vague reports in some of the newspapers suggested). The matter was raised in the House of Commons by Lieutenant Colonel Archer-Shee, who 'asked the Chief Secretary if he has any information with reference to the murder of ... Constable Shanley, murdered, and Sergeant Ryan, wounded, when returning from mass at Kildorrery, County Cork on 30 [*sic*] June 1921'? Greenwood had no answer, but what actually happened was that both men were walking in the middle of the road to ensure they were not attacked when they were fired on from behind. Ryan could not get his revolver out of his pocket and his auxiliary revolver was damaged by a bullet so he was effectively defenceless. Shanley had been wounded and was lying on his back in the middle of the road and according to one of the witnesses, Shea, he was shot three times by a man standing over him. The medical evidence does not confirm or refute this.[324]

## 27 June 1921

### Private Frederick Crowther

Yet again some soldiers out for a walk were picked up by the local IRA and taken away to be shot. The three were all privates in the Staffordshire Regiment, who were captured around Dillon's Cross and marched out into the countryside. Private Spooner made a successful bid to escape but Private Evans and Private Crowther were both shot. Crowther (25) died of his wounds and his body was returned to Heath, Staffordshire for burial. Evans survived.[325]

## 27 June 1921

### Volunteer Walter Leo Murphy

One surprising item of the court of inquiry into Leo Murphy's death, was the amount of detailed information that the British had about him. The official notice sent to Dublin Castle correctly identifies his rank and states that 'he was wanted for the kidnapping of Lieutenants Chambers, Green and Watts' at Waterfall; the 'murders of Captain Thompson and of Daniel McCarthy' and being 'present at the ambush in which Sergeant Bloxham was killed'. Major Evans of the Manchester Regiment told the court that Murphy had burst past him in the doorway of Mrs Donovan's public house in Waterfall and run down the road in an attempt to escape. His first six shots missed, but he reloaded and managed to shoot Murphy in the back, killing him. The time was 10.30 p.m. and it seems that the Manchesters had been looking for him all day after a tip-off. Murphy (25) was a senior commander of the IRA and had been on the run from as early as 1919. He was from Ballincollig and the barracks there was subsequently named after him.[326]

## 28 June 1921
### Volunteer Charles James Daly

Charlie Daly was captured at Waterfall in the raid during which Leo Murphy was shot. He was identified at Ballincollig and taken to Victoria Barracks. According to Military Cross winner Lieutenant Hammond of the Dorset Regiment, intelligence officer, at 10 p.m. he challenged Daly about the murder of Lance Corporal Hodnett, who was shot on 28 February 1921. Hammond stated that Daly started to cry and 'admitted to me that he was the Captain, "D" Company, 2nd Bn., 1st Brigade, IRA'. Hammond continued that at 11.30 p.m. he again questioned Daly, who offered to show him an arms dump. After further questioning they left with Captain Charles Humphreys Ricketts of the South Staffordshire Regiment and headed to Douglas. They arrived at a wooded area near Mount Vernon and Daly pointed out a clump of trees. Ricketts and a soldier went to investigate and turned around to see Daly running. According to his evidence Hammond fired, rushed after Daly and fired again. Daly fell, shot through the abdomen and head. The doctor recorded that Daly had a 'contusion of the right eye' and that the bullet to the head must have been fired at 'fairly close range'. The black eye must have been spectacular as every single soldier who gave evidence from the time of his capture at Waterfall, through to his eventual death, specifically remarked on it. The IRA dismissed Hammond's story and claimed that Daly had been summarily executed by the lieutenant after being beaten. It does seem incredible that two British officers would have thought it intelligent to go traipsing around a wood after midnight looking for an arms dump, when all they had to do was wait for first light at 3.30 a.m.[327]

## 28 June 1921
## William Horgan

The *Irish Independent* of 30 June 1921 states that Horgan was killed early on the morning of 28 June outside the Opera House in Cork city. He and another man called 'Lenihan' from Dillon's Cross had been arrested at their homes earlier in the evening in a raid by the South Staffordshire Regiment as a result of the killing of Private Crowther. The raid had taken place at 2.15 a.m. According to Lieutenant A. F. d'Ydewalle, their lorry had broken down on the way to the Bridewell RIC station. Apparently, the soldiers decided to search the two men and the officer was reading papers found on Horgan by the light of the gas lamp. While he was distracted Horgan attempted to escape by grabbing his revolver. After a short struggle Horgan was shot. The second man 'ran like a hare' down the quay and escaped. A second soldier corroborated the story. There were no other witnesses. Lavitt's Quay is within sight of the Bridewell. Horgan (29) worked as a fireman for the Great Southern and Western Railway and lived with his parents at 254 Dillon's Cross. The official report to Dublin Castle stated that he was a member of the IRA, but he does not appear on IRA membership lists.[328]

## 29 June 1921
## John Sullivan/O'Sullivan
## Patrick J. Sheehan

BMH WS 754 recorded: 'Sometime about May, 1921, two locals named Patrick J. Sheehan and a John O'Sullivan [*sic*] (nicknamed "Slag") came under grave suspicion of giving information to the enemy and were acting as spies, and had been used by the enemy as "stool-pigeons" by being placed in with

IRA prisoners in Tipperary town and Kildorney. The first information we obtained concerning them was from a Johnny White (since dead) who was catching a pony one night in a field at the rear of the R.I.C. barracks and saw Sheehan and Sullivan getting out very furtively over the barrack wall. The following day a Corporal Pepper, who was one of the garrison intelligence staff and who was practically always dressed in "civvies", warned White to keep his mouth shut regarding Sheehan and Sullivan coming from the barracks. Subsequently when the R.I.C. shifted quarters to another part of the town, a Volunteer named Joe Nagle, who had a harness shop near the barracks, saw the two boyos coming from the barracks. On another occasion Mick Geary and a Johnny Higgins saw them coming from the barracks. Confirmation was also obtained about them being used as "stool-pigeons" and, in fact, information was obtained from one of our lads working on the railway that Sheehan actually travelled from Charleville to Tipperary on an enemy rail warrant. Furthermore, in one of our raids on the mails a money order (I forget the amount) was caught addressed to a Mrs. Murphy in town and we were satisfied that this was for Sheehan as he was a frequent visitor to her house.

'It was decided in early June to arrest both of them, and about mid June Sullivan was arrested. Following Sullivan's arrest Sheehan did not stir out for at least a fortnight and then one day he took a chance of delivering a load of coal a few miles from the town when he was arrested. On arrest he collapsed completely and had to be bodily lifted over a hedge into a field. In the meantime while Sullivan was under arrest he admitted giving information to the enemy. Sheehan was a brainy and dangerous individual but Sullivan was almost an illiterate.

'They were both tried by Courtmartial at which the Battalion O.C. (Jim Brislane) presided, and the Brigade O.C. (Liam Lynch) who happened to be in our area at the time was present at the trial. Mick Geary and Tom Lyons of Buttevant gave evidence at the trial and both the accused were sentenced to death, which sentence was duly carried out on June 29th, 1921. They were attended by a priest immediately prior to the execution.'

Sheehan was twenty-five and John Sullivan was seventeen. Both lived in Charleville.[329]

## 29 June 1921
## Timothy (Patrick) Murphy

Timothy Murphy lived at 24 Blarney Street. Around 11 p.m. he was walking through Old Market Square, metres from his home, when a curfew patrol rounded the corner. He was ordered to halt but ran away and Corporal Finch of the South Staffordshire Regiment opened fire, killing him. When they searched the body they found army pension papers in the name of Jeremiah Mullane. Murphy had joined the South Irish Horse in the British Army in 1914 under that name. He was twenty-two when he died so would have been barely sixteen, if that, when he signed up during the Great War.[330]

## 30 June 1921
## Frank Sullivan

James 'Spud' Murphy, although getting the name wrong, recalled the events around Frank Sullivan's execution: 'Late in June 1921, Jim Hurley (Battalion O/C), Tim Donoghue, (Vice O/C) and I went to Rosscarbery to execute a spy named Frank O'Donoghue [sic]. This man had previously been working for Miss Whitley whose house had been burned after the attack on Burgatia House because of the part played by her in conveying information to the enemy regarding our occupation of Burgatia.

'The battalion staff had obtained definite information that this man had informed the Auxiliaries of the whereabouts of Jim Lane and myself on the occasion when we had to spend a day and a night in the potato garden. We had met him on that occasion in Regan's public-house and, when he left, it appears that he told the enemy of our presence in Rosscarbery. When we called to his house we were informed that he was in bed. We asked to see him in connection with the Rosscarbery Band and he came down to us. After a severe cross-examination, he admitted that he had informed the enemy of the whereabouts of Jim Lane and myself on the night mentioned above. We procured a priest to hear his confession and then executed him.' Sullivan's death was also reported in *The Skibbereen Eagle*.[331]

## 30 June 1921
### Bernard Moynihan

Little or nothing is mentioned about the death of Bernard Moynihan in any of the surviving documents. On 2 July a very brief report in *The Freeman's Journal* stated that as the Auxiliaries were passing Rathcoole Wood, Mill-street, a bomb was thrown at them. They shot dead the assailant, whom they claimed was Bernard Moynihan. He was shot dead on Rathcoole Bridge. If the story were true, his would have been an entirely reckless act, as the Auxiliaries had been attacked from the same wood only two weeks previously and were in the process of burning it on that Sunday – it was tinder dry from the extraordinary drought that had gripped the country since February. Local history states that Moynihan (19) was actually cutting hay when he was shot from a passing lorry. He was from Shankill, Kilcorney, and was the only son of Cornelius Moynihan.[332]

## June 1921 (date uncertain)
### Private John J. Walsh

The body of John J. Walsh was found in a drain south of Midleton in 1927. Rosary beads were found in his hand and a revolver casing beside the body. He appears to have gone missing in June 1921. Nothing is known about this shooting and it does not appear in the BMH witness statements or in the MSPC records. If the newspaper report is accurate he was a 'reserve' member of the British Army and was working as a labourer at the time of his death.[333]

## 1 July 1921 (date uncertain)
### Volunteer Batt Hegarty

Timothy Sexton told the BMH: 'Apart from the trenching of roads, there was little activity from then [May] to the Truce. Following the trenching of the roads one night, Volunteer Batt. Hegarty was killed by falling into one of the road trenches. He was buried with military honours.'[334]

## 3 July 1921
### Maurice Cusack

Some newspapers stated that the victim's name was Richard, but this was incorrect.[335] John Cusack (75) was sitting on the hill above his home in Ballycotton on the evening of Sunday 3 July 1921, when his son Maurice (41), a naval pensioner and 'privately against Sinn Féin' according to his father, came out of the house to fetch him. A military patrol had stopped just short of the village. As Maurice climbed up the steep hill, shots rang out and he was wounded. The military evidence is confused about whether he was waving a white handkerchief to signal to men at the top of the hill, but none was found at the scene. Evidence about whether a group of men was on the hillside was equally confused, with Lieutenants Rankin and Hannay of the Cameron Highlanders saying there was, but the enlisted men demurring. Bridget Sliney, Maurice's sister, agreed with the enlisted men, as did his father. However, the court found that, as the patrol had already been the victim of a mine attack, the men were entitled to be very suspicious and that Cusack should have known that waving and walking away from a military patrol more than 200 yards away was a very dangerous thing to do. Apparently he didn't and died for it.[336]

## 7 July 1921
### Constable James Connor

Sergeant Patrick Lavelle, stationed at Ballinhassig, heard three shots outside the police barracks and with two other constables went to investigate. When they went outside fire was directed at them and they retreated inside their fortress. The firing ceased after around five minutes and they again went outside. Lavelle then noticed that Constable Connor was missing and they went to search for him. They found his body a short distance away at Ripsdale. He had two bullet wounds from a rifle or revolver, and his body was also riddled with shotgun pellets. Connor had not been on duty but had been in uniform. His revolver and ammunition had been taken. He was married and was the father of two children.[337]

## 7 July 1921
### William McPherson

The court of inquiry heard that William McPherson had returned to Mallow in April 1921 after twenty-four years' service in the Royal Dublin Fusiliers and the Royal Engineers. He had picked up a chronic disease in India and this, according to his wife, required him to be outdoors. At 8 a.m. on 7 July he was kidnapped on Mallow Bridge and bundled into a horse and trap, which took off at speed down Broom Lane. Shortly before 8 a.m. the following day the local chemist, Dominic O'Connell, was exercising his horse along the Knockpogue Road to the south of the town when he found McPherson's body in a sitting position against an embankment. He had been shot dead. A local man, William O'Keeffe, told the RIC that David Barrow of Scarra, Dromahane, was one of the men who took McPherson, and the court of inquiry stated that he was at least an accessory before the murder. Many years later Cornelius O'Regan corroborated all this in his BMH witness statement and said that McPherson was tried by the battalion staff, found guilty of spying and shot.[338]

## 8 July 1921
### Volunteer Denis Spriggs

Pádraig Óg Ó Ruairc, who has researched the eve of Truce killings, explains what happened to Spriggs: 'A few hours after the Truce was announced, the British military abducted and killed an IRA Volunteer named Denis Spriggs. Spriggs, who was twenty years old and a plasterer and slater by trade, was a member of C Company, 1st Battalion of the IRA's Cork No. 1

Brigade. Spriggs' family home in Strawberry Hill, on the northern side of Cork city, was raided by the 2nd Battalion, South Staffordshire Regiment about midnight on 8 July. According to the British military inquest into the killing, the British Army had planned the raid, having received specific intelligence information, and had launched the operation specifically to capture Spriggs. Spriggs was asleep in his bed when the raid began. He was unarmed and, on being confronted, immediately surrendered to the raiders without offering any resistance. Second Lieutenant A. d'Ydewalle told the military inquest that Spriggs had been shot dead while attempting to escape.' Lieutenant d'Ydewalle, the officer who led the raid, told the court of inquiry that as the raiding party was descending Blarney Road the tailboard of the truck fell backwards and Spriggs ran. However, d'Ydewalle, had a history of involvement in the killing of unarmed prisoners and the likelihood is that Spriggs' killing was a premeditated and deliberate act. D'Ydewalle was criticised by GHQ for not securing the prisoner correctly and thus making it easy for him to escape.[339]

## 10 July 1921
### John Foley

Jamie Moynihan mentions the death of Foley, stating it happened at Coachford, but gives no further details. Foley from Leemount, Coachford, was killed by Private Smith of the West Yorkshire Regiment during a search operation. Every man between the ages of fifteen and forty-five found in any house was now being arrested. According to Smith, members of the regiment raided the Foley home at 6 a.m. but the door was barred. Along with Lance Corporal Pearson, Smith smashed in the door. The Foley family retreated to the bedroom. Smith got caught on the wrong side of the bedroom door with John Foley holding onto his rifle. Pearson managed to smash in the bedroom door and, as Foley ran at them, Smith shot him dead. Locals dismiss this version and state that Foley was shot in the back when he turned to put on his coat. In August 2015 a memorial was erected at his former home.[340]

## 10 July 1921
### Private Edward Larter

On Sunday 10 July Edward Larter (19) went for a walk. As he neared Doneraile he was captured by the local IRA. He was unarmed. William Regan told the BMH: 'On July 10, 1921, the Battalion Vice. O/C. (Patk. J. Luddy) in conjunction with the O/C. of the sub-battalion O/C. [*sic*] (Wm. Roche) at Mitchelstown, carried out an attack on a party of British military at Mitchelstown. The enemy party suffered a number of casualties while two members of the I.R.A. party were wounded. On the same date a British soldier was captured in the Doneraile area and executed in the vicinity of Ballyvonaire Camp.' The *Irish Independent* of 12 July says he was shot at Doneraile, which is a few miles east of Buttevant. He is buried in Swainsthorpe, Norwich, next to his brother who was killed in France in 1916.[341]

## 10 July 1921
### Lance Corporal Harold Daker
### Private Henry Morris
### Royal Engineer Alfred Camm
### Royal Engineer Albert Powell

Connie Neenan, the senior IRA officer in the area, was horrified by the deaths of these soldiers. He later stated: 'The night before the Truce, on July 10th … my mother brought me news about midnight that 4 young British soldiers had just been taken prisoner by our fellows. I felt alarmed. They were, I suppose, out for the first time in months with their guard down. One of them had gone into a shop to buy sweets. I gathered a group and we searched the fields from here to Togher. Around 2 a.m. we met some of our lads who told us the news was bad. I was astounded. Surely no one would shoot anyone at a time like this? I crept into a house, exhausted and filled with remorse.'[342]

Pádraig Óg Ó Ruairc writes: 'The verifiable facts are that all four soldiers left the British Army post at Cork jail on 10 July. They were travelling on foot and were unarmed. At 8 p.m. they were captured by a patrol of seven IRA Volunteers ... [who] had been patrolling an area from Donovan's Bridge along the Western Road in search of a suspected civilian informer.' This was probably a University College Cork student called Stevens, who was spying for the British. The only surviving account of the executions by an IRA participant is the official report sent to the IRA GHQ, which gave no indication as to the grounds for the executions. It simply reads: 'We held up four soldiers (2 Royal Engineers, 2 Staffs) and searched them but found no arms. We took them to a field in our area where they were executed before 9 p.m.' The author of this report, the captain of 'H' Company, 1st Battalion, Cork City Brigade, had led the operation and ordered the executions. However, like most contemporary IRA reports, it was signed with his rank, not his name, which made it practically impossible to identify him until recently. The release of the IRA organisation and membership files by the Military Archives has enabled us for the first time to identify who held what rank in the IRA at the time of the Truce. The captain of 'H' Company was Dan Hallinan (36), a plasterer from Bishopstown, Cork. This information allowed Ó Ruairc to suggest a motive for the Ellis Quarry killings. Hallinan was a close friend of Denis Spriggs, who had been killed a few days earlier by the Staffordshires. In truth, it is hard to see any possible value in these killings.[343]

## 10 July 1921
### Major George B. O'Connor

O'Connor was a unionist and a justice of the peace (JP), who lived on Hop Island in Rochestown. He was friendly with many of the wealthy individuals who were caught up in the 'Anti-Sinn Féin League' shootings. His good friend Alfred Reilly had been shot in February by the IRA. O'Connor had been a candidate for the Irish Unionist Alliance in Dublin in 1911 and was a retired member of the British Army. He had refused to resign as a JP in 1920 when the vast majority of Cork magistrates had. Yet he had survived the entirety of war unscathed, with the exception of an arms raid in 1920. Why then, within hours of the end of the war, was he taken from his home and shot? Various theories have been advanced, but it seems that his killing was a direct result of the workings of the sophisticated intelligence war in the city. IRA spymaster Florence O'Donoghue's new wife, Josephine Marchment Brown, was the stenographer in the British intelligence office in Cork. O'Donoghue stated that she passed on a letter written by a 'retired British officer' identifying a dugout occupied by senior IRA members, including her husband, near his home. As a result a man was shot. This happened 'at the end of the Tan War'. The only incident that this could be is the shooting of O'Connor. Suggestions, that an affidavit submitted to the trial of the Clonmult IRA prisoners was a cause of his targeting are incorrect, as this affidavit was for the defence.[344]

## 11 July 1921
### Constable Alexander Clarke

The sad task of recording the last British death fell to Colonel Peter Hudson of the King's Liverpool Regiment, who had been regarded as a thorough gentleman by Tom Barry and the Cork No. 3 Brigade, in complete opposition to the venom directed at Major Percival and the Essex Regiment. Constable Clarke (52), who was married, was walking along the street outside Coffey's shop at 8.30 a.m. on Townshend Street, Skibbereen, when he was shot dead. He had been a member of the RIC for thirty-four years and had been stationed in the town for many years. He had been shot in the chest and in the head.[345]

## 11 July 1921
### William J. Nolan

Nolan was reported missing on Thursday 14 July. While his exact fate is uncertain, it seems clear from the (closed) file of Volunteer Patrick Scannell that he was abducted for joining the RIC and suspected of spying. He was not alone in this and a number of individuals who had been killed, such as Finbarr O'Sullivan in February 1921, had also applied to join the RIC. The newspaper report in *The Cork Examiner* stated: 'A boy of about 17 years named Willie Nolan, of Annmount, Friars Walk, Cork, has been missing since about 11.30 a.m. on Monday, at which time he left his residence to post a letter. Nothing has since been heard of him. His father was formerly a member of the RIC, and a brother of his is at present serving with that force.' No trace of him was ever found.[346]

### July 1921 (date uncertain)
### John H. N. Begley

At 11.55 a.m. on 11 July John Begley was tracked down on St Patrick Street by members of the Cork IRA and bundled into a hackney cab. He was taken outside the city and shot a few days later as a spy. A year later his mother wrote to the Irish Department of Defence seeking information about the whereabouts of her son and was told that he had been 'informally' shot as a spy. The British government accepted liability for him, suggesting that he was an active supporter. His mother was awarded £1,500, an enormous sum for a family earning little more than £1 per week.[347]

### 12 August 1921
### Patrick Cronin

There is no record anywhere in Irish newspapers or in death records about the killing of Patrick Cronin. However, his parents lodged a claim with the Irish Grants Committee and were compensated for his death. He had been a member of the Royal Navy during the Great War. His mother, Mary T. Cronin, with an address at Castle Street, Dunmanway, was sixty when the claim was submitted in January 1927. Niall Meehan writes, '… the draper William Jagoe, who said his premises were fired upon, alleged that after the July 1921 Truce an IRA intelligence officer told Jagoe he was one of seven in Dunmanway "marked down for assassination". Jagoe was also informed of a "marked man", Patrick Joseph Cronin, a Catholic loyalist and formerly a Royal Navy rating, who was shot dead that same evening in August 1921. This significant information in Jagoe's compensation file corroborated a Grants Committee claim from Cronin's parents.'[348]

## 11 November 1921
### Volunteer Daniel Clancy

Daniel Clancy from Farrendoyle, Kanturk, died on 11 November 1921 in Cork Military Hospital, after punishment by outdoor exposure in the moat on Spike Island, Cork Harbour. The prisoners were protesting the conditions of detention imposed by the British authorities. They were kept in the moat overnight and Clancy was shot. When he collapsed he was initially refused treatment and later died of septicaemia. Tim Herlihy gave a detailed account of the events leading up to his death: 'In Spike Island were quite a large number of our boys, many high-ranking officers; Dick Barrett, Tom Crofts, Bill Quirke of Tipperary, Henry O'Mahoney were the selected leaders. We resisted the British by every means at our disposal, while the treatment the British meted out to us prisoners was brutal. A hunger-strike lasting eight days was, I believe, stopped from outside. Then we broke up and burned our huts. I took part in a fierce fight against soldiers armed with batons; our boys had pieces of boards. Casualties on both sides were serious. ...

'Eventually the soldiers drove us out of our partly destroyed huts and into the compound nearby. ... Then we were marched out under heavy guard to the "moat". ...

'Watching the movements of our guards stationed high above us, we noticed two particular soldiers watching one position as if they had special orders ... Soon we saw they were following Dick Barrett, Tom Crofts, Bill Quirke (Tipperary) and Henry O'Mahoney. We informed Dick Barrett of the special watching soldiers. "Good," he said, "we'll stay here until dark, then we will slip off and fool 'em." When darkness came we followed Dick Barrett and Co., slipping away one by one. Unfortunately, some more of our boys took our evacuated position. These men, weary, sat down, backs against the wall, legs out. Then about 2 a.m. those two soldiers opened rapid fire on that position, hitting one man, shooting off his big toe. Soldiers charged in but at the cry "man wounded" a stretcher came after a long delay and the wounded man was taken away. Sad to say, he died from the effects.'[349]

## 14 November 1921
## Alderman Tadhg Barry

Though technically not a Cork killing, no list of Cork's revolutionary dead would be complete without including senior IRA commander, trade union activist and city councillor Tadhg Barry. He was killed by a sentry at Ballykinlar Detention Camp in Co. Down, as he approached a fence to say goodbye to fourteen departing friends who had been released on parole after the Truce. The newspapers reported the inquest in detail: 'The Coroner's inquest into the shooting of Alderman Tadhg Barry, at Ballykinlar Camp, on November 15, was resumed on Monday. The military case presented was that "the deceased disobeyed the sentry's order to get back from the barbed wire, and was then shot". The case for the next of kin repudiated the suggestion that deceased contemplated an attempt to escape, and that the shooting was unjustifiable. The character of the act was shown, said Mr. Lynch, K.C., by the remark of the sentry to a man who picked up the deceased: "I will give you the same, you b." Col. Little, Adjutant of the Camp, admitted to Mr. Wood that it was the duty of the sentry to report and not to shoot. James Quigley, Co. Surveyor for Co. Meath, ex-internee, provided a map and model of the camp, the latter being constructed by internees under his direction. He had often been in the place where deceased was shot, and was never challenged. Everyone was quite free to go through that place … If an armed sentry ordered him away he would do so, as they were pretty quick in firing.' Barry is credited with the largest funeral ever held in Cork, with 30,000 in attendance. Michael Collins made a point of attending the Requiem Mass for Barry in Dublin's Pro-Cathedral and marched in the funeral cortège alongside Cathal Brugha and W. T. Cosgrave to Kingsbridge (Heuston) Station, even though it was a crucial moment in the Treaty negotiations in London.[350]

## 8 February 1922
### Michael Savage

*The Freeman's Journal* reported: 'The young man named Michael Savage, who was wounded in the shooting at Killaclova Bridge, near Carrigtwohill, on Monday evening, has died at Cork Military Hospital. Mr. Savage, who was 33 years of age, was married, and leaves a widow and child, 7 months old. He served in the R.G.A. [Royal Garrison Artillery] all through the war, and escaped without a wound. The bridge where the shooting took place was damaged during the Irish campaign, and recently the railway company had started its repair. Deceased, who was employed as a milesman on the line, lived in the village of Glounthaune. His duty was as watchman from 5.30 to 12 o'clock. As usual, he left his home at 4.45 Monday evening, and had only taken up duty at the foot of an embankment where railway material was stored. The occupants of the military car coming from Cobh state that an ambush was attempted, and that they fired in self-defence. The people living in the neighbourhood of the occurrence state they knew nothing of it until they heard the shooting, and were not aware that anyone had been shot until long afterwards. Savage was found shot at the foot of the embankment. He was removed in the military car to the Military Hospital in Cork.' The military did not attend the inquest.[351]

## 11 February 1922
### Inspector Michael Keany

On 27 July 1921 the *Irish Independent* reported: 'Our Clonakilty correspondent writes:– District Inspector Keeny [*sic*], who had been over eleven years Head Constable in Clonakilty, was deservedly promoted to the rank of District Inspector a few years ago. His authorities, appreciating his worth, have appointed him to the more important position in the City of Cork. As Head Constable in Clonakilty and District Inspector during the most strenuous and troublesome times of the past few years, he acted with great tact, prudence and common sense. Hence it was that matters got on very well in Clonakilty and district. His numerous friends on all sides wish him, his estimable wife and family, every success and happiness.'

Less than six months later Keany was dead. He had returned to Clonakilty to remove his wife and family from the RIC barracks. 'Shortly after his arrival he went to the local hotel and was walking down the street around 11 p.m. with his son Edward (Eddie) when he was fired on.' He was shot four times and Edward was also injured. The inquest jury tendered their sympathy to his widow, May, and his family. Uniquely, the inquest was attended by the IRA Inspector McCarthy and RIC DI Higman. Keaney had thirty-three years of service and was fifty-three according to his death certificate. He is buried in St Finbarr's Cemetery, Cork.[352]

## 17 February 1922
### Lieutenant Henry Genochio
Genochio left Victoria Barracks after tea around 5 p.m. on 15 February. He was probably an intelligence officer. He was in civilian clothes and brought his revolver, which was technically illegal as he would have needed permission from the Provisional Government that was now in charge of the state. On St Patrick Street, around 9.30 p.m., he was arrested by two members of the IRP, who were generally anti-Treaty. That was the last time he was seen alive by any military witnesses. He was imprisoned in the Lunatic Asylum on the Lee Road. He was missed from the barracks the following day but, as the Provisional Government was in charge, no attempt was made to search for him. On the following day the barracks contacted the Irish government only to be told that he had been shot on the Lee Road, Cork, about 200 yards east of the main gate of the asylum. He had been shot twice in the back, and it appears that he was shot while attempting to escape.[353]

## 16/17 March 1922
### Patrick Horgan

There is little doubt about what happened to Horgan. The *Irish Independent* reported on the inquest a few days after the event: 'The Inquest touching the death of Patrick Horgan, Wolfe Tone St., Cork, a member of the Parnell Guards' Band, mortally wounded on the night of the 16th–17th, when the [anti-Treaty] I.R.P. and the [pro-Treaty] band came into collision, was resumed and further adjourned. Evidence of members of the patrol was that any shots fired from the patrol were discharged in the air, and that only one shot came from the crowd. The inquiry, at which Mr. Denis Barry, O.C. I.R.P. represented the police, and Mr. P. F. Donovan, solr., appeared for the next-of-kin, was conducted by Mr. Coroner Murphy. David Keating, who was on duty with 4 others as members of a Republican patrol, said about 12.00 a fife and drum band playing, came through Castle St. towards Cornmarket St., at the corner of which the band was approached by Mr. Barry, the officer in charge, who asked for the man in charge of the band. Almost at the same moment members of the patrol were attacked by the crowd, who used sticks and stones. Shots were fired in the air by the patrol to frighten the crowd, but the latter continued to rush, and a shot was fired from their midst ... Members of the I.R.A. then came to the patrol's assistance and the crowd were forced back towards Castle Street, where they dispersed. He heard that two men had been wounded, but did not see them.'[354] The IRP later apologised for the shooting.

## 25 March 1922
### Sergeant William Gloster (retired)

Sergeant William Gloster had been stationed at College Road RIC Barracks for many years and was living on St Bridget's Street, just off Barrack Street, at the time of the 1911 census. He was a Kerryman and was married with four children. His wife, Eleanor, was from Tipperary. Typically for a densely packed city like Cork, their neighbours included republicans, such as future Sinn Féin TD Liam de Roiste and his new bride, Nóra, who had lived just seven doors away before they moved across the city to Sunday's Well. By August 1920 Gloster had retired from the RIC and was living inside the barracks in Elizabeth Fort on Barrack Street. On 25 March 1922 he was walking across South Gate Bridge when he was attacked and shot by a group of young men, receiving numerous wounds. Martin Higgins, a fireman who lived nearby, confirmed that Gloster died within a few minutes. No motive was advanced for the killing and IRP O/C Denis Barry stated that they had nothing 'whatsoever against the deceased' and the IRA 'condemned it [the murder] as strongly as anyone else'.[355]

**26–29 April 1922**
**John Bradfield**
**James Buttimer**
**John Buttimer**
**John Chinnery**
**Francis Fitzmaurice**
**James Greenfield**
**David Grey/Gray**
**Samuel Hornibrook**
**Thomas Henry Hornibrook**
**Robert Howe**
**Alexander Gerald McKinley**
**Robert Nagle**
**Volunteer Michael O'Neill**
**Captain Herbert Woods (retired) MC MM**
For details of their deaths, see Part 1: Massacre in West Cork.

**26 April 1922**
**Lieutenant Ronald A. Hendy**
**Lieutenant George R. A. Dove**

## Lieutenant Kenneth R. Henderson MC
## Private J. R. Brooks

On the morning of 26 April 1922, three British Army officers and their driver left Ballincollig Barracks in Cork, supposedly on a fishing expedition. It is likely that they called to an old friend of theirs, Major Clarke at Farran House, halfway to Macroom, for lunch.[356] They arrived in Macroom around 4 p.m. The local IRA became suspicious of the strange car without plates parked outside Dick William's hotel and went to investigate. The responses of the driver to their questions made them even more suspicious. The three officers were arrested in the snug of the hotel and interrogated. Their cover story was quickly exposed, as they had no fishing equipment with them. All four were shot and buried at Clondrohid four miles north-west of Macroom.

The officers may have been sent west in response to the kidnapping of the Hornibrooks. There is also little doubt that the shooting of the acting head of the IRA, Michael O'Neill, in Bandon by a former British officer would have prompted an investigation. James Murphy, who was a member of the Macroom IRA garrison, recalled that after they were captured they were held in the RIC barracks while the IRA garrison asked headquarters for instructions. The brigade ordered the killing of all four and this was carried out that night. The reason Murphy gives is: 'Two of these officers (Hendy and Dore [sic]) were members of the British intelligence who had tortured and shot unarmed prisoners during the fight. They were wanted men and were taken prisoners by our forces ...'. Many other BMH statements record similar information and all state that the men were shot the night they were captured after orders had been received from Cork IRA Brigade HQ.[357]

Unsurprisingly, on 27 April General Strickland sent Major (later Field Marshal) Bernard Montgomery to investigate the disappearance of his soldiers. This resulted, a few days later, in a tense stand-off between the IRA behind Macroom's castle walls and on house roofs and a British unit accompanied by at least one armoured car in the middle of the square, more than twenty-five miles inside enemy territory. A British officer found no evidence that the soldiers had ever been in the castle and Montgomery retreated. The bodies were recovered in December 1923 and taken back to army headquarters in Aldershot, Hampshire, for burial.[358]

## 27 April 1922
### Volunteer Seán Bullman

Seán Bullman was killed accidentally and was buried in the Republican Plot at St Finbarr's Cemetery on 30 April 1922. According to his death notice he was 'shot accidentally on duty'. The single newspaper report on his death did not explain exactly how he was killed, but he received a full military funeral. He was from Step Lane and was a member of 'D' Company, 1st Battalion, Cork No. 1 Brigade.[359]

## 20 May 1922
### Constable Timothy O'Leary (retired)

*The Southern Star* of 27 May 1922 reported that Timothy O'Leary (26), ex-RIC, was shot outside Ballinspittle when returning from Kinsale with his aunt, Mrs Fielding. 'Two boys' stopped their pony and trap and took him away. She never saw him alive again. O'Leary had been visiting his aunt for four or five weeks after the RIC was disbanded in the middle of April. He had been stationed in Cork city during the War of Independence. Coroner Neville held an inquest at Kilbrittain into the death. No motive was advanced for his killing.[360]

## 1 June 1922
### Constable Michael Williams (retired)

In 2007 the *Irish Independent* stated: 'An October 1924 memo from Chief Supt P. Fahy in Cork said he had received "reliable information" that Williams had been taken to Corry's farm, where a kangaroo court presided over by Seán Hegarty and involving Mrs McCurtain as a witness sentenced him to death. He gave details of where bodies were buried on the farm and in a nearby quarry.' According to Charles Cullinane's military service pension file, he was involved in the guarding and execution of Williams while he was attached to the Knockraha Company, after Christmas 1920. He stated: 'Execution (and guarding) of two victims brought from Cork by Crofts, Molyneux, Peter Donovan and Co. One was Head Constable Williams ex-Cork RIC captured in Tullamore, or somewhere, the other was a small rat of a fellow spying in Cork pre-truce but only captured [in Crosshaven, in a tent?] during Truce'.[361]

## 17 June 1922
### Na Fianna Frederick Grant

Frederick Grant (17) died from wounds received from a burst of revolver fire in Blackrock, Cork, on Saturday 17 June. The *Irish Independent* reported that a group of young men, all members of the anti-Treaty IRA or Na Fianna, were hunting rabbits. The incident took place at the rear of Dominick Daly's premises and it was his watchman, Mr Kenny, who shot Grant. One of the chief witnesses was R. H. Tilson JP, whose brother George had committed suicide the previous year after he received a threatening letter in relation to alleged spying activities against the IRA. Tilson stated that while Grant had threatened Kenny with the IRA, there had been no excuse for his shooting.[362]

## 28 June 1922
### Sergeant John Tehan RIC (retired)

John Tehan was kidnapped on the day that the Irish Civil War started. On 1 July *The Southern Star* reported that an ex-RIC man had returned to Killavullen on the previous Saturday and had been bundled into a car by armed men. He was found later that day shot through the head in a field at Killavullen. According to the report he had been stationed in the town for some time until demobilisation, but at the inquest he was still unidentified and his body was removed to Mallow workhouse, where it seems his identity was uncovered. As he had been stationed at nearby Castletownroche for many years it seems unlikely that he was unknown. Nobody ever admitted the killing. He has been recorded by the Mallow Archaeological and Historical Society as 'Tehan, John; Sergeant (retired) ... killed at Killavullen, Mallow, Co. Cork, 28 June 1922'. On 18 August his wife claimed £10,000 for his death against Mallow Rural Council.[363]

## 1 July 1922
### Anti-Treaty IRA William Spillane

Lieutenant William Spillane, on active service with Cork No. 1 Brigade, was accidentally shot dead by one of his comrades. The newspaper report stated: 'The remains of Lieut. Wm. Spillane, of the Cork First Brigade, were brought to Cork on Saturday evening ... An inquiry was opened at Buttevant on Saturday, and has not yet concluded the taking of evidence. The body was conveyed from Buttevant in a motor car, accompanied by a number of his comrades. The coffin was covered with the tricolour and the sad procession proceeded to The Church of the Immaculate Conception St. Finbarr's West where the remains were received by the Rvd Father O'Toole.'[364]

## 3 July 1922
### Anti-Treaty IRA Patrick McCarthy

*The Southern Star* reported on 8 July 1922 that 'Free State forces in Skibbereen had been besieged' in the town barracks by anti-Treaty IRA columns led by Commandant Gibbs Ross from Bantry and General Tom Hales. Uncharacteristically, this siege was substantial and was still progressing on the following Tuesday, with the anti-Treaty forces tightening their grip. On 4 July an agreement was reached between Gibbs Ross and Jeremiah McCarthy of the 'Dáil Troops' that the latter would 'vacate the building leaving their arms behind in the safe custody of Commandant Ross on the understanding that they would not be used in subsequent offensive action against them'. The Free State troops marched out at 8 p.m. and the anti-Treaty forces took control of the town. The only serious casualty was Patrick McCarthy on the anti-Treaty side. He had been injured early on Monday morning and succumbed to his injuries in Bandon Hospital the following day. Four members of the pro-Treaty troops were slightly injured.

The Free State troops retreated as far as the Town Hall and Emporium, where a stand-off developed until 29 July when some of their men were captured and they were forced to leave town. They returned on 4 August and forced the anti-Treaty men back into the barracks. Two days earlier Gibbs Ross had been captured, disarmed and given a warning before being released. He returned to the barracks to continue the fight. Despite the fact that the situation nationally was extremely serious, it is clear that at this early stage of the war neither side really wished to inflict serious harm on the other.[365]

## 14 July 1922
## Peter Cahill

The inquest jury returned the following verdict: 'That the said Peter Francis Cahill, aged 11½ years, late of 38 Thomas Davis Street, son of the late Peter Francis Cahill, of the same address, died on 14th July from internal hemorrhage [sic] and shock, resulting from a bullet wound received through the accidental discharge of a revolver at the hands of his brother Leo Cahill, whom we exonerate from all blame.' The revolver was owned by Daniel Mulroy, O/C of the 1st Battalion, Na Fianna, who had used it earlier during the funeral of Volunteer Jeremiah Pierce.[366]

## 18 July 1922 (date uncertain)
## Anti-Treaty IRA William O'Sullivan

William O'Sullivan's *Irish Independent* death notice states that he died at the Mercy Hospital from injuries received as the result of an accident. He is buried in the Republican Plot of St Finbarr's Cemetery, Cork. There are no other reports of what happened to him.[367]

## 30 July 1922
### Constable James O'Donovan (retired)

James O'Donovan (23) was shot dead on the Garretstown Road south of Ballinspittle. He was an ex-Irish Guard and a tram conductor in Cork. Denis Collins later recalled an incident that occurred when he was a prisoner in 'The Cage' in Victoria Barracks. A man came out to identify the prisoners: 'It was a man in civilian clothes and was actually a near neighbour of my own who had joined the Irish Guards and had fought through the 1914–1918 War.

'We looked steadily at one another, with only the wire between us. Neither of us gave a sign of recognition, I because I did not wish to show my fellow-prisoners that I would talk to someone who might have been there for no good reason. He might have been and probably was a spy, for on different evenings after that he used [to] come out of a doorway across the square, always dressed in civilian clothes, and come over and gaze in through the wire at us for quite a while and then without a word turn away. No soldier was allowed do this, so we were very suspicious.

'I heard afterwards he was seen in military police uniform down the city and also in civilian dress along with the Tans. He was also identified as being one of the principal actors in the burning of Cork in the previous December. He went home in 1922 and was shot very soon after. His name was Jimmy Donovan from Ballinspittal [*sic*].'[368]

## July 1922 (date uncertain)
### William Edward Parsons

Another disappeared, like William Nolan, this is one of the more controversial killings of the period.[369] There is no doubt that Parsons was captured and killed by the IRA. The difficulty arises because he was still alive long after the date of his supposed kidnapping in November 1920 and the evidence clearly shows that he was more than likely captured in July 1922.[370] Equally, there is little doubt that he was taken to the IRA prison managed by Martin

Corry in Knockraha and subjected to a mock execution before he confessed to his involvement in spying during the War of Independence. He was from the High Street area of Cork city and his family were from England. As he was only four years of age in the census records for 1911, he could have been no more than sixteen by the time of his death. Indeed, Michael Murphy, head of the IRA in Cork, stated that he was fifteen, so there is no doubt about the victim or the perpetrators.[371]

## 8 August 1922
**Anti-Treaty IRA Denis Coffey**

His father attempted to claim a pension for Denis Coffey but was unsuccessful. The Free State intelligence officer who commented in the pension file stated that Coffey was shot by 'the Irregulars' after they retreated from Bandon towards Kinsale, because they believed he intended to switch sides. Senior anti-Treaty IRA member Bob Hales told Coffey's father that he was shot in an ambush. There is no other information.[372]

## 9–11 August 1922
**National Army James Gavigan**[373]
**National Army Henry Quinn**
**National Army Patrick Maguire**
**National Army James Madden**
**National Army Patrick Perry**
**National Army Gerald McKenna**
**National Army Frederick McKenna**
**National Army William Nevin**
**National Army Christopher O'Toole**
**National Army Michael Collins**
**National Army Flood**
**National Army Unnamed (6)**
**Anti-Treaty IRA Ian MacKenzie-Kennedy**

## Anti-Treaty IRA James Maloney
## Anti-Treaty IRA Jeremiah Hourican (Hourigan)

The battle for Rochestown is comprehensively covered in *The Battle for Cork* by John Borgonovo, but there remains great confusion on all sides about the exact number of soldiers involved and the number of casualties. If the total number of claimed casualties is added up it comes to more than thirty. Only the National Army and anti-Treaty forces men definitely known to have died are recorded here.

When Free State forces landed near Cork city and along the south coast behind the anti-Treaty front line running from Waterford to Tralee, the anti-Treaty IRA was caught between two sets of National Army troops and did not have sufficient forces to oppose both. Indeed, the fighting in and around Cork city would not have proved so difficult for the National Army had seasoned IRA fighters not arrived by train from Kilmallock. Their move to Cork meant that the anti-Treaty IRA's northern front collapsed and the regular phase of the war quickly came to an end with a Free State victory.

The Free State forces landed at Passage West around 2 a.m. on 8 August with armoured cars and field guns, which later proved decisive in the battle. The anti-Treaty sentries at Passage mistook them for a ship that had gone out the night before, so it was only at the last minute that they offered any resistance. Once the troops had landed, they were fired on from the Cobh side of the narrow river channel and took casualties. Over the next two days they managed to work their way towards Cork city, despite fierce resistance. The crucial battle took place at Rochestown, where the anti-Treaty side was well dug in in the woods. A local doctor, James Lynch, described the battle in great detail, including the death of 'small' Michael Collins, a first cousin of the commander-in-chief, who charged a machine gun placed at the gates of Rochestown College but was shot when his gun jammed. On the anti-Treaty side the best-known casualty was Ian MacKenzie-Kennedy. Pádraig Óg Ó Ruairc writes: 'During the fighting in Rochestown, as the covering party of the IRA was evacuating to their second position near Douglas village, their lorry broke down at Belmont Cross ... One party of Free State soldiers who charged the cottage was forced to retire leaving one of their number by the name of Flood, a Dublin man, dying on the road. Frank O'Donoghue rushed from the cottage to Flood's aid, whispered an act of contrition into his ear, and the unfortunate Flood died grasping O'Donoghue's hand ... The cottage was later surrounded, and the three brave republican soldiers kept up an unequal fight against 64 Free State troops, killing 12, and wounding 15 according to the report. Only when the last bullet was fired did the battle cease. When further resistance was impossible, and having delayed the enemy until the republicans had taken up their position, the little party decided to surrender. MacKenzie-Kennedy opened the door and put up his hands in token surrender, but was shot dead, as was Moloney [*sic*]. O'Donoghue was captured and taken prisoner.'[374]

## 11 August 1922
### Unnamed child

The *Irish Independent*, which was the only newspaper able to report from Cork after the destruction of the *Cork Examiner*'s and *Cork Constitution*'s printing presses, stated that some young boys had found grenades at the Victoria Barracks after the anti-Treaty IRA had evacuated and burned the building. One was killed and the other 'had all his clothes blown off', and the way this report is written suggests that the reporter was an eyewitness.[375]

## 11 August 1922
### Mary Ann Curtin

As National Army soldiers moved to take Fermoy, they were ambushed at Rathcormac. Following a fierce battle the anti-Treaty IRA retreated to the rear of Mr Curtin's house and continued firing at the National Army troops. Dr Kiely of the South Infirmary was visiting the house at the time. A stray bullet came through the window and hit him in the shoulder before hitting Mary Ann Curtin in the head. Despite the assistance of Kiely, Dr

Barry and two medical staff from the National Army, she died on Friday 11 August.[376]

## 11 August 1922
### Anti-Treaty IRA Christie Olden

The only report of Christie Olden's death is a motion of condolence from the Cork Handball Association on his untimely death. As he is buried in the Republican Plot it is not unreasonable to assume he was shot during the battle for Cork earlier in the month, but the report does not provide this information nor is there any death notice. His official death certificate states that he was nineteen.[377]

## 18 August 1922
### National Army Jeremiah McDonald

The weapon that won the Civil War was the field gun. General Seán Hales had landed at Union Hall on the morning of 8 August and fought his way into Skibbereen, arriving around 3 a.m the next day. He brought with him a sixteen pounder, which he used to good effect on his 'triumphant march' through South Cork to Bandon. However, throughout the march he was careful to allow his opponents time to escape rather than seek confrontation. The only point of serious opposition was at Bandon, where the gun was fired into the barracks to excellent effect as the anti-Treaty garrison surrendered. According to his second-in-command, John L. Sullivan, the shells were filled with blanks, so achieved their aim of demonstrating the threat without the risk of casualties. However, as the National Army moved through West Cork it suffered some fatalities. On 18 August, halfway between Rosscarbery and Clonakilty, the column was ambushed, resulting in a firefight. Jeremiah McDonald was shot in the head and died instantly, while Michael Collins was injured. Both were from Rosscarbery. The anti-Treaty side retreated and again attacked the column just outside Clonakilty, where they were routed. McDonald is buried in Rosscarbery.[378]

## 18 August 1922
### National Army Patrick Breen

Patrick Breen Junior (19), a National Army soldier from Drogheda, was killed in action at Kildorrery, Co. Cork. The *Irish Independent* report was glowing. Breen was part of a 'rounding up' party of thirty soldiers that was ambushed by around fifty anti-Treaty troops and suffered two casualties, one fatal. Despite the fact that they were outnumbered, 'their better discipline allowed them to surround [half] the ambushers and these surrendered. Twenty-five prisoners were taken.' The remaining anti-Treaty men retreated.[379]

## 20 August 1922
### National Army Patrick Corcoran

Corcoran's file in the MSPC is the only official record of his death. It records Mary Corcoran's receipt of a partial dependants' gratuity of £50. The file suggests that Private Corcoran died on 20 August 1922 in the South Infirmary, Cork, from wounds received near Macroom on 10 August. As Macroom was occupied on 17 August without a shot being fired it is more probable that Corcoran was another victim of the Rochestown fighting. Prior to joining the National Army, Corcoran had served with the British Army.[380]

## 20 August 1922
### National Army Edward Cregan

Lieutenant Commandant Edward Cregan was killed on 20 August 1922 at Curraghs, Kanturk, in an attack by the anti-Treaty IRA on a National Army party of which he was a member. They were travelling from Drumcollagher to Kanturk. His father, Edmund Cregan, stated that 'the Irregulars' attempted to burn his son's body. The truth seems to be worse, according to an *Evening Herald* report, which stated: 'An official bulletin, issued by Field G.H.Q., South Western Command, last night says:– While a detachment of 7 men under Lieut.-Comdt. E. Cregan, of the West Limerick Brigade, was returning from Liscarroll to Kanturk on Sunday evening they were ambushed at 7.30 o'clock by 60 irregulars with 2 Thompson guns and rifles at a place called Curraghs, 3 miles from Liscarroll. Lieut-Comdt. Cregan was seriously wounded. The driver of the car remained with the wounded officer while the others of the party engaged the attackers. The driver was taken from the car by the irregulars and made a prisoner. The irregulars then proceeded to set the car on fire while the wounded officer was still in it. The driver, however, made good his escape, and returned to find the dying officer in the burning car. He carried his officer from the car, and Lieut.-Comdt Cregan died immediately on the roadside. Meanwhile the remainder of the party made a fierce resistance, and fought their way through the ambushers, inflicting severe casualties, and all succeeded in reaching Kanturk, fighting a rearguard action for over a mile. Two of the troops were slightly wounded.'[381]

## 21 August 1922
## William Levingstone Cooke

In 1911 William Levingstone Cooke was the next-door neighbour of James Blemens, who was kidnapped and shot by the IRA during the November killings of 1920. *The Cork Examiner* recorded: 'A verdict of wilful murder against an unknown man who shot him was returned in the case of William Levingstone Cooke, who was shot dead when a group of men called to his house demanding subscriptions for a football club. Mr Levingstone Cooke lived at Rock Lodge, Old Blackrock Road, Cork.' Collections for such organisations were euphemisms used by those collecting for the IRA and Sinn Féin. Cooke was a justice of the peace and had been a member of the last British Grand Jury on 14 July 1921, according to the *Cork Constitution*. In a 1923 interview with the Irish Grants Committee, Thomas Hunter Harte stated that he and Cooke had 'received threats from the Sinn Féin element in Cork'. Compensation of £8,000 was granted to Cooke's wife and six children by the courts.[382]

**21 August 1922**

**Patrick Burns**

According to John Borgonovo, Patrick Burns was asleep in Ballincollig Barracks on the night it was burned by the anti-Treaty IRA. None of the newspapers record details of the event, but there is an October 1922 death certificate for Burns, which confirms the cause of the death and the date.[383]

**22 August 1922**

**National Army Commander-in-Chief Michael Collins**

For details of Collins' death, see Part 1: Michael Collins: 'The Man Who Couldn't Be Killed'.

**27 August 1922**

**National Army Cyril Lee**

National Army officer Cyril Lee was shot in the head during an anti-Treaty ambush at Clondrohid, seven miles from Macroom, on Sunday 27 August and died several hours later. The troops came under fire on arrival in the village. Lieutenant Lee was a native of Belfast. A report by the Dublin Metropolitan Police in his MSPC file states that Lee was a lieutenant in the British Army and had served for twelve years prior to joining the National Army. He had to leave Belfast as a result of the 'pogroms' according to the news reports.[384]

**27 August 1922**

**Jeremiah O'Callaghan**

Under an *Irish Independent* heading 'Mallow Tragedy, Man Fatally Shot', it was reported that 'while a young soldier of the detachment of National troops at present doing duty in Mallow was examining his rifle in a room at the Police Barracks on Sunday, the weapon accidentally went off, a young man named Jeremiah O'Callaghan from the town who happened to be in the room at the time being mortally wounded. The remains were subsequently taken to the mortuary chapel of the Parish Church.'[385]

## 29 August 1922
## National Army Denis McCarthy

Denis McCarthy had returned home to 20 Rochford's Lane off Barrack Street to visit his family. After he left to return to barracks, he was shot 'through and through' on nearby Barrack Street. His cousin had left around 9.20 p.m. and passed three young men in trench coats with velour hats pulled down over their heads standing at the corner of Vicar Street. Twenty minutes later she heard shots and found McCarthy dead in a pool of blood in Mrs Kennefick's public house at 48 Barrack Street. He had been carried into the pub by locals.[386]

## 29 August 1922
## National Army Hugh Thornton

Thornton had a long association with West Cork, having trained and organised the Volunteers there after the 1916 Rising. He was a personal friend of most of the senior leadership but as a member of the Dublin Guard and close associate of Michael Collins had taken the pro-Treaty side. Given his high level of activity during the War of Independence, it is perhaps particularly sad that he lost his life in the way he did. Initial reports stated that he was being driven through Clonakilty in an open-topped Lancia touring car when it was fired on. Thornton was shot in the head and another soldier was wounded before the attackers ran off. However, the inquest stated that he was shot accidentally by a rifle that discharged inside the armoured car between Bantry and Skibbereen. Many years later Michael Crowley, who was one of the senior fighters in the Cork No. 3 Brigade flying column, paid him tribute: 'Late in 1916, G.H.Q. sent Hugh Thornton, a young officer who had participated in the Rising, as Volunteer organiser for West Cork. He made Kilbrittain his base for training of existing units and forming new ones and I spent a considerable portion of my time assisting him in his work in adjoining areas. To his enthusiasm and tireless energy West Cork owes a debt of gratitude as he laid the foundation of the later formed Cork III Brigade.'[387]

**30 August 1922**

**Anti-Treaty IRA Gibbs Ross**

**Anti-Treaty IRA Patrick Cooney**

**Anti-Treaty IRA Donal (Daniel) McCarthy**

**Anti-Treaty IRA Michael Crowley**

**National Army John Hourihane**

Denis Keohane told the BMH: 'On August 30th 1922 we decided to endeavour to recapture the town [Bantry]. We succeeded in driving in the outposts from the eastern end, but in the absence of suitable armament we were unable to push the attack to a successful conclusion. In this engagement the Brigade O/C (Gibbs Ross) was killed.' *The Freeman's Journal* reported: 'During the last attack on Bantry the Irregular leader, Mr. Gibbs Ross, was killed leading an attack on the Post Office. An entrance had been tunnelled from the adjacent building, and bombs were about to be exploded if the National garrison failed to surrender. However, just at this moment a shot rang through the fanlight of the Post Office side entrance and struck the Irregular leader in the head. He lived for but 20 minutes and was attended by Canon Murphy. Three other Irregulars were also killed during the attack, viz., Patrick Cooney, Daniel McCarthy and Michael J. Crowley.' One of the defenders, John Hourihane from Drimoleague, was also killed in the attack, dying from gunshot wounds according to his death certificate. He was a vice-commandant in 2nd Battalion, Cork No. 5 Brigade. Gibbs Ross was buried in his family's plot in Careagh.[388]

**30 August 1922**

**National Army Albert Redvers Cottle**

The *Irish Independent* reported on 31 August 1922: 'A party of twelve National troops, proceeding from Cork to Fermoy, left the city about 8 o'clock yesterday morning in a Crossley tender and a Lancia car, and at a place called Tubbcreenmire, near Watergrasshill, a mine was exploded under the Crossley tender, which reduced it practically to matchwood. Driver

Cuddell [*sic*], of the Motor Transport Department was killed, and three injured.' His name was, in fact, Cottle. His mother, Bessie, unsuccessfully applied for an award under the Army Pensions Act 1923 as a dependant.[389]

## 31 August 1922
**National Army James Murray**

James Murray failed to hear a challenge to stop at a National Army checkpoint on the Bandon Road in Cork city. A member of the army, he was shot by Private Thomas Coughlan from his own side and killed. He had been driving a lorry to Bandon and probably did not hear the soldiers over the noise of the engine.[390]

## 1 September 1922
**National Army Nicholas Ward**
**National Army Richard (Dick) Kearns**

On Friday 1 September 1922, while recovering the wreckage of a National Army lorry destroyed in an earlier ambush, two soldiers of the National Army were killed in Watergrasshill on their return journey. The troops stopped to inspect a bump in the road, which was in fact a mine. It exploded while it was being examined. Incredibly, the soldier standing on the mine was blown clear and survived. However, the anti-Treaty IRA then opened fire and during the exchange of fire Private Ward of No. 1 Company, 1st Dublin Brigade, and Richard Kearns (26) were both mortally wounded by shots to the head. Kearns was married with two children.[391]

## 2 September 1922
**National Army Francis Neary**
**National Army John O'Leary**

The anti-Treaty IRA launched an attack on Macroom on 2 September. At Codrum Cross, just to the west of the town, a National Army patrol was strafed by machine-gun fire from behind Leary's public house. The patrol was led by Commandant Peadar O'Conlon of the Dublin Guard, who stated that 'in all my experience I have never seen a body of men to advance under machine-gun fire, with all its demoralising effects, as did the 30 men I brought down the road that morning'. As the party moved forward they also came under fire from two snipers and John O'Leary took up a position to silence them, while O'Conlon led the patrol towards the safety of the town 200 metres away. When O'Conlon looked back he saw O'Leary stretched on the ground, probably having been shot in the back by yet another sniper to his rear. Sergeant Francis Neary attempted to shoot another sniper who was hiding behind a wall just on the edge of the town and as he looked over the wall to get a better shot he was killed. O'Leary was buried a couple of days later in Clondrohid and Neary's body was returned to Dublin.[392]

**2 September 1922**

**National Army Michael Francis Behan**

**National Army Thomas Conway**

**14 September 1922**

**National Army James McCann**

**National Army James Yates**

Sixteen members of the National Army were machine-gunned at 10.15 a.m. on this Saturday, with two of them, Behan and Conway, shot dead. Two days later the *Irish Independent* had an extraordinarily detailed account of the shooting: 'They are all members of the Curragh Reserve. Inquiries into the terrible occurrence have brought to light the fact that the soldiers when attacked were unarmed. Just about ten o'clock they were sitting or standing in groups on the Grand Parade, outside the [Cork City] Club premises, when the officer in charge came out and told them to fall in and go inside to draw their pay. The soldiers paraded in front of the club, between it and the National Monument, with the intention of going into the building one by one. They were facing the South Mall. Just as they paraded the attack was opened on them from the opposite side of the river – Sullivan's Quay.

A motor bicycle and sidecar was proceeding slowly up the quay from Parliament Bridge in a westerly direction. A machine-gun was mounted in the sidecar attachment and trained on the Grand Parade. As soon as the soldiers came into view of the two men in this vehicle the machine-gun opened fire. At the same moment two men with rifles were seen to fire on the unarmed soldiers from the roof of a house a little to the Parliament Bridge side of Friary Lane, which turns off Sullivan's Quay at right angles, almost opposite the National Monument. Two other men opened fire from another low roof on the western side of the corner of Friary Lane. These four snipers commenced to fire at the same moment that the man in the sidecar attachment began using the machine-gun, and their shots passed over the heads of the two men on the road. The motor bicycle continued all the time moving westwards, and when the machine-gun ceased firing, jumped forward at a terrific pace and disappeared in the direction of Barrack Street. Heavy firing by the four snipers covered the retreat of these two men.' Incredibly, at 9.30 p.m. on 30 August a grenade had been dropped between a group of soldiers outside the City Club, yet nobody had thought to increase security.[393]

A further two casualties from the machine-gun attack on soldiers outside the City Club were reported in the newspapers on 15 September. The bodies of Privates Yates and McCann were removed to Dublin for burial in Glasnevin. McCann was from Glasgow. Yates was from Dublin and was married with a young daughter.[394]

## 8 September 1922
### Anti-Treaty IRA Timothy Kennefick

According to *The Freeman's Journal*: 'Another shooting affray is reported from Coachford, which is situated in Mid-Cork, where a young man named Timothy Kennefick, of 1, Lady's Well Place, Cork, described as being prominent in the Irregulars, died as a result of wounds on Friday. Kennefick, it is stated, was returning to Cork from Ballingeavy [*sic*] by motor-car and was arrested by National troops. Later in the evening the dead body of Kennefick was found in some briars on the land of Mr. O'Sullivan, Galgey, Nadrid, with two bullet wounds in the body. It is believed that he was shot while attempting to escape. The remains were subsequently removed, to Cork, and were interred in the Republican Plot in the cemetery to-day.' Kennefick was unarmed when he was arrested. The army gave the usual excuse of 'shot while trying to escape' when explaining his death. He left behind a wife and young family.[395]

## 9 September 1922
### Anti-Treaty IRA Patrick Murphy

The mystery surrounding the shooting of Patrick Murphy was finally cleared up two weeks after it happened. According to *The Freeman's Journal*, a pro-Treaty soldier 'and his companion went for a cycle spin in the country, intending to proceed to Healy's Bridge, Blarney. Near the Leemount Bridge they were challenged by a party of nine Irregulars, whose assembly at this place, it was subsequently ascertained, was to raid the mails being conveyed from Donoughmore, Coachford, Blarney and other centres to Cork. The two cyclists refused to halt when called upon to do so, with the result that the Irregulars fired upon them. The Volunteer, who had a revolver and six rounds of ammunition, replied to the attack without dismounting from his bicycle. In the exchange of shots Murphy was hit through the stomach and another of the attackers, Sullivan, was shot in the wrist. After the third shot the Volunteer was struck from behind in the hip. The Irregulars in the meantime had taken shelter behind a wall, and it was from their concealed position that they continued the attack on the two young men, whose ages have been given as 20 and 24 years. When an Irregular advanced with a bomb in his hand, the cyclists, seeing the futility of further resistance, surrendered.' They were taken prisoner, but escaped on Monday 18 September and walked the eighteen miles back to Cork.[396]

**14 September 1922**

**Anti-Treaty IRA John O'Brien**

**17 September 1922**

**Anti-Treaty IRA Denis Creedon**

Eight National Army troops were returning from Donoughmore to Blarney when they were attacked by two ambush parties around 3.15 p.m. just to the east of the village. They drove through the second ambush but stopped to engage the ambushers. Unbeknownst to them a third ambush party was waiting and engaged the Lancia drivers. This nearly led to disaster, as the six troops got cut off from the car which had stalled. However, they managed to escape and headed into Blarney, where they gathered reinforcements and returned to the ambush site around 7 p.m. A running fight over three miles developed and only finished as darkness fell. During the battle John O'Brien from Evergreen Road, Cork city, was shot dead and Denis Creedon was seriously injured. He died a few days later in the Mercy Hospital. The National Army captured William Healy, who was subsequently executed in Cork Gaol (see page 354).[397]

**14 September 1922**

**Edward Williams**

On Thursday 14 September 1922 a young merchant sailor, Edward Williams (18) from 15 Burley Street, Liverpool, who was serving on the Cork Steam Packet Company's SS *Kenmare* as a wireless watcher, was shot dead on the corner of Bridge Street in Cork. He was in uniform. Williams had left the ship with another young man, John William Cave of 8 Howe Street, Liverpool. As they were talking to some girls at the corner of Bridge Street, a man emerged from a public house and fired on them with a revolver. The captain of the *Kenmare* stated that Williams had only joined the ship on Tuesday and this was his first trip to Cork. *The Freeman's Journal* reported on 18 September that a National Army patrol had passed the spot a few minutes before the murder and a soldier had been wounded.[398]

**16–17 September 1922**

**National Army Thomas Keogh**

**National Army Tom Manning**

**National Army Dan O'Brien**

**National Army William Murphy**

**National Army Ralph Conway**

**National Army Patrick O'Rourke**

**National Army John Riordan**

**National Army Unknown**

For details of these men's deaths, see Part 1, The Door to Madness.

**16/17 September 1922**

**Anti-Treaty IRA James Buckley**

For details of Buckley's death, see Part 1, The Door to Madness.

**18 September 1922**

**National Army Bernard (Patrick) Gray (Grey)**

National Army sentry Bernard Gray was 'cleaning a rifle with some inflammable liquid, with the result that when he discharged it [during an attack] the weapon burst, the stock striking him and inflicting a compound fracture to the jaw and a fracture to the base of the skull, to which he speedily succumbed at Coachford.[399] He was from Belfast and it took four years for compensation to be paid to his mother, Catherine Gray, who with increasing irritation pointed out that he had died in the service of the Department of Defence. The department replied that the delay was a result of the difficulties conducting investigations in the 'northern area'. He was a member of the Scottish Brigade of the National Army.[400]

**19 September 1922**

**National Army David O'Sullivan**

According to the *Irish Independent* of 20 September: 'About 12 o'clock yesterday a party of National troops went to Crookstown for the purpose of lifting some land mines. They succeeded in lifting several. On the way out the convoy, which consisted of about 40 men, were ambushed four times. At various places along the Crookstown road they were attacked by parties of irregulars, stated to number at least 200. The party of National troops, however, succeeded not only in getting through without any casualties but they captured five irregulars on the outward journey. On their return journey, one of the National troops was killed at Aherla, and another was slightly wounded. The troops claim to have killed seven irregulars, as well as to have captured a large quantity of war material.'[401]

## 21 September 1921
### National Army Robert O'Sullivan

All that is known about O'Sullivan's death is that he was accidentally shot in Kinsale Barracks.[402]

## 22 September 1922
### Frances Haynes

On 23 September the *Irish Independent* reported: 'At the inquest on Mrs. Haynes (73), who died of wounds received during an attack by Irregulars on Moore's Hotel, Cork, Mrs. R. Dalton, 12 Morrison's Island, said during the firing she heard a scream from upstairs and found Mrs. Haynes standing outside her bedroom door. She said "I am badly hit, Mrs. Dalton" and fell. Sergt. J. Browne, National Army, stationed at the A.O.H. Hall, Morrison's Island, said he saw a Ford car coming up on the opposite side. After going down about 50 yards it stopped and a crowd came round the corner of Buckingham Pl. The car backed towards the crowd, and then he heard a Lewis gun played on the quay between the A.O.H. Hall and Moore's Hotel. He put his men in positions at each window at once. An armoured car went in pursuit of the Ford car. Medical evidence was that deceased died of shock following receiving 7 bullets.'[403]

## 22 September 1922
## Timothy Collins

Nothing at this stage would be known of the death of Timothy Collins, because it was never reported in the newspapers and there is no evidence that an inquest was held, except for a single question asked in the Dáil. On 15 May 1924 Tadhg Ó Murchadha 'asked the Minister for Finance whether he is aware that a claim for compensation made by Timothy Collins, Hollyhill, Glengarriffe [*sic*], Co. Cork, in respect of the kidnapping and murder of his son on the 22nd of September, 1922, was rejected; whether the victim was employed at the Eccles Hotel, Glengarriffe, and contributed ten shillings per week to his parents' support, and whether the case will be reconsidered with a view to giving Collins some compensation'. Ernest Blythe answered: 'This case was fully and carefully investigated by the Compensation (Personal Injuries) Committee, who considered that the applicant was not dependent upon the deceased. The application was, therefore, refused. I see no reason why the case should be reopened.'[404]

## 24 September 1922
## Anti-Treaty IRA Patrick Mangan

The IRA prisoners in Cork Gaol went on hunger strike over conditions in the prison, which were acknowledged by all sides as dire. At 7 p.m. on Saturday evening they informed the governor that they would refuse food and at 10.30 a.m. the following day they refused to leave the exercise yard. The stand-off lasted almost an hour and a half with the head guard going as far as firing shots over the heads of the prisoners. The guards eventually managed to clear the yard but had great difficulty in getting the rioting prisoners back into their cells. At 11.50 a.m. the sentries were ordered to fire to frighten them back into their cells. Some, including Mangan, still refused and one of the sentries fired again, hitting and killing Mangan.[405]

**24 September 1922**

**Anti-Treaty IRA Jeremiah Long**

Long died in a motorcycle accident at Myrtleville. He is buried in the Republican Plot according to the *Irish Independent*.[406]

**25/28 September 1922**

**National Army Bernard Murphy**

Bernard Murphy was accidentally shot and killed in Victoria Barracks, Cork, on 25 or 28 September 1922 (his pension file records both dates). Murphy had served in the Royal Garrison Artillery of the British Army and enlisted in the National Army on 18 July 1922. On 30 September 1922 the *Irish Independent* reported: 'Yesterday there took place to the National Army Plot in Glasnevin the funeral of Pte. Bernard Murphy, of the Volunteer Reserve, 8, Lr. Mercer St., Dublin, who was accidentally killed in Cork. The coffin, covered with the Tricolour and numerous wreaths, had reposed overnight in Whitefriars St. Church and the funeral took place after the celebration of Requiem Mass. The cortege included the Pipers' Band, Beggar's Bush, under Acting-Lieut. Lawlor, and a guard of honour and firing party from Portobello Barracks.'[407]

**27 September 1922**

**National Army Edward Searls**

*The Southern Star* of 30 September stated: 'On Saturday evening, about seven o'clock, a Crossley tender with troops, on the way from Ballinhassig through Innishannon, was ambushed on the Bandon side of Innishannon, the Irregulars using a Thompson gun in addition to rifles, from the heights across the river. One of the soldiers was hit by an explosive bullet in the head, part of the skull being blown away, and it is feared that there is no hope for his recovery.' The reporter was clearly unaware that Searls was already dead, having succumbed to his injury on 27 September.[408]

## 28 September 1922

### Anti-Treaty IRA Seán O'Donoghue

On Thursday 28 September 1922 Seán O'Donoghue was shot dead when attempting to ambush National Army forces two miles outside Cork city. He was acting O/C of Cork No. 1 Brigade. It was reported that O'Donoghue was one of thirty-nine prisoners recently escaped from Cork Gaol. Subsequent reports stated that he was shot in a Free State lorry after his recapture. The evidence given at the military inquiry is shocking. Seamus Collins, who had been captured and put in the back of a military truck along with O'Donoghue, gave evidence that O'Donoghue was threatened, assaulted and then murdered by a soldier. As Collins himself had been shot and seriously wounded, his evidence carried great weight with the military court. He identified the murderer at an identity parade and the court found that there was a *prima facie* case of murder to be answered. The soldier was taken into custody.[409]

## 29 September 1922

### National Army Stephen Donovan

'Stephen O'Donovan [*sic*], Kilbarry, Dunmanway, was killed near Inchigeela on Friday. He was the victim of a sniper's bullet. Further particulars concerning the advance of the National troops from Inchigeela on Ballingeary and Ballyvourney go to show that the Irregulars were in very large numbers on hills beyond Inchigeela, and occupied fortified positions. By a flanking movement they were driven into a confined area. While one party of Irregulars was coming out of a cave, artillery was brought into action against them. The shrapnel took a heavy toll, and the Irregulars suffered many casualties, the dead and wounded, being taken away on horse.' In contrast to this newspaper report, the pension claim from Donovan's mother claimed that he was killed by machine-gun fire. While there is no doubt about the death of Stephen Donovan and his burial in Dunmanway, two weeks after his death, there is no evidence that the anti-Treaty IRA suffered any serious casualties in this action.[410]

## 4 October 1922
## Jeremiah Holland

During a National Army offensive in Kealkill against anti-Treaty forces, who had retreated there after the unsuccessful attack on Bantry in which Gibbs Ross was killed, a farmer named Holland was shot through the head and died instantly. He had either been ploughing or was walking into town when he was shot. It is not known by whom he was shot but it is likely to have been National Army troops. His death certificate stated that he died from a gunshot wound a few days after the shooting, was from Cahirmountain, and that there was no inquest.[411]

## 4 October 1922
## Patrick Burns
## Daniel O'Hanlon

The deaths of these two young men were described at the court of inquiry into their deaths as 'the cruellest murder'. Evidence given to the court of inquiry stated that the anti-Treaty IRA had shot them. Locals believed that their deaths were the result of a boycott on a local man (unnamed), whom the two men used to work with. However, the evidence also presents other plausible reasons for the targeting of Burns. Burns apparently had found a shotgun buried in a hayrick the day before he was taken away and it is likely that this belonged to the anti-Treaty forces. The *Irish Independent* recorded that a witness 'saw the bodies in a turnip field two miles away, tied by the arms with a handkerchief. Witness's opinion was that they were tied before being shot. Witness repeated that he had no doubt that the men were shot by irregulars – the neighbours would not do it. The deceased (O'Hanlon) had been a Volunteer during the war with England, and the brother of the other deceased was a member of the National Army at present. O'Hanlon was aged about 38. Witness thought the whole thing was a local conspiracy over the threshing.'[412]

**5 October 1922**

**Anti-Treaty IRA Patrick Pearse**

**Anti-Treaty IRA Daniel Sullivan**

**Anti-Treaty IRA Michael Hayes**

On 5 October 1922 three anti-Treaty soldiers were shot dead near the village of Upton, Co. Cork. The men died when they attempted to cut off a small National Army outpost but were surprised by a larger force of troops. The official communiqué stated: 'On Thursday evening, while troops of the Kinsale command, were operating between Innishannon and Upton, three irregulars attempted to cut off a small post. They were fully armed and called on to halt, and on refusing to do so were fired on by the outposts. The irregulars were shot dead, and on their bodies being searched, over 300 rounds of ammunition were found. One of them was in uniform. Later on in the evening when reinforcements arrived, the whole district was searched, and a new Ford taxi was discovered hidden in a hollow of a field. The National forces brought back the bodies to Kinsale.'[413]

**6 October 1922**

**Anti-Treaty IRA Francis Power**

The only place that the death of Francis Power is recorded is on the IRA Cork No. 1 Brigade monument in Donoughmore Cemetery, Co. Cork. According to this he was 'killed in battle' at White's Cross. There is no other record to explain what happened to Power. It is possible that he was an unidentified victim of the ambush of 28 September during which Seán O'Donoghue was killed, but this is only speculation. A death certificate for a Francis Power is recorded in Dublin on 2 November and as this man died of a gunshot wound it is possible that it is the same man.[414]

**6 October 1922**

**Anti-Treaty IRA Daniel O'Donovan**

On Friday 6 October anti-Treaty forces were demolishing the main bridge allowing access to Timoleague. As Daniel O'Donovan removed the keystone to collapse the arch he failed to get clear and was buried under seven tons of masonry, which killed him instantly.[415]

## 8 October 1922
### National Army Charles Kearns

Kearns' mother, Annie, claimed for the death of her son in the Imperial Hotel on 8 October 1922. It seems that the wound may have been self-inflicted through accident, as the part of the standard declaration that states the wound was not attributable to his own negligence was crossed out by Adjutant General Gearóid O'Sullivan.[416]

## 11 October 1922
### National Army Joseph (James) Claffey

Sergeant Joseph Claffey was shot dead accidentally in Bandon by a colleague. He was a member of the Dublin Brigade. His father, who had also been in the army, but had been demobilised, claimed for compensation but this was rejected as he had no dependency on his son.[417]

## 11 October 1922
### Anti-Treaty IRA Richard Noonan

A military court inquired into the death of Richard Noonan (18), who was a prisoner in Cork Gaol. 'Michael Carey (political prisoner) stated: "Richard Noonan was a prisoner with me. I saw him on the day of his death. He died about 4.30 p.m. It may be a few hours before this I saw I him. From information I gathered he suffered from a slight complaint before. He never made any complaint to me. I knew him for a considerable time and long before he came to prison. He never made any complaint, and I had no reason to believe he would die suddenly." The Court found that the deceased died of cardiac failure.' Noonan is buried in the Republican Plot at St Finbarr's Cemetery.[418]

## 12 October 1922
### National Army Patrick Byrne

On 11 October 1922 two soldiers of the National Army were shot during an anti-Treaty ambush when marching between Dunmanway and Clonakilty, Co. Cork. Seán Hales was in charge of the column, which was ambushed at Ballygurteen by 'a large party of irregulars who opened fire from the cover of a low hill'. According to the report the National Army troops engaged their attackers and, after 'a very hot engagement', the attackers withdrew. Initial reports stated that two men were mortally wounded in the attack – Private Hayes of Clonakilty who died from his wounds at the scene and Private Byrne who died from 'very serious wounds' in Dunmanway Hospital the following day. However, *The Cork Examiner* corrected this and stated that Hayes was still alive on 16 October. This, combined with the absence of a death certificate and no MSPC record, suggests that he survived.[419]

## 16 October 1922
### John (Patrick) Walsh

The newspapers initially reported that at about 10 o'clock on the night of 16 October 1922 armed men shot dead John Walsh of Gerald Griffin Street, Cork, at his home.[420] In fact, he was killed on Great William O'Brien Street coming home from the pictures with his wife. The *Irish Independent* on 19 October reported that he occasionally drove National Army troops, which is presumably the reason for his shooting. On 28 October the newspaper reported: 'ten arrests have been made by National troops on the north side of the city. They include some men who are alleged to have been implicated in the murder of Patrick J. Walsh … [it is] alleged that one of the men, now in custody, was seen crouching in a doorway near the scene of the shooting on the night that Mr. Walsh was fatally shot.'

## 16 October 1922
### National Army Jeremiah Driscoll

Jeremiah Driscoll died following the accidental discharge of Private Hurley's rifle in 'The Rink', Bantry, on 16 October 1922. There appears not to have been an inquest, so there are no details of what exactly happened.[421]

## 17 October 1922
### Anti-Treaty IRA James O'Callaghan

'National troops travelling in a Crossley tender from Mallow were ambushed near Castletownroche last night by a party of Irregulars, who attempted [to] hold up their car on the road. One of the attackers was shot dead. Darkness having fallen, the ambushers apparently mistook the tender for a civilian motor. Some of the party having come into the middle of the road to hold up with revolvers, the driver of the tender was ordered to speed ahead, and the troops opened fire with a Lewis gun and rifles on the Irregulars, who now realising what they were up against, crossed the ditch and returned the fire. The tender, which was conveying an armed escort for a Government aeroplane forced to come down in the district because of engine trouble, never halted, and its passengers suffered no casualties. Subsequently a stronger force proceeded to the scene of the attack, and discovered a dead Irregular named Callaghan [*sic*], lying behind a ditch with his revolver beside him. Part of his hand was blown away apparently by the fire of the Lewis gun. A roadside memorial in Killavullen identifies him as James O'Callaghan, who was killed on 16 October [*sic*].'[422]

## 20 October 1922
### National Army Daniel Sullivan

Daniel Sullivan (18) from Burgita, Rosscarbery, was shot while removing a roadblock at Curragh Hill, three miles to the west of Clonakilty. According to his MSPC file he died on 17 October, but *The Southern Star* stated that he died on 20 October in Donovan's Hotel, where he had been taken after the ambush. His parents, who were in poor circumstances, were awarded £60 in compensation.[423]

## 22 October 1922
### Anti-Treaty IRA Daniel O'Halloran

The irishmedals.org website states: 'On Sunday the 22nd of October 1922 anti-Treaty Volunteer Daniel O'Halloran aged 34 was killed in an ambush on Free State troops at Carrigaloe, County Cork. A Lieutenant of the National Army gave evidence at the inquest that he had left Queenstown at 9.30 to visit troops at Belvally and on his return journey a bomb was thrown at the car he was travelling in; one of the men in the car was wounded. On reaching Queenstown the Lieutenant got some reinforcements and returned to the scene of the ambush. When they returned fire was opened on them, which they returned. During this exchange of fire O'Halloran was killed. O'Halloran's brother stated at the inquest "he was probably killed in armed opposition to the National Forces" and added "he was killed in a fair fight".'[424]

## 22 October 1922
### National Army Thomas O'Mahony

The *Irish Independent* reported on 24 October that on the previous 'Sunday morning a party of troops, under Brig. Comdt. Ahern, marched to Rathduane, where, after Mass, they arrested Denis Murphy (carpenter), and J. Twohig (farm labourer). As the party, on their return with the prisoners, reached Annagloor, about a mile from the town, fire was opened on them from both sides of the road at a point where little or no shelter was available … In the opening fire Private Thomas O'Mahony, a native of Midleton, received a serious bullet wound in the stomach. A priest and doctor from Millstreet were promptly in attendance, and after the wounded man received careful attention he was removed in a military ambulance to Cork. It is not known what casualties the irregulars may have sustained. Later the soldier died on the way to a Cork hospital from Millstreet. He was being removed to the Mercy Hospital for an operation, but succumbed to the wound before reaching that institution.' He was buried in the Republican Plot in Midleton.[425]

## 23 October 1922
### National Army James Marum

James Marum was shot and killed in Charleville. Marum joined the National Army in May 1922. Both his wife, Isabella, and his mother, Ellen, made claims as dependants for a pension. His mother stated in her application that Marum had been a member of the British Army for eleven and a half years previous to joining the National Army. He was from Bray, Co. Wicklow. There were a number of possible incidents in Charleville around this time, but no soldiers were stated to have been killed. However, three soldiers were wounded on 18 October and it is possible that Marum was one of these.[426]

## 23 October 1922
### Ellen (Lily) Gallagher

A grenade or bomb was thrown at a Free State Crossley tender in Cork city on 18 October, but bounced off into the street at the Lee Boot Factory before it exploded, seriously injuring two young girls. Ellen (Lily) Gallagher from Western Road sustained a head wound from the shrapnel and, despite regaining consciousness the following morning, passed away a few days later at the Mercy Hospital. She was approximately thirteen.[427]

## 25 October 1922
### Anti-Treaty IRA William Cox

Cox (23) was shot during a firefight when National Army troops raided a house. On their approach they were attacked by rifle and machine-gun fire. Cox died that night in Midleton Hospital. The *Irish Independent* reported: 'A court of inquiry held ... into the circumstances of the death of a young man named William Cox, who was fatally wounded near [Mount Uniake] Killeagh during a search carried out by military the previous afternoon, found that he died from shock and haemorrhage caused by a bullet fired by a member of the National forces in the execution of his duty, the said William Cox being at the time engaged in an attack on National troops.'[428]

## 26 October 1922
### David Nolan

'A military inquiry was held in Cork into the death of David Nolan, who died from an injury received on 22 October when a military lorry collided with a trap in which he and another were occupants on Washington Street. The accident apparently occurred after bombs were thrown and shots fired at National Army troops. The court was of the opinion that the circumstances in the case were such as to warrant a recommendation that the widow and children of the deceased should receive reasonable compensation from the army authorities.' Nolan, who was secretary of the Lee Boot Company, lived at Homeville, Magazine Road, and was married with young children.[429]

## 28 October 1922
### National Army Peter Byrne

There is much confusion about this killing. In a letter sent to the Ministry of Defence, a man called Michael Hanley stated that the man buried as Peter Byrne was, in fact, his son, also called Michael. The newspapers and Michael Hanley Senior stated that the shooting was in Galway, but the claim made by Mary Francis Morgan, the aunt and foster mother of Peter Byrne, suggests that the dead man was shot in Buttevant. Although there is no mention in the newspapers of any incident in Buttevant that would match this event, the pensions file includes a letter from the records office in Portobello Barracks, Dublin, confirming that a Peter Byrne was killed on 28 October 1922. The letter gives no further details.[430]

## 28 October 1922
## Daniel Griffin

Shots were fired on a military truck on Patrick's Bridge and Daniel Griffin (29) of Roche's Buildings was struck by one of the bullets and killed. The bullet had passed through the coat pocket of his friend. 'He was on his way home from work at Ford's. While none of the occupants of the military car was hurt a shot, however, struck, Mr. Griffin, who was crossing the bridge, and he fell seriously wounded in the right buttock.' He died subsequently from blood poisoning.[431]

## 30 October 1922
## National Army Daniel Dennehy

The *Cork Examiner* recorded: 'Yesterday morning about 4.30 the little military post at Monard, about three or four miles from Cork, which was established for the protection of the railway and bridge, was attacked by irregulars. One soldier named Daniel Dennehy, Old Youghal Road, Cork, was killed. The irregulars were eventually put to flight, and it is known that at least two of them were hit.' On 13 November the same newspaper reported: 'The Irish Transport and General Workers' Union Fife and Drum Band, accompanied by Ald. Kenneally, the officials of the Union, and some members marched to Rathcooney graveyard yesterday to pay tribute to one of their members, the late Volunteer Dennehy, of the National Army. Vol. Dennehy was fatally wounded in the recent attack on the outpost at Monard Bridge.'[432]

## 1 November 1922
## National Army Jeremiah O'Sullivan

The facts of Jeremiah O'Sullivan's death were simple. While he was on guard at Cork Female Prison he was shot and killed by the accidental discharge of another soldier's rifle. The other soldier, Donovan, was exonerated of any blame at a military inquiry. Jeremiah (20), whose brother also served in the

National Army, was from Deanrock, Togher, Cork. His mother was awarded a small pension.[433]

**4 November 1922**
**Anti-Treaty IRA John Howell**
**Anti-Treaty IRA Timothy (Tadhg) O'Leary**
**National Army Thomas Gallagher**
**National Army Michael Woods (Wolfe)**
**7 November 1922**
**National Army Andrew Horgan**

The newspapers provided a graphic account of an intense anti-Treaty attack on the twin villages of Ballineen/Enniskeane, during which all five casualties occurred.[434] At 5 a.m. the National Army posts in the villages were attacked. The main attack was concentrated on the hotel, where the officer in charge, Captain Byrne, was upstairs. The anti-Treaty IRA captured the ground floor and besieged the men above. They brought a Lewis gun into the building and fired through the ceiling. Captain Byrne jumped out a window, which was 20 feet above ground level, with a Lewis gun and opened fire on the ground floor. However, both he and the rest of the troops were taken prisoner. Other National Army soldiers fought a fierce house-to-house defence until about ten o'clock, when the anti-Treaty forces retreated. The fighting left two dead on each side and Horgan badly wounded.

O'Leary's death was the subject of a Dáil question in May 1937. Tadhg Ó Murchadha 'asked the Minister for Defence if he would state the present position of the claim lodged by the late John O'Leary, South Square, Macroom, in respect of the death of his son, Timothy, killed in action at Ballineen, County Cork, on 4th November 1922'. The minister, Frank Aiken, replied that a claim for Anthony O'Leary was being now considered. Timothy was twenty-five when he died and his young brother Anthony was twelve and an invalid.[435]

John Howell's death notice stated that he was the second son of Edmond

Howell, Broaght, Doneraile and that he had been interred in Old Court Cemetery on 6 November. He was recorded as aged ten in the 1901 census, making him thirty when he died. This is confirmed by his death certificate, which was issued in 1933. Andrew Horgan died on 7 November in Bandon Hospital.[436]

**5 November 1922**
**Samuel Jones**
**James Lack**

*The Freeman's Journal* reported: 'Samuel Jones, aged 15, son of Captain Jones, of the ketch *Isabella*, of Gloucester, and James Lack, aged 40, mate of the same vessel, were fatally wounded in Youghal on Sunday night. They were proceeding through Grattan Street with the skipper when they were challenged by the sentry at the Constabulary Barracks. Not thinking that the challenge was meant for them they failed to halt. A shot was fired from the barracks. The bullet struck Lack in the breast, emerged and penetrated the boy's jaw. They were immediately brought into the barracks and Drs. Twomey and Kevin and the Rev. Mr. Elliott, Methodist minister, were called. Lack died almost immediately, and Jones succumbed on his way to hospital. The *Isabella* was to have left Youghal on Sunday morning but was delayed through the illness of one of the crew. The tragedy created a painful sensation in the town.'[437]

**7 November 1922**
**William Aherne**

*The Southern Star* reported on 11 November that William Aherne of Model Cottages was shot by the IRA as a spy: 'The body of a man named William Aherne, aged 30, was found at Bishopstown, near Cork, at about 9.30 o'clock on Tuesday evening. On the body was a label inscribed, "Shot as spy – IRA". Aherne was a native of the district. The body was brought by national soldiers into Cork Hospital. A military inquiry will be held.'[438]

## 10 November 1922
## Helena Barry

*The Cork Examiner* reported: 'A Military Court of Inquiry in lieu of inquest was held yesterday morning into the circumstances of the death of Miss Helena Barry [26], who died in the Mercy Hospital on Saturday as a result of a bullet wound received on the 3rd October in her home near Bantry. Her mother, Mrs. Brigid Barry, gave evidence of identification. She told the Court that on the day her daughter was shot irregulars passed the road and asked for a drink of milk. She gave them a drink, and when they were at the door, she said she saw National troops fire at them. It was about 9 a.m. when the irregulars called. The firing went on about half an hour. Then the irregulars went away and the National troops came in and searched the house, but they found nothing and went out again. After that more firing started and lasted about three hours. Her daughter, who was in the kitchen washing when the firing began, went under the table for protection, but she was struck by a bullet. After some time, the irregulars came back and sent for a priest and doctor.' Helena's brother, who had been an anti-Treaty fighter, refused to confirm that National Army troops had fired into the house after searching it, despite the court asking him repeatedly about this allegation.[439]

## 10 November 1922
## James Murphy

The *Evening Herald* reported: 'A military inquiry here into the death of James Murphy, an ex-soldier, who died as a result of wounds received while standing at the gateway of Murphy's Brewery, Leitrim St., when an attack was made on Cork Barracks on Friday night, found that death was due to shock and haemorrhage caused by a wound in the abdomen.' The inquiry concluded that he could not have been hit by fire from the barracks and must have been shot by the attackers. However, there is a direct line of sight from the barracks gates to the brewery around 500 metres away, and although to hit Murphy from the barracks would have been difficult, it was not impossible, so the inquiry may have been incorrect.[440]

## 11 November 1922
### National Army Frank Creegan

The death of Frank Creegan was an accident: 'A military inquiry was held at the Imperial Hotel, Cork, yesterday, into the circumstances of the death of Vol. Frank Creegan, a native of Cobh, who was injured in a motor smash at Castletownroche last Saturday week, and died in Fermoy Hospital last Saturday morning. A military doctor stated that on receiving a report on the date mentioned he went to Castletownroche and found four injured men there, amongst them being the deceased, who had a bad fracture of the right leg. [They had run into a tree felled across the road.] Witness treated him provisionally and had him removed to Fermoy Hospital. On Friday last complications set in and an operation was performed, but he died on Saturday morning. Death, in his opinion, was due to septic poisoning. A commandant stationed in Rathcormac stated that on the date of the accident he was in charge of certain military operations in that district. Those under his command divided into two parties, one going to Anakissa and the other to Doneraile. There was some indiscriminate firing from a Ford car in which some of the soldiers travelled. From other evidence it appeared that the Crossley car in which the deceased and others were driving when the accident occurred had been left on the roadside while the lieutenant in charge of it and the official driver went into a house for tea, and was taken by this party of soldiers without authority. A captain said that deceased, whom he saw in hospital, gave as an explanation for taking the Crossley that they were all "fairly tight".'[441]

## 13 November 1922
### Eileen O'Driscoll

Perhaps one of the most tragic events of the Civil War occurred in Riverstown on 13 November. Three days later the *Irish Independent* reported: 'Heavy firing was heard during the Tuesday [14 November] night in Glanmire direction, and it appears the military barracks in that village were attacked. The troops replied to the firing and after an exchange of shots the attackers were forced to withdraw. The troops suffered no casualties.' On the previous day two boys had found cartridges in Riverstown Graveyard, which were probably left there for use in this attack, and took them home. One of the boys threw a bullet onto the fire and when it exploded it filled the room with smoke. A little girl in the room was hit and collapsed, the place where she fell covered with blood. She was just three years and three months old. Her mother wrapped her in a sheet and put her on the bed, then went to get a pony and trap. The child was taken to the Mercy Hospital where it was found that she had been shot through the intestines. There was no hope for her as the bullet and casing had passed through her body. She died between 7.30 and 8 p.m.[442]

## 13 November 1922
## Mary (Molly) Egan

According to *The Freeman's Journal*, Molly Egan was driving a horse and car through Newtownshandrum when she was called on to halt by Private Breen of the National Army, which was raiding the town. An account given later by Michael Shine, who was in the village at the time, contests this. He said that Egan had been given a lift in the car by two IRA men, Edmond McCarthy and Thomas Creagh, who were armed. He also claimed that two other civilians, Nora Fitzgerald and Hugh Aherne, were in the car when fire was opened on it. According to *The Freeman's Journal*, Breen stated that 'he saw a rifle in the car being pointed at one of our men about ten yards distance'. Both Breen and Captain Hannan fired on the car. Shine recorded that the two IRA men fled, McCarthy returning fire with his revolver but leaving his rifle behind in the car. When reinforcements arrived they approached and found Egan's body 'lying across the car'. She had no arms or ammunition on her person, but Private Considine stated that he found 'a rifle, five cartridges and a flat nosed bullet in the car'. Molly lived locally and was twenty-four when she died.[443]

## 14 November 1922
### National Army John F. Cronin

John Cronin was working for the National Army's Labour Corps on the railway line at Rathduff Station. The anti-Treaty IRA attacked the post and the troops guarding it returned fire. The battle lasted about ten minutes. At 7 p.m. Cronin and two of the soldiers went into the waiting room and a few minutes later the soldiers began to unload their rifles. One of them pressed the trigger (thinking the gun was empty) and the rifle discharged. The bullet went through the other soldier's clothing before lodging in Cronin's body. He was shot through the armpit. The soldier was arrested but at the inquiry Cronin's father stated that he accepted it was an accident and this was noted by the court.[444]

## 14 November 1922
### National Army William Cronin

*The Southern Star* reported: 'We regret to have to announce the death of Volunteer W. Cronin, of the National Forces, who succumbed to injuries received in an ambush near Durrus Road, Bantry, on last Saturday [11 November]. The deceased, who was wounded in the abdomen, was convoyed to Bandon, where he passed away on Tuesday evening. The remains were removed to the Pro-Cathedral, Skibbereen, on Wednesday, and on Thursday the funeral took place to the family burying place in Abbeystrowrey. The deceased, who was a son of the late Mr. John Cronin, carriage builder, was a very respectable young man, and the greatest sympathy is felt with his bereaved relatives. May he rest in peace. The funeral was attended by a large gathering of town folk. Rev. P. McCarthy officiated. The coffin, which was draped in the tricolour and bore on it the deceased's military cap, was carried on the shoulders of stalwart and loving comrades-in-arms.'[445]

**16 November 1922**

**National Army William Francis Woulahan**

One of the great problems in finding evidence for the deaths in this book is that many of the people involved could neither read nor write. This leads to difficulties that are often impossible to solve. In this case the bad handwriting of the person who filled in her claim denied Mrs Mary Woulahan a pension. To the authorities her surname appeared to be Wonlahan, and there was no record of a William Francis Wonlahan in the military files. His name is correctly inscribed on the plinth around Michael Collins' grave. There is no mention in the available sources about what happened to Woulahan (33), other than that he was shot in action in Bandon. The brief *Irish Independent* report simply stated: 'The funeral of Pte. W. F. Woulahan, National Army, late of 49, Charlemont St., killed in action in Bandon, took place with full military honours at Rathmines Church, after Requiem Mass, to Glasnevin. The cortege was headed by the Fife and Drum Band of the 2nd Eastern Div. under Sergt. Healy, Wellington Barracks. A bodyguard was furnished by deceased's comrades under Capt. O'Doherty. The firing party was in charge of Co. Sergt-Major Duffy. Rev. R. Concannon, C.F., said the prayers at the grave. The funeral arrangements were in charge of Staff Capt. Stafford.' Woulahan was living in Rathdrum with his family at the time of the 1911 census.[446]


**17 November 1922**

**Anti-Treaty IRA Patrick Duggan**

The only public record of the shooting of Patrick Duggan is in *Rebel Cork's Fighting Story*, which states he was killed by Free State forces on 17 November 1922. The place of death given is Glengarriff.[447] His death certificate (issued in 1933) stated that Duggan died instantly from gunshot wounds.

**20 November 1922**

**Madge Daly**

**National Army Daniel Desmond**

Madge Daly (24) was the eldest of three orphaned children. She worked in the Edinboro Hotel in the city and her two younger siblings lived at 37 Cathedral Walk. She was a member of the Confraternity and visited St Mary's on Pope's Quay most evenings after checking on her siblings. She was walking down Mulgrave Road and as she was passing a National Army patrol, which included Daniel Desmond, shots rang out. A sentry had challenged a man coming out of Devonshire Street and the man had opened fire from a distance of 20 yards. One bullet struck the soldier's rifle but the others hit both Daly and Desmond in the head, killing them instantly. Compensation was paid to Daly's family and they emigrated to the United States, where their descendants still live. Trooper Desmond (20) was from nearby 2 Knapps Square.[448]

**23 November 1922**

**National Army Henry Stringer**

The only newspaper report of Stringer's death stated: 'National forces operating in North Cork report that on Thursday a party of troops under Capt. Delaney on their way from Millstreet to Kanturk, were ambushed near Kilcornery, one of their number being fatally wounded. The troops were travelling in a lorry and when they reached a damaged bridge in Kilcorney district they got out to push the lorry across a temporary bridge which had been put up. As they were getting into the lorry fire was opened on them from three sides. One soldier named Stringer, a native of Mallow, was wounded. He was placed in the lorry, where he died shortly afterwards. Other members of the party immediately took cover, and vigorously replied. An exchange of shots lasted about 20 minutes, after which the attacking party withdrew. It is not known if they suffered any casualties. The remains of Private Stringer were conveyed to Kanturk, and were subsequently removed to Mallow for interment.'[449]

**24 November 1922**
**National Army Thomas McCann**
**National Army John Walsh**

The court of inquiry was told what happened: 'A military witness said he was with the party that travelled on a Crossley tender to White's Cross on the day in question. The night previous to that day he had also visited the scene with a party of soldiers. They went there for the purpose of dislodging a mine which they were told was laid there. After some time they decided to let it alone until the following day when they would have the advantage of the daylight. The deceased, McCann and Walsh, expressed the wish to accompany the party, as they had experience of lifting mines. When the place was visited on the second occasion, bombs were fired at the mine to explode it. Three bombs were fired, when McCann shouted: "It's a dud" and walked towards it. Witness advised him to be cautious, and in answer he said: "It's all right". McCann then procured a shovel, and was in the act of unearthing the mine when it exploded. The concussion threw witness a considerable distance away, dazing him. The military chaplain attended McCann. There were two cables attached to the mine, continued witness, but these were removed before any attempt was made to lift it. Witness thought three of the bombs which were fired at the mine went into the hole alongside it, but the splinters of them did not touch it. Machine gun fire had been directed at it from an elevation. Some nine rounds were fired at the mine, which did not appear to be laying there long. Witness identified the remains of Volunteer McCann at the hospital. Walsh was also badly injured on the occasion.' McCann served with the North Lancashire Regiment, Dublin Fusiliers and finished up in the King's Liverpool Regiment with the rank of company sergeant major. He fought in the First World War, seeing action at Gallipoli. Private John Walsh was from Blarney Street. The MSPC file states that John Walsh had also served with the British Army for a period of time prior to joining the National Army and his father, William Walsh, is stated to have served with the Royal Navy.[450]

**25 November 1922 (date uncertain)**
**Anti-Treaty IRA Patrick Healy**

Patrick Healy (30) was fighting with the anti-Treaty forces in and around Kanturk when he was killed. He was from High Street, Limerick. There are no other details available.[451]

**25 November 1922**
**James Delaney**

The *Irish Independent* recorded this death: 'A painful tragedy occurred in Cork on Saturday night, when John Delaney, Volunteer in the National Army, shot dead his brother James, 32 Warren's Lane. Evidence given at a military inquiry was to the effect that Volunteer Delaney left a patrol without permission and went to his mother's home, Warren's Lane. In the house at the time were two brothers, Thomas and James, the former being in bed and the latter engaged in the kitchen. Thomas Delaney stated that he heard his brother, John, ask his mother for a cup of tea. The next thing was that the soldier brother rushed out into the street, and the mother, "knowing how excitable John was", told James to go out after him. Witness also knew how excitable he was and how he was not responsible for his actions. Accordingly, he jumped out of bed and put on his pants. Rushing downstairs he caught his brother James at the door and threw his arms around him in order to pull him in from the door. "As I did so", concluded witness, with emotion, "a shot was fired and James fell dead in my arms. John was in the lane at the time … John held the rifle in an awkward position – partly under his arm – and did not mean to shoot". Further military evidence was that Volunteer John Delaney returned to Cork Co. Gaol, his headquarters, after midnight, and made a statement. He was then disarmed and placed under arrest. The court found that death was due to laceration of the brain, caused by a bullet inflicted by Volunteer John Delaney and recommended that John Delaney be arrested and court-martialled.'[452]

**27 November 1922**

**Daniel O'Meara (Mara)**

'On Saturday evening between 6 and 7 o'clock, two civilians were wounded, one very seriously, in Sunday's Well. They were Mr. O'Meara, a milkman, in the employment of Mr. T. Corcoran, ex-M.C.C, Leemount House, and Mr. Doocey, who is employed by Mr. Murphy, of Mount Desert. It appears that they were called upon to halt but failed to obey and were fired on with the unfortunate result mentioned. At the time of the shooting O'Meara was on his way back from the city in his milk car, while Doocey was walking in the opposite direction, towards the approaching milk car. O'Meara was called upon to halt by a military sentry on duty near the City Gaol, but did not obey the challenge, presumably having failed to hear it owing to the noise of the cart. The sentry fired and hit both O'Meara and Doocey, the latter as he was just turning round to return home on hearing the shots. The horse attached to the milk cart was also hit, so seriously that the animal had to be destroyed. Both of the wounded men were removed to the Mercy Hospital.' O'Meara, from Bishopstown, died two days later.[453]

**27 November 1922**

**National Army William Williamson**

**National Army Unknown**

Mrs Florence Payne, who lived at Upton House, was angry when she wrote to the newspapers on 29 November 1922. An ambush in which two National Army soldiers were killed had taken place at Cashel Hill, Upton, where many of her tenants lived. Three of the houses had been taken over and fortified by a large force of anti-Treaty IRA. As a National Army convoy headed to Bandon from Cork a 'hurricane of fire was opened on the passing troops'.[454]

Half the National Army convoy engaged the anti-Treaty men, while the other half went for reinforcements. When they arrived, the anti-Treaty IRA withdrew. Though neither of the troopers killed is named in the newspaper reports, it is probable that one was William Williamson, the only National Army soldier known to have been killed at this time in the Bandon area.[455]

The Bandon Command of the National Army seems to have been particularly poor at reporting events or following correct procedures. Williamson was a member of the 1st Scottish Brigade (and had been during the War of Independence, when there was a Scottish Brigade based in Glasgow) when he was shot. His body should have been shipped to Dublin for inspection by Captain Stafford of the burial section before funeral arrangements were made, but instead it was sent directly to Glasgow. William Fullerton, adjutant of the Scottish Brigade, found himself with a body, no grave and a family who did not have the money to pay for one, so he took it upon himself to sort out the mess. Adjutant General Gearóid O'Sullivan agreed with his decision, stating that to do otherwise would give 'propaganda value to the enemy'. However, a small life policy, which would have covered the cost of the burial, could not be paid as Captain Stafford could not issue a death certificate when he had not seen the body. Williamson was also the father of a young baby and had applied for permission to get married, which led to complications when compensation was sought. Unfortunately the MSPC file relating to this claim gives no details of how he died.[456]

## 30 November 1922
## National Army Daniel O'Leary

On 26 November 1922 Lieutenant O'Leary led a National Army column to take over Drimoleague after the Free State offensive had moved on towards Bantry. According to Colonel Murphy of the Cork Command: 'On November 30th something approaching a mutiny broke out in the ranks of his Column.' Murphy noted that it was not clear how Lieutenant O'Leary was killed, but that a shot was fired 'in the endeavour to quell the trouble' and he 'fell, mortally wounded'.[457]

**30 November 1922**

**Anti-Treaty IRA William Buckley**

Acting on information, National Army troops raided the Buckley home in Riverstown. William Buckley was a member of the anti-Treaty IRA. The *Irish Independent* reported: '… the military party under Lieutenant Hurley arrived at 7 o'clock and surrounded the village of Riverstown. Captain Farrelly, accompanied by Lieut. Hurley, proceeded to Buckley's house where they knocked at the door. The knock was answered by Buckley senior, who in reply to a question where his sons were, replied that one of them was upstairs. The officer then called on young Buckley to come down, and he answered "Yes, I will". At the same time he appeared at the top of the stairs, and without warning fired a revolver at the officer. Captain Farrelly escaped the bullet, which passed over Lieut. Hurley's head. Buckley fired again, and this time Lieut. Hurley was struck on the thigh. Fearing that Lieut. Hurley would be further wounded Capt. Farrelly dragged him from the house, and then called up his men, ordering them to rush the house.

'Buckley, availing of the brief absence of the military, escaped through a back window. The sentry placed outside called on him to halt, but instead he fired at the sentry. The sentry then fired, wounding Buckley in the stomach. Notwithstanding his wound he continued to run and got over a high fence, where he was fired at and wounded by another sentry. In all, he received three dangerous wounds. When arrested Buckley was found to be in possession of a Webley revolver … Buckley succumbed to his injuries late yesterday afternoon at the Mercy Hospital.'[458]

**4 December 1922**

**National Army Unknown**

A party of sixty anti-Treaty fighters ambushed a Free State convoy of two lorries accompanying General Ennis on the main Drimoleague to Dunmanway road in West Cork and a National Army sergeant was killed. The machine-gun on an armoured car accompanying General Ennis failed to fire and he had to retreat using the cover of his Lancia touring car. Gunner McPeake later explained that it was jammed. The troops called for air support and an aeroplane arrived, which bombed and machine-gunned the anti-Treaty fighters. They dispersed in a panic, abandoning their arms. The *Irish Independent* interviewed Lieutenant Fitzmaurice, who confirmed that this was the first action by the newly formed Irish Air Corps. The newspaper stated that the anti-Treaty side suffered many casualties, but there is no other evidence for this.[459]

**6 December 1922**
**National Army Thomas Nolan**
**Cornelius O'Leary**
**7 December 1922**
**National Army William McNeice**

An attack on Ballymakeera by anti-Treaty forces (often called the battle of Ballyvourney in the sources) to rescue one of their men resulted in the death of Thomas Nolan and the wounding of fifteen other National Army troops. Each side had an armoured car; the anti-Treaty one was 'Sliabh na mBan', which been stolen from Bandon the previous night by Jock McPeake, who had been driving it at Béal na Bláth when Michael Collins was killed three months earlier. National Army troops rolled two grenades under the Sliabh na mBan, but while the explosion lifted it off the ground, it was not put out of action. Anti-Treaty IRA soldiers forced their way into the Hibernian Hotel, firing shots up through the ceiling and rescuing their colleague. Jamie Moynihan recorded that a civilian, Cornelius O'Leary, was shot and killed, and that Volunteer McNeice was badly wounded in the abdomen and unlikely to live.[460] Private Thomas Nolan was killed by gunfire in the house where he was billeted. Private William McNeice died subsequently in the Mercy Hospital in Cork.[461]

## 6 December 1922
### National Army Daniel Hurley

Daniel Hurley was guarding the mail lorry from Fermoy to Cork. To get to Victoria Barracks required the lorry to stop before negotiating a steep hill. At this point fire was opened on the lorry and Hurley was shot. He was taken to the Mercy Hospital, where he was examined by Dr Hamilton, but as the wounds were abdominal, nothing could be done and he died that evening. He had fought in the Great War as part of the Leinster Regiment and was a native of Fermoy; he is buried in Castlehyde. His funeral was notable, as eighty veterans of the Great War marched in the cortège.[462]

## 6 December 1922
### Anti-Treaty IRA Daniel (Jeremiah) Casey

Timothy Buckley stated: 'With about five men from Clondrohid company, I was on outpost duty during the attack by our battalion column on the Free State forces in Ballyvourney on December 6th, 1922. Enemy forces raided Gortnalicka late in the evening of the day of this attack. They opened fire from a distance on Daniel Casey who was alone in the district and was armed with a rifle. Casey was wounded and, when the officer in charge of the Free State forces reached the wounded man, he (the officer) shot him through the heart. This officer's name was Conlan. My sister and my wife were the first people to reach the dead man.'[463]

## 7 December 1922
### National Army General Seán Hales

The Free State started executing anti-Treaty IRA members found in possession of weapons after a Public Safety Resolution was passed by the Dáil on 28 September. Erskine Childers, the Dáil's director of publicity during the War of Independence, was executed in Beggar's Bush for possession of a small revolver, which had apparently had been given to him by Michael Collins. On 30 November anti-Treaty Chief of Staff Liam Lynch issued the 'orders of frightfulness', which stated that anyone who had voted for the Public Safety Resolution was a legitimate target for reprisal. Seven days later Seán Hales was its first victim.[464]

On 6 December 1922 Hales, who had been commanding an army unit in Co. Cork but was also a TD, arrived in Dublin for the formal establishment of the Irish Free State. Hales had been a close friend of Michael Collins and one of the most senior IRA fighters in the Cork No. 3 Brigade during the War of Independence. He took the pro-Treaty side, famously declaring, 'If it's good enough for Mick Collins, it's good enough for me.' His brother Tom rejected the Treaty and was in charge of the ambush where Collins was shot. Seán's arrival at the Dáil had caused amusement among Dubliners, who 'marvelled' at the sight of a man in full military uniform wearing a homburg hat.[465]

On 7 December Hales and the new deputy speaker of the Dáil, Pádraig Ó Máille, went for lunch in the Ormond Hotel. At 2.40 p.m. they hailed a side-car to take them to Leinster House. As they were seated, six men 'opened fire from 12 yards away'. Hales was fatally wounded while Ó Maille was shot in the back and arm.[466] Hales was rushed to Jervis Street Hospital, just 750 metres away, but died within minutes. He had been shot in the temple, throat, left lung, arm and thigh.[467]

Less than an hour later, a clearly shocked President Cosgrave informed the Dáil 'that Deputy Sean Hales has been shot dead and that Deputy Padraig Ó Máille has been wounded. I just got information a few moments ago and I give it to the Dáil now officially.'

Minister for Defence Richard Mulcahy commented: 'There was neither Press present, nor were the Deputies asked if they would like to see their relatives, nor were they asked would they like to see a clergyman, nor were they asked had they any private business of their own that they would like to transact.'[468] His remarks were prompted by criticisms of the government in denying such rights to Republican prisoners who had previously been executed and those under sentence of death.

## 8 December 1922
### Anti-Treaty IRA Richard (Dick) Barrett

What happened after the death of Seán Hales almost beggars belief.[469] During the evening of 7 December members of the government met to discuss what they would do. The heads of the army proposed that four prisoners – Rory O'Connor (Connaught), Liam Mellows (Leinster), Joseph McKelvey (Ulster) and Dick Barrett (Munster) – should be executed the following morning by order of the government. Barrett was from Ballineen, West Cork. Ministers Kevin O'Higgins and Joseph McGrath demurred and had to be persuaded that there was no other option. A communiqué was issued stating the killings were a reprisal for the murder of Hales.[470]

At 1.30 a.m. each of the four condemned men was visited by National Army chaplains to 'prepare them for execution', and before dawn all four were shot, with officers having to provide the coup de grâce to McKelvey.[471] A stark official notice was issued for the afternoon papers announcing the four deaths. The Dáil debate which followed made clear that the killings were illegal, as the men had not been tried. The justification was simple and was summed up by Minister Ernest Blythe in 1968. He believed 'that if the Dáil was not to be reduced to a shadow by the shooting of the bolder members and by the resignation of the timorous, terrorism would have to be stopped by a stern application of counter-terror'.[472]

The threat to the Oireachtas was very real. Senator Oliver St John Gogarty was kidnapped while taking a bath at the end of January 1923 and taken away to be shot. He escaped by swimming across the freezing Liffey at Chapelizod.[473] Senator John Bagwell was also kidnapped from outside his home on the Hill of Howth on 6 February. He escaped by climbing out a window and 'being an old cross country runner he soon left his prison, and his captors behind'.[474] During the same week Senator Dr George Sigerson resigned, stating: 'I attended the Senate day after day taking the same risk as my colleagues, but if I continue to act my house is to be burned.' Free State legal advisor Hugh Kennedy's home was bombed and the sentry outside the home of the chief state solicitor was also attacked.[475] On 10 December the home of Seán McGarry TD was set on fire by the anti-Treaty IRA and his son was killed in the blaze. The following night Dr Thomas Higgins, the father of Kevin O'Higgins, was shot at his home in Laois.[476]

The execution of the prisoners was particularly troubling for Cork anti-Treaty leader Liam Deasy, who described them many years later as 'such an act of savagery that it seemed all principles of war were abandoned'.[477] Deasy had fought alongside Barrett in Cork No. 3 Brigade, where Deasy was adjutant and Barrett was quartermaster.[478]

## 8 December 1922
### Anti-Treaty IRA George Dease
### Anti-Treaty IRA John Dwyer

*Rebel Cork's Fighting Story* records these deaths but gives no details. After the battle of Ballyvourney, National Army troops launched an all-points offensive on the anti-Treaty stronghold of Kealkill, north-east of Bantry. The aim was to recapture the Sliabh na mBan armoured car, but they also wanted to force the anti-Treaty IRA westwards into the Beara peninsula, where they could be cut off. As the Bantry column moved north they were attacked from a wood about three miles down the road to Kealkill and after a sharp exchange of fire lasting two hours the anti-Treaty side retreated, 'leaving one dead with rifle and ammunition'. A second anti-Treaty soldier was killed as he retreated from a house. It is not made clear which man was shot where, nor is there any record of their deaths in the official files.[479]

## 9 December 1922
### Anti-Treaty IRA James Malone

James Malone was living in his sister's house at 31 Gerald Griffin Street. His brother William was a prisoner in the Curragh Camp. James had been assisting in drilling the anti-Treaty forces in Cork 'before the National Troops had arrived'. He had been arrested a few weeks previously by National Army troops, but it had been discovered that he had a serious heart condition and he was released into his sister's care. According to her he had been nervous in the days leading up to his death. It was also claimed that two men had visited the house enquiring if he was the only brother in the house a few days before the shooting. At 2 a.m. on 9 December two men 'thundered' on the door and forced him to get dressed. He knew what was going to happen and said to his sister, 'they are going to shoot me'. He was taken to the bottom of Fair Hill and shot five times. He died instantly. The family stated that the men who took him away wore National Army uniforms.[480] Miraculously, in January an IRA arms dump was found at Dublin Pike, which contained three National Army great-coats. The news report confidentially stated that these had been used in the murder of James Malone.[481]

## 13 December 1922
### National Army Thomas Mooney

The *Irish Independent* stated that Private Thomas Mooney was in a military lorry proceeding along the North Mall in Cork city, when 'it was halted by a picket on duty in the district. Believing that he should have been recognised as a soldier, the driver did not pull up sufficiently quickly, with the result that the picket, seemingly having mistaken the occupants of the car, fired and wounded the driver of the lorry, a soldier named Kelly of Cobh, as well as another of the car's occupants named Mooney, of Dublin.' Mooney (19) was shot in the thigh and the bullet shattered the bone. Both men were taken to the Mercy Hospital, where Mooney died early the following morning. He was buried in Glasnevin.[482]

## 15 December 1922
### National Army John Travers

Private John Travers (20) was walking along Mill Road in Youghal around 8.30 p.m. on 13 December when he was challenged to halt. It appears from the evidence that the time between the challenge and the shooting was extremely short. Travers was shot in the left hip and the bullet had lodged in his groin. In the era before antibiotics, wounds in the abdomen almost inevitably proved fatal and this case was no different. Travers died two days after the shooting, in the workhouse hospital in Youghal.[483]

## 15 December 1922
### National Army Laurence Galvin

Laurence Galvin was accidentally shot at the New Barracks, Fermoy, by a Private Leary. The *Irish Independent* reported: 'Vol. Galvin, who was accidentally wounded by a rifle shot at Fermoy on Thursday evening, died subsequently at the District Hospital. It appears that the bullet entered the stomach and came out at the back, injuring the spinal column. Deceased was a native of Kilworth, and had seen service in the Irish Guards.'[484]

## 15 December 1922
### James Roche

A trench coat appears to have been fatal for James Roche. 'Mrs. Roche, widow, gave evidence of identification. When she saw the deceased he was dead. He left the house at 8.15 on the night of the occurrence to get cigarettes. It was unusual for him to go himself, as witness generally went for the cigarettes. He worked in the Passage Docks for five or six years, and belonged to Wexford. He was 38 years of age. He took no part in politics; in fact he was disgusted with politics. Witness had three children, the eldest of whom was five years. The deceased was the sole support of witness and the children.'

Roche was standing outside O'Leary's public house talking to a shipwright who also worked in the Passage West dockyard where he was an engineer, when a military tender approached and there was a lot of shouting and confusion. As the tender got to within 30 yards, the two men tried to run into the pub, but got stuck in the half door. As they did so Roche was shot in the left groin and collapsed. His last words were 'I am shot'. Some witnesses about 2 yards from Roche had heard a shout to halt, but it appears that Roche did not, even though the lorry was only yards from him. A man in a trench coat had entered the pub in front of them and left by the back door. The lieutenant in charge of the patrol said that 'all the civilians looked suspicious. The man in the trench coat was the most suspicious, and got away.' The military tribunal issued a warning to civilians that they needed to halt when called on.[485]

## 16 December 1922
### Eric Wolfe

The inscription on the plain stone cross that marks Eric Wolfe's grave in St Multose's churchyard in Kinsale records: 'Eric Seymour Wolfe: shot 16 December 1922'. *The Freeman's Journal* stated: 'A report reached Cork on Sunday morning that Eric Wolfe, farmer, residing near Kinsale, was shot dead on Saturday night. As far as can be learned, Mr. Wolfe was driving home in a pony and trap and in a shaded avenue near his home was accosted by armed men. He was apparently ordered out of the trap, and the next known of him was the discovery of his body riddled with bullets. The shocking discovery was made by his brother, who later in the night was also driving home. There were at least five wounds in the body. The tragic circumstances of his death have created a great sensation in the district. Mr. Wolfe was a popular figure at point-to-point meetings and at jumping competitions in the South.'

The *Irish Independent* reported: 'The funeral of Mr. Eric Wolfe, of Ringnane, Kinsale, took place on Tuesday from the residence to the Cemetery, Kinsale. The cortege was of large dimensions. The people from the town and district attended in large numbers and bore testimony to the popularity of the deceased young man and to the sympathy felt for the family on the loss they have sustained under such tragic circumstances. The Rev. H. H. Canon Pearson, L.L.D [Church of Ireland], officiated at the graveside.'

Wolfe (31) was single. Other than the fact that he was an ex-soldier and that his father claimed in his Irish Grants Commission compensation claim that there had been a long-running land dispute, there seems no motive for this murder. However, the fact that his father was compensated suggests this murder was over more than simply land.[486]

## 19 December 1922
### Michael Nagle

'The funeral of Mr. Ml. Nagle, Millfield House, took place yesterday morning from the Cathedral after Requiem Mass at 10 o'clock, for St. Joseph's Cemetery. The exceptionally distressing circumstances of his death stirred the deepest and widest sympathy. Last Saturday night he was in bed in his home at Millfield House when an outbreak of firing consequent on an attack on the Barracks and the National Army garrison at Garvey's Bridge took place. Several bullets struck Mr. Nagle's residence and some went through the windows and partition walls of the rooms. One bullet hit Mr. Nagle in the ankle while in bed, and then as he was leaving to seek more security three more bullets came through the window and one of those pierced his thigh and shattered the bone. After some hours only was it possible to have him removed to the Mercy Home for treatment. Here everything that surgical skill could do was done to alleviate his sufferings and save his life. But in vain, and though under three severe operations, that the patient suffered with wonderful fortitude, he passed away peacefully on Tuesday night.' Given the location of the various forces it is likely that Nagle was hit by fire from the National Army when they responded to the attack.[487]

## 20 December 1922
### Katherine Feehely

As a church holiday, 8 December was traditionally the day farmers came into Cork to start shopping for Christmas, so the main shopping street was packed with people even though half of it was still burnt out. Despite the crowds, a bomb was thrown at a car on St Patrick's Street, outside Thompson's restaurant, and a large number of civilians were injured, including Katherine

Feehely (24) of 19 Bachelor's Quay, who subsequently died. At the inquest, held on the same day as her death, 'an officer stated that on the occasion of the bomb attack he left the County Gaol, accompanied by another officer, escort and driver. Opposite Paul Lane a bomb was thrown, and hit the door of the car. Some revolver shots also rang out from Paul Lane and from Mutton Lane. The bomb ricocheted off the door of the car onto the mud-guard and rolled into Lipton's window. The bomb was a seven second Mill's. The bomb exploded. They ran after the men who had thrown the bomb, but lost them in the crowd, and the soldiers could not fire, owing to the crowded streets. There were ten civilians hit. The military went to the Mercy Hospital afterwards and were so informed. The soldiers did not fire at all. Witness got a splinter under the right eye. There were more than three men in the attack.'[488]

## 22 December 1922
### John O'Sullivan

A car accident took the life of John O'Sullivan: 'Mary Agnes Regan, NT, Leap deposed "I knew the deceased child, he was under my charge in school. I was standing on the steps of the school on the day in question. I saw the motor car pass the school. The motor car passed the school slowly. I did not see anything of the child until I saw him lying flat on the ground."' The car was being driven by a member of the military when it struck the child.[489]

## 22 December 1922
### National Army Jeremiah Desmond

Jeremiah Desmond (35) was on active service around Macroom on 16 December when he was shot in the knee. It is not explained on the file whether the wound was accidental or whether he was attacked. He was taken to the Mercy Hospital in Cork, where an operation to save the leg was not successful. On the day after the shooting his left leg below the knee was amputated, but he died (probably as a result of septicaemia) on 22 December 1922. His brother Timothy had served in the Royal Navy.[490]

## 22 December 1922
### Robert Baylor

The *Irish Independent* reported Baylor's death: 'Mr. R. S. Baylor, LL.D., solicitor, died yesterday at the Mercy Home, Cork, from wounds received on 4th inst. at Ballinrush, Kilworth. On that date Dr. Baylor received a letter requesting him to go to Ballinrush to draw the will of a farmer there. Approaching the man's house he was fired at and wounded by two men, whose faces were masked in handkerchiefs. He was promptly taken to the military hospital, Fermoy, and thence to the Mercy Home, Cork. A few days ago his leg was amputated in an effort to save his life. Dr. Baylor was admitted a solicitor in 1889 after a brilliant final examination in which he secured the silver medal and the Findlater Scholarship. In 1910 he received the LL.D. degree. He enjoyed a great reputation as a lawyer, and, as a result, a very large practice. Recently he was appointed solicitor to the Fermoy UDC in succession to Mr. Seán Troy appointed a District Justice. He leaves a widow and four young children to mourn his loss.' The motive for his shooting seems to have been his work for the Free State. Richard Corish raised the matter in the Dáil on 9 March 1923. He asked if the Minister for Finance knew that 'Dr. R.S. Baylor, of Fermoy, died from wounds received when he was lured from his home by masked men; if he is aware that the late Dr. Baylor acted as a servant of the State in local Referee Courts and as solicitor for the Troops in Fermoy area; if any claim for compensation has been made on behalf of his widow and three young children; and, if so, what was the result?'[491]

## 23 December 1922
### National Army Samuel Crawford

Eight nights after the death of James Roche in the centre of Passage West a cycle patrol was attacked in nearby Monkstown and Samuel Crawford, a native of Cappoquin, was shot through the heart and killed. The two other members of the patrol were disarmed and beaten. In a previous incident the military had come under rifle fire at the same location so it is possible that this incident was a revenge killing for the death of Roche. Crawford's body was subsequently removed to the Mercy Hospital, Cork, where he was pronounced dead.[492]

## 25 December 1922
### James Byrne

The violence of the Civil War did not stop even on Christmas night, when James Byrne was killed. There was much confusion about this shooting in the newspapers. The *Irish Independent* believed that Byrne was a Free State supporter, but all the other papers said he was anti-Treaty. According to the reports he and another man called Walsh were walking through Whitegate when an altercation developed. Both men were shot and James Byrne was fatally wounded. Walsh was shot in the stomach and was taken to Cork but whether he survived is not clear.[493]

## 26 December 1922
### National Army Michael McDonald

'A National soldier was killed, and an Irregular badly wounded in a skirmish during a raid on a public-house at Ring near Clonakilty, on St. Stephen's Night. A patrol of National troops was on duty around the village of Ring towards nightfall. It was decided to raid a licensed premises, where suspicious circumstances were noted. When the troops entered the house they found seven prominent local Irregulars within. Immediately, one of these drew a revolver and fired on the soldiers. One bullet hit Vol. McDonnell [*sic*], a native of Thurles, and killed him almost instantaneously. The soldier nearest to McDonnell then fired at the Irregular, and he fell with a severe wound in the side. In the course of a further exchange of shots all lights in the house went out and a hand-to-hand scuffle ensued in the darkness. Ultimately the soldiers got the lights on, and found that the Irregulars were moving off carrying their wounded comrade with them. The soldiers gave pursuit and arrested three of them. In a subsequent search of the house a Thompson gun was found under the bar counter.'[494]

## 31 December 1922
## Michael Downey

A *Cork Examiner* report states: 'According to an official statement in Cork an armed party shot dead a civilian named Downey at Pearson's Bridge near Bantry on December 31.'[495]

## 4 January 1923
## National Army Jeremiah O'Mahony
## 19 January 1923
## National Army Henry Pomeroy
## 5 February 1923
## National Army James Nolan

An attack led by Tom Barry was made on the National Army forces stationed in Millstreet early in the new year. Major Galvin of the National Army made a detailed report of what happened: 'The main body of the Irregulars came from the Kerry border, a large proportion from Ballyvourney. They were assisted by local Irregulars from Millstreet and a party from North Cork. L. Lynch and T. Barry were the two principal leaders in the attack. The first object of the attack was to destroy the wireless station, which was erected at the end of the town, 300 yards from the HQ at the Carnegie Hall. This post was taken completely by surprise and captured, the sentry [Pomeroy] being shot by Thompson gunfire, receiving ten bullet wounds ... The next attack was launched on HQ at the end of the town, known as the Carnegie Hall. On this post the most determined attack was made. The Irregulars used six machine-guns and concentrated a heavy fire on the building from various vantage points. Our troops, who numbered twenty-three, had only one Lewis gun in the building and replied vigorously to the fire of the attackers who advanced under cover of machine-gun fire as far as the entrance of the hall and succeeded in setting fire to the door. Were it not for the bravery of Sgt Maj. J. O'Mahony, who rushed in the face of machine-gun fire and succeeded in quenching the fire, the whole building would have been burned to the ground. It was whilst engaged in putting out the fire that this gallant W.O. was killed, leaving the army to mourn the loss of a very brave soldier.' Pomeroy died on 19 January 1923 in the Mercy Hospital in Cork. According to his mother's application for a dependant's pension, his leg had been 'riddled with machine-gun bullets'. Nolan's death certificate stated that he died on 5 February in the Mercy Hospital of sepsis from gunshot wounds.[496]

## 5 January 1923
## Robert Tobin

The *Irish Independent* provided exceptional details of this shooting: 'Last night, shortly after ten o'clock, Robert Finbarr Tobin, of St. Mary's Villas, Western Road, was shot dead walking near the Courthouse. From the details which have transpired concerning the tragedy, it appears that the deceased man was with his wife at the time. They walked down Washington Street, and after making some small purchases in a fruiter's shop, they turned in towards Sheares Street, when they reached the Courthouse. It was in the thoroughfare connecting Washington Street with Sheares Street, that is in Courthouse Street, that the shooting occurred. Three men who had been walking behind Mr. Tobin drew revolvers when they saw him turn into Courthouse Street, and, opening fire, discharged several shots point blank at him. Mr. Tobin fell dead, and his three assailants quickly disappeared from the scene. At the time of the shooting the streets were practically deserted. Hearing the shots a priest hurried from the adjoining presbytery of St. Francis Church and administered the last rites of the Church. The body was removed to the Mercy Hospital, where it was found that the unfortunate man had received no less than eight bullet wounds. The deceased had been a member of the National army for a brief period since the arrival of the troops in Cork but left the army some time ago. He was an employee of the Cork City Pensions Office.'[497]

## 6 January 1923
### National Army Denis Coakley

Denis Coakley (41), from Lissane, Dunmanway, died in Skibbereen Barracks from asthma and bronchitis caused by continuous active service in bad weather. Coakley had taken part in a series of raids across West Cork from early December. It appears from the file that his illness was contracted on these raids. After initially being rejected, because his death was not from a wound received in battle, his was one of the few natural causes claims allowed by the Military Service Pensions Board. There is no logical reason given for this change of heart on the file. It appears that one of the civil servants there felt sorry for his invalid sister.[498]

## 8 January 1923
### National Army Denis Minogue

Once again the *Irish Independent* was able to provide great detail: 'A fierce engagement took place on Monday evening between a small party of National troops and irregulars at a place a few miles north of Ballineen. The irregulars were in large force, and the fighting was fierce for about twenty minutes, when the National troops by skilful manoeuvring beat them out of their very strong positions. A running fight ensued, the irregulars being followed up by the National troops until darkness set in. One of the National troops, Sergeant B. [*sic*] Minogue, was shot dead and a lieutenant wounded. The irregular casualties, which must have been heavy, could not be ascertained, but they were seen taking away at least four bodies with them. The National troops captured a quantity of ammunition and equipment. A large amount of blood was seen around the positions occupied by the irregulars.' There is no actual evidence for any anti-Treaty deaths in this ambush. Minogue was from Scarriff, Co. Clare and was twenty-five when he died.[499]

**19 January 1923**

**National Army Christopher Smith**

*The Freeman's Journal* recorded: 'A column of National troops from Rathluirc [Charleville] on Wednesday proceeded on a round-up operation between Dromina and Freemount, Co. Cork. In a house near the former place they captured four men with rifles and about 50 rounds of ammunition … Following the arrests the troops proceeded towards Freemount in extended formation and had not gone far when intensive fire was opened on them from Thompson guns, Peter the Painters, and rifles. The advance was maintained, and the attackers, who numbered between 50 and 100 retreated towards the hills. They fought a rearguard action which lasted several hours until they gained a commanding position, and then made a stand, and the fire became more intense. After half an hour's desperate fighting the attackers were driven from their positions, and were forced to scatter, carrying many wounded with them. The military sustained but one casualty – Vol. O'Gorman [*sic*] who was rather seriously wounded, and who is being treated at St. John's Hospital, Limerick, for a bullet wound in the lung.' According to the newspapers Smith died on 19 January and was a native of Limerick.[500]

**3 February 1923**

**Seámus O'Leary**

**Patrick Murray**

**22 February 1923**

**John Desmond**

When National Army troops arrived in the village of Newcestown around Mass time on Sunday 3 February, they ordered some local men to clear the road of a barricade left by the anti-Treaty forces. As they did so, a trigger mine exploded and two men – Murray and O'Leary – were killed instantly. John Desmond was buried in Templemartin after his death in hospital in Cork three weeks later. John Allen, Denis O'Brien, Tim Murphy, Michael Murphy, Patrick Boyle and John Long were seriously injured. Two National

Army troops were slightly injured. The troops claimed that the men used to clear the mine were part of the anti-Treaty forces, an opinion backed up by Ernest Blythe in the Dáil for Boyle at least, when asked why Boyle had received no compensation for his injuries. However, locals dismissed this and said that they had merely been at Mass when the raid happened. Given that all the victims lived in the parish, the latter is more likely to be the case.[501]

## 7 February 1923
## Michael Cusack

The *Irish Independent* reported: 'Coroner Murphy, solicitor, resumed at the Mercy Hospital, Cork, yesterday, the inquiry into the death of Michael Cusack, who died in hospital on Feb. 7, from a wound received near the Courthouse on the evening of Feb. 6, when an attack on soldiers guarding the Courthouse was made. Corporal John Boyle stated that about 7 p.m. on Feb. 6 he was standing inside the Courthouse front door, talking to another soldier. He was not on duty, and he had not a view of the street at the time. He heard the noise of a bomb exploding and ran out with Private Robinson. When they got outside they heard Mauser shots and saw a civilian lying on his side on the flags in front of the Courthouse. They went to him and saw he was wounded. Dr. O'Riordan ... Mercy Hospital, stated that deceased was brought to hospital at 7.20. Witness found a bullet wound in the left side behind, just above the pelvis. That was an entrance wound. There was no exit wound, but he found a bullet under the skin in front of the abdomen. The man died at 2 a.m. the next morning. Mrs. Cusack said that her husband was never connected with any political organisation. He had no enemies and never received a threatening letter. The officer representing the military said ... no less than 20 peaceable citizens had been killed in Cork during the past few months owing to those attacks, while the military casualties had been nil.' Cusack (48) lived at 187 Old Youghal Road.[502]

**13 February 1923**

**Ellen (Nellie) Patricia Hayes**

Nellie Hayes (17) of Tracton Park, Montenotte, Cork, was talking to National Army troops with some other children when one of their rifles discharged accidentally and she was shot through the neck. The soldier had been fired at earlier in the day and had asked his corporal for permission to fire at a log 'to frighten anybody that might be around'. The corporal refused and the private apparently 'put the safety back on the rifle'. However, as he turned around the gun went off. Ellen was pronounced dead on arrival at the North Infirmary.[503]

**15 February 1923**

**Anti-Treaty IRA Laurence Cunningham**

On 11 February, at Lyre, halfway between Ballineen and Clonakilty, 'Spud' Murphy and Larry Cunningham called into the local pub for a rest. National Army troops surrounded the building and as Cunningham attempted to escape he was shot. 'Spud' Murphy was also wounded but was removed to safety before he could be arrested. Laurence Cunningham later died in the Mercy Hospital from septicaemia.[504]

**16 February 1923**

**National Army Michael Ahern**

Lieutenant Ahern was shot in the abdomen during a firefight in Drimoleague. He was taken to the Mercy Hospital in Cork, where he died. As his body was being returned home for burial in Knocknagoshel, the Red Cross Ambulance was fired upon near Barraduff, Co. Kerry, by anti-Treaty forces.[505]

**18 February 1923**

**Michael Gorman (Charles McIlgorm)**

Michael Gorman, a crewman on the *Carrigan Head*, was shot on Albert

Quay by National Army soldiers. He had been trying to fight another man and two young women. One of the women complained to the guard at the Albert Road Power Station, who went to arrest him. Seeing the soldiers he ran and was shot dead when he failed to halt. Dr Riordan, resident surgeon at the Mercy Hospital, said the man was admitted at 11.30 on Saturday night. He died at 5.30 on Sunday morning.[506]

**19 February 1923**

**National Army David Lehane**

David Lehane from Macroom was a member of the 1st Cork Reserves and was guarding the military barracks situated at the workhouse when it was fired on by anti-Treaty forces. He was killed outright and buried in the local churchyard a few days later. His elder brother, Stephen, had been killed on 22 November 1917 on the Western Front.[507]

**19 February 1923**

**National Army Patrick Harford**

Quartermaster Patrick Harford of the Dublin Guard was accidentally shot on 18 February 1923 in Collins Barracks. No details of the shooting were given. He died the following day in the Mercy Hospital.[508]

**28 February 1923**

**National Army Denis Galvin**

*An t-Óglách* reported: 'Commandant [General] Galvin, wounded by an accidental bomb explosion at Mallow on the 20th ult., died at the Mercy Hospital, Cork, on the 28th ult. His record with the Army goes back to 1914. He was out in 1916. During the intense portion of the Anglo-Irish War he was O/C. of the Active Service Unit of the 4th North Cork Brigade. North Cork people remember the conflicts at Rathcoole, Cloonbanin [*sic*], and Rathmore and the parts Denis Galvin played in them. He was in the thick of everything and never found wanting. He had no hesitation in following the late Chief on the Treaty question, and his influence brought hundreds of men from his district into the National Ranks. It is hard that he should go with the end so near at hand.'[509]

## 10 March 1923
## Michael Hickey

Seven days after Hickey's death *The Southern Star* reported: 'Michael Hickey, aged about 25, of Limerick City, residing near Edward Street, Limerick, was shot dead in Cork on Saturday night. Accompanied by some friends, he was returning to the hotel at which he was staying, when they were held up at Patrick's Bridge by some soldiers engaged in searching passers-by. The deceased was ordered to put up his hands, and did so. An altercation then ensued, and in a few seconds deceased was fighting one of the soldiers. Shots then rang out, and the persons on the street, including two friends who were with Hickey, fled for cover. Later they returned to look for their comrade, and found him lying on the pavement, wrapped in his overcoat, and quite dead. The remains were removed to the Mercy Hospital. It was at first thought that the deceased had died from heart failure or from the effects of a blow, but when the body was examined a bullet wound was seen on the left arm near the shoulder, the bullet having apparently passed into the body in the region of the heart and this injury was the cause of death. The tragic death of Mr. Hickey, who was very popular, will be learned with sincere regret, and his relatives will have widespread sympathy in their great bereavement.'[510]

## 13 March 1923
## Anti-Treaty IRA William Healy

Healy was executed in Cork Gaol on 13 March 1923. He enlisted in the Irish Volunteers, 'E' Company, 1st Battalion, Cork No. 1 Brigade in 1918. He was involved in the attacks on Blarney RIC Barracks and on city police barracks in Cork city in 1921. At the outbreak of the Civil War, he went anti-Treaty and was captured at the Donoughmore ambush in September 1922. He was court-martialled on a charge of possession of arms and was executed by firing squad. His was the only anti-Treaty Civil War execution in Cork. Writing before his execution he discussed the dilemma facing many of the anti-Treaty IRA in the first months of 1923, as the full force of the government's executions policy was driven home: 'If I had told on one of the boys, I would not be executed but, as you know, I would not have it said that there was a spy in our family, because as you know I was out for a Republic and I sincerely hope it will be got some day.' He was initially buried in Cork Gaol, but his body was handed over to his relatives in 1924.[511]

**17 March 1923**
**Ben McCarthy**
**20 March 1923**
**William Goff Beale**

Though many miles apart these two deaths are linked by the motive behind them – the execution of William Healy. On 20 March 1923 John H. Bennett, a Midleton businessman, wrote a note 'in memory of a good friend and fellow sportsman William Goff Beale who was shot by Republicans as a reprisal for an execution in Cork'. A Free State intelligence report suggested the same motive. 'Two murders took place. One in Cork; an old man unidentified with any movement. The reason given was Healy's Execution. One in Bantry, a boy of sixteen years. The reason given was [a] reprisal for [the] execution of our comrades.'[512]

The *Irish Independent* agreed: 'Coroner Neville, Solr., Bandon, held an inquest on Monday at one o'clock in the Bantry Town Hall, into the circumstances touching the death of a young lad, aged about 17 years, son of Florence McCarthy, Ardra, farmer, whose dead body was found on Saturday morning near Lough Bofinna lake, on the public road, about three miles east of Bantry, and some four or five miles from his parent's residence, from which he was taken. Evidence was given that he was taken by armed men from his parents' house about three o'clock on Saturday morning; that his dead body was found as stated lying on the side of the public road, with several bullet wounds, and on the body was a card with the words "Convicted spy. Shot as a reprisal for the execution of our comrades [*sic*] during the week". Medical, military and civilian evidence bearing on the foregoing having been heard, the jury returned a verdict of wilful murder against some person or persons unknown. Sympathy was tendered to the deceased's parents. The remains were subsequently removed for interment, and the funeral procession was a large one.'[513]

William Goff Beale (52) died in the South Infirmary on 20 March 1923. He had been walking home from work and reached the gates of his home at Elmgrove on the Ballyhooley Road. He had been followed by two men from town and they rushed up and shot him in the back from point-blank range. He was shot in the abdomen and twice in the arms and his killers had told him that 'this was a reprisal for the executions'. The murder shocked the city as not only was Beale a prominent businessman, but as a Quaker he would have been non-violent. The only possible reason advanced was that Beale was a first cousin of Mr Justice Pim, who was a High Court judge of the Free State.[514]

## 18 March 1923
### National Army Peter Clune

Peter Clune was accidentally shot in Dunmanway on 5 March 1923: 'A young National Volunteer named Clune, from the Clare or Limerick district belonging to the Western Division met with a rather serious accident on Monday at the local headquarters, Carbery House, a bullet from a revolver which a comrade was holding accidentally going off and passing through his forehead when he was lying in bed. He was attended promptly by Dr. O'Donovan, but being in a serious condition he was removed to Bandon military hospital, where he is progressing fairly well under the circumstances, and hopes are entertained of his recovery. He was a most popular and brave soldier, who has a splendid record with the old IRA and National forces.' Sadly he did not recover and died in Bandon Military Hospital on 18 March.[515]

## 25 March 1923
### National Army Cornelius O'Driscoll

Cornelius O'Driscoll was wounded on 24 March 1923 at Green Barracks, Bandon, Co. Cork and died the following day. It was stated in documents in his MSPC file that he was killed by a sniper. *The Southern Star* noted that a half-hour sniping attack on Green Barracks at 5 a.m. had resulted in a serious injury to a sentry and it is probable that this was O'Driscoll. His death certificate recorded that he was shot in the groin.[516]

## 28 March 1923
### National Army Bernard O'Brien

On 31 March the *Irish Independent* reported the death of a National Army soldier called O'Connor who resided at 3 Sullivan's Lane off Barrack Street. He had been guarding the army post at Ballinspittle and had been shot in the head by a sniper. The body was conveyed to the Mercy Hospital at 4 p.m. on Thursday 29 March and an inquest was expected but none happened. However, there is no record in the MSPC of a soldier named O'Connor who died at this time and it seems likely the newspaper got the name wrong. There is a record of an application by Mrs Edith Luther for a dependant's pension in relation to her brother, Bernard O'Brien, who was shot by a sniper while on patrol duty in Ballinspittle on the previous day.[517]

## 1 April 1923
### National Army John Flynn

Yet another rifle accident killed another National Army trooper. *The Southern Star* reported: 'on Monday Volunteer John Flynn, aged 20, of the 15th Infantry Battalion was killed at the Devonshire Arms, Hotel, Bandon, by the accidental discharge of a comrade's rifle. It appears that a soldier had the rifle in his hands, when the weapon suddenly went off and the bullet hit Flynn, killing him. The body has been brought to the Mercy Hospital.' On 6 April the *Irish Independent* reported: 'After 1 o'clock Mass at St. Laurence O'Toole's Church yesterday the funeral took place to Glasnevin of Vol. John Flynn, 2 Irvine Tce. East Rd who was accidentally killed at Bandon on April 1. The cortege was accompanied by the brass and reed band from Collins Barracks [Dublin], and firing party in charge of Capt. T. O'Doherty.'[518]

## 3 April 1923
### National Army Michael O'Brien

On 5 April a military inquiry was held in Cork into the death of Private Michael O'Brien (25) from Grenagh. O'Brien was a member of the Railway Protection and Maintenance Corps. He was fatally wounded by a bomb thrown at the military post at the Cork, Blackrock and Passage Railway Station and the Albert Road Power Station which were next to one another. A verdict of wilful murder was returned at the inquiry.[519]

## 7 April 1923
### Michael Barry

*The Cork Examiner* report stated: 'A sensational shooting of a postman occurred at Carrigtwohill, East Cork, on Saturday morning, the victim being so dangerously wounded that he is not expected to recover. The injured postman's name is Michael Barry. He was on his customary round of delivery at Carrigtwohill when the attack was made upon him. Almost a mile from the village he was held up by a party of armed men, who had evidently lain in wait for him, for they sprang out on to the road from the fence just as Barry was passing. In response to a shout of "hands up" Barry halted. What happened next is not quite clear, one version stating that Barry resisted the efforts of the raiders to take away the post bag and mails, while a second story, probably the correct one, is that the men immediately opened fire.

At any rate Barry fell on the roadway, badly wounded in several places. The fact that his postbag was not tampered with or letters abstracted, and that a notice was left attached to it bearing the inscription "Convicted spy. Spies and informers beware. – I.R.A" seem to indicate that the shooting was not consequent on a mere raid for mails; and the additional circumstance that several wounds were inflicted on the unfortunate postal official is corroborative of this. Barry was subsequently removed to Midleton Hospital, where it was found that his condition was extremely precarious. He has very serious wounds in the head, and is not expected to live.' By this stage he was already dead.[520]

## 9 April 1923
### Margaret Dunne
### Anti-Treaty IRA Unknown (uncertain)
### Anti-Treaty IRA Unknown (uncertain)

According to *The Cork Examiner*, a fight at Adrigole resulted in the death of two irregulars and Margaret Dunne (26), who was buried in Adrigole a few days later. On 23 April an attempt to have an inquest into the death of Dunne was postponed when the National Army officer who had been in charge of the column when she was shot could not attend. Aside from the initial report there is no further mention of the dead irregulars. On 15 May 1924 Tadhg Ó Murchadha asked Minister for Finance Ernest Blythe 'whether a claim for compensation in respect of the fatal shooting of his daughter, Margaret Dunne, in an armed conflict between National Forces and Irregulars on April 8th, 1923, has been received from Daniel Dunne, Dromlave, Adrigole, Co. Cork, and if so, whether any award has yet been made'. Blythe replied that such an application had been 'received by the Compensation (Personal Injuries) Committee. After full investigation, the Committee came to the conclusion that there was no dependency of the applicant upon the deceased, and they have recommended that no compensation should be paid. The applicant was informed accordingly.'[521]

## 9 April 1923
### National Army James Mahony

The *Irish Independent* reported: 'A motor lorry with National troops when passing along by the Bantry Quay got overturned near the deal yard. One of the men was so badly injured that he died subsequently. The others received a bad shaking, and had had a narrow escape with their lives.' An MSPC file relates to Margaret Mahony's application in respect of the death of her husband, James Mahony, who was killed in a motor accident on 9 April 1923 in Bantry. Lieutenant Hayes was injured in the same incident. Margaret Mahony claims that her husband joined the National Forces on 10 August 1922 and that he was in receipt of a pension from the British government for service in the military/police force. Margaret Mahony went on to marry Private Denis Dennehy on 24 August 1923.[522]

## 10 April 1923
### Anti-Treaty IRA Chief of Staff Liam Lynch

Liam Lynch was born on 9 November 1893 near Anglesboro, Co. Limerick. By 1919 he was O/C of Cork No. 2 Brigade and was part of the group of IRA men who attempted to steal arms on 7 September outside the Methodist Church in Fermoy. In the ensuing scuffle Private William Jones was killed and Lynch was shot by his own side. He was lucky to survive. Following this he went on the run.

Lynch was captured on 12 August 1920, but his captors failed to recognise him and he was released. Shortly afterwards he was appointed to the seven-strong Supreme Council of the IRB. He served alongside Michael Collins, who was a good friend of his. Although he took the anti-Treaty side, he worked hard to avoid civil war. However, once it broke out, he resumed command of the 1st Southern Division of the IRA, which made up one-quarter of the anti-Treaty's total force, and soon became chief of staff of the anti-Treaty IRA.

His attempt to hold the line of a 'Munster Republic' in the first month of the war was fatally undermined by the capture of Cork from the sea. Following this he ordered the anti-Treaty forces to form small flying columns and to conduct a guerrilla war against the Free State. Despite his attempts to prevent the war before it broke out, when a number of attempts were made to end the fighting Lynch always cast his vote in favour of continuing.

In early April 1923, with Frank Aiken, Lynch travelled to Cork to attend a meeting to discuss the impossible military situation for republican troops. On 10 April National Army troops surrounded the small republican party at Crohan West on the slopes of the Knockmealdown Mountains.[523] National Army Lieutenant Larry Clancy described what happened: 'As we moved again in the new direction uphill a burst of firing opened up on us, from an eminence on the right and a few yards in front of us splinters flew from the rocks along with whizzing bullets. I ordered the men to take cover and running up a nearby rock took out my field glasses to scan the hillside ... About four hundred yards in front and higher up I was surprised to see a group of men daringly standing on rocks above us wearing big black overcoats and hats and firing from Peters and Parabellum autos with arms out-stretched. ... using my glasses, I saw them running down the hill towards the skyline. I then observed a man fall forward and remain there. ... When we got near to where the man was lying on his back with a topcoat folded under his head, one of our men said "We have Dev". ... the man answered, "I'm Liam Lynch, get me a priest and a doctor, I'm dying".' Lynch died that evening in Clonmel and is buried next to his great friend Michael Fitzgerald at Kilcrumper Cemetery outside Fermoy.[524]

## 17 April 1923
## Anti-Treaty IRA Denis Kelly
## Anti-Treaty IRA Unknown Coughlan

The *Irish Independent* reported: 'Bantry, Thursday. Night: Considerable excitement was caused here this evening, when large forces of National troops arrived here from the Kealkill and the Pass of Keimanigh [*sic*] direction, bringing close on twenty prisoners, some of them stated to be active and prominent Irregulars belonging to the West Cork Brigade. It is stated that another large batch captured further out in the mountainous district, which includes some prominent leaders, were taken on to Macroom. There appears to have been a large encircling movement of the troops from the Kerry side, working in conjunction with the Bantry force and other districts. Two Irregulars named Kelly and Coughlan, natives of Bantry, were killed. No casualties are reported on the National forces' side. It is thought that the backbone of the Irregular resistance in that difficult mountainous area is broken, and that peace will soon be fully restored all round.' The Castletownbere monument suggests that Lieutenant Kelly was killed on 17 April.[525] Nothing further is known about Coughlan.

## 21 April 1923
### William Murphy

The *Irish Independent* recorded the events of that Saturday. The report shows that the citizens of Cork city had become inured to mayhem on the streets: 'William Murphy, a rather elderly man, and a resident of Ninety-eight Street (off Bandon Road), was fatally shot in Patrick Street, Cork, on Saturday night. ... It appears that an attack was made by a number of armed youths on a military officer passing through Patrick Street. Several shots were fired at him from revolvers, and the deceased was unfortunate in coming into the line of fire, with the result that he was struck in the side by one of the bullets. He ran from a point close to the corner of Robert Street and Patrick Street, where he had been hit, as far as Cook Street ... and he collapsed near the Victoria Hotel. With all possible speed he was conveyed to the Mercy Hospital, but it was obvious to everyone that his injury was a fatal one, and less than an hour after being wounded, he succumbed. The officer upon whom the attack was made was not injured, and there was no other casualty ... The shooting created considerable alarm in the centre of the city, which was being promenaded by the usual Saturday evening crowds at the time, but when there was no repetition of the shots people became reassured, and again moved about as before.'[526]

## 1 May 1923
## National Army Michael Monahan

In 1923 the most dangerous place for the National Army was anywhere near one of their own comrades who had a loaded rifle. Once again a soldier was killed by the accidental discharge of a weapon, this time in Mallow Barracks. The *Irish Independent* reported: 'About midnight last night the body of Volunteer Moynihan [*sic*], of the Railway Corps, of the National Army, Mallow, was brought to the Mercy Hospital. It was stated that the deceased, who had been dead about two hours on admission, was accidentally shot. A later report stated that Vol. Moynihan who, as already reported, was accidentally shot dead at Mallow, was one of the guard on an armoured train operating between Cork and Mallow and was killed by the discharge of a rifle. He was formerly a resident of Lower Road.'[527]

## 4 May 1923
## National Army John Duggan

John Duggan (17) from Clashmaguire, Clondrohid was part of Commandant Peadar O'Conlon's column based at Macroom. On operations at Inchigeela he was accidentally shot by a cousin of his who was also a soldier. There is no record in the newspapers as it appears that no inquest or military inquiry was held.[528]

## 28 June 1923
## Thomas Dinan
## 30 June 1923
## Jeremiah Dinan

Although the war had officially ended on 24 May, with the IRA's dump arms order, the conflict continued to take its toll, with a number of accidental deaths and deliberate shootings right up to the end of the year. There were also many anti-Treaty men still interned in various places, which also led to a number of deaths.

Around 8 p.m. on Thursday 28 June Thomas Dinan, from Gowlane, Donoughmore, was returning home with his two sons when he picked up an object. It exploded, killing him instantly and seriously wounding Jeremiah, whose left hand was shattered and who had perforation wounds in his abdomen. Jeremiah was able to walk into the kitchen of the house. The unnamed seven-year-old with them was not seriously injured. Jeremiah was taken to the North Infirmary, where he was operated on, but when it was discovered that the intestines were cut there was little hope and he died on 30 June.[529]

## 17 July 1923
### John 'Jack' O'Donovan

On 17 July at Dunmanway John O'Donovan (21) was at a house party with his sister and some friends. They had attended an 'American wake' and were walking home around 11.30 p.m. when they heard a cart approaching from behind. They took little notice of it until suddenly challenged by armed men whom they did not recognise as National Army troops. The troops apparently opened fire immediately the order to halt was given and it took a few minutes to get them to stop firing. The 'night was not too bright or too dark either'. According to the evidence the soldiers were angry that the people would not come back. 'Jack' was shot in the leg. When his sister went to help him he told her it was broken. He died on 17 July in hospital from haemorrhage and shock. He was from Milanes, just to the west of the town.[530]

## 14 August 1923
### Michael Coakley

The *Irish Independent* details what happened: 'Michael Coakley (23), unmarried, Woods Place, York Street, Cork, was shot dead, and five others, including an officer and two soldiers of the National Army were wounded in a shooting affair at Kealkill, near Bantry, on Tuesday night. Whilst a dance was in progress in a licensed house it was surrounded by troops from Bantry. It is not known who fired the first shot, but the troops say they were shot at from within. The soldiers rushed to the house and in doing so Lieut. P. Connolly, Bantry, was shot in the back and seriously wounded. He was removed to Cork for treatment. Two other soldiers it is stated were also wounded. The civilian Coakley, one of the dancers, who was shot dead, was employed as a confectioner's assistant at Messrs. Thompson's, Cork and was on a week's holidays in the Kealkill district. Two other civilians named McCarthy and Connolly, from the Bantry district, are reported to be dangerously wounded. Consternation reigned in the little village, and all who could went home as soon as possible.'[531]

## 18 August 1923
### Abina Murphy

A party of armed men shot at a member of the National Army on Gerald Griffin Street in Cork city and he returned fire. A second party of men opened fire from behind him. Two civilians were caught in the crossfire – Abina Murphy (33) of St James's Square was shot in the abdomen and Kathleen Deasy of Spangle Hill was shot in the throat. Murphy died the following day in the North Infirmary.[532]

## 22 August 1923
### National Army Christopher Henry Burke

An outbreak of typhus occurred in the Cork Harbour Board premises where some National Army troops had been billeted during the war. The victim, Burke, was moved, first to the Mercy Hospital and thence to the Union (Workhouse) Hospital. Sir John Scott, who was a candidate in the general election, pointed to the disgusting conditions of the lavatory and blamed the soldiers quartered at the premises for this. On 28 August a panicked Cork

Harbour Board decided to evict the few remaining military still guarding the docks.[533]

## 15 November 1923
## William O'Sullivan

*The Southern Star* report is one of the few newspaper reports that goes to the heart of the terror to which the victims of the summary executions that were a hallmark of the Irish revolution were subjected: 'Richard White stated that he lived in Droumdrastil [*sic*] and was a farmer's son. He remembered the night of the 15th when he was in the kitchen in the deceased's house. About 9.30 a knock came to the door and a masked member of the IRA came in carrying a rifle, and ordered all of them to put up their hands, which they did. There were six people in the kitchen, and they were asked their names, a rifle being pointed at each in turn. When the deceased answered his name the stranger asked him was he the owner of the house, and deceased said he was. He asked deceased if he had a gun, and deceased told him he hadn't as it was taken away by the Guards a few days ago. The stranger then said: "If you don't give the gun you will be dead in a short time." The stranger then said, "Come out here in the yard" and deceased did so and whilst walking from the fire-place to the door deceased said, "Oh, sir, what have I done? Don't shoot me. Give me time to prepare." Witness heard the deceased being ordered by the stranger to get on his knees. This was outside the door. Witness then heard O'Sullivan praying, he said: "Oh Jesus, save me. Oh Jesus have mercy on me," and said "I have no gun sir. That is as true as God is in Heaven." Witness heard the stranger then tell the deceased to say an Act of Contrition, and deceased did so, and he heard the deceased being ordered to "Get up and keep back out from me." He heard the deceased say: "Oh, I will, sir," or words to that effect. He then heard a shot and a moan, and he thought the deceased called him by name to go for a priest. They all rushed out and found the deceased on his back in the yard.'[534]

## 20 November 1923
## Anti-Treaty IRA Denis Barry

James Durney provides one of the best descriptions of the events that led up to the death of Denis Barry: 'Commandant Denis Barry, of Cork, died on 20 November 1923 in the Curragh Military Hospital while on hunger-strike. During the Irish Civil War scores of republican prisoners were interned in Newbridge Barracks and the Curragh Camp. Despite the ending of the Civil War in May, by 1 July 1923 the number of republican prisoners in the Free State was officially estimated as 11,316. On October 10, as a protest against conditions and the continued incarceration of the prisoners, prisoners in Mountjoy Jail began a hunger-strike. An order of the day was issued by Frank Aiken, I.R.A. chief of staff, asking for support for the Mountjoy hunger-strikers, which was interpreted in the jails and internment camps throughout Ireland as an invitation to support the Mountjoy prisoners by joining the hunger strike. As many as 8,000 prisoners decided to do so ...

'Denis joined the mass hunger-strike on 17 October 1923 in support of his protesting comrades. On 6 November he wrote his final letter to his brother Bartholomew or "Batt" ... "I hope there is nobody worrying over-much, as for the present, thank God, I am as strong as can be expected, not having eaten for 21 days, but otherwise can sit up in bed, and get out while it is being dressed. The general state of my health, now at any rate, is really very good. I need nothing for the moment as friends I have by those who attend me so my advice to ye is to do everything with a light heart, trust God for His hand is greater than those who hold me here."'

On Saturday 17 November the Barry family received a telegram, which read: 'Your brother is now seriously ill in Newbridge Internment Camp, Co. Kildare. Every facility will be given to his family to visit him on making a personal application to the Governor.' Batt left immediately and on arrival at the Curragh was escorted by Seán Hayes, the governor, to a hut where he saw his brother. Denis was conscious but unable to speak. Batt decided to try to save his brother's life and arranged for Denis to be taken to the

Curragh Military Hospital on 19 November. However, Denis (40) died at 2.45 a.m. the following morning. Initially the authorities refused to hand over the remains but on 26 November, following a High Court action, the body of Denis Barry, which had been buried in the internment camp, was exhumed. The remains arrived in Cork the following afternoon, but Bishop Daniel Cohalan decreed that 'the remains were not permitted to enter any church in his diocese' and forbade 'any of his priests to officiate at any religious ceremonies for the deceased'. Instead, Barry's remains were taken to 56 Grand Parade, the headquarters of Sinn Féin. His funeral, to the Republican Plot in St Finbarr's Cemetery, was one of the largest ever seen in Cork. Prayers were recited at the graveside by David Kent, TD, who also sprinkled the grave with holy water.[535]

## 22 November 1923
### Anti-Treaty IRA Andrew O'Sullivan

If the death and burial of Denis Barry is now understood as a major event in the Civil War, the death of Andrew O'Sullivan is overshadowed by the controversy surrounding the arrival in Cork of Barry's body. The two were buried on the same day. This is the detailed record of O'Sullivan's death in the *Evening Herald*: 'At St. Bricin's Hospital today Oswald J. Murphy, Deputy Coroner, held an inquest into the circumstances of the death of Andrew O'Sullivan, aged about 37 of the West End, Mallow, Co. Cork, who died in the hospital at 3.40 p.m. yesterday. The deceased was on hunger strike in Mountjoy. He was removed to St. Bricin's on Thursday, and when admitted was unconscious. Michael Joseph O'Sullivan, The Creamery, Tarelton, Macroom, Co. Cork stated the deceased was single and was an instructor under the Department of Agriculture and Technical Instruction.' Originally from Co. Cavan, he had been living in Mallow for thirteen years. Michael had been informed that his brother was dangerously ill on 22 November. The 'Leader' in *The Anglo-Celt* newspaper paid Andrew a glowing tribute on 1 December, stating that he had been 'discovered' by them when he submitted articles as secretary of the United Ireland League in 1903 when he was eighteen. According to *The Anglo-Celt* he was possessed of a 'most marvellous memory'. In a long report on his death it stated that he had been 'barely recognisable' to his brother because he was 'so emaciated'. He had started his hunger strike on 11 October and ended it on 21 November. He was moved to the prison hospital and took lemon juice and food but it was too late. O'Sullivan had very rapidly developed pneumonia due to his weakened state and was unconscious by the time he left the prison hospital for St Bricin's. He was buried in the Mallow Republican Plot after Requiem Mass in St Patrick's church.[536]

## 22 December 1923
### Anti-Treaty IRA George Burke

Only the *Irish Independent* recorded the death of George Burke. 'Mr. George Burke died at the South Infirmary, Cork, of peritonitis. He was interned at Newbridge, and was released on November 12. The remains were removed to the Church of the Immaculate Conception, and were escorted by a large cortege headed by the MacCurtain Pipers' Band. The funeral took place on Christmas Day to the Republican Plot.'[537]

# POSSIBLES

Due to a scarcity of sources, there are a number of individuals whose deaths cannot be definitively established, and others whose deaths cannot be definitively linked with either side in the war but who warrant a mention as the connection is possible. They are listed here.

## 13 August 1920
### Private H. Ward
A British soldier called H. Ward apparently went missing from Cork on 13 August 1920, yet the Cameron Highlanders have no record of anyone missing at that time.[1]

## Uncertain 1920
### Denis Lehane
In his interview with Ernie O'Malley, Michael Leahy suggests that he 'executed' Constable Denis Lehane in 1920. Lehane had been captured after being found on an RIC supply boat. However, in his BMH file Leahy makes no mention of this. Equally, nobody on the British side seems to have missed the man and no body was ever found, so in truth it is impossible to decide on the accuracy of this claim.[2]

## January 1921
### Daniel (uncertain) Lynch
According to Tadg O'Sullivan, a spy called Lynch had given information that led to the death of Volunteer Tim Fitzgerald at the Brinny ambush. In an interview with Ernie O'Malley, Flor Begley stated that IRA suspicions about this man's connection with British forces were confirmed when he warned a 'young lad' about an impending raid. Lynch was shot in early 1921

and secretly buried in Killeady Quarry. John O'Driscoll also mentions the execution of a spy name Lynch in his BMH witness statement, but provides no further details. Although none of the sources provide a first name, Andy Bielenberg and James Donnelly have suggested this was Daniel.[3]

## 30 April 1921
### Stephen O'Callaghan

Stephen O'Callaghan (28) died in the South Infirmary having been rushed there shortly before 10 p.m. He had been shot on Anderson's Quay by unknown men. He was an ex-soldier and had been a member of the Munster Regiment in the war. He had just drawn his pension on the day he was killed. He lived with his mother at 23 Rutland Street. Despite his army links, there was no claim of responsibility by anyone in the IRA so it is impossible to say who shot him or why. The divisional commander of the RIC stated that he had no involvement with the security forces.[4]

## 21 May 1921
### Peter O'Callaghan

The only place that this death is recorded is on the IRA memorial at Donoughmore. There is no mention of how he died.[5]

## Uncertain 1921
### Jimmy Devoy

It was claimed that Devoy was shot in 1921 at Ovens by the IRA.[6]

## Uncertain 1921
### Privates Pincher, Mason and Caen

David Grant of 'The Cairo Gang' website has suggested that some members of the Manchester Regiment stationed at Ballincollig were executed by the IRA in early 1921. According to Michael O'Regan: 'On 15th November 1920, I got word that four unarmed British soldiers were in the area of Ovens.

I mobilised "A" Company and proceeded to Ovens where we found the four soldiers. We arrested them, questioned them and held them prisoners for about a week in Farran Company area, after which they were shot dead on the instructions of the brigade O/C. and were buried in the Aherla company area.' As three British Army intelligence officers were captured on the same day at Waterfall (about four miles away but in the same battalion area) it may be that O'Regan is referring to them. However, the details appear to be very different, so these can't be ruled out as separate deaths.[7]

## 9 March 1922 (date uncertain)
## Thomas Roycroft

On 11 March 1922 a small advertisement appeared in the *Cork Constitution* seeking the whereabouts of Thomas Roycroft, who had gone missing on 9 March. His father had resigned from the RIC in February 1921 and Thomas had been dismissed from the same body in June 1921. He had 'gone for a walk around 8.15 p.m. and had not been seen since'. Given his background it is possible that he was shot by the IRA but there is no evidence whatsoever to support this other than his father's claim to the Irish Grants Committee.[8]

## 3 September 1922
## Jeremiah Coleman

*The Freeman's Journal* reported: 'Mystery surrounds the death of a carter named Jeremiah Coleman, of George's Quay, Cork, whose dead body was found yesterday morning in a cart outside a stable which he had rented near Fort Elizabeth. ... He left Cork on Saturday morning as usual, and nothing was heard of him until yesterday morning, when some people who were passing noticed the horse and cart outside the stables. In the cart was Coleman's dead body, with a bullet hole in his head. He had evidently been dead for some time. How he met his death is not known.' The inquest on the following day was told he was actually shot twice in the back. The next report of 12 September stated that he was last seen alive at Kilumney about eight miles from Cork and that he had left the pub there around 11 p.m. It is possible that he was hit by stray bullets between Kilumney and Cork, or he may have been a victim of an armed robbery. However, as he had money on him at the autopsy, this is unlikely.[9]

## September 1922 (date uncertain)
## Unnamed

The body of a young man (likely an anti-Treaty soldier) was found just outside Macroom. 'The remains were badly decomposed and appeared to have been gnawed by rats. It was likely that the victim had been shot during the recent fighting in the town.'[10]

## 20 January 1923
## V. Sweeney

The *Irish Independent* of 22 January 1923 records: 'Details obtained from official sources state that an irregular leader named V. Sweeney of Castlefreake was killed, another irregular named Mead(e) was captured, and a soldier (Volunteer Curran) was rather seriously injured in a fight near Clonakilty on Saturday evening.'

'The Cairo Gang' website also has a long list of possible killings: 'Bodies of British Soldiers missing and never found (or exhumed and reburied)', www.cairogang.com/soldiers-killed/CAUSE_OF_DEATH/MISSING/exhumed-missing.html. It also has a 'List of kidnapped officers and other ranks not accounted for on 1st July, 1921', www.cairogang.com/soldiers-killed/CAUSE_OF_DEATH/MISSING/hansard.html, taken from Hansard.

# ADDENDUM

Dr Andy Bielenberg and I have corresponded regularly about the circumstances of the deaths recorded in this book, and also about his research with John Donnelly on the period from 1919 to July 1921, now published under 'The Cork Digital Memorial for the War of Independence' at http:// theirishrevolution.ie/digital-memorial/#.WPZCsIX0qHk. Some entries that they managed to clarify after this book was finalised for print, and which needed to be included, are:

**13 June 1920**
**Private Edward Statton**
Private Statton was accidentally shot at Ballincollig Barracks before he went on patrol. He was seventeen and a member of the Seventeenth Lancers. For details see *The Cork Examiner*, 15 June 1920 and *The Freeman's Journal*, 15 June 1920.

**15 June 1920**
**Daniel Fitzgerald**
Daniel Fitzgerald was killed by a military truck as he was crossing Leitrim Street, Cork city. For details see *The Cork Examiner* of 16 and 17 June 1920.

**1 July 1920**
**Private William Entwistle**
According to his death certificate Private Entwistle died on 1 July 1920 of a gunshot wound. There is no information as to how the wound was inflicted.

**25 July 1920**

**Coastguard Philip William Snewin (Snowden)**

**Coastguard Charles Brown**

Liam O'Dwyer, who shot both men dead in a proper wild-west style gunfight inside Ballycrovane Coastguard Station, gives a very detailed account of the planning, execution and successful outcome of this IRA raid for arms outside Ardgroom. The fight took place on the ground floor of the station in the presence of Brown's wife, who threw herself between Brown and O'Dwyer to try to stop the shooting. When the ten enlisted men upstairs saw that their officers were dead, and faced with the IRA's threat to burn the building around them, they surrendered. For full details see Liam O'Dwyer, BMH WS 1527, pp. 9–14.

**4 August 1920**

**Private Herbert Charles Jerrum**

Private Jerrum was accidentally shot by a sentry at Cork Military Barracks. For details see *The Cork Examiner*, 6 August 1920.

**18 October 1920**

**Edward Turner**

Edward Turner was shot and killed by wild firing from British forces in the town park at Mallow after the wounding of a British soldier at the barracks by the IRA. For details see *The Cork Examiner* of 19 and 23 October 1920.

# ENDNOTES

## INTRODUCTION

1 'Detailed list of captured Sinn Fein documents', National Archives Kew (hereafter NAK) CO 904/24/3.

2 Barry Keane, 'Protestant Cork 1911–1926: Summary Courts of Inquiry Irish War of Independence', https://sites.google.com/site/protestantcork191136/summary-courts-of-inquiry-irish-war-of-independence (accessed 14 September 2016).

3 Military Archives of Ireland (hereafter MAI), 'Medals Awarded, 1916–1923', www.militaryarchives.ie/collections/online-collections/military-service-pensions-collection/about-the-collection/new-medals-awarded-1916-1921 (accessed 14 September 2016).

4 David Grant, 'The Cairo Gang', www.cairogang.com and 'The Auxiliary Division of the Royal Irish Constabulary', www.theauxiliaries.com.

5 On Bloody Sunday thirty-one people were killed in Dublin. The day began with an IRA operation organised by Michael Collins to assassinate British intelligence officers who had been drafted in to Dublin after the assassination and resignation of many senior RIC men. Later that afternoon RIC trainees, supported by members of the Auxiliaries, opened fire on a crowd at a Gaelic football match in Croke Park. The Auxiliaries' officer later claimed that his men did not open fire and he saw no reason to have done so. That evening two IRA members and an innocent civilian were beaten and killed in Dublin Castle by their captors, who claimed they were trying to escape.

6 *Irish Examiner*, 15 August 2013, 'British forces will not be commemorated at Kilmichael ambush site', www.irishexaminer.com/ireland/british-forces-will-not-be-commemorated-at-kilmichael-ambush-site-239891.html (accessed 14 September 2016).

7 Eunan O'Halpin and Daithí Ó Corráin, *The Dead of the Irish Revolution, 1916–21* (Yale University Press, forthcoming).

## THE IRISH REVOLUTION AND CIVIL WAR
## 24 APRIL 1916–24 MAY 1923

1 Seamus Kavanagh, Bureau of Military History Witness Statement (hereafter BMH WS) 1670, p. 43. The use of England rather than Britain here is deliberate.

2 House of Commons debate, 3 May 1916, vol. 82 c30, http://hansard.millbank systems.com/commons/1916/may/03/resignation-of-mr-birrell (accessed 14 September 2016).

3 www.aoh61.com/history/easter_trials.htm; 'The dramatic tale of Thomas Kent – the forgotten 1916 rising patriot', *Irish Examiner*, 15 May 2015, www.irish

examiner.com/lifestyle/features/the-dramatic-tale-of-thomas-kent--the-forgotten-1916-rising-patriot-330661.html (accessed 14 September 2016).

4  Anne-Marie Ryan, *16 Dead Men: The Easter Rising Executions* (Cork, 2014), pp. 229–30.

5  Under a general amnesty the final convicted rebels, including Countess Markievicz and Seán MacEntee, were freed by the British government in June 1917. Such was the change in attitude during the previous year that the released prisoners were mobbed by welcoming crowds at Westland Row (Pearse) Station on their return to Dublin.

6  'Those that Set the Stage: Augustine Birrell, Chief Secretary for Ireland, 1907–16', www.nli.ie/1916/exhibition/en/content/stagesetters/homerule/augustinebirrell/; *Report of the Royal Commission on the Rebellion in Ireland*, available at www.garda.ie/Documents/User/Royal%20Commission%20on%20the%20Rebellion%20in%20Ireland%201916.pdf (accessed 14 September 2016).

7  William O'Brien, 'Chapter XV: The Easter Rebellion (1916)', *The Irish Revolution and How It Came About* (London, 1923), available at www.libraryireland.com/irish-revolution/easter-week-rebellion-1916.php (accessed 14 September 2016).

8  'Easter 1916: Monday', www.easter1916.ie/index.php/rising/monday/ (accessed 14 September 2016).

9  O'Brien, 'Chapter XV: The Easter Rebellion (1916)', available at www.libraryireland.com/irish-revolution/easter-week-rebellion-1916.php (accessed 14 September 2016).

10  House of Commons debate, 3 May 1916, vol. 82 cc30–9, http://hansard.millbanksystems.com/commons/1916/may/03/resignation-of-mr-birrell (accessed 14 September 2016). Sir Edward Carson's contribution is notable because of his clear warning about the implications of a reckless response. He stated, 'it would be a mistake to suppose that any true Irishman calls for vengeance. It will be a matter requiring the greatest wisdom and the greatest coolness, may I say, in dealing with these men, and all that I say to the Executive is, whatever is done, let it not be done in a moment of temporary excitement, but with due deliberation in regard both to the past and to the future.' It is also of note that William O'Brien selectively quotes both Redmond and Carson to claim that both men did not understand the implications of shooting the rebels in his discussion of this incident, which is clearly incorrect as it places Redmond speaking after Carson, rather than before, as was the case.

11  HMSO, *Report of the Proceedings of the Irish Convention, 1918*; '1916 Llyod [*sic*] George Negotiations', www.qub.ac.uk/sites/irishhistorylive/IrishHistoryResources/Shortarticlesandencyclopaediaentries/Encyclopaedia/LengthyEntries/1916LlyodGeorgeNegotiations/ (accessed 14 September 2016).

12  This is the accepted start date. 'Commemoration of the first Dáil and launch of the Irish War of Independence', www.museum.ie/Corporate-Media/Media-Information/Media-Releases-Archives/Media-Releases-2009/March-2009/

Commemoration-of-the-first-Dail-and-launch-of-the. For the text of the declaration see http://www.difp.ie/docs/1919/Declaration-of-independence/1.htm (accessed 14 September 2016).

13 House of Lords debate, 21 June 1921, vol. 45 cc659-704, http://hansard.millbank systems.com/lords/1921/jun/21/the-government-of-ireland#S5LV0045P0_1921 0621_HOL_97 (accessed 14 September 2016).

14 Broken down, the figure of 2,819 comes from: 1919 (67), 1920 (423), 1921 (1,230), 1922 (630), 1923 (386), 1924 (83). The figure for 1922 is an estimate as there are no obvious statistics available for Northern Ireland, but D. P. Sharma, *Countering Terrorism* (New Delhi, 1992), p. 13, states that there were eighty murders in April 1922 in Northern Ireland and one in September. The figures for 1923 and 1924 are for the twenty-six counties only, consisting of murders and executions, and are therefore an underestimate, but apparently not by much. For yearly deaths, see 'Annual Reports on Marriages, Births and Deaths in Ireland from 1864 to 2000', www.cso.ie/en/statistics/birthsdeathsandmarriages/archive/ annualreportsonmarriagesbirthsanddeathsinirelandfrom1864to2000/ (accessed 14 September 2016).

15 'Annual Reports on Marriages, Births and Deaths in Ireland from 1864 to 2000', www. cso.ie/en/statistics/birthsdeathsandmarriages/archive/annualreportsonmarriages birthsanddeathsinirelandfrom1864to2000/ (accessed 14 September 2016).

16 'Key Issues in the Treaty Document', http://treaty.nationalarchives.ie/exhibition-topics/key-issues-in-the-treaty-document/ (accessed 14 September 2016).

17 Such was the confusion created by the Treaty that the Parliament of Southern Ireland was convened by the head of the Treaty delegates appointed by an illegal assembly (Arthur Griffith as president of Dáil Éireann) and not by the lord lieutenant as required by the 1920 Government of Ireland Act. (For the full text of the Government of Ireland Act, 1920 see www.legislation.gov.uk/ukpga/Geo5/10-11/67/contents (accessed 10 October 2016).) Equally, given all the difficulties the oath of loyalty to the king had caused during the Treaty debates in the Dáil over the previous few weeks, no formal oath seems to have been administered, with the members merely answering their name and signing the attendance register. The oath would have been the equivalent to that taken by members of the Northern Home Rule Parliament: 'I, A.B., swear by Almighty God that I will be faithful and bear true allegiance to His Majesty, King George the Fifth, his Heirs and Successors, according to law.' Two of the four Dublin University members, none of whom attended the Dáil, answered their names in Irish at the Parliament of Southern Ireland meeting, much to the amusement of their pro-Treaty colleagues: *Irish Independent, Yorkshire Post* and *Leeds Intelligencer,* 16 January 1922. For the official text of the oath of allegiance see British Nationality and Status of Aliens Act, 1914, www.legislation.gov.uk/ukpga/1914/17/pdfs/ukpga_19140017_en.pdf (accessed 14 September 2016).

18 House of Lords debate, 'Irish Free State Agreement Bill', 16 March 1922, vol. 49 c592,

http://hansard.millbanksystems.com/lords/1922/mar/16/irish-free-state-agreement-bill-hl#S5LV0049P0_19220316_HOL_16 (accessed 14 September 2016).

19    *Derry Journal*, 24 April 1922; *The Cork Examiner*, 18 and 20 April 1922.

20    House of Commons debate, 'Easter recess (adjournment), Ireland', 12 April 1922, vol. 153 c529, http://hansard.millbanksystems.com/commons/1922/apr/12/ireland-1 (accessed 14 September 2016).

21    Maryann Gialanella Valiulis, *Portrait of a Revolutionary: General Richard Mulcahy and the Founding of the Irish Free State* (Lexington, 1992), pp. 142–59, especially pp. 151–5.

22    Liam Lynch had been based in the 1st IRA Southern Division headquarters at the Clarence Hotel (across the River Liffey from the Four Courts), having been banned from entering the Four Courts after his rejection of Barry's proposal. He was able to escape to the south after the attack on the Four Courts began and led the anti-Treaty IRA in the Civil War from there.

## CORK 1916–1919

1    Seán Murphy, Thomas Barry, Patrick Canton, James Wickham, BMH WS 1598, pp. 7–13; apparently, not all the guns were surrendered: see p. 17.

2    *Ibid.*, pp. 3, 5–6.

3    *Ibid.*, pp. 16–17.

4    *The Cork Examiner*, 25 June 1917; *Cork Constitution*, 25 and 26 June 1917; *The Freeman's Journal*, 25, 26 and 27 June 1917; Cork City and County Archives (hereafter CCCA) U97, Head Constable John Brown Papers; John Borgonovo, *The Dynamics of War and Revolution: Cork City 1916–1918* (Cork, 2013), pp. 64–7.

5    Major John O'Connell, BMH WS 1444, p. 2.

6    The Cabinet meeting of 23 April 1918 outlined the widespread opposition to conscription in Ireland and the government plan to introduce a new Home Rule Bill. Such was the manpower crisis in the war that the Cabinet called up all British resident men born in 1874–5 (i.e men aged up to forty-eight), 'War Cabinet 397: Man-Power: Military Service Acts, 1916–1918', NAK CAB 23/6, filestore. nationalarchives.gov.uk/pdfs/small/cab-23-6-wc-397-19.pdf (accessed 14 September 2016).

7    Patrick Murray, BMH WS 1584, p. 10. For example, 'There were now nine battalions in Cork 1 Brigade: Cork City (two), Whitechurch, Ovens, Passage, Donoughmore, Macroom, Ballyvourney, Midleton.'

8    Borgonovo, *The Dynamics of War and Revolution*, p. 210.

9    'Cork Union Letterbook, August 1911–February 1918, 29 May 1918', CCCA BG69/B/9.

10   Danny Denton, 'On the Truth of the "German plot"', *Journal of the Galway Archaeological and Historical Society*, vol. 59 (2007), pp. 122–33.

11   The nominees included the party's president, Éamon de Valera, Vice-President Arthur Griffith, Countess Markievicz, Desmond FitzGerald, Ernest Blythe and

Seán MacEntee. See Jill Evans, 'Sinn Fein leaders in Gloucester Prison, 1918', for those imprisoned in Gloucester Gaol, https://gloscrimehistory.wordpress. com/2014/01/23/sinn-fein-leaders-in-gloucester-prison-1918/ (accessed 14 September 2016).

12   Gary Evans, 'The Raising of the First Internal Dáil Éireann Loan and the British Responses to It, 1919–1921', Masters thesis, National University of Ireland Maynooth, 2012, p. 17. Available at http://eprints.maynoothuniversity.ie/4012/1/ MLitt_-_Gary_Evans.pdf (accessed 14 September 2016).

13   Representation of the People Act 1918, www.parliament.uk/about/living-heritage/ transformingsociety/electionsvoting/womenvote/parliamentary-collections/ collections-the-vote-and-after/representation-of-the-people-act-1918/ (accessed 14 September 2016).

14   The IPP was singularly unused to fighting elections. In December 1910, out of 103 Irish seats, fifty-three were uncontested. Little more than 200,000 people voted in Ireland, with the IPP getting eighty-two seats with 92,709 votes.

15   'The Irish Election of 1918', www.ark.ac.uk/elections/h1918.htm (accessed 14 September 2016). Cork city voters had two votes, as it was a two-seater, first-past-the-post constituency. 60,723 votes were cast, which represented a 67 per cent turnout.

16   Oireachtas Éireann, Dáil Debates 3, An Rolla, Tuesday 21 January 1919, http:// oireachtasdebates.oireachtas.ie/debates%20authoring/debateswebpack.nsf/takes/ dail1919012100005?opendocument (accessed 14 September 2016). Michael Collins, TD for Cork South, was too busy rescuing de Valera, while four of the others were in prison.

17   Seán T. O'Kelly, 'Letter to Clemenceau 22 February 1919', www.ucc.ie/celt/Website/ E900014/text001.html (accessed 14 September 2016).

18   'Irish Delegate arrives in Paris; Sean O'Kelly inquires about Recognition of the "Provisional Government"', *The New York Times*, 14 February 1919, http://query. nytimes.com/gst/abstract.html?res=9501E3DF1331E433A25757C1A9649C94 6896D6CF (accessed 14 September 2016).

19   http://hansard.millbanksystems.com/C20 (accessed 14 September 2016).

20   University College Dublin Archives (hereafter UCDA), Éamon de Valera Papers P150, Chronology, p. xxi, http://www.ucd.ie/t4cms/p0150-devalera-eamon-descriptive-catalogue.pdf (accessed 14 September 2016).

21   The prisoners had sent out a drawing of the prison key, which they had copied from a soap impression of the chaplain's key obtained while he was saying Mass. A blank was smuggled into the prison inside a cake. As they left they locked each door behind them. See Erik Grigg, 'Éamon de Valera's Escape from Lincoln Prison', *Lincolnshire Past & Present*, no. 86 (Winter, 2011), https://manchester. academia.edu/ErikGrigg/Papers. A misleading version of events given at the Paris Peace Conference appeared in 'Irish Girls aided De Valera's escape', *The New York Times*, 1 March 1921, available at http://query.nytimes.com/mem/archive-free/ pdf?res=9900EED7113BEE3ABC4A53DFB5668382609EDE. The Australian

*Daily Telegraph* of 7 February 1919 also had a small piece headed 'De Valera's Escape, 1919', http://nla.gov.au/nla.news-article153049652. All websites accessed 14 September 2016.

22    Tim Pat Coogan, *The Man who Made Ireland: The Life and Death of Michael Collins* (Colorado, 1992), p. 99.

23    *An t-Óglách*, 1 February 1919, http://antoglach.militaryarchives.ie/ (accessed 4 November 2016). See also Valiulis, *Portrait of a Revolutionary*, p. 40 for an extended discussion of this.

## THE MURDER OF LORD MAYOR TOMÁS MacCURTAIN AND THE 'STOLEN' JURY

1    Patrick A. Murray, BMH WS 1584, pp. 11–12.

2    Peg Duggan, BMH WS 1576, p. 10.

3    Terence MacSwiney Collection, CCCA PR4/3/7.

4    Michael J. Feeley, BMH WS 68.

5    *The Cork Examiner*, 22 March 1920.

6    Harry Lorton, BMH WS 77, p. 1; 'List of Irish Volunteers extracted from U271', Liam de Roiste Papers, CCCA U271, www.corkarchives.ie/media/Irish%20Volun teers%20Cork%20List-by%20name.pdf (accessed 21 September 2016).

7    Online facial recognition software suggests that this is O'Donoghue, but it is impossible to be absolutely certain.

8    For instance, it was reported in the *Poverty Bay Herald* of 22 May 1920, National Library of New Zealand – Papers Past.

9    'The Killing of Lord Mayor Tomas MacCurtain', http://homepage.eircom. net/~corkcounty/Timeline/MacCurtain.htm (accessed 21 September 2016).

10    Daniel Healy, BMH WS 1656, p. 4, states that Pa McGrath was manufacturing pikes in his forge along with 'slugs for shotguns'. In an email to the author, his grandson identified him in the contemporary picture. Similarly, Peter O'Donovan's grandson also identified his grandfather in the photograph.

## THE DEATH OF COLONEL SMYTH

1    Bill Smyth, Glasheen, Cork, interview with author, 16 August 2015. Mr Smyth's father-in-law was the telegraph officer and an IRA courier.

2    Seán Culhane, BMH WS 746, p. 6.

3    Daniel Healy, BMH WS 1656, p. 11.

4    Seán Culhane, BMH WS 746, p. 6. There have been claims that one of the men said, 'Our orders were to shoot on sight. You are in sight now so make ready', but the men who actually did the shooting make no mention of this: see www. historyireland.com/volume-23/when-the-black-and-tans-came-calling-to-our-school-1920-1/ (accessed 10 October 2016).

5    Paul McCandless, 'Smyths of the Bann. Appendix C: Lieutenant-Colonel Gerald Brice Ferguson Smyth, DSO & BAR', www.sinton-family-trees.com/smyths

ofthebann/apx-c.php (accessed 21 September 2016). For more on Tudor see 'The Last Inspector General of the Royal Irish Constabulary: Major General Sir Henry Hugh Tudor (1870–1965) K.C.B., C.B., C.M.G', www.policehistory.com/tudor.html (accessed 21 September 2016).

6    Jeremiah Mee, BMH WS 379, p. 10.

7    *Ibid.*, pp. 12–13.

8    *Ibid.*, p. 16.

9    For the refutation see House of Commons debate, 14 July 1920, vol. 131 c2386, http://hansard.millbanksystems.com/commons/1920/jul/14/police-listowel (accessed 21 September 2016).

10   House of Commons debate, 22 June 1920, vol. 130 c2130, http://hansard.millbank systems.com/commons/1920/jun/22/maintenance-of-law-and-order-1 (accessed 21 September 2016).

11   *The Irish Times*, 30 July 1920.

12   *The Cork Examiner* from 18 June 1920 onwards covers the shooting of Smyth and the subsequent events in great detail.

## THE DISAPPEARANCE OF JOHN COUGHLAN

1    Interview with Michael Leahy, Ernie O'Malley Notebooks, UCDA P17b/112. I published my list of disappeared on the Internet in July 2015 and was contacted by John Coughlan's grandchildren, who had been searching for information about him since 2009. The family had also contacted Gerard Murphy, author of *The Year of Disappearances: Political Killings in Cork 1921–1922* (Dublin, 2010), who provided them with much of the information about the abduction contained here: email from John Coughlan's granddaughter.

2    'Prosecution of John Glanville, William Leary and Andrew Moore; kidnapping, assault and false imprisonment; conspiracy; 12th October, 1920; Queenstown, Cork', NAK WO 35/125/4 1920, discusses action to be taken against these men and others.

3    *Lincolnshire Post*, 6 September 1920.

4    This is four kilometres from Inch Strand, the location mentioned in the Leahy interview.

5    St James's Cemetery is on the north side of the town. The very short period before burial of unidentified remains was not unusual, as the same happened to Timothy Quinlisk in Cork. He was also buried in a pauper's grave within two days of being killed. While Quinlisk's father was given special permission to exhume the body and return it to Waterford, in the case of John Coughlan his wife was accorded no such privilege. The family state that when she went to Midleton to claim the body, she was told it was too late.

## THE FUNERAL OF TERENCE MacSWINEY

1    Maighread Bean Uí Luasa (Mrs Margaret Lucey), BMH WS 1561, p. 1 of Áine

MacSwiney's diary. The BMH uses the anglicised Annie McSwiney.

2    For a dramatic reconstruction of the hunger strike and death of MacSwiney, go to RTÉ Radio 1, 'Documentary on One: The Death of a Lord Mayor' (1960), available at www.rte.ie/radio1/doconone/2013/0908/647512-podcast-lord-mayor-terence-MacSwiney-cork/ (accessed 21 September 2016).

3    *The Irish Times*, 26 October 1920. William Murphy, *Political Imprisonment and the Irish, 1912–1921* (Oxford, 2014), pp. 174–91, gives a very good and detailed account of the progress and impact of the hunger strikes.

4    *The Irish Times*, 26 October 1920.

5    Maighread Bean Uí Luasa (Mrs Margaret Lucey), BMH WS 1561, p. 20 of the diary.

6    Maurice Walsh, *The News from Ireland: Foreign Correspondents and the Irish Revolution* (London, 2008), p. 80.

7    Maighread Bean Uí Luasa (Mrs Margaret Lucey), BMH WS 1561, pp. 24–6 of the diary.

8    'Fight over the Body at Holyhead Station: Call Officials Body-Snatchers. Woman Bruised in Melee', *The New York Times*, 30 October 1920.

9    Maighread Bean Uí Luasa (Mrs Margaret Lucey), BMH WS 1561, p. 27 of the diary.

10   There can be little doubt that the Cork hunger strikers were being fed supplements in their water, as so many could not have survived for ninety-three days otherwise. MacSwiney had refused prison water once he suspected this might be happening and would only accept 'certified' water. While the use of supplements was denied by the Brixton Prison doctor, it is of note that MacSwiney died shortly after this incident.

## THE KILMICHAEL AMBUSH

1    This was not always the case. In Dorothy Macardle's *The Irish Republic: A Documented Chronicle of the Anglo-Irish Conflict and the Partitioning of Ireland, with a Detailed Account of the Period 1916–1923* (New York, 1965) it merited one sentence.

2    Peter Hart, *The IRA and its Enemies: Violence and Community in Cork, 1916–1923* (Oxford, 1998), pp. 32 and 36. Despite suggestions that Hart was related to Auxiliary Vernon Hart, who murdered Canon Magner of Dunmanway, this is untrue. Peter Hart was from a British Army and Ulster Unionist background, while Vernon Hart was from a Liverpool business family. The list of those involved in the debate over Kilmichael includes Kevin Myers, Eoghan Harris, Jack Lane, Brendan Clifford, Fr Brian Murphy, Meda Ryan, Eve Morrison, John Borgonovo, Niall Meehan, John Regan, David Fitzpatrick, Gerard Murphy, Stephen Howe, Brian Walker, Andy Bielenberg, Charles Townsend and Eugenio Biagini.

3    F. P. Crozier, *Ireland Forever* (London, 1932), p. 128. It was not explained who was telling the story in 1921 and Hart attaches no significance to this. He was

unaware at the time that on 26 November 1932 *The Irish Press* had run an article on Kilmichael and the lack of mention of a false surrender in this had incensed Barry. See correspondence between Meda Ryan, who uncovered evidence of Barry's anger, and Hart in *The Irish Times*, 'Letters to the Editor', 10 November and 10 December 1998. On 10 December Hart accepted that 'legitimately different accounts exist of what happened' and the possibility that some of the IRA had been tricked or that some of the Auxiliaries might have tried to surrender, but he continued to insist that there was no 'false surrender' as depicted by Barry. This seems a long way from 'riddled with lies and evasions'. See also Meda Ryan, 'The Kilmichael Ambush, 1920: Exploring the *"Provocative Chapters"*', *History*, vol. 92, issue 306, April 2007, p. 239 fn. 15; Eve Morrison, 'Kilmicheal Revisited: Tom Barry and the "False Surrender"', in David Fitzpatrick (ed.), *Terror in Ireland 1916–1923* (Dublin, 2012), pp. 158–80. Brian P. Murphy OSB, 'Poisoning the Well or Publishing the Truth?', in *Troubled History: A 10th Anniversary Critique of Peter Hart's The IRA and its Enemies* (Millstreet, 2008) provides a full critique.

4    *Round Table* (June 1921), p. 500. It might be suggested that *Round Table* was an obscure source, but it was discussed in Lord Longford's *Peace by Ordeal* (Pakenham, 1972) as early as 1933, a source referenced by Hart himself.

5    Patrick O'Brien, BMH WS 812, p. 14. See also Liam Deasy, *Towards Ireland Free: the West Cork Brigade in the War of Independence, 1917–1921* (Dublin, 1973), pp. 115–17.

6    James 'Spud' Murphy, BMH WS 1684, pp. 5–6. The main sources all number the sections differently but there is agreement between the British and the Irish evidence about their locations. By numbering them sequentially Murphy's description is the easiest to follow. The members of the column at Kilmichael according to Murphy (pp. 7–8) were: 'Denis Cronin, Bantry; Mick O'Driscoll, Ballineen; Denis O'Sullivan, Ardfield; John Hegarty, Leap; Tim O'Connell, Ahakeera; Tim McCarthy, Durrus; Ned Young, Dunmanway; Dan Hourihan, Ballinacarriga; Pat Donovan, Dunmanway; John O'Sullivan, Kealkil; Mick Herlihy, Union Hall; Stephen O'Neill, Clonakilty; James Murphy (witness), Clonakilty; Paddy O'Brien, Ballineen; Jack Hennessy, Ballineen; M. Donovan, Skibbereen; 'Neilus' Cotter, Dunmanway; David Crowley, Ballineen; Jack Roche, Kilbrittain; Jerome O'Hea, Barryroe; Denis O'Brien, Newcestown; Tim Crowley, Ballygurteen; Patrick O'Donovan, Inchafune; James O'Mahoney, Corran; John O'Donovan, Dunmanway; Sonny Crowley, Dunmanway; Denis O'Neill, Baltimore; John D. O'Sullivan, Caheragh; John Falvey, Upton; Michael O'Donovan, Clogagh; Batty Coughlan, Dunmanway; Michael O'Driscoil, Bantry; Michael McCarthy, Dunmanway (killed); James O'Sullivan, Knockawadra, Clonakilty (killed); Pat Deasy, Bandon (killed); Jerh Mahoney, Coppeen; Michael McCarthy, Schull; John Lordan, Newcestown; John 'Flyer' Nyhan, Clonakilty; Jack Hourihan, Ballineen, and Tom Barry (column O/C.)'. This is four more than Barry stated (but he did

exclude the scouts) and eight more than the figure given in a report of the ambush contained in the Strickland Papers in the Imperial War Museum, London. One notable omission is Tim Keohane, whose participation was questioned around the time of his death. However, Jim O'Driscoll (Keohane's O/C) stated in his BMH WS (1250, p. 15): 'Kilmichael Ambush 28th November, 1920. Timothy Keohane, Ballinroher, Armed', so it appears that Keohane was there.

7       Tom Barry, *Guerilla Days in Ireland*, (Dublin, 1949), pp. 42–5. See also Deasy, *Towards Ireland Free*, p. 115, which states that McCarthy was only 2 yards above the road when the Auxiliary lorry stopped opposite him; Terence O'Reilly, *Our Struggle for Freedom: Eye-witness Accounts from An Cosantóir* (Cork 2009), pp. 93–108.

8       There is constant dispute about where the grenade landed, but it is patently obvious from the wounds to the Auxiliaries recorded in their death certificates that it landed in the body of the truck. While this may seem like an extremely lucky throw given that the distance from Barry to the truck was approximately 35 metres, in a county where 28-ounce cannonballs are used in road bowling this is not particularly spectacular.

9       Barry, *Guerilla Days in Ireland*, pp. 43–4.

10      'Kilmichael Ambush – 28 Nov 1920', www.theauxiliaries.com/INCIDENTS/kilmichael-ambush/kilmichael.html (accessed 27 September 2016).

11      Jack Hennessy, BMH WS 1234, pp. 5–6.

12      Meda Ryan, 'The Kilmichael Ambush, 1920', p. 241 fn. 19. Ryan states that Deasy had been grazed in the abdomen earlier, but the fatal chest wound occurred at this point.

13      Murphy, Seán A., *Kilmichael: A Battlefield Study* (Cork, 2014), pp. 100–2.

14      O'Sullivan and Deasy. Meda Ryan, *Tom Barry: IRA Freedom Fighter* (Cork, 2005), p. 66. If this was, in fact, the case, then questions about the false surrender are irrelevant as this is clear evidence of one. See also a letter in James Sullivan's military pension collection file (Military Service Pensions Collection, Military Archives Ireland (hereafter MSPC) 1D117) from James Cullinane, dated 21 September 1923, which states O'Sullivan died from a bullet through the head.

15      Timothy Keohane, BMH WS 1295, pp. 6–7.

16      Stephen O'Neill, 'Auxiliaries Annihilated at Kilmichael', in Brian Ó Conchubhair (ed.), *Rebel Cork's Fighting Story* (Cork, 2009), p. 142.

17      Patrick O'Brien's account of the fight can be found in BMH WS 812, pp. 15–16. In yet another controversy it is claimed by Dr Eve Morrison that because other veterans make no mention of a false surrender, including Paddy O'Brien in the account he gives in Deasy, *Towards Ireland Free*, pp. 115–17, then Hart's suggestion that Tom Barry made up the 'false surrender' gains credibility. O'Brien says that 'the remaining sixteen [out of the eighteen Auxiliaries at the ambush] had been killed outright', i.e. before the end of the ambush, which clearly means that no prisoners were taken to be executed, as Hart claimed. Therefore O'Brien is no help

to Hart's theory and is little more than a red herring in the debate. See also John Regan, 'West Cork and the Writing of History: In reply to Eve Morrison', *Dublin Review of Books* (2014), http://www.drb.ie/essays/west-cork-and-the-writing-of-history (accessed 18 October 2016); Eve Morrison, 'Reply to John Regan', http://www.drb.ie/reviews/reply-to-john-regan (accessed 14 January 2017).

18  James 'Spud' Murphy, BMH WS 1684, pp. 6–7.

19  Ryan, *Tom Barry*, p. 56. If prisoners were shot out of hand at Kilmichael this would have been unusual for the West Cork Brigade. Surrenders from British forces were taken at Toureen, Laurel Walk (partially), Rosscarbery and Skibbereen, both before and after Kilmichael. At Crossbarry one veteran recalls Barry warning his men not to shoot wounded soldiers or to use exploding or 'dum-dum' bullets: William Norris, BMH WS 595, p. 10.

20  For the definition of axilla (armpit), see the Merriam-Webster Medical Dictionary, www.merriam-webster.com/medical/axilla (accessed 1 September 2015).

21  *The Skibbereen Eagle*, 15 January 1921 and *The Irish Times*, 1 December 1920 both carried reports of Dr Kelleher's evidence on the autopsies.

22  'Cecil James Guthrie', www.theauxiliaries.com/men-alphabetical/men-g/gutherie/guthrie.html (accessed 27 September 2016).

23  *Irish Independent*, 17 January 1921.

24  *The Irish Times*, 12 January 1921.

25  Hart stated this in *The IRA and its Enemies*, so it is not in contention.

26  For other versions of the false surrender story see Piaras Béaslaí, *Michael Collins and the Making of a New Ireland*, vol. 2 (London, 1926), p. 97; Crozier, *Ireland Forever*, p. 168; Ernie O'Malley, *On Another Man's Wound* (Dublin, 1979), p. 217; Stephen O'Neill, 'Auxiliaries Annihilated', in Ó Conchubhair, *Rebel Cork's Fighting Story*, pp. 140–3; Lionel Curtis (ed.), 'Ireland', *Round Table*, June 1921, p. 500.

27  Crozier, *Ireland Forever*, pp. 128–33. Crozier had resigned as head of the Auxiliary police in February 1921 over the reinstatement of men he had dismissed following the burning of Tuam the previous year. He stated that he had investigated Kilmichael while in plain clothes in 1921 and had been told this by the IRA. Reasonably, Peter Hart questioned the likelihood of this happening before the resignation. However, he incorrectly dismisses Crozier. After all, Crozier shows that the false surrender was part of the story from the outset. Eve Morrison (*op. cit.*) also wonders how believable these reports of a false surrender in 1921 should have been to British commentators like Crozier and Lionel Curtis, yet the fact that the reports were circulating appears to be a critical point in favour of Tom Barry's version of events. Put simply, if someone is telling you an unbelievable story, they are still telling you the story. It is also of note that Morrison emphasises phrases such as 'it is alleged by Sinn Féin' and 'ex parte' but chooses to downplay 'when the attacking party approached to take the surrender fire was opened upon them'.

# THE BURNING OF CORK

1    'Vernon Anwyl Hart', www.theauxiliaries.com/men-alphabetical/men-h/hart-va/
     hart.html (accessed 11 October 2016). The make-up and formation date of 'K'
     Company is important as they were directly involved in a series of incidents which
     undermined the credibility of the Auxiliary force. These included the murder of
     Nicholas de Sales Prendergast in Fermoy on 1 December, and following this, in
     Cork, various shooting incidents, arson attacks, the humiliation of a priest on St
     Patrick's Street, the burning of the city centre, the murder of the Delaney brothers
     at Dublin Hill and, subsequently, in Dunmanway, the murder of Canon Magner
     two days after they were transferred out of the city, followed by a series of petty
     crimes around Dunmanway. As with most events in this story, the formation of
     'K' Company led to an 'academic debate' between David Leeson and John Bor-
     gonovo. Borgonovo claimed, in *Spies, Informers and the 'Anti-Sinn Féin Society'*:
     *the Intelligence War in Cork City, 1920–1921* (Dublin, 2007), that the company
     had 'gone rogue' within days of being formed. According to him this pointed to
     poor training or a deliberate policy to take the gloves off. Leeson dismissed this
     and pointed to General Crozier's statement that 'the men were not "new men" as
     they had all served together in other companies elsewhere'. Research by David
     Grant has proved that the first platoon of the company was formed in late August
     1920 and served with 'E' Company until its transfer to 'K' in November 1920; the
     second platoon was formed from new recruits who joined after 17 November; the
     third platoon was not formed (again from new recruits) until after the burning
     of Cork. So it is clear that Crozier's version of events is at least partially inaccu-
     rate. See 'K Company ADRIC – Individual Platoons', http://theauxiliaries.com/
     companies/k-coy/platoon-detailed/men-by-platoon.html (accessed 10 October
     2016).

2    Alan J. Ellis *et al.*, *The Burning of Cork: an Eyewitness Account by Alan J. Ellis, and
     Other Items* (Millstreet, 2004). Available at http://aubanehistoricalsociety.org/au-
     bane_collection/burning.pdf (accessed 27 September 2016).

3    Samuel Baster, Gerald Fitzgerald, Albert Coates, Bert Carre, Herbert Quinn,
     Vernon Hart and Eric Cummings were all under arrest in Dunmanway at
     that time. For more details on these men see 'K Company ADRIC', http://the
     auxiliaries.com/companies/k-coy/k-coy.html (accessed 13 October 2016).

4    See NAK CAB/23/24, 'Cabinet Conclusions', 14 February 1921 and minutes
     of the meeting about the burning of Cork, 15 February 1921, in the same
     document. See also the House of Commons debate on the king's speech, where
     Lloyd George blamed the poor of the city for some of the fires. Where the poor
     would have got this petrol during a curfew is not explained. House of Commons
     debate, 15 February 1921, vol. 138 c43, http://hansard.millbanksystems.com/
     commons/1921/feb/15/debate-on-the-address (accessed 27 September 2016).

5    For information on Horgan, see Gerry White and Brendan O'Shea, *The Burning
     of Cork* (Cork, 2006), pp. 99–100.

6   *Ibid.*, pp. 89–99.
7   Anon., *Who Burnt Cork City? A Tale of Arson, Loot, and Murder. The Evidence of Over Seventy Witnesses* (Dublin, 1921). Published by the Irish Labour Party and Trade Union Congress, this is an essential primary source for many of the incidents covered in this book, including the Delaney Brothers' killings, the Dillon's Cross ambush, and of course the burning of Cork: http://archive.org/stream/whoburntcorkcity00dubl#page/65/mode/2up, pp. 65–7. See also http://homepage.eircom.net/~corkcounty/brothers.html (accessed 27 September 2016).

## THE INCIDENT AT MALLOW STATION

1   In contrast, the entrance to Fermoy Station was sandbagged and guarded by armed sentries. As the station was next to the entrance to New Barracks, Fermoy, this may have been the cause of the extra security.
2   Jeremiah Daly, BMH WS 1015, p. 5.
3   House of Commons debate, 15 February 1921, vol. 138 c32, http://hansard.mill banksystems.com/commons/1921/feb/15/debate-on-the-address (accessed 27 September 2016).
4   'Ireland Civil Registration Indexes, 1845–1958', database, FamilySearch (https://familysearch.org/ark:/61903/1:1:FRGM-X66 : 4 December 2014), DEATHS entry for Joseph Greensmyth; citing Mallow, Jul–Sep 1921, vol. 5, p. 269, General Registry, Custom House, Dublin; FHL microfilm 101,608 (accessed 31 August 2015). Thanks to Peter Rigney for alerting me to this.
5   House of Commons debate, 15 February 1921, vol. 138 cc30–35, http://hansard.millbanksystems.com/commons/1921/feb/15/debate-on-the-address (accessed 27 September 2016).
6   HMSO, 'Report of the Mallow Court of Inquiry', www.dippam.ac.uk/eppi/documents/22737/page/737414 (accessed 27 September 2016).

## CASCADING DEATH

1   In *Massacre in West Cork: The Dunmanway and Ballygroman Killings Cork* (Cork, 2014), I stated that Frank Busteed was at the viaduct and had shot Din-Din but, in fact, he was reporting the story second-hand and was not involved in the shooting.
2   James Charles Beale (the name on his death certificate), a.k.a. James Charles Beal or James Beal; *Cork Constitution*, 16 February 1921.
3   Seán O'Callaghan, *Execution* (London, 1974), pp. 60–2. See also Hart, *The IRA and its Enemies*.
4   Mick Murphy, BMH WS 1547, p. 33. See also Jeremiah Kelleher, BMH WS 1657, p. 8, and Borgonovo, *Spies, Informers and the 'Anti-Sinn Féin Society'*, pp. 28–33.
5   O'Callaghan, *Execution*, p. 63.
6   Interview with Michael (Mick) Murphy, Ernie O'Malley Notebooks, UCDA P17b/112. 'On 1.12.1920, the house of a man named Blemings was raided on my directions and Blemings and his son taken away. They were both shot. These two

were members of the senior spy section in the Y.M.C.A. Their names were given to me by Parsons. We also had information about them from letters captured by our lads in raids on postmen for mails', Mick Murphy, BMH WS 1547, p. 33. Murphy is incorrect about the date of the shootings.

7    'England and Wales Marriage Registration Index, 1837-2005,' database, FamilySearch (https://familysearch.org/ark:/61903/1:1:2DNS-3R5 : 13 December 2014), James Charles Beal, 1909; from "England & Wales Marriages, 1837-2005," database, findmypast (www.findmypast.com : 2012); citing 1909, quarter 3, vol. 1D, p. 2319, Woolwich, London, England, General Register Office, Southport, England (accessed 27 September 2016).

8    William Barry, BMH WS 1708, pp. 6–7. There was apparently much surprise among Sinn Féin members at the shooting of Reilly, who, as a prominent Methodist Home Ruler and the organiser of a petition to save Terence MacSwiney, would not have been a likely member of a conspiracy involving members of Anglican church organisations.

9    Jeremiah Keating, BMH WS 1657, p. 8: 'This man, Beale, lived on College Road, Cork, and on 16th February, 1921, Pat Collins, John Horgan and I, with two others, watched the approaches to College Road. John Horgan and I spotted Beale as he was crossing Southgate Bridge en route to his home. I went and got revolvers, picked up Beale and brought him by car to the Wilton district; where he was shot. We found in his possession papers giving valuable information relating to the spy organisation with which he was connected. In my opinion the shooting of Beale broke the back of the anti-I.R.A.-Sinn Féin organisation in Cork City.' See also Patrick Collins, BMH WS 1707, pp. 7–8, and Michael Murphy, BMH WS 1547, p. 37.

10   Patrick Collins, BMH WS 1707, p. 8.

11   'Civilians Killed', www.irishmedals.org/civilians-killed.html (accessed 27 September 2016).

12   *The Irish Times*, 21 February 1921.

## THE CLONMULT SHOOTOUT

1    Ó Conchubhair, *Rebel Cork's Fighting Story*, p. 234.

2    James Coss, BMH WS 1065, p. 11.

3    Patrick Higgins, BMH WS 1467, pp. 4–6.

## 28 FEBRUARY 1921

1    *The Irish Times*, 17 October 1978. See also 'Inniscarra: Ambush at Dripsey', www.inniscarra.org/styled/page42/ (accessed 28 September 2016).

2    The assailant was Frank Busteed according to his recollections in O'Callaghan, *Execution*, p. 154. Frank had been the officer in charge at the Dripsey ambush.

3    'Cork Shootings – 28 February 1921', www.cairogang.com/soldiers-killed/cork-street-feb-21/Cork-streets.html (accessed 28 September 2016).

4    *The Freeman's Journal*, 30 March 1921.

5    *Irish Independent*, 30 March 1921. See also 'Cork Shootings – 28 February 1921', www.cairogang.com/soldiers-killed/cork-street-feb-21/Cork-streets.html (accessed 28 September 2016).

6    *The Cork Examiner*, 30 March 1921.

7    Also listed as Wyse in some of the news reports.

8    *Irish Independent*, 30 March 1921. Michael V. O'Donoghue, BMH WS 1741 Pt 1, p. 147, states that he killed Gill. His account of this event differs slightly from the *Irish Independent*'s.

9    *Irish Independent*, 30 March 1921; *The Irish Times*, 30 March 1921. See also 'Cork shootings – 28 February 1921', www.cairogang.com/soldiers-killed/cork-street-feb-21/Cork-streets.html (accessed 28 September 2016).

10   *The Irish Times*, 17 October 1978.

11   For the date of Mrs Lindsay's shooting see *The Southern Star*, 30 July 1921.

## THE CROSSBARRY AMBUSH

1    Ryan, *Tom Barry*, p. 133.

2    The number of British soldiers involved in the operation according to Barry was nearly 1,400: see *Guerilla Days in Ireland*, p. 124. This was disputed by Flor Begley who put the figure at nearer 300 based on the number of lorries that had been involved: BMH WS 1771, p. 3. William Sheehan in *A Hard Local War: The British Army and the Guerrilla War in Cork, 1919–1921* (Stroud, 2011), pp. 147–51, suggests that the figures involved were no more than 150 based on the number of troops in barracks in July 1921.

3    Imperial War Museum, London, Peter Strickland Papers, EPS.

4    John O'Driscoll, BMH WS 1250, p. 9.

5    For the full story of Charlie Hurley see Ó Conchubhair, *Rebel Cork's Fighting Story*, pp. 163–9. To ensure Hurley's safety William Desmond was sent from the main party by Barry to guard him. However, just before he reached Forde's he was captured by the Hampshires, who did not recognise him. He was brought to Major Percival, intelligence officer of the Essex Regiment, at Forde's to be questioned and saw a dead body in a trap. When the firing started at Crossbarry, Percival immediately departed with the Essex Regiment, and the Hampshires attempted to block the IRA retreat to the north. William Desmond, BMH WS 832, pp. 37–9.

6    Michael O'Driscoll, BMH WS 1297, pp. 6–7.

7    William Morris, BMH WS 595, p. 11: 'We had a lot of stuff to remove and we had two wounded men – these were Dan Corcoran and James Crowley. Corcoran was seriously wounded. We left three men behind, dead – Peter Monaghan, Jeremiah O'Leary of Leap, and Con Daly of Ballinascarthy.'

8    Despite claiming to be an explosives expert, few of the mines placed by Monaghan worked, leading to speculation that he was a spy. See 'Peter Monaghan Deserter

from British Army', www.cairogang.com/ira-men/monaghan-deserter.html (accessed 2 September 2015). However, Ewan Butler, in *Barry's Flying Column* (London, 1972), pp. 49–50, states that the reason that the mines did not work was an absence of a gun cotton primer, which suggests that the problem occurred during manufacture. Monaghan is buried in the Republican Plot in Bandon and there is no other suggestion that he was anything but genuine.

9    Cornelius Calnan, BMH WS 1317, pp. 7–8.

10   Peter Kearney, BMH WS 444, pp. 7–9.

11   William Sheehan, *British Voices from the Irish War of Independence 1918–1921: The Words of British Servicemen Who Were There* (Cork, 2005), pp. 96–140.

12   *Connacht Tribune*, 26 March 1921. The description includes the second 'Hotblack' battle. As the Beazleys and Harolds were Church of Ireland and the Healys Roman Catholic, presumably it was the latter who provided the rosary beads. The Beazley family was large by Church of Ireland standards (though not in West Cork) with nine children.

13   *The Irish Times*, 21 March 1921.

14   *Ibid.*, 23 April 1921. Both families were compensated and remained in West Cork long after the War of Independence. It is often presented that these were reprisal or sectarian burnings by the IRA but, given their central role in the ambush, it is more likely that the culprits were on the British side, especially because the IRA headquarters at Crosspound was burned on the same night.

## THE DESTRUCTION OF ROSSCARBERY POLICE BARRACKS

1    David Fitzpatrick, *Descendancy: Irish Protestant Histories Since 1795* (Cambridge, 2014), p. 204.

2    James 'Spud' Murphy, BMH WS 1684, p. 13.

3    *Ibid.*, p. 14.

4    *Ibid.*, pp. 14–15.

5    Michael Coleman, BMH WS 1254, p. 17.

6    The Auxiliaries reoccupied Rosscarbery on 28 June but when they were attacked by the flying column they withdrew. This was followed by a 'sweep' by Major Percival's flying column, which trapped James 'Spud' Murphy among others on the cliffs at Dunny Cove, Ardfield, Clonakilty. However, the IRA men made their escape as night fell: James 'Spud' Murphy, BMH WS 1684, p. 26.

## TOM BARRY'S TRENCH COAT

1    Barry, *Guerilla Days in Ireland*, pp. 90–1, p. 157.

2    Stephen O'Brien, BMH WS 603, pp. 1–2.

3    Tom Barry Collection, CCCA UI6/1/5. Butler, *Barry's Flying Column*, pp. 81–2, also comments about the relationship between the IRA and the King's Liverpool Regiment.

4    Denis Lordan, BMH WS 470, p. 18.

5    In contrast, two weeks after the release of the Skibbereen troops, Barry's column
     shot two Essex Regiment troops and handed a letter addressed to Major Percival
     to two captured members of the Royal Navy, declaring all-out war on his regiment
     for their torture and murder of prisoners: Jack Hennessy, BMH WS 1234, p. 12.

6    Maurice Donegan recalled of his capture by the Liverpools (BMH WS 639, p.
     6): 'Abandoning the car we tried to make our escape and were fired on. Only by
     throwing ourselves flat did we avoid the bullets and we were quickly surrounded
     and had the mortification of being hauled off as prisoners to the military barracks
     – Bantry Workhouse. Here we were lodged in a galvanized iron hut attached
     to and in front of the guardroom and that night the R.I.C. from their barracks
     alongside tried to get at us, but the British Sergeant in charge of us – Nash by
     name and married to an Irishwoman – turned out the Guard and drove off the
     R.I.C.'

7    For Crowley's intelligence-gathering operation, see Keane, *Massacre in West Cork*,
     p. 154. See also Patrick O'Brien, BMH WS 812, p. 19.

8    Dunmanway Historical Society, 'Extracts from the Memoirs of Florence John
     Crowley', *Dunmanway Doings* (4) 2010, pp. 21–2.

9    There is no reason to doubt Crowley given that much of the rest his story as an
     IRA spy is corroborated by BMH statements, for example Patrick O'Brien, WS
     812, p. 19. Crowley also stated that, as Brownie sat opposite him in the workhouse
     office, he was inadvertently the main source of his information.

10   For more on this, see Keane, *Massacre in West Cork*, pp. 66–74.

## MASSACRE IN WEST CORK

1    *The Corkman*, 16 May 2015, available at www.independent.ie/regionals/corkman/
     news/appeal-to-help-solve-mystery-of-mid-cork-killings-31219202.html   (ac-
     cessed 10 October 2016). Full details of these deaths can be found in Keane, *Mas-
     sacre in West Cork*; most of the details in this chapter come from this book.

2    'Four victims', *The Irish Times*, 2 May 1922.

3    'West Cork tragedies', *The Southern Star*, 6 May 1922.

4    See *Massacre in West Cork* and Barry Keane, 'The IRA and loyalist co-operation
     with British forces in Cork 1920-1923', www.academia.edu/16377450/The_
     IRA_and_loyalist_co-operation_with_British_forces_in_Cork_1920-1923 (ac-
     cessed 28 September 2016).

5    This is hardly surprising as he was a justice of the peace and crown solicitor, but he
     is also described as 'a frequent visitor to the barracks' in Dunmanway during the
     war. See Michael Collins Papers, MAI A0897.

6    This claim was made by Meda Ryan in *Tom Barry*, pp. 213–14, but the quality of
     the evidence for this is disputed.

7    MSPC MSP34REF52679. Thanks to Niall Murray for alerting me to this.

8    Ryan, *Tom Barry*, pp. 213–14.

9    For a detailed analysis of how the murder victims of April 1922 were selected see

Keane, 'The IRA Response to Loyalist Co-operation in County Cork during the Irish War of Independence', www.academia.edu/27954537/The_IRA_response_to_loyalist_co-operation_in_County_Cork_during_the_Irish_War_of_Independence (accessed 1 March 2017).

10  'Disturbances in Ireland: Irish Distress Committee for the aid of refugees and Irish Grants Committee to provide compensation for victims of the troubles who had lost their homes etc.', NAK TS 18/236; Fitzpatrick (2014), p. 226.

## MICHAEL COLLINS: 'THE MAN WHO COULDN'T BE KILLED'

1  The chapter title quote is from Collins' great friend John L. Sullivan, who met him in Bandon on the day he was killed. University College Cork, Boole Library, John L. Sullivan Collection, IE BL/SC/JLS/4, transcript of cassette tape.

2  Frank Thornton, BMH WS 615, p. 2.

3  See British Commander-in-Chief Nevil Macready's comments to London on 19 July 1921, 'Report by the General Officer Commanding-in-Chief on the Situation in Ireland for Week Ending 16th July, 1921', NAK CAB 24/126/56.

4  *The Southern Star*, 23 July 1921.

5  Contemporary Documents, MAI, Cathal Brugha Barracks, Dublin.

6  Meda Ryan, *Michael Collins and the Women who Spied for Ireland* (Cork, 2006), p. 92.

7  *The Skibbereen Eagle*, 23 April 1921.

8  *The Freeman's Journal*, 17 September 1921.

9  'War Cabinet and Cabinet: Minutes. Conferences of Ministers. Conclusion, 13 October 1920', NAK CAB 23/38/2.

10  Lord Longford, the first scholar to cast a cold eye over the negotiations, understood its full significance – that with this fiscal concession, an oath of faithfulness to the king instead of the legally required allegiance, the use of Commonwealth instead of Empire for the first time, and a Boundary Commission in the event of James Craig rejecting essential unity, this was a substantially different and stronger document than that presented to the Dáil Cabinet a few days before. However, Longford did have the benefit of hindsight not available to the men of 1921. See Francis Pakenham, Earl of Longford, *Peace by Ordeal: An Account, from First-Hand Sources of the Negotiation and Signature of the Anglo-Irish Treaty 1921* (London, 1972), pp. 229–43. In truth, the British knew that at least one of the Irish leaders (most likely Collins) had recognised that fiscal autonomy meant independence as far back as January 1921. A memorandum seized at Collins' headquarters concerning a proposal by Justice O'Connor for fiscal autonomy states, 'We would have a 26 County Republic, in effect, without the sword': 'Detailed list of documents seized at Sinn Fein HQ', NAK CO/904/24/3. After a meeting between Justice O'Connor and Edward Carson, this proposal was then put to the British according to the Lloyd George Papers in the British Parliamentary Archive. See memo from Judge O'Connor about his meetings with Carson and

the outcome, De Valera Papers, UCDA P150/1902, www.difp.ie/docs/1921/
Anglo-Irish-Treaty/129.htm (accessed 28 September 2016).

11  HMSO, *Papers Respecting Negotiations with the Egyptian Delegation* (London,
1921), available at https://archive.org/stream/papersrespecting00egyp#page/n1/
mode/2up (accessed 28 September 2016). The British deeply regretted 'that the
maintenance of British troops in Egypt and the association of British officials
with the Ministries of Justice and Finance should be so gravely misunderstood' (p.
13), which, to say the least, is a massive understatement of the control demanded
in return for 'sovereignty'.

12  Robin J. Moore, 'Curzon and Indian Reform', *Modern Asian Studies*, vol. 27,
no. 4 (October 1993), pp. 719–40. Curzon is blamed for removing the phrase
'self-government' as being potentially lethal for British control of India, only to
replace it with the even more dangerous 'responsible government', which could be
interpreted as a path to parliamentary democracy. Curzon was in favour of Indian
self-government 'in say 500 years'.

13  See Martin Mansergh, 'The Freedom to Achieve Freedom?', in Gabriel Doherty
and Dermot Keogh (eds), *Michael Collins and the Making of the Irish State* (Cork,
1998) for a good overall analysis of this dilemma for the Treaty negotiations.
Of course, if either Collins or Griffith had known that the British Cabinet had
expressed its determination to retain Fermanagh and Tyrone 'within the area of
the Northern Ireland Parliament' at a meeting in Inverness on 9 September 1921,
despite their nationalist majorities, there is no doubt that they would not (and
indeed could not) have signed the Treaty. Given this much-overlooked British
decision, it must be concluded that Lloyd George was negotiating in bad faith by
suggesting a Boundary Commission which was so open to manipulation, and that
his government never had any intention of ceding any Northern Ireland territory.
See NAK CAB 23/27/1 for the Inverness meeting.

14  Lady Eleanor Smith, the daughter of Lord Birkenhead, F. E. Smith, recalls the
comment and another anecdote about the friendship that had developed between
the two men: 'F. E. Smith', *The West Australian*, 4 November 1939, http://nla.gov.
au/nla.news-article46435673 (accessed 28 September 2016).

15  *The Irish Times*, 7 March 1922.

16  *Ibid.*, 13 March 1922. A month later, when the 'dream team' were speaking in
Tralee, shots were again fired at the start of the speeches. Collins had had to im-
provise the previous day by addressing the crowd in Killarney from a donkey and
cart, after the platform from which he was to speak was burned down: *The Irish
Times*, 22 April 1922.

17  Coogan, *Michael Collins*, p. 316.

18  Collins was not the target of this attack. It was in response to a 'drive-by' shooting
earlier. See *The Irish Times*, 18 April 1922.

19  Charles Townshend, *The Republic: The Fight for Irish Independence* (London, 2013)
available at https://books.google.co.uk/books?id=oVl5AAAAQBAJ&q=thin+ve

neer#v=snippet&q=thin%20veneer&f=false (accessed 10 October 2016).

20  *The Irish Times* of 15 June 1922 records the speech in a brief report of a single paragraph. This report shows that the speech was Collins expressing his personal opinion. It is little more than the usual eve of election speech to which little attention is paid. Collins is implying that the people should vote for him because he will meet the situation that needs to be met 'as it should be met', which could be interpreted as a threat to the Four Courts garrison.

21  The election was a triumph for the pro-Treaty party in his constituency, with Collins getting 17,000 of the pro-Treaty Sinn Féin total of 25,403 votes. Anti-Treaty Sinn Fein got 12,587, barely staying ahead of Labour on 10,737. The Farmers Party got 6,372. Pro-Treaty Sinn Féin took 3 seats, Labour 2 and the Farmers 1, with anti-Treaty Sinn Féin taking 2. This gave a 6:2 majority for the pro-Treaty parties. While most of the West Cork IRA was anti-Treaty, 77 per cent of the electorate voted the other way.

22  Pictures of this can be found at 'Civil War in Cork City', www.corkpastandpresent. ie/mapsimages/corkphotographs/civilwarphotographsofcorkcity/civilwar/ (accessed 28 September 2016).

23  The new state was desperately short of cash and was kept afloat only by British lines of credit. According to the unsigned typescript, the coffin sat on the floor of the touring car and was placed in a secret vault in Dublin shortly after his death: Desmond FitzGerald Papers, UCDA P80/300. That gold was collected and handed to Collins is not in doubt. See Mary Flannery Woods, BMH WS 624, p. 33.

24  'What matter if for Ireland Dear we Fall', 24 August 2014, http://blog.mercier press.ie/what-matter-if-for-ireland-dear-we-fall-liam-deasy/#sthash.bXdpcpbu. dpuf (accessed 8 September 2015).

25  *Ibid.* For further details on this day see T. Ryle Dwyer, *Michael Collins and the Civil War* (Cork, 2012), pp. 271–81.

## THE DOOR TO MADNESS

1  *The Irish Times*, 23 September 1922.

2  T. Ryle Dwyer, *The Squad and the Intelligence Operations of Michael Collins* (Cork, 2006), pp. 80–1.

3  Militaria Archive, Vinny Byrne Collection, www.militaria-archive.com/indepen dence/vb-docu/content/Vincent_Byrne_Scrapbook_225_large.html (accessed 3 November 2016).

4  UCD Archives, Mulcahy papers, P7/B/82, Commandant Conlon to Dalton, quoted in Timothy Breen Murphy, 'The Government's Executions Policy during the Irish Civil War 1922–23', PhD thesis, National University of Ireland Maynooth, p. 83, http://eprints.maynoothuniversity.ie/4069/1/The_Government%27s_Executions _Policy_During_the_Irish_Civil_War_1922_-_1923_%28Breen_Murphy_ -_62129007%29.pdf (accessed 21 September 2015).

5  *Ibid.*, pp. 83–4.

6   'How the State turned a blind eye to the Ballyseedy killings', *Irish Examiner*, 5 March 2013, www.irishexaminer.com/viewpoints/analysis/how-the-state-turned-a-blind-eye-to-the-ballyseedy-killings-224525.html (accessed 3 November 2016).

7   For more information on some of the men killed see MSPC 2D224 (Keogh), 2D28 (Conway), 2D438 (O'Rourke), 2D143 (Riordan), 2D107 (Manning), 2D335 (Murphy) and 2D120 (O'Brien).

## PART 2: THE DEAD

1   Frank King, BMH WS 635, p. 2.

2   *Ibid.*, p. 4.

3   'RTÉ to screen live State funeral of 1916 rebel Kent', *Irish Examiner*, 3 September 2015, www.irishexaminer.com/ireland/rte-to-screen-live-state-funeral-of-1916-rebel-kent-351724.html (accessed 4 November 2016).

4   *The Cork Examiner*, 28 June 1917; Mike Rast, 'Tactics, Politics, and Propaganda in the Irish War of Independence, 1917–1921', Masters thesis, Georgia State University, 2011, http://scholarworks.gsu.edu/history_theses/46 (accessed 29 September 2016), p. 12.

5   Charles Browne, BMH WS 873, p. 7.

6   'History of the E Company Inchigeela from 1917 to the end of the Civil War', *Cumann Staire Bhéal Átha'n Ghaorthaidh* (1997), available at www.ballingearyhs.com/journal1997/inchigeelavolunteers.html (accessed 29 September 2016). See also *The Cork Examiner*, 16 May 1918; *Leitrim Observer*, 18 May 1918.

7   P. J. Murphy, BMH WS 869, p. 17; Irish Volunteers Commemorative Organisation, 'Fian Seamus Courtney, Passage West, Cork', http://irishvolunteers.org/fian-seamus-courtney-passage-westcork/ (accessed 29 September 2016).

8   James Allan Busby, BMH WS 1628, p. 3.

9   *Ibid.*

10  *The Cork Examiner*, 25 November 1918. The inquest is reported in *The Cork Examiner* of 30 November 1918. See also 'Na Fianna Eireann in Cobh, Co. Cork', https://fiannaeireannhistory.wordpress.com/2014/06/30/na-fianna-eireann-in-cobh-co-cork/ (accessed 2 November 2016).

11  *The Cork Examiner*, 17 December 1918; Hart, *The IRA and its Enemies*, p. 69.

12  James McCarthy, BMH WS 1567, pp. 6–7.

13  *The Skibbereen Eagle*, 12 April 1919.

14  Seán O'Connell, BMH WS 1706, pp. 3–4; *The Cork Examiner*, 22 May 1919.

15  *The Cork Examiner*, 9 September 1919; 'British Regiments with War of Independence dead in Ireland', www.cairogang.com/soldiers-killed/REGIMENTS/regiments.html for details of all British soldiers killed during the Irish War of Independence (accessed 15 October 2016); 'British Soldiers KIA', www.irishmedals.org/british-soldiers-kia.html (accessed 15 October 2016) also lists British soldiers killed in Ireland.

16   *The Cork Examiner*, 10 September 1919; *Irish Independent*, 10 September 1919.

17   Hart, *The IRA and its Enemies*, p. 70.

18   See *The Freeman's Journal*, 10 September 1919 for the arrest of the IRA men, and *The Cork Examiner*, 26 January 1920 for details of the court case.

19   *Irish Independent*, 29 December 1919.

20   *The Cork Examiner*, 14 February 1920.

21   *The Kerryman*, 21 February 1920. For a good account of this attack from an IRA perspective see James Sullivan, BMH WS 1528, pp. 4–5.

22   Richard Walsh, BMH WS 400, pp. 102–9. See also *The Freeman's Journal*, 20 February 1920 for information on the discovery of the body; *Irish Independent*, 24 February 1920 for identification; and *The Cork Examiner*, 5 March 1920 for its exhumation. Quinlisk is also mentioned in many other BMH witness statements, including Maurice Forde *et al.* (719, p. 9), Liam Archer (819, p. 9), Michael Murphy (1547, pp. 12–18) and Daniel Breen (1739, pp. 28–9).

23   *The Freeman's Journal*, 3 March 1920; Michael Burke, BMH WS 1424, pp. 13–14.

24   Joseph Cashman, BMH WS 1466, p. 2. For the inquest see *The Freeman's Journal*, 15 March 1920.

25   There is much confusion about this death, but the general consensus among researchers is that Patrick Morrissey is the victim. See *The Cork Examiner*, 9 April 1920 for his arrest, and 13 April for identification. See also the death certificate of Patrick Morrissey; Cork, Apr–Jun 1920, vol. 5, p. 84, General Registry, Dublin.

26   *Irish Independent*, 23 April 1920 and 1 May 1920.

27   Tom Crean, 'On This Day – 25th April 1920: The Death of Cornelius Crean', http://tomcreandiscovery.com/?p=1764 (accessed 2 November 2016).

28   *Weekly Irish Independent*, 15 May 1920; John O'Driscoll, BMH WS 1250, p. 9.

29   Daniel Healy, BMH WS 1656, pp. 6–7. See also *Evening Herald*, 12 May 1920; *The Cork Examiner*, 15 May 1920.

30   Seán Cotter, BMH WS 1493, p. 10.

31   Ted O'Sullivan, BMH WS 1478, p. 16.

32   House of Commons debate, vol. 130 c1425, http://hansard.millbanksystems.com/commons/1920/jun/17/murder-constable-king (accessed 29 September 2016).

33   *Evening Herald*, 22 June 1920; *The Skibbereen Eagle*, 26 June 1920. Ted O'Sullivan also gives a short account of this attack: see BMH WS 1478, p. 16.

34   *The Times*, 30 September 1920.

35   Ted O'Sullivan, BMH WS 1478, p. 16.

36   *Sunday Independent*, 27 June 1920.

37   For the first report of the events see *Irish Independent*, 20 July 1920.

38   *The Cork Examiner*, 23 and 28 July 1920.

39   'Civilians Killed', http://irishmedals.org/civilians-killed.html (accessed 29 September 2016).

40   *The Struggle of the Irish People: Address to the Congress of the United States* (Washington,

1921), available at https://archive.org/stream/struggleofirishp00wash/struggleof
irishp00wash_djvu.txt (accessed 29 September 2016).

41  For photographs of the dead see *Irish Independent*, 23 July 1920 (O'Brien); 26 July
1920 (Bourke); 2 August 1920 (McGrath).

42  *The Struggle of the Irish People*, https://archive.org/stream/struggleofirishp00wash/
struggleofirishp00wash_djvu.txt (accessed 29 September 2016). The site is mistaken in listing McGrath's age as eighteen.

43  *The Cork Examiner*, 24 and 27 July 1920; Patrick J. Luddy, BMH WS 1151, p. 10.

44  'Captain James Osmund Airy, 1st Bn. Manchester Regiment', www.cairogang.
com/soldiers-killed/manchesters-macroom/airy/airy.html; 'Private Ernest Francis Barlow 64159 1st Bn. Manchester Regiment', www.cairogang.com/soldiers-
killed/manchesters-macroom/barlow/barlow.html (accessed 29 September 2016).

45  Patrick Lynch, BMH WS 1534, pp. 9–10.

46  Frank Neville, BMH WS 443, p. 4; *The Cork Examiner*, 16 July 1920; Collins
Papers, MAI A0535.

47  *The Skibbereen Eagle*, 31 July 1920; Frank Taffe's Athy Eye on the Past website,
'Bandon, Co. Cork', http://athyeyeonthepast.blogspot.ie/2014/02/bandon-co-
cork.html (accessed 29 September 2016). The blogspot incorrectly states that
Mulherin was thirty-nine when he died. For the bishop's condemnation see *The
Liberator*, 27 July 1920.

48  *Guy's Almanac 1921*, p. 133, www.corkpastandpresent.ie/places/streetandtrade
directories/1921citycountyalmanacanddirectoryguys/1921pages9to199/1921%20
126-133.pdf.

49  Michael Riordan, BMH WS 1638, pp. 11–12.

50  James 'Spud' Murphy, BMH WS 1684, pp. 3–4. See also *The Skibbereen Eagle*, 14
August 1920.

51  *Weekly Irish Independent*, 7 August 1920.

52  Edward Tobin, BMH WS 1451, pp. 51–3.

53  *The Cork Examiner*, 16 August 1920; Jeremiah Murphy, Michael Courtney and
Denis Mulchinock, BMH WS 744, p. 6.

54  Jeremiah Murphy *et al.*, BMH WS 744, pp. 7–8; *Irish Independent*, 27 August
1920. See also *The Struggle of the Irish People*, https://archive.org/stream/struggle
ofirishp00wash/struggleofirishp00wash_djvu.txt (accessed 29 September 2016).

55  'Second Lieutenant Frederick Clarence Sharman MSM', www.cairogang.com/
soldiers-killed/sharman/sharman.html (accessed 30 September 2016). For more
on this ambush see Mícheál Ó Súilleabháin, *Where Mountainy Men Have Sown:
War and Peace in Rebel Cork in the Turbulent Years 1916–21* (Cork, 2013), pp. 138–
41.

56  Patrick Collins, BMH WS 1707. There is also a discussion of Herlihy's death in
the Collins Papers, MAI A0897.

57  Deasy, *Towards Ireland Free*, pp. 135–6; Michael Riordan, BMH WS 1638, p. 13.

58  Royal Irish Constabulary Forum, http://irishgenealogyqueries.yuku.com/reply/

1202/Sgt-Daniel-Maunsell-RIC#.Vyz_ePkrLIU (accessed 30 September 2016); *Irish Independent*, 23 August 1920; *The Kerryman*, 28 August 1920.

59    'IRA Killed', www.irishmedals.org/IRA-killed.html (accessed 30 September 2016).

60    'Private Joseph Evans – 181848 MGC', www.cairogang.com/soldiers-killed/evans-j/evans-j.html (accessed 30 September 2016); *Limerick Leader*, 27 August 1920; Charles Browne, BMH WS 873, p. 22.

61    Maurice Donegan, BMH WS 639, p. 4; *The Skibbereen Eagle*, 29 January 1921.

62    'Pte John Kelly, 43681 Manchester Regt', www.cairogang.com/soldiers-killed/kelly/kelly.html; 'Inquest into death of John Kelly, Manchester Regiment', www.cairogang.com/soldiers-killed/kelly/inquest.html (accessed 30 September 2016).

63    Michael O'Driscoll, BMH WS 1297, pp. 2–3; *The Cork Examiner*, 28 August 1920. This shooting made news in New Zealand, being mentioned in the *Marlborough Express*, 27 August 1920, http://paperspast.natlib.govt.nz/cgi-bin/paperspast?a=d&d=MEX19200827.2.29.4 (accessed 30 September 2016).

64    'Private Charles Edward Hall, M/45295, 1155th M.T. Coy. Royal Army Service Corps', www.cairogang.com/soldiers-killed/hall-ce/ce-hall.html (accessed 30 September 2016); Michael Kearney, BMH WS 1418, pp. 17–18.

65    Pat Barry, 'Cork and "The Trouble", 1919–1921', *By Bride and Blackwater: Local History & Traditions* (Miltown Malbay, 2003); Seamus Fitzgerald, BMH WS 1737, p. 30. See also *The Struggle of the Irish People*, https://archive.org/stream/struggleofirishp00wash/struggleofirishp00wash_djvu.txt (accessed 29 September 2016); *The Freeman's Journal*, 30 August 1920.

66    *The Struggle of the Irish People*, https://archive.org/stream/struggleofirishp00wash/struggleofirishp00wash_djvu.txt (accessed 29 September 2016); *The Freeman's Journal*, 31 August 1920; *Ulster Herald*, 4 September 1920. See also *The Cork Examiner*, 6 September 1920.

67    *The Struggle of the Irish People*, https://archive.org/stream/struggleofirishp00wash/struggleofirishp00wash_djvu.txt (accessed 29 September 2016). There seems to be some confusion over Hegarty's first name, with some sources using Patrick and others Liam.

68    Manus O'Riordan, 'Forget Not The Boys Of Kilmichael!', *Cumann Staire Bhéal Átha'n Ghaorthaidh* (2004), available at www.ballingearyhs.com/journal2004/forgte_not_kilmichael.html (accessed 30 September 2016); Ó Súilleabháin, *Where Mountainy Men Have Sown*, pp. 262–3.

69    *Irish Independent*, 16 September 1920.

70    Patrick Collins, BMH WS 1707, p. 9; 'Private Persons Injured etc.', NAK CO 905/15.

71    Quoted in Bill Hammond, 'Attack on Mallow Barracks' (taken from *Soldier of the Rearguard*), available at http://homepage.eircom.net/~berfen/mall.html (accessed 30 September 2016).

72    Charles Browne, BMH WS 873, pp. 25–6. Brady the printer is also mentioned by Murphy in *The Year of Disappearances*, p. 40.

73    *The Struggle of the Irish People*, https://archive.org/stream/struggleofirishp00wash/struggleofirishp00wash_djvu.txt (accessed 29 September 2016).

74    Historic Graves, 'CO-KLBG-0060', http://historicgraves.com/kilbrogan/co-klbg-0060/grave (accessed 30 September 2016).

75    Irish Volunteers Commemorative Organisation, 'Cork IRA Memorials', http://irishvolunteers.org/cork-IRA-memorials/ (accessed 30 September 2016).

76    *Irish Independent*, 6 October 1920; 'Attack on Black and Tans at Patrick Street', http://homepage.eircom.net/~corkcounty/Timeline/chave.htm (accessed 30 September 2016); *The Cork Examiner*, 6 October 1920.

77    Michael O'Regan, BMH WS 1524, p. 5.

78    Tim Herlihy *et al.*, BMH WS 810, pp. 15–16. See also *The Skibbereen Eagle*, 9 October 1920; *The Cork Examiner*, 6 October 1920.

79    *Irish Independent*, 9 October 1920; *The Freeman's Journal*, 9 October 1920; 'Barrack Street Ambush', http://homepage.eircom.net/~corkcounty/barrack.html (accessed 30 September 2016).

80    William Desmond, BMH WS 832, p. 21; *The Freeman's Journal*, 12 October 1920; *Irish Independent*, 15 October 1920.

81    'Private Edward Wade Cowin, EMT/44943 1155th M.T. Coy. (Cork) Royal Army Service Corps', www.cairogang.com/soldiers-killed/cowin/cowin.html; Bill Hammond, 'Ballydrochane' (taken from *Soldier of the Rearguard*), available at http://homepage.eircom.net/~berfen/bally.html (accessed 30 September 2016). See also *Irish Independent*, 12 November 1920.

82    *Irish Independent*, 11 and 16 October 1920; *The Struggle of the Irish People*, https://archive.org/stream/struggleofirishp00wash/struggleofirishp00wash_djvu.txt (accessed 29 September 2016). Both of these articles mistakenly call him Michael. See also *The Cork Examiner*, 11 October 1920.

83    Hart, *The IRA and its Enemies*, p. 299.

84    *The Skibbereen Eagle*, 29 January 1921.

85    Daniel Harrington, BMH WS 1532, pp. 11–12.

86    Eilis Bean Uí Chonaill (Ní Riain), BMH WS 568, p. 11; 'The Four Courts Reilly's Fort Garrison', www.irishmedals.org/the-four-courts-reilly-s-fort.html (accessed 30 September 2016); MSPC 1D400. See Bean Mhicil Uí Fhoghludha (née Smartt), BMH WS 539, p. 1, for McNestry's membership of the Keating Branch of the Gaelic League, which included virtually every senior leader of the Irish revolution.

87    George Power, BMH WS 451, p. 5. Power gets his timing wrong, claiming that the officer was captured because Fitzgerald was already on hunger strike.

88    'Brigadier General Lucas', www.cairogang.com/soldiers-killed/Lucas-ambush/lucas.html; 'Lucas ambush', www.cairogang.com/soldiers-killed/Lucas-ambush/lucas-ambush.html (accessed 30 September 2016).

89    'Commandant Michael Fitzgerald', http://homepage.eircom.net/~corkcounty/fitzgerald.html (accessed 30 September 2016).

90    Ó Conchubhair, *Rebel Cork's Fighting Story*, pp. 135–8; 'Ballinhassig Ambush', www.

cairogang.com/soldiers-killed/ballinhassig/ballinhassig.html (accessed 30 September 2016).

91 Patrick O'Sullivan, BMH WS 1481, p. 7. Thanks to John O'Donovan, University College Cork, for additional information.

92 *The Anglo-Celt*, 30 October 1920.

93 Charles Browne, BMH WS 873, p. 31. For more details on the two men who died see 'Possible Intelligence men who died', www.cairogang.com/soldiers-killed/REGIMENTS/INTELLIGENCE/intelligence.html (accessed 3 October 2016).

94 Jeremiah Keating, BMH WS 1657, p. 7; *Irish Independent*, 15 October 1920; *The Cork Examiner*, 10 November 1920.

95 *The Freeman's Journal*, 8 November 1920; *Irish Independent*, 10 November 1920.

96 Seán Healy, BMH WS 1479, pp. 31–2. Walsh is listed in the official British list of the missing published in the *Irish Independent* of 22 August 1921.

97 *The Struggle of the Irish People*, https://archive.org/stream/struggleofirishp00wash/struggleofirishp00wash_djvu.txt (accessed 29 September 2016).

98 'Pte Percy Victor Starling, 13560 RMA', www.cairogang.com/soldiers-killed/starling/starling.html (accessed 3 October 2016); Mitchell Families Online, http://mfo.me.uk/getperson.php?personID=I13133&tree=E1 (accessed 3 October 2016).

99 *Irish Independent*, 10 November 1920; Mark Wickham, John J. Lucey, Patrick J. Deasy and Maurice Fitzgerald, BMH WS 558, p. 3.

100 *The Cork Examiner*, 15 November 1920.

101 Laurence Nugent, BMH WS 907, p. 242 – he gets the Hales brother wrong, mentioning Seán not Tom; Michael Murphy, BMH WS 1547, p. 29. See also White and O'Shea, *The Burning of Cork*, pp. 70–1.

102 'Agnew and Mitchell are abducted', www.theauxiliaries.com/INCIDENTS/agnew-mitchel/agnew-mitchell.html (accessed 3 October 2016).

103 This particular set of killings has been exhaustively parsed and analysed by every author who has examined the Cork IRA in recent years. See White and O'Shea, *The Burning of Cork*, pp. 71–4; Hart, *The IRA and its Enemies*, pp. 5–10; 'Death of James Coleman; 18th [*sic*] November, 1920; North Mall, Cork,' NAK WO 35/147A/86.

104 Royal Irish Constabulary Forum, http://irishgenealogyqueries.yuku.com/topic/956/BMDs?page=11#.VzO50PkrLIU. Thanks to John O'Donovan, University College Cork, for additional information.

105 'Volunteer Paddy McCarthy, 90th Anniversary Commemoration', www.millstreet.ie/blog/2010/10/21/paddy-mccarthy-90th-anniversary-commemoration (accessed 3 October 2016).

106 Tim Herlihy *et al.*, BMH WS 810, pp. 13–14.

107 *The Cork Examiner*, 23 November 1920.

108 Michael V. O'Donoghue, BMH WS 1741, Pt 1, pp. 80–1.

109   *Irish Independent,* 29 November 1920; *The Cork Examiner,* 30 November 1920.

110   Maurice Forde *et al.,* BMH WS 719, p. 6; *Irish Independent,* 29 November 1920.

111   Thomas Barry, BMH WS 430, pp. 10–12; 'The Glanworth Ambush', www.cairogang.com/soldiers-killed/glanworth/glanworth.html (accessed 3 October 2016).

112   Joseph Aherne, BMH WS 1367, pp. 33–4; 'Liam Heffernan', http://homepage.eircom.net/~corkcounty/Who%27s%20Who%20First.html (accessed 3 October 2016).

113   *Irish Independent,* 29 November 1920.

114   'Sing Sing prison', a vault in Knockraha graveyard where IRA prisoners were held before execution and burial in the nearby bog.

115   *Irish Independent,* 27 and 29 November 1920.

116   'Historical Plaques in Kilmichael', *The Lee Valley Outlook,* 28 November 2013, www.macroom.ie/news/lee-valley-outlook-2013/267-lee-valley-outlook-nov-28-13-v10e24; 'Activities of Ballingeary IRA 1920–1921', *Cumann Staire Bhéal Átha'n Ghaorthaidh,* www.ballingearyhs.com/journal1998/activitiesIRA2021.html (accessed 3 October 2016).

117   Maurice Forde *et al.,* BMH WS 719, pp. 6–7; Edward Maloney, MSPC 34REF27648; Pádraig Óg Ó Ruairc, *Truce: Murder, Myth and the Last Days of the Irish War of Independence* (Cork, 2016), p. 119.

118   *The Cork Examiner,* 2 December 1920; *Irish Independent,* 3 December 1920; *Edinburgh Evening News,* 3 December 1920; *Weekly Irish Independent,* 11 December 1920; *The Struggle of the Irish People,* https://archive.org/stream/struggleofirishp00wash/struggleofirishp00wash_djvu.txt (accessed 29 September 2016);

119   Barry, *Guerilla Days in Ireland,* pp. 52–5; MSPC 1D281 (Begley); *The Cork Examiner,* 7 December 1920.

120   *The Southern Star,* 5 November 1921; *The Struggle of the Irish People,* https://archive.org/stream/struggleofirishp00wash/struggleofirishp00wash_djvu.txt (accessed 29 September 2016). A. K. Watson, E. S. Radford, A. O. Jackson, and possibly C. M. Cautley have been identified by David Grant as the most likely Auxiliaries involved: 'Nicholas de Sales Prendergast – 1 Dec 1920', http://theauxiliaries.com/INCIDENTS/prendergast-murder/prendergast-murder.html (accessed 2 November 2016).

121   Terence O'Reilly, *Rebel Heart: George Lennon, Flying Column Commander* (Cork, 2009), p. 77; *Irish Independent,* 4 December 1920.

122   Barry, *Guerilla Days,* p. 55; John L. Sullivan in Kenneth Griffith and Timothy O'Grady (eds), *Curious Journey: An Oral History of Ireland's Unfinished Revolution* (Cork, 1998), available at www.bbc.co.uk/history/british/easterrising/witnesses/wh09.shtml (accessed 3 October 2016); 'Private Thomas Charles Watling, Essex Regt, 11544/5998506', www.cairogang.com/soldiers-killed/essex-deserters/watson/watson.html (accessed 3 October 2016); Frank O'Connor, *Guests of the Nation* (New York, 1931), pp. 1–12.

123 *Irish Independent*, 11 December 1920; *The Struggle of the Irish People*, https://archive.org/stream/struggleofirishp00wash/struggleofirishp00wash_djvu.txt (accessed 29 September 2016).

124 Patrick O'Brien, BMH WS 812, p. 17.

125 Edward Young, BMH WS 1402, pp. 17–18. For more on this see also *Irish Independent*, 11 December 1920; Joseph McKenna, *Guerrilla Warfare in the Irish War of Independence, 1919–1921* (Jefferson, NC, 2011), p. 159; 'IRA Killed', www.irishmedals.org/IRA-killed.html (accessed 3 October 2016) – the name is misspelled in this source as McClean.

126 *The Struggle of the Irish People*, https://archive.org/stream/struggleofirishp00wash/struggleofirishp00wash_djvu.txt (accessed 29 September 2016). This source mistakenly calls him Michael J. Murphy. See also 'Death of Michael Murphy; 8th December, 1920; Cork', NAK WO35/156/11; *The Cork Examiner*, 11 December 1920.

127 *The Struggle of the Irish People*, https://archive.org/stream/struggleofirishp00wash/struggleofirishp00wash_djvu.txt (accessed 29 September 2016); *Irish Independent*, 13 December 1920.

128 *The Cork Examiner*, 14 December 1920.

129 'Irish Incidents', *The Mail*, 11 December 1920, http://nla.gov.au/nla.news-article 63884167 (accessed 3 October 2016).

130 His father, Denis Horgan, was a Roman Catholic and his mother, Anna, was Church of Ireland: National Archives of Ireland (hereafter NAI), Census 1901, www.census.nationalarchives.ie/pages/1901/Kerry/Killarney/High_Street__West_Side_/1414551/ (accessed 3 October 2016); NAI, Census 1911, www.census.nationalarchives.ie/pages/1911/Cork/Blackrock/Ballintemple/400890/ (accessed 3 October 2016).

131 Murphy, *The Year of Disappearances*, p. 92.

132 James Brennock, BMH WS 1113, pp. 10–11.

133 *Irish Independent*, 13 December 1920; 'Death of Sarah Medaile; 10 December, 1920; Cork', NAK WO 35/155A/31.

134 John Kelleher, BMH WS 1456, p. 21.

135 Pat Whelan, BMH WS 1449; Murphy, *Year of Disappearances*, p. 160.

136 As always there are many versions of the sequence of events. See Neil O'Mahony, 'The Life & Death of Canon Magner', *Times Past: Journal of the Muskerry Local History Society*, vol. 9, 2010–11, pp. 59–61, for a particularly good examination of this event.

137 It is usually suggested that the Auxiliaries were on their way to the funeral of those shot at Kilmichael, but this took place on 2 December. Hart was found guilty but insane. The case would never have got to trial except for Brady's insistence on making a statement. In fairness to the Auxiliaries, Hart had been arrested by his commanding officer, who had turned back once the second lorry was missed and before anyone else arrived on the scene.

138 House of Commons debate, 17 February 1921, vol. 138 c246, http://hansard.

millbanksystems.com/commons/1921/feb/17/murder-court-martial (accessed 3 October 2016).

139 *Irish Independent*, 29 December 1920; 'Death of Patrick Tarrant; 21st December, 1921; Cork', NAK WO 35/159B/18. The NAK file has got the year of Tarrant's death wrong.

140 Patrick Whelan, BMH WS 1449, pp. 46–7.

141 Denis Dwyer, BMH WS 713, p. 4; 'A/Cpl Belchamber RASC', www.cairogang. com/soldiers-killed/belchamber/belchamber.html.

142 Michael Walsh, BMH WS 1521, p. 12; 'Courts in lieu of inquest: individual cases SAD–STO', NAK WO 35/159A; 'Death of Constable Francis Shortall, RIC; 7th January, 1921; Cork', NAK WO 35/159A/21; the date on this NAK file is incorrect.

143 'Courts in lieu of inquest: individual cases BUC–COL', NAK WO 35/147A; *The Struggle of the Irish People*, https://archive.org/stream/struggleofirishp00wash/ struggleofirishp00wash_djvu.txt (accessed 29 September 2016); *Irish Independent*, 5 January 1921.

144 *The Liberator*, 6 January 1921; 'Death of Finbar D'Arcy; 4th January, 1921; Cork City', NAK WO 35/148/77; Robert C. Ahern, BMH WS 1676, p. 13; Eoin 'Pope' O'Mahony, BMH WS 1401, pp. 4–5.

145 There is some divergence in the sources about the spelling of his surname, and he is recorded as both MacSwiney and McSweeney. *The Struggle of the Irish People*, https://archive.org/stream/struggleofirishp00wash/struggleofirishp00wash_djvu. txt (accessed 29 September 2016); *Irish Independent*, 7 January 1921; Ireland Civil Registration Indexes 1845–1958, database, FamilySearch (https://familysearch. org/ark:/61903/1:1:FRL5-B2D : 4 December 2014), DEATHS entry for John Mcsweeney; citing Kanturk, Jan–Mar 1921, vol. 5, p. 165, General Registry, Custom House, Dublin; FHL microfilm 101,608 (accessed 7 October 2016).

146 *Irish Independent*, 19 January 1921. Evidence of Harold C. Pring: 'Courts in lieu of inquest: individual cases O'DEM–PUR', NAK WO 35/157A.

147 John O'Driscoll, BMH WS 1250, p. 20; 'Death of Patrick Donovan; 16th/17th January, 1921; Cullinagh, Courtmacsherry, County Cork', NAK WO 35/149A/31. Michael Coleman, BMH WS 1254, pp. 9–10, gives a detailed account of the round-up.

148 *The Skibbereen Eagle*, 22 January 1921; 'Death of Denis Hegarty; 18th/19th January, 1921; Barryshall, County Cork', NAK WO 35/151A/53. Hegarty is listed by Charles O'Donoghue as one of the dead of the Timoleague Company in BMH WS 1607, p. 9.

149 Edward Neville, BMH WS 1665, pp. 4–5; 'List of missing', *Irish Independent*, 22 August 1921.

150 William Desmond, BMH WS 832, p. 28; *The Skibbereen Eagle*, 16 April 1921. 'Death of Michael Dwyer; on or about 22nd January, 1921; Bandon, County Cork', NAK WO 35/149A/70. Denis Lordan also mentions this incident in BMH WS 470, p. 13. *The Skibbereen Eagle* of 16 April 1921 includes details of the

deaths of shooting victims Thomas Bradfield, Michael Dwyer, William Johnston and James and Tim Coffey.

151 'Death of Sergeant Henry Bloxham, RIC; 21st January, 1921; near Waterfall, County Cork', NAK WO 35/146A/44.

152 *The Freeman's Journal*, 14 January 1922.

153 *The Skibbereen Eagle*, 29 January 1921; 'Death of Richard Morey; 23rd January, 1921; Cork', NAK WO 35/155A/46.

154 Anna Hurley O'Mahony, BMH WS 540, p. 4. This incident is also mentioned in BMH WS 470 (Denis Lordan) and WS 1607 (Charles O'Donoghue). See also 'Death of Thomas Bradfield; 23rd January, 1921; Carhue, Bandon, County Cork', NAK WO 35/146A/26.

155 Daniel Canty, BMH WS 1619, p. 24; Denis O'Brien, BMH WS 1353, p. 8.

156 'Death of Francis Barnane; 26 [*sic*] January, 1921; Cork', NAK WO 35/146A/14.

157 'Death of Philip Armstrong Holmes; 29th January, 1921; Cork', NAK WO 35/152/12. For a detailed description of this ambush see Aideen Carroll, *Seán Moylan: Rebel Leader* (Cork, 2010), pp. 80–5.

158 *The Freeman's Journal*, 16 May 1921; 'Death of Constable Patrick William Joseph O'Connor RIC; 1st February, 1921; Drimoleague, County Cork', NAK WO 35/156/57.

159 *The Freeman's Journal*, 2 and 4 February 1921.

160 James 'Spud' Murphy, BMH WS 1684, pp. 12–13.

161 Denis Lordan, BMH WS 470, p. 16.

162 *Cork Constitution*, 27 January 1921.

163 *Lancashire Evening Post*, 8 February 1921; Edward Sisk, BMH WS 1505, p. 4; 'Deaths of Constables E. Carter and W.H. Taylor, RIC; 3rd February, 1921; Ballinhassig, County Cork', NAK WO 35/160/10.

164 Mary Walsh, BMH WS 556, p. 5.

165 *The Skibbereen Eagle*, 12 February 1921. For details of the Crowley brothers' actions during the War of Independence, see J. J. O'Mahony *et al.*, BMH WS 560.

166 *Derry Journal*, 9 February 1921; Ireland Civil Registration Indexes, 1845–1958, database, FamilySearch (https://familysearch.org/ark:/61903/1:1:FRL5-GY4 : 4 December 2014), DEATHS entry for Alfred Kidney; citing Youghal, Jan–Mar 1921, vol. 4, p. 544, General Registry, Custom House, Dublin; FHL microfilm 101,608 (accessed 7 October 2016).

167 Ireland Civil Registration Indexes, 1845–1958, database, FamilySearch (https://familysearch.org/ark:/61903/1:1:FRL5-LJQ, DEATHS entry for Daniel Moloney; citing Clonakilty, Jan–Mar 1921, vol. 5, p. 46, General Registry, Custom House, Dublin; FHL microfilm 101,608 (accessed 7 October 2016); *Irish Independent*, 8 February 1921.

168 *The Freeman's Journal*, 8 February 1921; 'Death of Michael John Kelleher; 6th February, 1921; Knocknagree, County Cork', NAK WO 35/152/61.

169 'Death of Patrick O'Sullivan; 7th February, 1921; Cork', NAK WO 35/157A/47.

170   Denis Lordan, BMH WS 470, p. 17; Patrick O'Sullivan, BMH WS 1481, p. 8.

171   Email from C. Darts, Arabella's granddaughter, 10 September 2013; *The Skibbereen Eagle*, 16 April 1921.

172   William Barry, BMH WS 1708, pp. 6–7; 'Death of Alfred Charles Reilly; 9th February, 1921; Douglas, County Cork', NAK WO 35/157B/15; *The Cork Examiner*, 6 June 1921; 'Compensation (Ireland) Commission (Shaw and Wood-Renton Commission) and Related Bodies: Registers, Indexes and Papers, Private Persons Injured', NAK CO 905/15.

173   Con Meany, BMH WS 787, pp. 15–16; 'Private John Joseph Holyome, 6446476. 1st Bn. Royal Fusiliers', www.cairogang.com/soldiers-killed/millstreet-train/holyome/holyome.html (accessed 7 October 2016).

174   'Activities of Ballingeary IRA 1920–1921', *Cumann Staire Bhéal Átha'n Ghaorthaidh*, www.ballingearyhs.com/journal1998/activitiesira2021.html (accessed 7 October 2016); 'Death of Thomas Miles RIC; 28th January, 1921; Castle Ireland, Dublin', NAK WO 35/155A/32. This NAK file is misnamed.

175   *Connacht Tribune*, 19 February 1921.

176   Ted Hayes, BMH WS 1575, p. 8; *Cork Constitution*, 14 February 1921. See also Hart, *The IRA and its Enemies*, p. 298; *The Skibbereen Eagle*, 16 April 1921; Thomas Earls Fitzgerald, 'The Execution of Spies and Informers in West Cork, 1921', in David Fitzpatrick (ed.), *Terror in Ireland: 1916–1923* (Dublin, 2012), pp. 181–93. Earls Fitzgerald notes Keany's further claim that Eady had not given information to the police.

177   *Irish Independent*, 15 February 1921; Jerome Coughlan, BMH WS 1568, pp. 9–10.

178   The only type of bullet that could inflict this type of wound was a dum-dum or soft-tip bullet. *Vide* means see in Latin.

179   *Cork Constitution*, 15 February 1921; *The Skibbereen Eagle*, 16 April 1921; 'Death of Thomas Bradfield; 1st February, 1921; Castle Derry, County Cork', NAK WO 35/146A/52. See also Keane, *Massacre in West Cork*, pp. 88–9.

180   'Death of John O'Leary; 15th February, 1921; Cork', NAK WO 35/157A/24; Michael Murphy, BMH WS 1547, p. 36.

181   'Serious reverse for I.R.A. at Mourneabbey', http://homepage.eircom.net/~cork county/Timeline/Mourne%20Abbey.htm (accessed 7 October 2016); Jerome Buckley, BMH WS 1063, pp. 9–12.

182   'Civilians Killed', http://irishmedals.org/civilians-killed.html (accessed 7 October 2016).

183   Evidence of Major Percival and Dr Harrison, 'Deaths of John McGrath, Tim Connolly, Jeremiah O'Neill, and Con McCarthy; 17th February, 1921; Kilbrittain, County Cork', NAK WO 35/154/1; 'Four IRA Volunteers Shot Dead Near Kilbrittain', http://homepage.eircom.net/~corkcounty/Timeline/Crois%20 na%20Leanbh.htm (accessed 7 October 2016). As this was a police action according to the British government, and the military were merely operating in support of the civil power, then they would argue that the Geneva Convention

did not apply. Of course, there were no RIC regulations that allowed constables to shoot people in the back of the head from close range with impunity.

184 *The Skibbereen Eagle*, 26 February 1921; P. J. Murphy, BMH WS 869, p. 19.

185 There is much confusion about Sweetman's second name in the news reports and it varies between Sweetnam and Sweetman, but his death certificate says Sweetman. William Connell is often confused with Thomas Connell (his first cousin), who owned a large shop in Skibbereen.

186 Patrick O'Sullivan, BMH WS 1481, p. 8; *The Skibbereen Eagle*, 23 April 1921.

187 'Death of William Mohally; 20th February, 1921; near South Infirmary, Cork', NAK WO 35/155B/15.

188 William Barry, BMH WS 1708, p. 7.

189 *The Skibbereen Eagle*, 4 June 1921.

190 'Death of George Fletcher; 25th February, 1921; Cork', NAK WO 35/149B/17.

191 Daniel Canty, BMH WS 1619, p. 25. For further descriptions of the attack and the reasoning for the shooting of the unarmed Essex Regiment soldiers see William McCarthy, BMH WS 1255, p. 2; John (Jack Hennessy) BMH WS 1234, pp. 11–12; Con Flynn, BMH WS 1621, pp. 19–20.

192 'Coolavohig [*sic*] Ambush – 25 Feb 1921', http://theauxiliaries.com/INCIDENTS/coolavohig-ambush/coolavohig-ambush.html (accessed 7 October 2016); 'Death of Constable William Arthur Cane, RIC; 26th February, 1921; Cork', NAK WO 35/147A/33. There is a lot of confusion over Cane's name: he is alternatively called Lane, Kane and Keane in various newspaper reports.

193 *Irish Independent* 28 February 1921; MSPC MSP34REF26441, Patrick Carroll; Jack Hennessy, BMH WS 1234, p. 12; Collins Papers, MAI A0897.

194 Roadside memorial Passage West; 'Death of Michael John O'Mahoney; 28th February, 1921; Passage West, County Cork', NAK WO 35/157A/28.

195 Patrick Crowe, BMH WS 775, pp. 4–5.

196 *Irish Independent*, 1 March 1921.

197 National Police Officers Roll of Honour, www.policerollofhonour.org.uk/forces/ireland_to_1922/ric/ric_roll.htm (accessed 7 October 2016); James 'Spud' Murphy, BMH WS 1684, p. 18.

198 Michael O'Regan, BMH WS 1524, p. 7.

199 Richard Smith, BMH WS 754, pp. 22–4. Michael Sheehy also mentions the murder of O'Brien, BMH WS 989, pp. 7–8.

200 'Courts of inquiry in lieu of inquest: Individual cases: BUC–COL', NAK WO 35/147A; *Irish Independent*, 3 March 1921.

201 *The Irish Times*, 17 March 1921; 'Death of Thomas Cotter; 1st March, 1921; Curraclough, County Cork', NAK WO 35/147B/14.

202 'Death of Denis O'Brien; 2nd March, 1921; Cork', NAK WO 35/156/39; House of Commons debate, 2 June 1921, vol. 142 cc1259-60W, http://hansard.millbanksystems.com/written_answers/1921/jun/02/casualties#S5CV0142P0_19210602_CWA_49 (accessed 7 October 2016).

203 *The Skibbereen Eagle*, 28 January 1922. This issue of the newspaper is particularly useful for evidence of the incidents that happened in West Cork in the last weeks of the war, as the courts worked their way through the compensation claims.

204 Philip Chambers, BMH WS 738, p. 6; MSPC 1D184.

205 William Reardon, BMH WS 1185, p. 10.

206 Charles Browne, BMH WS 873, p. 40; 'Death of Cornelius Foley; 6th March, 1921, Toames, County Cork', NAK WO 35/150/44.

207 Denis Mulchinock *et al.*, BMH WS 744, pp. 13–14. 'Death of Constable Nicholas Somers, RIC; 8th March, 1921; Shronbeha, near Banteer, County Cork', NAK WO 35/159A/32.

208 Leo O'Callaghan, BMH WS 978, pp. 18–19; 'Deaths of David Herlihy, Michael Kiely and Ned Waters; 10th March, 1921; Nadd, County Cork', NAK WO 35/151A/60.

209 'Death of John Good; 10th March, 1921; Barryshall, Timoleague, County Cork', NAK WO 35/149B/29. John O'Driscoll *et al.*, BMH WS 1250, p. 24, stated that the armed party who did the shooting comprised James Hodnett, Company Captain Daniel Minihane and 2nd Lieutenant Con Lehane.

210 Philip Chambers, BMH WS 738, pp. 7–8; 'Death of Timothy Hourihan; 13th March, 1921; West Coppeen, County Cork', NAK WO 35/152/17.

211 *The Skibbereen Eagle*, 19 March 1921.

212 'Death of Richard Newman, 14th March, 1921; Allihies, 1921; County Cork', NAK WO 35/156/25.

213 'Death of Thomas Hennessy; 13th March, 1921; Crosshaven, County Cork', NAK WO 35/151A/57.

214 'Death of Michael Joseph Murray; 13th March, 1921; Cork', NAK WO 35/155B/32; *Irish Independent*, 16 March 1920.

215 'Civilians Killed', www.irishmedals.org/civilians-killed.html (accessed 7 October 2016). The *Irish Independent* of 18 March 1921 reported that the death notice stated he was a member of the IRA.

216 'Courts of inquiry in lieu of inquest: Individual cases: BUC–COL', NAK WO 35/147A/38.

217 'Death of Constable William Elton, RIC; 19th March, 1921; Castletownroche, County Cork', NAK WO 35/149A/73.

218 'Death of Cornelius Sheehan; 19th March, 1921; Cork', NAK WO 35/159B/3; P. J. Murphy, BMH WS 869, p. 24; *The Freeman's Journal*, 21 March 1921.

219 Tim Herlihy, BMH WS 810, p. 31; Michael O'Regan, BMH WS 1524, p. 5; Patrick Cronin, BMH WS 710, p. 2; *Irish Independent*, 14 January 1922. The *Independent* article also deals with the compensation cases for William McCarthy (Mallow), John Sullivan Lynch (Carrigrohane), George Horgan (Ballintemple) and Patrick Rea (Passage West).

220 *The Skibbereen Eagle*, 26 March 1921; *Irish Independent*, 26 March 1921; 'Death of Jeremiah Mullane; 20th March, 1921; Cork', NAK WO 35/155B/26.

221  *Irish Independent*, 22 March 1921; 'Death of John Sheehan; 5th [*sic*] March, 1921; Kanturk, County Cork', NAK WO 35/159B/4.

222  William Buckley, BMH WS 1009, p. 19; 'Death of Arthur Mulcahy; 22nd March, 1921; Currabeha, County Cork', NAK WO 35/155A/57; Barry, 'Cork and "The Trouble"' in *By Bride and Blackwater*; *Irish Independent*, 11 May 1921. Mulcahy's name is recorded on the Kilcrumper Liam Lynch Memorial, which states he is buried at Tallow.

223  Midleton Graveyard War of Independence Memorial; *Irish Independent*, 7 April 1921.

224  Seamus Fitzgerald, BMH WS 1737, Appendix D. Appendices B to H in Fitzgerald's statement reproduce various eyewitness statements about what happened that night. See also 'Murder of Six Volunteers at Clogheen', http://homepage. eircom.net/~corkcounty/clogheen.html (accessed 11 October 2016); 'Deaths of William Deasy, Jeremiah [O']Mullane, Thomas Dennehy, Daniel Murphy, Michael [O']Sullivan, Daniel Crowley; 23rd March, 1921; Kerry Pike, near Cork, County Cork', NAK WO 35/149A/1.

225  Hart, *The IRA and its Enemies*, p. 293. Hart appears to imply that the revenge notice was posted by the IRA, which is incorrect. 'Death of John Cathcart; 25th March, 1921; Youghal, County Cork', NAK WO 35/147B/8; 'Robert George Torrens – A Biographic Note', www.torrens.org.uk/Biography/rgt.html (accessed 10 October 2016).

226  'IRA Volunteer Commemorated at Shannonvale', *An Phoblacht*, www.anphoblacht. com/contents/9885 (accessed 11 October 2016). See p. 30 of MSPC 1D201 for Burke's letter.

227  'Death of William Good; 26th March, 1921; Ballycatteen, Timoleague, County Cork', NAK WO 35/149B/30.

228  Richard Russell, BMH WS 1591, p. 21; 'Death of Frederick Stenning; 30th March, 1921; Innishannon, County Cork', NAK WO 35/159A/40.

229  'Death of Denis Dounovan or Donovan; 29th [*sic*] March, 1921; Bandon, Cork', NAK WO 35/149A/40; *Evening Herald*, 29 March 1921; *The Cork Examiner*, 1 April 1921.

230  Denis Mulchinock *et al.*, BMH WS 744, p. 14.

231  'Death of Constable Frederick H. Lord; 8th April 1921; Carrigadrohid, County Cork', NAK WO 35/153A/44; *The Cork Examiner*, 11 April 1921. See also Charles Browne, BMH WS 873, p. 43.

232  *Nenagh Guardian*, 16 April 1921.

233  'Death of William Hoare; 8th April, 1921; Ballymacoda, near Youghal, County Cork', NAK WO 35/151A/75.

234  Kevin Murphy, BMH WS 1629, p. 8. Murphy gives the date as 7 January 1921, which is a mistake. The *Dungarvan Leader* of 9 March 1946 mentions the setting up of a memorial fund for Liam Hoare: http://snap.waterfordcoco.ie/collections/ enewspapers/dungarvan_leader/1946/DUNGARVAN_LEADER_03_MAR_ 09.PDF (accessed 11 October 2016).

235 Leo Buckley, BMH WS 1714, pp. 7 and 12. See also 'Death of Denis Finbar Donovan; died between 9th and 12 the April [*sic*], 1921; Ballygassen, County Cork', NAK WO 35/149A/29; *The Cork Examiner*, 15 April 1921.

236 'Deaths of Constables Joseph Boynes and George Woodward, RIC; 10th April, 1921; Kildowny [*sic*], County Cork', NAK WO 35/160/2; George Power, BMH WS 451, p. 19; *Irish Independent*, 12 April 1921 (where Boynes is named Boyne).

237 Collins Papers, MAI A0649.

238 'Death of William Kenefick; 12th April 1921; Cork', NAK WO 35/152/74; *Irish Independent*, 14 April 1921 (where the name is spelled Kennefick).

239 Michael Murphy, BMH WS 1547, p. 41; 'Death of Timothy O'Sullivan; 19th April, 1921; Cork', NAK WO 35/157A/49.

240 *Irish Independent*, 11 May 1921.

241 'Death of Constable John C. McDonald [*sic*], RIC; 22th April, 1921; Central Military Hospital, Victoria Barracks, Cork', NAK WO 35/154/33; *Irish Independent*, 26 April 1921.

242 'Drummer John Henry George Marquis, Gloucester Regt', www.cairogang.com/soldiers-killed/marquis/marquis.html (accessed 11 October 2016).

243 Denny Mullane, BMH WS 789, p. 26; 'Private Norman Thornton Fielding 3379143 2nd Bn. East Lancashire Regiment', www.cairogang.com/soldiers-killed/fielding/fielding.html.

244 *The Freeman's Journal*, 26 April 1921 (for the court case) and 29 April 1921 (for the executions). See also Barry, 'Cork and "The Trouble"' in *By Bride and Blackwater*.

245 'Death of Constable John Edward Bunce, RIC; 29th April, 1921; Cork', NAK WO 35/147A/7.

246 Felix O'Doherty, BMH WS 739, pp. 50–2; Historic Graves, 'Major Geoffrey Lee Compton Smith', http://historicgraves.com/story/major-geoffrey-lee-compton-smith (accessed 11 October 2016).

247 'Civilians Killed', http://irishmedals.org/civilians-killed.html (accessed 11 October 2016); 'RIC Report Cork East Riding, April 1921', University College Cork Boole Library & Archives; Francis Healy, BMH WS 1694, p. 17; *Irish Independent*, 2 May 1921. Healy incorrectly records the date as 1 May.

248 *The Cork Examiner*, 14 May 1921; *Irish Independent*, 18 October 1921; Collins List, MAI A0909; *The Freeman's Journal*, 21 May 1921.

249 Daniel F. O'Shaughnessy, BMH WS 1435, pp. 87–92; Donnchadh Ó hAnnagain, BMH WS 600, p. 35; 'Death of Patrick Casey; 2nd Mary, 1921', NAK WO 35/147B/7.

250 'Civilians Killed', http://irishmedals.org/civilians-killed.html (accessed 11 October 2016); 'Death of Joseph Coughlan; 1st May, 1921; Sunford, County Cork', NAK WO 35/148/34; MSPC 1D269.

251 *The Freeman's Journal*, 2 May 1921; 'Death of Constable William Albert Smith, RIC; 1st May, 1921; Castlemartyr, County Cork', NAK WO 35/159A/28; 'Death of Constable John Thomas Webb, RIC; 2nd May, 1921; Cork', NAK WO 35/160/54.

252   Commandant Patrick O'Brien, BMH WS 764, pp. 42–4; MSPC 1D115.

253   *Irish Independent*, 9 May 1921; 'Death of James Lynch; 6th May, 1921; Whitegate, County Cork', NAK WO 35/153 B/8.

254   *The Freeman's Journal*, 3 June 1921; 'Death of Private Thomas Collins, Cheshire Regiment; 7th May, 1921; Youghal, County Cork', NAK WO 35/147A/92; *Irish Independent*, 12 May 1921.

255   Michael Murphy, BMH WS 1547, p. 42; *Evening Herald*, 9 May 1921; 'Death of William Purcell; 7th May, 1921; Cork', NAK WO 35/157A/78. See also *Irish Independent*, 12 May 1921; *The Freeman's Journal*, 3 June 1921.

256   Robert Ahern, BMH WS 1676, pp. 10–12. The story is also recorded by Jerome Coughlan in BMH WS 1568, pp. 13–14. See also 'Death of Constable Frederick Sterland, RIC; 8th May, 1921; Cork', NAK WO 35/159A/42; *The Cork Examiner*, 4 June 1921.

257   House of Commons debate, 24 May 1921, vol. 142 cc21–22, http://hansard. millbanksystems.com/commons/1921/may/24/murders-and-outrages (accessed 11 October 2016). There is little information about the death of John Hodnett other than a single line in the newspapers.

258   'Death of William Bransfield; 8th May, 1921; Carrigtwohill, County Cork', NAK WO 35/146B/12; Francis Healy, BMH WS 1694, pp. 17–18.

259   James 'Spud' Murphy, BMH WS 1684, p. 22; 'Death of Constable James Cullen, RIC; 9th May, 1921; Cork', NAK WO 35/148/54. The *Irish Independent* of 11 May 1921 suggests that a Constable Fallon was killed, but this is more likely a misprint as no other source appears to record this.

260   Barry, *Guerilla Days in Ireland*, p. 165.

261   Charles O'Donoughe, BMH WS 1607, p. 7; Anna Hurley O'Mahony, BMH WS 540, p. 3. There is also some information about his death on the Historic Graves website, http://historicgraves.com/kilbrogan/co-klbg-0034/grave (accessed 11 October 2016).

262   John O'Connor, BMH WS 1250, p. 14; Michael Coleman, BMH WS 1254, pp. 18–19.

263   Seán Moylan, BMH WS 838, p. 247; William McCarthy, BMH WS 1255, pp. 11–12. This general shoot-up might be described as an early version of the Vietnamese 'Tet Offensive' of 1968.

264   *Irish Independent*, 16 May 1921; John Kelleher, BMH WS 1456, p. 26.

265   David Cashman, BMH WS 1523, p. 12; *Sussex Agricultural Express*, 27 May 1921.

266   *The Skibbereen Eagle*, 21 May 1921; 'Prosecution of Peter O'Keefe; purchase of rifles from soldiers at Cork; 1917; Cork; Penal Servitude', NAK WO 35/95/2; Patrick A. Murray, BMH WS 1584, p. 24.

267   Christopher O'Connell, BMH WS 1530, p. 26; 'Beara Peninsula Ambush, 15 [*sic*] May 1921', www.cairogang.com/soldiers-killed/beara-peninsula/beara-peninsula. html (accessed 11 October 2016); *Irish Independent*, 25 May 1921.

268   Peter Kearney, BMH WS 444, p. 13; Barry, *Guerilla Days in Ireland*, pp. 169–72;

'5998780 Pte Francis William Shepherd 1st Bn. Essex Regiment', www.cairogang.com/soldiers-killed/shepherd/shepherd.html (accessed 11 October 2016).

269 *The Skibbereen Eagle*, 21 May 1921.

270 Con Flynn, BMH WS 1621, p. 24. See also *The Cork Examiner*, 18 May 1921.

271 House of Commons debate, 23 June 1921, vol. 143 c1519, http://hansard.millbank systems.com/commons/1921/jun/23/military-operations#S5CV0143P0_19210 623_HOC_38 (accessed 11 October 2016).

272 John Kelleher, BMH WS 1456, p. 27; *The Cork Examiner*, 17 May 1921 – this report spells the name McNamara. Intentionally, or otherwise, it seems that Henry misled the House of Commons. According to the Dáil record no compensation was paid to Richard Barry's father, as there had been no dependency on his son: Dáil Éireann Debate, Vol. 9 No. 21, Ceisteanna – Questions. [Oral Answers.] – Compensation Claims, Thursday, 4 December 1924, http://oireachtasdebates.oireachtas.ie/debates%20authoring/DebatesWebPack.nsf/takes/dail1924120400004?opendocument (accessed 11 October 2016).

273 *The Cork Examiner*, 19 May 1921.

274 *The Skibbereen Eagle*, 21 May and 22 October 1921.

275 *Cork Constitution*, 16 May 1921. See also The Diocese of Cork and Ross, 'Rev. Seamus (James) Ó Ceallacháin CC', http://corkandross.org/priests.jsp?priestID=713# (accessed 17 January 2017); 'Reprisal Killing of Cork Priest', http://homepage.eircom.net/~corkcounty/ocallaghan.html (accessed 11 October 2016).

276 *The Cork Examiner*, 18 May 1921; Irish Volunteers Commemorative Organisation, 'Cork County Gaol, IRA Volunteers Executed Memorial', http://irishvolunteers.org/cork-county-gaol-ira-volunteers-executed-memorial/ (accessed 11 October 2016).

277 James Coss, BMH WS 1065, p. 11; William Buckley, BMH WS 1009, p. 21. Patrick J. Higgins, BMH WS 1467, p. 7, also records that Walsh was the person who informed the British Army about Clonmult. See NAK CO 904/156B for the British view.

278 'L/Cpl Arthur Wilfrid Lavington Hill, 5486595, No. 7 Coy. S Bn. Hampshire Regiment', www.cairogang.com/soldiers-killed/hill/hill.html (accessed 11 October 2016).

279 *Irish Independent*, 25 May 1921. Seán O'Connell, BMH WS 1706, p. 9, stated that Hawkins was shot as a spy on the Lee Road but survived.

280 *Irish Independent*, 21 May 1921; Daniel Healy, BMH WS 1656, p. 14.

281 Barry, 'Cork and "The Trouble"' in *By Bride and Blackwater*; *Irish Independent*, 23 May 1921.

282 'Attack on four workers near Douglas Street', http://homepage.eircom.net/~corkcounty/dorman.html (accessed 11 October 2016); Ellis, *The Burning of Cork*, http://aubanehistoricalsociety.org/aubane_collection/burning.pdf (accessed 27 September 2016).

283 Michael Geary *et al.*, BMH WS 754, p. 25. The story of these two men is also recorded on 'The Cairo Gang' website: 'Charleville Deserters', www.cairogang. com/soldiers-killed/deserters/charleville/charlville-deserters.html (accessed 11 October 2016).

284 *The Cork Examiner*, 21 July 1921; *The Freeman's Journal*, 14 January 1922.

285 George Power, BMH WS 451, pp. 15–16. James Hackett, BMH WS 1080, pp. 6–8, records how he collected a bag belonging to Vincent from Fermoy Railway Station which contained evidence that he was an intelligence officer. David Grant's comprehensive work on Vincent can be found on 'The Cairo Gang' website: 'Lt. Seymour Lewington Vincent', www.cairogang.com/soldiers-killed/vincent/vincent.html (accessed 11 October 2016).

286 'Death of Patrick Hickey; 24th May, 1921; Laravotta, near Inniskeane, County Cork', NAK WO 35/151A/70; House of Commons debate, 23 June 1921, vol. 143 cc1519–20, http://hansard.millbanksystems.com/commons/1921/jun/23/military-operations#S5CV0143P0_19210623_HOC_43 (accessed 11 October 2016).

287 'Death of Patrick Keating, 24th May 1921; Cork', NAK WO 35/152/55.

288 *Irish Independent*, 6 June 1921.

289 Tim Herlihy, BMH WS 810, pp. 32–3; 'Tramp's death', *The Skibbereen Eagle*, 9 July 1921.

290 Patrick J. Whelan, BMH WS 1449.

291 *The Cork Examiner*, 6 October 1921.

292 *Ibid.*, 14 January 1922; Tim O'Keeffe, BMH WS 810, p. 32.

293 Michael Leahy, BMH WS 1421, pp. 28–9. See also *Irish Independent*, 31 May 1921.

294 'Death of Patrick White; 31st May, 1921; Spike Island Internment Camp', NAK WO 35/159B/35; Pádraig Óg Ó Ruairc, 'Captain Patrick White, Meelick Company of the IRA; East Clare Brigade Commemoration', http://irishvolunteers.org/tag/captain-patrick-white-meelick-company-of-the-i-r-a/ (accessed 12 October 2016).

295 *The Freeman's Journal*, 1 June 1921; 'Hampshire Band Murders 31 May 1921', www.cairogang.com/soldiers-killed/youghal/youghal.html (accessed 12 October 2016).

296 Patrick J. Whelan, BMH WS 1449.

297 'Death of John Kenure; 31st May 1921; Youghal, County Cork', NAK WO 35/152/81. *The Freeman's Journal* of 1 June 1921 calls him Patrick rather than John.

298 Timothy Sexton, BMH WS 1565, pp. 6–7; http://the irishrevolution.ie/wp-content/uploads/2016/08/CorkSpyFiles-Database-27.08.2016.pdf.

299 House of Commons debates, 2 June 1921, vol. 142 cc1221–3, http://hansard.mill banksystems.com/commons/1921/jun/02/murder-colonel-peacocke (accessed 12 October 2016). Fans of the sitcom *Yes Minister* will recognise that, much like Sir Humphrey, Hamar Greenwood does not answer the question asked by Colonel

Willoughby, but gives an answer that allows him to suggest that Peacocke was an innocent.

300 Richard Russell, BMH WS 1591, pp. 25–6. Peacocke's name is recorded in many sources without the final e, which is incorrect.

301 *Irish Independent,* 5 July 1921; 'Death of Joseph C. Holman; 1st June, 1921; Kilworth, County Cork', NAK WO 35/152/10.

302 *Irish Independent,* 8 June 1921.

303 Tim O'Keeffe, BMH WS 810, p. 18; 'Manchester Regiment Band Boy Murders – 5 June 1921', www.cairogang.com/soldiers-killed/band-boy-murders/band-boy.html (accessed 12 October 2016).

304 Dónal Ó hÉalaithe (ed.), *Memoirs of an Old Warrior: Jamie Moynihan's Fight for Irish Freedom 1916–1923* (Cork, 2014), pp. 145, 213; 'Death of Dan Riordan; 5th June, 1921; Carrigaphooka Bridge, County Cork', NAK WO 35/158/33; 'Death of John Kelleher; 5th June 1921; Cork', NAK WO 35/152/59. See also *The Cork Examiner,* 10 June 1921 for O'Riordan and *Irish Independent,* 14 June 1921 for Kelleher.

305 'Death of Daniel Buckley; 8th June, 1921; Toames, near Macroom, County Cork', NAK WO 35/147a/2; Charles Browne, BMH WS 873, pp. 47–8. Michael O'Sullivan, BMH WS 793, p. 27, repeats the collecting water story, only he claims it was for the mother rather than the father. Halahan is also sometimes spelled Hallahan in the sources.

306 *The Freeman's Journal,* 10 June 1921.

307 *Ibid.,* 13 June 1921; *The Anglo Celt,* 18 June 1921.

308 'Death of David Fitzgibbon; 9th June, 1921; Killinane, Liscarroll, County Cork', NAK WO 35/150/30. See also *The Freeman's Journal,* 13 June 1921.

309 *Evening Herald,* 10 June 1921.

310 *The Southern Star,* 18 June 1921.

311 Charles Browne, BMH WS 873, p. 49; Charles O'Donoghue, BMH WS 1607, p. 10; 'Death of Matthew Donovan; 10th [*sic*] June, 1921; Quarry's Cross, Ballinablath, Macroom, County Cork', NAK WO 35/149A/30; *The Southern Star,* 18 June 1921.

312 *The Cork Examiner,* 15 June 1921; 'Death of Michael Driscoll; 13th June, 1921; Waterlands, Kinsale, County Cork', NAK WO/35/149A/54. There is some confusion about Driscoll's age at the time of his death; *The Cork Examiner* says fifty-five and the military says sixty.

313 'Echo of Tragedy', *Irish Independent,* 11 March 1922.

314 'Private F. Roughley, 3514304, 1st Bn. Manchester Regiment', www.cairogang.com/soldiers-killed/band-boy-murders/roughley/roughley.html (accessed 12 October 2016).

315 Millstreet.ie, 'On this day: The Rathcoole Ambush', www.millstreet.ie/blog/2014/06/16/on-this-day-1921-the-rathcoole-ambush (accessed 11 October 2016); 'Death of Temporary Cadets Frederick Edgar Shorter and William Arthur

Halmerston Boyd; 16th June, 1921; near Millstreet, County Cork', NAK WO 35/159A/22.

316  Patrick 'Pa' Murray, BMH WS 1584, pp. 25–6.

317  *Weekly Irish Independent*, 24 June 1921; 'Death of Josephine Scannell; 23rd [*sic*] June, 1921; Cork', NAK WO 35/159A/6.

318  'Letter from Thomas Cotter', Seamus Fitzgerald Collection, CCCA PR6/32; 'Death of Daniel O'Callaghan; 21st June, 1921; Carrigtwohill, County Cork', NAK WO 35/156/49.

319  *Irish Independent*, 29 June 1921; *The Southern Star*, 25 June 1921.

320  Daniel Corkery, BMH WS 1719, p. 25.

321  Timothy Buckley, BMH WS 1641, pp. 18–19.

322  Millstreet.ie, 'On this day in 1921 – June 23rd', www.millstreet.ie/blog/2014/06/23/on-this-day-in-1921-june-23rd (accessed 12 October 2016).

323  'Death of Mary Parnell; 26th June, 1921; Cork, County Cork', NAK WO 35/157A/57.

324  The name on the court of inquiry is Thomas Stanley, but Shanley is correct. 'Death of Constable Thomas Stanley, RIC; 26th June, 1921; Kildorrery, County Cork', NAK WO 35/159A/36; House of Commons debate, 30 June 1921, vol. 143 c2312, http://hansard.millbanksystems.com/commons/1921/jun/30/murders#S5CV0143P0_19210630_HOC_62 (accessed 11 October 2016).

325  'Private Frederick Crowther 4906896, South Staffordshire Regiment', www.cairogang.com/soldiers-killed/crowther/crowther.html (accessed 3 November 2016).

326  'Death of Walter Leo Murphy; 27th June, 1921; Waterfall, County Cork', NAK WO 35/155B/31. Michael O'Regan, BMH WS 1524, provides details of Murphy's IRA activities and also has a brief record of his death.

327  'Death of Charles Daly alias McCarthy; night of 28th/29th June, 1921; Cork', NAK WO 35/147B/6; Michael Murphy, BMH WS 1547, p. 38, although he confuses the date with that of Charlie Daly who was killed in the tunnel of Cork railway station at the end of February. Daly's death is also mentioned in Jerome Coughlan, BMH WS 1568, p. 3.

328  'Death of William Horgan; 28th June, 1921; Lavitts Quay, Cork', NAK WO 35/152/16; *Evening Herald*, 30 June 1921.

329  Michael Geary and Richard Smith, BMH WS 754, pp. 25–7; 'Death of Patrick John Sheehan and John Sullivan; 28th [*sic*] June, 1921; Drews Court, County Limerick', NAK WO 35/159B/5; *Irish Independent*, 30 June 1921.

330  'Death of Timothy Murphy, 29th June, 1921; Cork', NAK WO 35/156/14.

331  James 'Spud' Murphy, BMH WS 1684, p. 24; *The Skibbereen Eagle*, 9 July 1921.

332  *The Freeman's Journal*, 2 July 1921; Millstreet.ie, 'The Rathcoole Ambush', www.millstreet.ie/blog/2014/06/16/on-this-day-1921-the-rathcoole-ambush (accessed 12 October 2016); NAI, Census 1911, www.census.nationalarchives.ie/pages/1911/Cork/Kilcorney/Shanakill/437629/ (accessed 12 October 2016).

333  *The Cork Examiner*, 19 October 1927.

334  Timothy Sexton, BMH WS 1565, p. 7.

335  For example, *Irish Independent*, 5 July 1921.

336  'Death of Maurice Cusack; 3rd July, 1921; Ballycotton, County Cork', NAK WO 35/148/72.

337  'Death of Constable James Connor; 7th July, 1921; Rigsdale, County Cork', NAK WO 35/148/16.

338  'Death of William Alexandra MacPherson; 8th July, 1921; Knockpogue, Mallow, County Cork', NAK WO 35/153 B/14; Cornelius O'Regan, BMH WS 1200, p. 14. O'Regan mistakenly calls Barrow Denis rather than David.

339  Ó Ruairc, *Truce*, pp. 233, 240; 'Death of Dennis [*sic*] Joseph Spriggs; 8/9th July, 1921; Cork', NAK WO 35/159A/34. See also 'Cork City Volunteer Shot Dead by British', http://homepage.eircom.net/~corkcounty/spriggs.html (accessed 12 October 2016.

340  John Foley is incorrectly called Jeremiah in some newspaper reports. Ó hÉalaithe, *Memoirs of an Old Warrior*, p. 275; *The Freeman's Journal*, 11 July 1921; 'Death Notice', *Irish Independent*, 12 July 1921; 'Death of John Foley; 10th July, 1921; Coachford, County Cork', NAK WO 35/150/46; Ó Ruairc, *Truce*, pp. 249–51.

341  William C. Regan, BMH 1069, p. 13; 'Private Richard Edward Larter, 1st Bn. Machine Gun Corps', www.cairogang.com/soldiers-killed/larter/larter.html (accessed 12 October 2016).

342  'Cork Executions – 10 Jul. 1921', www.cairogang.com/soldiers-killed/cork-jul-21/cork-executions.html (accessed 12 October 2016).

343  Ó Ruairc, *Truce*, pp. 162–74. David Grant and Pádraig Óg Ó Ruairc succeeded in uncovering the correct details by co-operating as evidence appeared. Even the most cynical commentator should accept the killings were unlikely to have had any military or propaganda value for the IRA.

344  Ó Ruairc, *Truce*, pp. 88–90; *Irish Independent*, 21 and 22 April 1921.

345  'Courts of inquiry in lieu of inquest: Individual Cases: BUC–COL', NAK WO 35/147A.

346  Ó Ruairc, *Truce*, pp. 92–3; *The Cork Examiner*, 14 July 1921.

347  Ó Ruairc, *Truce*, pp. 93–4.

348  'Irish Distress Committee and Irish Grants Committee: Files and Minutes. William Jagoe, County Cork, No. 11', NAK CO 762/4/1; 'Irish Distress Committee and Irish Grants Committee: Files and Minutes. Mr and Mrs Cronin, County Cork, No. 1515', NAK CO 762/92/2; Niall Meehan, 'Distorting Irish History, Two: The Road from Dunmanway. Peter Hart's Treatment of the 1922 "April killings" in West Cork', https://www.academia.edu/612672/Distorting_Irish_History_Two_the_road_from_Dunmanway_Peter_Hart_s_treatment_of_the_1922_April_killings_in_West_Cork (accessed 12 October 2016).

349  Tim Herlihy, BMH WS 810, pp. 19–21; MSPC 1D11; 'Death of Dave [*sic*] Clancy; 10th [*sic*] October 1921, Cork', NAK WO 35/147A/61.

350  *The Freeman's Journal*, 21 November 1921. For a full history of his life see Irish

Congress of Trade Unions, www.ictu.ie/download/pdf/a_brief_insight_into_the_life_of_a_great_trade_unionist.pdf (accessed 12 October 2016).

351 *The Freeman's Journal*, 9 February 1922; *Irish Independent*, 18 February 1922.

352 *The Skibbereen Eagle*, 18 February 1922.

353 'Henry Marion Genochio', www.cairogang.com/other-people/british/castle-intelligence/genochio/genochio.html (accessed 12 October 2016).

354 *Irish Independent*, 22 March 1922.

355 *Ibid.*, 28 March 1922.

356 It has also been suggested that they had lunch at the Hornibrooks or the Tonson-Ryes at Cloughduv just south of the Thady Inn where Frank Busteed claims he captured them. As the Hornibrooks had already been arrested and Ryecourt had been burned in 1921, this is unlikely. For information on Farran House's location see www.farranhouse.com/rental/location.html (accessed 18 October 2016).

357 James Murphy, BMH WS 1633, p. 15. Other accounts include Tim Buckley (WS 1674), Maurice Brew (WS 1695), Dan Corkery (WS 1719) and Nora Cunningham (WS 1690).

358 Keane, *Massacre in West Cork*, pp. 174–8; *The Southern Star*, 15 December 1923; 'Kilgobnet Killings', www.cairogang.com/incidents/kilgobnet%201922/kilgobnet-1922.html (accessed 12 October 2016). See Michael Walsh, BMH WS 1521, p. 17, for evidence of the three officers' interrogation methods.

359 *The Cork Examiner*, 29 April 1922 (for vote of condolences) and 1 May 1922 (for funeral).

360 *The Southern Star*, 27 May 1922; *The Skibbereen Eagle*, 27 May 1922.

361 *Irish Independent*, 1 July 2007; Charles Cullinane, MSPC MSP34REF59839, p. 34.

362 *Irish Independent*, 20 June 1922.

363 *The Southern Star*, 1 July and 18 August 1922; Mallow Archaeological and Historical Society, 'Royal Irish Constabulary, Casualties in the Mallow Area, 1916–22,' www.rootsweb.ancestry.com/~irlmahs/mric.htm (accessed 18 November 2016). Tehan was born in Co. Kerry in 1872 and his RIC Number was 57533 (information available at Findmypast.ie).

364 *Irish Independent*, 3 July 1922.

365 For more on the siege see Ted O'Sullivan interview in Andy Bielenberg *et al.*, *The Men Will Talk to Me: West Cork. Interviews by Ernie O'Malley* (Cork, 2015), pp. 126–7; *The Cork Examiner*, 4 and 5 July 1922; *Irish Independent*, 9 August 1922; *The Southern Star*, 23 September 1922.

366 *Irish Independent*, 17 July 1922.

367 *Ibid.*, 18 July 1922.

368 *The Southern Star*, 5 August 1922; Denis Collins, BMH WS 827, pp. 20–1.

369 Murphy in *The Year of Disappearances* claims the misdating of the Parsons killing allowed the anti-Treaty IRA to cover up secret killings between March and August 1922 when they were in complete control of Cork city. However, the evidence is tenuous. Many of his claimed disappeared and victims had either

emigrated before, during or after the revolution, or survived it. See Barry Keane, 'The Undead: Cork's Missing War of Independence Freemasons 1920–1926' in 'Protestant Cork 1911–1926', https://sites.google.com/site/protestantcork191136/ the-undead-cork-s-struck-off-freemasons-1920-1926 (accessed 13 October 2016).

370   Mick Murphy, BMH WS 1547, p. 33.

371   Murphy, *The Year of Disappearances*, pp. 175–80; NAI, Census 1911, www.census. nationalarchives.ie/pages/1911/Cork/Cork_No__5_Urban__part_of_/High_ Street/399066/ (accessed 3 November 2016).

372   MSPC 1D13.

373   Alternatively called Gannaghann/Cunningham/Galvin in the sources.

374   *Irish Weekly Times*, 19 August 1922; John Borgonovo, *The Battle for Cork* (Cork, 2011), pp. 102–4; *The New York Times*, 12 August 1922, available at http://query. nytimes.com/mem/archive-free/pdf?res=9D00EEDB1E3EEE3ABC4A52DFB E668389639EDE (accessed 13 October 2016); Pádraig Óg Ó Ruairc, 'British IRA Volunteers 1921', http://theirishwar.com/british-i-r-a-volunteers-1921/ (accessed 13 October 2016). For James Lynch's eyewitness report of the Battle of Douglas, see http://homepage.eircom.net/~corkcounty/douglas.html (accessed 13 October 2016). For more details on some of those who died, see MSPC 2D383 (Gavigan); MSPC 2D450 (Quinn); MSPC 2D371 (Maguire); MSPC 2D82 (Madden); MSPC 2D133 (Perry); MSPC 2D17 (O'Toole).

375   *Irish Independent*, 12 August 1922.

376   *Ibid.*, 20 August 1922.

377   *Ibid*, 18 August 1922.

378   McDonald is sometimes called McDonnell in the sources. *Irish Independent*, 22 August 1922; MSPC 2D379.

379   *Irish Independent*, 21 August 1922; MSPC 2D14; Everafter, www.discovereverafter. com/uploads/graveyards/droghedatest_115/E173.JPG (accessed 13 October 2016).

380   MSPC 2D31. See *Irish Independent*, 19 August 1922, for details of the capture of Macroom.

381   MSPC 2D37; *Evening Herald*, 23 August 1922.

382   *The Cork Examiner*, 24 August and 19 October 1922; *Cork Constitution*, 15 July 1921; Murphy, *The Year of Disappearances*, pp. 200–2; NAK TS18/236. See also NAK CO 762/152/2.

383   Borgonovo, *The Battle for Cork*, p. 116.

384   'National Army Killed', www.irishmedals.org/national-army-killed.html (accessed 13 October 2016); MSPC 2D378.

385   *Irish Independent*, 29 August 1922.

386   *Ibid.*, 30 August 1922; MSPC 2D413.

387   'Day by Day', War Special, *An t-Óglách*, 2 September 1922, p. 1, available at http:// antoglach.militaryarchives.ie/PDF/1922_09_02_Vol_IV_No_13_An_t-Oglac. pdf; MSPC 2D477; *The Freeman's Journal*, 4 September 1922; Michael J. Crowley, BMH WS 1603, p. 2.

388   Denis Keohane, BMH WS 1469, p. 5; *The Freeman's Journal*, 5 September 1922; *The Southern Star*, 9 September 1922.

389   'National Army Killed', www.irishmedals.org/national-army-killed.html; MSPC 2D34.

390   MSPC 2D276; *Irish Independent*, 1 September 1922.

391   'National Army Killed', www.irishmedals.org/national-army-killed.html; MSPC 2D80 (Kearns). The MSPC file for Kearns says he died on 5 September, but the *Evening Herald* of that date records his burial in Glasnevin on that day and says he died on 1 September.

392   *The Cork Examiner*, 7 September 1922. See also MSPC 2D206 (Neary); MSPC 2D88 (O'Leary); 'Day by Day', War Special, *An t-Óglách*, 9 September 1922, p. 2, http://antoglach.militaryarchives.ie/PDF/1922_09_09_Vol_IV_No_14_An_t-Oglac.pdf (accessed 13 October 2016).

393   *Irish Independent*, 31 August and 4 September 1922; MSPC 2D191; MSPC 2D172; 'Day by Day', War Special, *An t-Óglách*, http://antoglach.militaryarchives.ie/PDF/1922_09_09_Vol_IV_No_14_An_t-Oglac.pdf (accessed 14 October 2016).

394   *Irish Independent*, 15 September 1922; MSPC 2D208; MSPC 2D397; 'National Army Killed', www.irishmedals.org/national-army-killed.html (accessed 14 October 2016); the Irish Army plot in Glasnevin incorrectly claims Yates died on 16 September.

395   *The Freeman's Journal*, 14 September 1922; CCCA SM698 Commemorative Brochure for Captain Timothy Kenefick/Kennefick. See also Tomás Nogla's question in the Dáil about Kennefick's death on 1 November 1922 and the reply: http://oireachtasdebates.oireachtas.ie/debates%20authoring/debateswebpack.nsf/takes/dail1922110100025?opendocument (accessed 14 October 2016).

396   *The Freeman's Journal*, 22 September 1922.

397   *The Cork Examiner*, 16 September 1922; *Irish Independent*, 18 September 1922; Irish War Memorials, 'Creedon, O'Brien and Healy Memorial', www.irishwarmemorials.ie/Memorials-Detail?memoId=408 (accessed 14 October 2016).

398   *The Freeman's Journal*, 16 and 18 September 1922.

399   *Irish Independent*, 23 September 1922.

400   MSPC 2D289.

401   *Irish Independent*, 20 September 1922. See also MSPC 2D369.

402   MSPC 2D212.

403   *Irish Independent*, 23 September 1922.

404   Ceisteanna – Questions. Oral Answers. Glengarriffe Compensation Claim. Thursday, 15 May 1924, http://oireachtasdebates.oireachtas.ie/debates%20authoring/debateswebpack.nsf/takes/dail1924051500005?opendocument (accessed 14 October 2016)

405   *Irish Independent*, 28 September 1922; *The Southern Star*, 30 September 1922.

406   *Irish Independent*, 26 September 1922.

407   MSPC 2D367.

408  *The Southern Star*, 30 September 1922; MSPC 2D305.

409  *The Southern Star*, 28 October 1922; 'Anti-Treaty Killed', www.irishmedals.org/anti-treaty-killed.html (accessed 14 October 2016).

410  *The Freeman's Journal*, 6 October 1922; MSPC 2D163.

411  *Irish Independent*, 6 October 1922. The death certificate was not issued until 1933.

412  *Ibid.*, 17 October 1922.

413  *The Cork Examiner*, 10 October 1922.

414  Irish Volunteers Commemorative Organisation, 'IRA 1 Cork Brigade, Donoughmore Cemetery, Co. Cork', http://irishvolunteers.org/IRA-1-cork-brigade-donoughmore-cemetery-co-cork/ (accessed 14 October 2016).

415  *Irish Independent*, 9 October 1922.

416  MSPC 2D298.

417  MSPC 2D216.

418  *Irish Independent*, 13 October 1922.

419  *The Southern Star*, 14 October 1922 (initial report); *The Cork Examiner*, 16 October 1922 (correction). See also 'National Army Killed', www.irishmedals.org/national-army-killed.html (accessed 14 October 2016); MSPC 2D189 (Byrne). In the MSPC file on Byrne there seems to be some confusion over the date of death, with some of the documents claiming he died on 5 October.

420  'Civilians Killed, Civil War', www.irishmedals.org/civilians-killed-civil-war.html (accessed 14 October 2016).

421  MSPC 2D54.

422  *The Freeman's Journal*, 20 October 1922.

423  MSPC 2D153; *The Southern Star*, 28 October 1922.

424  'Anti-Treaty Killed', www.irishmedals.org/anti-treaty-killed.html (accessed 14 October 2016). See also *The Irish Times*, 25 October 1922; *Irish Independent*, 25 October 1922.

425  *Irish Independent*, 24 October 1922; MSPC 2D377.

426  MSPC 2D218. There are some contradictions in the documents in the MSPC file, but the details presented here are correct.

427  *The Cork Examiner*, 19 and 24 October 1922.

428  *Irish Independent*, 27 October 1922.

429  *Ibid.*, 27 and 30 October 1922.

430  MSPC 2D320; 'National Army Killed', www.irishmedals.org/national-army-killed.html (accessed 14 October 2016).

431  *Irish Independent*, 16 November 1922.

432  *The Cork Examiner*, 1 and 13 November 1922; MSPC 2D284.

433  MSPC 2D384.

434  For example, *Irish Independent*, 6 November 1922.

435  Dáil Debate, Written Answers – Mortality Claims. Tuesday, 4 May 1937, http://oireachtasdebates.oireachtas.ie/debates%20authoring/debateswebpack.nsf/takes/dail1937050400026?opendocument (accessed 14 October 2016).

436  *The Cork Examiner*, 11 November 1922; MSPC 2D73 (Horgan); MSPC 2D239 (Gallagher); MSPC 2D181 (Woods). Ó Conchubhair, *Rebel Cork's Fighting Story*, p. 180, records the two anti-Treaty men.

437  *The Freeman's Journal*, 7 November 1922.

438  *The Southern Star*, 11 November 1922.

439  *The Cork Examiner*, 13 November 1922.

440  *Evening Herald*, 13 November 1922.

441  *Irish Independent*, 14 November 1922. Some of the other newspaper reports use the spelling Cregan.

442  *Ibid.*, 16 November 1922.

443  *The Freeman's Journal*, 22 November 1922; Michael Harrington, *The Munster Republic: The Civil War in North Cork* (Cork, 2009), pp. 98–102. As well as the eyewitness account, Harrington provides a comprehensive outline of the contradictory evidence given at the inquest into this shooting, including the suggestion by Hannan that their men were fired on from the trap and Private Breen's failure to mention this.

444  *Irish Independent*, 18 November 1922; MSPC 2D299.

445  *The Southern Star*, 18 November 1922; MSPC 2D39. Although the MSPC file mentions varying dates of death, the Tuesday mentioned in *The Southern Star* as the day of death was 14 November.

446  *Irish Independent*, 23 November 1922; MSPC 2D319 (Wonlahan).

447  Ó Conchubhair, *Rebel Cork's Fighting Story*, p. 180.

448  *Irish Independent*, 22 November 1922; email with family in author's possession.

449  *Irish Independent* 30 November 1922. See also MSPC 2D321.

450  *The Cork Examiner*, 25 November 1922; *Irish Independent*, 1 December 1922; MSPC 2D351 (McCann); MSPC 2D223 (Walsh); 'National Army Killed', www.irishmedals.org/national-army-killed.html (accessed 14 October 2016).

451  *Limerick Leader*, 27 November 1922.

452  *Irish Independent*, 28 November 1922.

453  *The Southern Star*, 25 November 1922.

454  *The Irish Times*, 29 November 1922.

455  *The Freeman's Journal*, 29 November 1922; *Irish Independent*, 30 November 1922.

456  MSPC 2D214.

457  MSPC 2D265.

458  *Irish Independent*, 1 December 1922.

459  *Ibid.*, 6 December 1922.

460  Ó hÉalaithe, *Memoirs of an Old Warrior*, pp. 240–8.

461  For more information on Nolan and McNeice, see MSPC 2D119 (Nolan); MSPC 2D458 (McNeice). Although some accounts credit Nolan with being a sergeant, the record from Portobello Barracks contained in his pension file lists him as a private. McNeice's pension file lists both 6 and 7 December as possible dates of death. For other accounts of the battle see *Irish Independent*, 7 December 1922; Brother P. J. Kavanagh, 'Carlow Men in Cork Ambush', *Cumann Staire*

*Bhéal Átha'n Ghaorthaidh* (2010) www.ballingearyhs.com/pdf_folder/2010_BallingearyJournal.pdf#page=25 (accessed 14 October 2016).

462 *The Cork Examiner*, 11 December 1922; MSPC 2D437.

463 Timothy Buckley, BMH WS 1674, p. 10.

464 For a comprehensive treatment of the executions see Murphy, 'The Government's Executions Policy during the Irish Civil War 1922–1923'.

465 *The Irish Times*, 7 December 1922.

466 *Ibid.*, 8 December 1922.

467 *Ibid.*, 9 December 1922.

468 Dáil Éireann Debate, vol. 2 no. 2, http://oireachtasdebates.oireachtas.ie/debates%20authoring/debateswebpack.nsf/takes/dail1922120700015?opendocument (accessed 3 November 2016).

469 The intent was to perpetrate an act of such utter ruthlessness that members of the Dáil would be off-limits, and until the assassination of Kevin O'Higgins in 1928 this turned out to be the case.

470 'Birth Pangs of a Nation – 1', *The Irish Times*, 19 November 1968.

471 Murphy, 'The Government's Executions Policy during the Irish Civil War 1922–1923', pp. 141–2.

472 Birth Pangs of a Nation – 1', *The Irish Times*, 19 November 1968.

473 'Colourful Gogarty escapes death by a whisker', *Galway Advertiser*, 14 August 2014, www.advertiser.ie/galway/article/71637/colourful-gogarty-escapes-death-by-a-whisker (accessed 17 September 2015).

474 *Weekly Irish Times*, 10 February 1923.

475 *Ibid.*

476 *Ibid.*, 17 February 1923.

477 Liam Deasy, *Brother against Brother* (Cork, 1998), p. 112.

478 James Hurley, BMH WS 1354, p. 8.

479 Ó Conchubhair, *Rebel Cork's Fighting Story*, p. 180; *The Cork Examiner*, 9 December 1922.

480 *Irish Independent*, 18 December 1922.

481 *Ibid.*, 19 January 1923.

482 *Ibid.*, 15 December 1922; MSPC 2D296.

483 *Irish Independent*, 19 December 1922; MSPC 2D193.

484 *Irish Independent*, 16 December 1922; MSPC 2D295.

485 *Irish Independent*, 20 December 1922.

486 Historic Graves, 'CO-MULT-0259', http://historicgraves.com/st-multose-s/co-mult-0259/grave; *The Freeman's Journal*, 20 December 1922; *Irish Independent*, 23 December 1922; 'Irish Distress Committee and Irish Grants Committee: Files and Minutes. William Wolfe, County Cork, No. 2468', NAK CO 762/147/1; 'Protestant Farmer Shot Dead', *Glasgow Herald*, 20 December 1922, http://news.google.com/newspapers?nid=2507&dat=19221220&id=0ZxAAAAAIBAJ&sjid=NqUMAAAAIBAJ&pg=4073,6205018 (accessed 14 October 2016).

487  *Irish Independent*, 22 December 1922.

488  *Ibid.*, 23 December 1922. Her name is spelled Fehily in this article, but her death certificate says Feehely.

489  *The Southern Star*, 23 December 1922.

490  MSPC 2D345; NAI, Census Ireland 1911, Commons Road, Cork, www. census.nationalarchives.ie/pages/1911/Cork/Cork_No__4_Urban__part_of_/ Commons_Road/387881/ (accessed 18 November 2016).

491  *Irish Independent*, 23 December 1922; Dáil Éireann debate, vol. 2 no. 40, Ceisteanna – Questions. [Oral Answers.] – Fermoy Fatality, Friday 9 March 1923, http://oireachtasdebates.oireachtas.ie/debates%20authoring/debateswebpack. nsf/takes/dail1923030900006?opendocument (accessed 15 October 2016).

492  *Irish Independent*, 27 December 1922; MSPC 2D176.

493  *Irish Independent*, 1 January 1923; *The Freeman's Journal*, 30 December 1922; *Irish Examiner*, 1 January 1923.

494  *The Freeman's Journal*, 29 December 1922. There seems to be some real confusion over McDonald's name, with many of the files in his military pension file, MSPC 2D210, also calling him McDonnell or MacDonnell, including the registrar of births and deaths.

495  *The Cork Examiner*, 3 January 1923.

496  Harrington, *The Munster Republic*, pp. 109–10. See also MSPC 3D245 (O'Mahony); MSPC 3D292 (Pomeroy); MSPC 3D74 (Nolan).

497  *Irish Independent*, 6 January 1923.

498  MSPC 3D199. It is possible to calculate his age at the time of death from his entry in the 1911 census records: www.census.nationalarchives.ie/search/ (accessed 17 October 2016).

499  *Irish Independent*, 10 January 1923. See also MSPC 3D149.

500  *The Freeman's Journal*, 22 January 1923; *Irish Independent*, 22 January 1923. There is some confusion in his pensions file, MSPC 3D201, over the date of death, with his sister Annie's claims varying from 19 or 20 January to 19 April.

501  *Irish Independent*, 6 February 1923; *The Cork Examiner*, 10 February 1923; Dáil Éireann debate, vol. 13 no. 18, Ceisteanna – Questions. [Oral Answers.] – Co. Cork Mine Explosion, Friday 11 December 1925, http://oireachtas debates.oireachtas.ie/debates%20authoring/debateswebpack.nsf/takes/dail1925 121100004?opendocument (accessed 15 October 2016).

502  *Irish Independent*, 8 February 1923.

503  *The Freeman's Journal*, 15 February 1923; *Irish Independent*, 16 February 1923.

504  *Evening Herald*, 12 February 1923; *Irish Independent*, 16 February 1923.

505  MSPC 3D306; Tom Doyle, *The Civil War in Kerry* (Cork, 2008), p. 265.

506  *Irish Independent*, 20 February 1923. The second name, Charles McIlgorm, comes from the Historical RFA (Royal Fleet Auxiliary) site and says he was killed on 17 February, www.historicalrfa.org/requisitioned-auxiliaries/162-requisitioned-auxiliaries-c/1349-requisitioned-auxiliary-caarrigan-head (accessed 3 November 2016).

507  MSPC 3D241.

508  MSPC 3D252.

509  *An t-Óglách*, vol. 1 no. 2 (new series), 10 March 1923, http://antoglach.military archives.ie/PDF/1923_03_10_Vol_1_No_2_An_t-Oglac-2.pdf. For more information see 'Gen Denis Galvin', www.findagrave.com/cgi-bin/fg.cgi?page=gr&GR id=80888928 (accessed 17 October 2016).

510  *The Southern Star*, 17 March 1923.

511  *The Corkman*, 23 May 2013, www.independent.ie/regionals/corkman/news/the-last-man-to-be-executed-at-cork-gaol-honoured-29290339.html (accessed 17 October 2016).

512  Bennett Papers, CCCA B609/9/A/43 and B609/9/A/42; Irish Civil War Operation/Intelligence reports, Cork Command, Box11/1, General weekly report from the Cork command, 26 March 1923, MAI.

513  *Irish Independent*, 21 March 1923.

514  *The Freeman's Journal*, 21 March 1923; Murphy, *The Year of Disappearances*, pp. 203–6. See also Murphy, 'The Government's Executions Policy during the Irish Civil War 1922–1923'.

515  *Irish Independent*, 10 March 1923; MSPC 3D190.

516  *The Southern Star*, 31 March 1923; MSPC 3D61.

517  *Irish Independent*, 31 March 1923; MSPC 3D278.

518  *The Southern Star*, 7 April 1923; *Irish Independent* 6 April 1922.

519  'National Army Killed', www.irishmedals.org/national-army-killed.html; MSPC 3D56; *The Cork Examiner*, 4 April 1923.

520  *The Cork Examiner*, 9 and 12 April 1923.

521  *Ibid.*, 11 April and 23 April 1923; Dáil Éireann, Ceisteanna – Questions. Oral Answers. Cork Fatality Compensation Claim. Thursday, 15 May 1924 http://oireachtasdebates.oireachtas.ie/debates%20authoring/debateswebpack.nsf/takes/dail1924051500006?opendocument (accessed 17 October 2016).

522  *Irish Independent*, 12 April 1923; MSPC 3D79; personal email with author.

523  For a more detailed description of this see letter from Frank Aiken outlining the circumstances of Liam's death on 10 April 1923, 6 July 1923, National Library of Ireland, MS 36,251/30.

524  National Graves Association, 'Death of Liam Lynch', www.nga.ie/Civil%20War-Liam_Lynch-Death.php (accessed 4 November 2016).

525  *Irish Independent*, 21 April 1923. Rebel Cork's Fighting Story (website), 'Plaques and Monuments of Ballydehob, Bantry and Castletownbere', https://rebelcorksfightingstory.wordpress.com/2014/04/05/plaques-and-monuments-of-ballydehob-bantry-and-castletownbere/ (accessed 17 October 2016).

526  *Irish Independent*, 23 April 1923.

527  *Ibid.*, 2 May 1923; MSPC 3D50. In the MSPC file Monahan's name is also spelled Monaghan in some of the official papers, but since his mother signs her name without the g, that is the spelling chosen here. See also *Irish Independent*, 4

May 1923.

528  MSPC 3D16.

529  *The Southern Star*, 7 July 1923.

530  *Ibid.*, 28 July 1923.

531  *Irish Independent*, 16 August 1923.

532  *The Cork Examiner*, 22 and 25 August 1923.

533  *Irish Independent*, 30 August 1923. There seems to be some confusion over his cause of death, with many of the documents in the MSPC file (3D237) claiming he died of scarlatina, or scarlet fever. However, the register of births and deaths says typhus.

534  *The Southern Star*, 24 November 1923.

535  James Durney, 'Comdt. Denis Barry in Newbridge and the Curragh', *Kildare Online Electronic History Journal*, www.kildare.ie/library/ehistory/2011/10/comdt_denis_barry_in_newbridge.asp The article is edited and paraphrased for space reasons. I would like to thank James Durney for his kind permission to use it. See also Denis Barry, *The Unknown Commandant: The Life and Times of Denis Barry 1883–1923* (Cork, 2010); Michael Biggs, *Cork Hunger Strikes by Irish Republicans, 1916–1923* (University of Illinois at Urbana-Champaign, 2004).

536  *Evening Herald*, 24 November 1923; *The Cork Examiner*, 26 November 1923; *The Anglo-Celt*, 1 December 1923.

537  *Irish Independent*, 27 December 1923.

## POSSIBLES

1  '33713 H Ward, Cameron Highlanders', www.cairogang.com/soldiers-killed/ward-h/ward-h.html (accessed 3 November 2016).

2  Interview with Michael Leahy, Ernie O'Malley Notebooks, UCDA P17b/108.

3  Tadg O'Sullivan, BMH WS 792, p. 5; O'Malley Notebooks, UCDA P17b/111; John O'Driscoll, BMH WS 1250, p. 21; http://the irishrevolution.ie/wp-content/uploads/2016/08/CorkSpyFiles-Database-27.08.2016.pdf.

4  'Death of Stephen O'Callaghan; 29th April, 1921; South Infirmary, County Cork', NAK WO 35/156/51; *Weekly Irish Independent*, 5 May 1921.

5  http://irishvolunteers.org/IRA-1-cork-brigadedonoughmore-cemetery-co-cork/ (accessed 3 November 2016).

6  Patrick Cronin, BMH WS 710, p. 2.

7  Michael O'Regan, BMH WS 1524, p. 5.

8  *Cork Constitution*, 11 March 1922; 'William Roycroft, County Cork, No. 2928', NAK CO 762/170/21.

9  *The Freeman's Journal*, 4 and 5 September 1922; *The Cork Examiner*, 12 September 1922. No record could be found of any fighting between Kilumney and Cork on this day.

10  *Evening Herald*, 23 September 1922.

# BIBLIOGRAPHY

## BOOKS AND ARTICLES

Anon., *Who Burnt Cork City? A Tale of Arson, Loot, and Murder. The Evidence of Over Seventy Witnesses* (Irish Labour Party and Trade Union Congress, Dublin 1921)

Barry, Denis, *The Unknown Commandant: The Life and Times of Denis Barry 1883–1923* (Collins Press, Cork 2010)

Barry, Pat, *By Bride and Blackwater: Local History & Traditions* (Donal de Barra, Miltown Malbay 2003)

Barry, Tom, *Guerilla Days in Ireland* (Irish Press, Dublin 1949)

Barry, Tom, *The Reality of the Anglo-Irish War, 1920–21 in West Cork: Refutations, Corrections and Comments on Liam Deasy's Towards Ireland Free* (Anvil Books, Tralee 1974)

Béaslaí, Piaras, *Michael Collins and the Making of a New Ireland,* vol. 2 (Harrap, London 1926)

Bielenberg, Andy, Borgonovo, John and Ó Ruairc, Pádraig Óg (eds), *The Men Will Talk to Me: West Cork Interviews by Ernie O'Malley* (Mercier Press, Cork 2015)

Biggs, Michael, *Cork Hunger Strikes by Irish Republicans, 1916–1923* (University of Illinois at Urbana-Champaign 2004)

Borgonovo, John, *Spies, Informers and the 'Anti-Sinn Féin Society': the Intelligence War in Cork City, 1920–1921* (Irish Academic Press, Dublin 2007)

Borgonovo, John, *The Battle for Cork* (Mercier Press, Cork 2011)

Borgonovo, John, *The Dynamics of War and Revolution: Cork City 1916–1918* (Cork University Press, Cork 2013)

Butler, Ewan, *Barry's Flying Column* (Leo Cooper, London 1972)

Carroll, Aideen, *Seán Moylan: Rebel Leader* (Mercier Press, Cork 2010)

Coogan, Tim Pat, *The Man who Made Ireland: The Life and Death of Michael Collins* (Roberts Rinehart, Colorado 1992)

Crozier, Frank P., *Ireland Forever* (Jonathan Cape, London 1932)

Deasy, Liam, *Towards Ireland Free: the West Cork Brigade in the War of Independence, 1917–1921* (Mercier Press, Dublin 1973)

Deasy, Liam, *Brother against Brother* (Mercier Press, Cork 1998)

Denton, Danny, 'On the Truth of the "German plot"', *Journal of the Galway Archaeological and Historical Society*, vol. 59, 2007, pp. 122–33

Doherty, Gabriel and Keogh, Dermot, *Michael Collins and the Making of the Irish State* (Mercier Press, Cork 1998)

Doyle, Tom, *The Civil War in Kerry* (Mercier Press, Cork 2008)

Dunmanway Historical Society, 'Extracts from the Memoirs of Florence John Crowley', *Dunmanway Doings*, vol. 4, 2010, pp. 21–2

Durney, James, 'Comdt. Denis Barry in Newbridge and the Curragh', *Kildare Online Electronic History Journal*, www.kildare.ie/library/ehistory/2011/10/comdt_denis_barry_in_newbridge.asp

Dwyer, T. Ryle, *The Squad and the Intelligence Operations of Michael Collins* (Mercier Press, Cork 2006)

Dwyer, T. Ryle, *Michael Collins and the Civil War* (Mercier Press, Cork 2012)

Ellis, Alan J. *et al.*, *The Burning of Cork: an Eyewitness Account by Alan J. Ellis, and Other Items* (Aubane Historical Society, Millstreet 2004)

Evans, G., 'The Raising of the First Internal Dáil Éireann Loan and the British Responses to It, 1919–1921', Masters thesis, National University of Ireland Maynooth, 2012

Fitzpatrick David (ed.), *Terror in Ireland: 1916–1923* (Lilliput Press, Dublin 2012)

Fitzpatrick, David, *Descendancy: Irish Protestant Histories Since 1795* (Cambridge University Press, Cambridge 2014)

Griffith, Kenneth and O'Grady, Timothy (eds), *Curious Journey: An Oral History of Ireland's Unfinished Revolution* (Mercier Press, Cork 1998)

Grigg, Erik, 'Eamon de Valera's Escape from Lincoln Prison', *Lincolnshire Past & Present*, no. 86, winter 2011, pp. 16–18

Harrington, Michael, *The Munster Republic: The Civil War in North Cork* (Mercier Press, Cork 2009)

Hart, Peter, *The I.R.A. and its Enemies: Violence and Community in Cork, 1916–1923* (Clarendon Press, Oxford 1998)

Hart, Peter, *The I.R.A. at War, 1916–1923* (Oxford University Press, Oxford 2003)

Hittle, J. B. E., *Michael Collins and the Anglo-Irish War: Britain's Counterinsurgency Failure* (Potomac Books, Washington D.C. 2011)

HMSO, *Papers Respecting Negotiations with the Egyptian Delegation* (His Majesty's Stationery Office, London 1921)

Kautt, W. H., *The Anglo-Irish War, 1916-1921: A People's War* (Praeger, Westport 1999)

Kautt W. H., 'Militarising Policemen: The Various Members of the RIC and Their Response to IRA Violence in Ireland, 1919–21', www.academia.edu/1686881/_The_Auxies_Black_and_Tans_and_the_RIC_and_their_response_to_IRA_violence_in_Ireland_1919-21_

Keane, Barry, *Massacre in West Cork: The Dunmanway and Ballygroman Killings Cork* (Mercier Press, Cork 2014)

Keane, Barry, 'Protestant Cork 1911–1926: Summary Courts of Inquiry Irish War of Independence', https://sites.google.com/site/protestantcork191136/summary-courts-of-inquiry-irish-war-of-independence

Keane, Barry, 'The IRA and Loyalist Co-operation with British forces in Cork 1920–1923', www.academia.edu/16377450/The_IRA_and_loyalist_co-operation_with_British_forces_in_Cork_1920-1923

Keane, Barry, 'The IRA Response to Loyalist Co-operation in County Cork during the Irish War of Independence', www.academia.edu/27954537/The_IRA_response_to_loyalist_co-operation_in_County_Cork_during_the_Irish_War_of_Independence

Macardle, Dorothy, *The Irish Republic: A Documented Chronicle of the Anglo-Irish Conflict and the Partitioning of Ireland, with a Detailed Account of the Period 1916–1923* (Farrar, Straus and Giroux, New York 1965)

Mansergh, Martin, 'The Freedom to Achieve Freedom?', in Gabriel Doherty and Dermot Keogh (eds), *Michael Collins and the Making of the Irish State* (Mercier Press, Cork 1998)

Martin, Hugh, *Ireland in Insurrection: An Englishman's Record of Fact* (Daniel O'Connor, London 1921)

McKenna, Joseph, *Guerrilla Warfare in the Irish War of Independence, 1919–1921* (Jefferson, NC 2011)

Meehan, Niall, 'Distorting Irish History, Two: The Road from Dunmanway. Peter Hart's Treatment of the 1922 "April killings" in West Cork', https://www.academia.edu/612672/Distorting_Irish_History_Two_the_road_from_Dunmanway_Peter_Hart_s_treatment_of_the_1922_April_killings_in_West_Cork

Moore, Robin J., 'Curzon and Indian Reform', *Modern Asian Studies*, vol. 27, no. 4, October 1993, pp. 719–40

Morrison, Eve, 'Kilmicheal Revisited: Tom Barry and the "False Surrender"', David Fitzpatrick (ed.), *Terror in Ireland 1916–1923* (Lilliput Press, Dublin 2012)

Morrison, Eve, 'Reply to John Regan', *Dublin Review of Books*, 2014, http://www.drb.ie/reviews/reply-to-john-regan

Murphy, Breen Timothy, 'The Government's Executions Policy during the Irish Civil War 1922–1923', PhD thesis, National University of Ireland Maynooth, 2010

Murphy, Brian P., OSB, 'Poisoning the Well or Publishing the Truth?', in *Troubled History: A 10th Anniversary Critique of Peter Hart's The IRA and its Enemies* (Aubane Historical Society, Millstreet 2008)

Murphy, Gerard, *The Year of Disappearances: Political Killings in Cork 1921–1922* (Gill & Macmillan, Dublin 2010)

Murphy, Seán A., *Kilmichael: A Battlefield Study* (Four Roads Publishing, Cork 2014)

Murphy, William, *Political Imprisonment and the Irish, 1912–1921* (Oxford University Press, Oxford 2014)

O'Brien William, *The Irish Revolution and How It Came About* (Allen & Unwin, London 1923)

O'Callaghan, Seán, *Execution* (Muller, London 1974)

Ó Conchubhair, Brian (ed.), *Rebel Cork's Fighting Story* (Mercier Press, Cork 2009)

O'Connor, Frank, *Guests of the Nation* (Macmillan Co., New York 1931)

O'Halpin, Eunan and Ó Corráin, Daithí, *The Dead of the Irish Revolution 1916–21* (Yale University Press, Newhaven CT forthcoming)

Ó hÉalaithe, Dónal (ed.), *Memoirs of an Old Warrior: Jamie Moynihan's Fight for Irish Freedom 1916–1923* (Mercier Press, Cork 2014)

O'Mahony, Neil, 'The Life & Death of Canon Magner', *Times Past: Journal of the Muskerry Local History Society*, vol. 9, 2010–11, pp. 59–61

O'Malley, Ernie, *On Another Man's Wound* (Anvil Press, Dublin 1979)

O'Reilly, Terence, *Our Struggle for Independence: Eye-witness accounts from the pages of An Cosantóir* (Mercier Press, Cork 2009)

O'Reilly, Terence, *Rebel Heart: George Lennon, Flying Column Commander* (Mercier Press, Cork 2009)

Ó Ruairc, Pádraig Óg, *Truce: Murder, Myth and the Last Days of the Irish War of Independence* (Mercier Press, Cork 2016)

Ó Ruairc, Pádraig Óg, 'Captain Patrick White, Meelick Company of the IRA; East Clare Brigade Commemoration', http://irishvolunteers.org/tag/captain-patrick-white-meelick-company-of-the-i-r-a/

Ó Ruairc, Pádraig Óg, 'British IRA Volunteers 1921', http://theirishwar.com/british-i-r-a-volunteers-1921/

Ó Súilleabháin, Mícheál, *Where Mountainy Men Have Sown: War and Peace in Rebel Cork in the Turbulent Years 1916–21* (Mercier Press, Cork 2013)

Pakenham, Francis (Earl of Longford), *Peace by Ordeal: An Account, from First-Hand Sources of the Negotiation and Signature of the Anglo-Irish Treaty 1921* (Sidgwick & Jackson, London 1972)

Rast, Mike, 'Tactics, Politics, and Propaganda in the Irish War of Independence, 1917–1921', Masters thesis, Georgia State University, 2011

Regan, John M., 'West Cork and the Writing of History: In reply to Eve Morrison', *Dublin Review of Books*, 2014, www.drb.ie/essays/west-cork-and-the-writing-of-history

Ryan, Anne-Marie, *16 Dead Men: The Easter Rising Executions* (Mercier Press, Cork 2014)

Ryan, Meda, *The Day Michael Collins was Shot* (Poolbeg, Swords 1989)

Ryan, Meda, *Tom Barry: IRA Freedom Fighter* (Mercier Press, Cork 2005)

Ryan, Meda, *Michael Collins and the Women who Spied for Ireland* (Mercier Press, Cork 2006)

Ryan, Meda, 'The Kilmichael Ambush, 1920: Exploring the "Provocative Chapters"', *History*, vol. 92, issue 306, April 2007, pp. 235–49

Sharma, D. P., *Countering Terrorism* (Lancers Books, New Delhi 1992)

Sheehan, William, *British Voices from the Irish War of Independence 1918–1921: The Words of British Servicemen Who Were There* (Collins Press, Cork 2005)

Sheehan, William, *A Hard Local War: The British Army and the Guerrilla War in Cork, 1919–1921* (The History Press, Stroud 2011)

*The Struggle of the Irish People: Address to the Congress of the United States* (Government Printing Office, Washington 1921)

Townshend, Charles, *The Republic: The Fight for Irish Independence* (Allen Lane, London 2013)

Valiulis, Maryann G., *Portrait of a Revolutionary: General Richard Mulcahy and the Founding of the Irish Free State* (University Press of Kentucky, Lexington 1992)

Walsh, Maurice, *The News from Ireland: Foreign Correspondents and the Irish Revolution* (I.B. Tauris, London 2008)

White, Gerry and O'Shea, Brendan, *The Burning of Cork* (Mercier Press, Cork 2006)

## NEWSPAPERS

*Anglo-Celt, The*
*Connacht Tribune*
*Cork Constitution*
*Cork Examiner, The*
*Corkman, The*
*Daily Telegraph* (Australian)
*Derbyshire Courier*
*Derry Journal*
*Dungarvan Leader*
*Edinburgh Evening News*
*Evening Herald*
*Freeman's Journal, The*
*Galway Advertiser*
*Glasgow Herald*
*Irish Examiner*
*Irish Independent*

*Irish Times, The*

*Irish Weekly Times*

*Kerryman, The*

*Lancashire Evening Post*

*Leeds Intelligencer*

*Leitrim Observer*

*Liberator, The*

*Limerick Leader*

*Lincolnshire Post*

*Mail, The* (Australian)

*Marlborough Express*

*Nenagh Guardian*

*New York Times, The*

*Poverty Bay Herald*

*Skibbereen Eagle, The*

*Southern Star, The*

*Sunday Independent*

*Sussex Agricultural Express*

*Times, The*

*Ulster Herald*

*Weekly Irish Independent*

*West Australian, The*

*Yorkshire Post*

## WEBSITES

*An Phoblacht*, www.anphoblacht.com

*An t-Óglách*, http://antoglach.militaryarchives.ie

Auxiliary Division of the Royal Irish Constabulary, The, www.theauxiliaries.com

Bureau of Military History, www.bureauofmilitaryhistory.ie

Cairo Gang, The, www.cairogang.com

Central Statistics Office, www.cso.ie

Cork City and County Archives, www.corkarchives.ie

Cork Past and Present, www.corkpastandpresent.ie

Cork's War of Independence, http://homepage.eircom.net/~corkcounty

*Cumann Staire Bhéal Átha'n Ghaorthaidh*, www.ballingearyhs.com

Documents in Irish Foreign Policy, www.difp.ie

Easter 1916, www.easter1916.ie

FamilySearch, https://familysearch.org

Findmypast, www.findmypast.com

Garda Síochána Historical Society, www.policehistory.com

Glasnevin Trust, www.glasnevintrust.ie

Hansard 1803–2005, http://hansard.millbanksystems.com

Historic Graves, http://historicgraves.com

History Ireland, www.historyireland.com

Houses of the Oireachtas debates, http://oireachtasdebates.oireachtas.ie

Irish Congress of Trade Unions, www.ictu.ie

Irish Genealogy.ie (for death certificates), https://civilrecords.irishgenealogy.ie/
churchrecords/civil-search.jsp

irishmedals.org, www.irishmedals.org

Irish Volunteers Commemorative Organisation, http://irishvolunteers.org

Millstreet.ie, www.millstreet.ie

Military Service Pensions Collection, www.militaryarchives.ie/collections/
online-collections/military-service-pensions-collection

National Archives of Ireland, Census of Ireland 1901/1911, www.census.
nationalarchives.ie

National Library of Ireland, www.nli.ie

National Museum of Ireland, www.museum.ie

National Police Officers Roll of Honour, www.policerollofhonour.org.uk

Royal Irish Constabulary Forum, http://irishgenealogyqueries.yuku.com

The National Archives (UK), www.nationalarchives.gov.uk

Tom Crean: An Irish Antarctic Explorer, http://tomcreandiscovery.com

Treaty Exhibition, http://treaty.nationalarchives.ie

www.legislation.gov.uk

# INDEX

## A

Aghada 33

Agnew, Bertram 149

Ahern, John 124

Ahern, Michael (Ballyrichard) 238, 239

Ahern, Michael (Drimoleague) 350

Aherne, James 63, 192

Aherne, Jeremiah 192

Aherne, Liam 63, 192

Aherne, William 321

Aiken, Frank 19, 320, 359, 365

Airy, James O. 120, 121

Allen, Abraham 21, 106

Allen, Seán 67, 195

Allihies 111, 206

Angliss, James 100

Arthur, Richard 188, 191

Asquith, Herbert H. 15

## B

Baker, Harold 208

Ballincollig 65, 120, 151, 172, 178, 198,
204, 247, 248, 268, 286, 298, 369, 372

Ballineen 86, 87, 194, 199, 205, 320, 336,
347, 350

Ballingeary 148, 156, 167, 183, 303, 310

Ballygroman House 85, 86

Ballykinlar Internment Camp 100, 209,
281

Ballymakeera 120, 257, 333

Ballymurphy 69, 71

Ballyvourney 99, 120, 121, 128, 135, 142,
194, 256, 257, 310, 333, 334, 337, 345

Bandon 53, 69, 70, 72, 74–76, 84, 86, 88,
96, 97, 110, 122, 123, 129, 130, 138,
144, 149, 157, 159, 160, 174, 193, 214,
221, 232, 236, 237, 243, 255, 256, 258,
260, 286, 290, 292, 295, 301, 309, 313,
325, 326, 330, 331, 333, 353–356

Bantry 81, 84, 111, 115–117, 131, 132,
146, 164, 247, 289, 299, 300, 311,
315, 322, 325, 331, 337, 345, 353,
358–360, 363

Barlow, Ernest F. 120, 125

Barnane, Francis 174

Barnes, William T. 44, 46, 154

Barrett, Daniel 27, 28

Barrett, James 65, 211

Barrett, Richard (Dick) 27, 28, 280, 336,
337

Barry, Denis 284, 285, 365, 366

Barry, Gerald 216

Barry, Helena 322

Barry, Michael 356, 357

Barry, Richard 238, 239

Barry, Tadhg 209, 281

Barry, Tom 19, 39, 40, 41, 43, 44, 46, 47,
49, 50, 70, 76, 78, 81–83, 91, 150, 157,
159, 171, 176, 177, 186, 193, 205, 236,
237, 250, 278, 345

Barry, William 182, 186, 191

Barry, W. J. 27

Barton, Robert 24

Bayley, Cecil James 44, 154

Baylor, Robert 343

Beale, James Charles  58–60, 189

Beale, William Goff  353, 354

Béal na Bláth  90, 91, 96, 97, 99, 333

Béaslaí, Piaras  24, 93, 143

Beattie, John Edward Lawrence George  67, 195

Beazley, William  74, 75

Begley, Flor  72, 368

Begley, John H. N.  279

Begley, Joseph  157

Behan, Michael Francis  302

Bennett, Denis  57, 176

Bennett, Thomas  144

Birrell, Augustine  16

Blemens, Frederick  59, 155

Blemens, James  59, 155, 297

Bloxham, Henry  171, 172, 268

Boland, Harry  24

Bolger, Edward  110, 111

Bourke, James  32, 118, 119

Bourke, William  243

Bowden, George Stokes  67, 195

Bowles, Charles  79, 80, 215

Bowles, Michael  107, 108, 115

Boxold, Frederick  182, 183

Boyd, William  262, 263

Boynes, Joseph  218

Bradfield, John  88, 89, 285

Bradfield, Thomas  76, 176, 177, 186, 205

Bradfield, Thomas J.  173

Bradfield, William  88, 89

Bradshaw, Leonard Douglas  45, 154

Brady (executed)  137, 138

Bransfield, William  229, 230

Breen, Dan  24, 210

Breen, Patrick  296

Brett, James  116

Brick, William  114

Brixton Prison  9, 35, 36

Brock, Alfred V. G.  197

Brooks, J. R.  286

Brown, John  106

Brown, Bernard  146, 149

Brown, Charles  373

Browne, Josephine Marchment  59, 278

Bryan, George 'Appy'  86, 89

Buckley, Batt  134

Buckley, Daniel  257, 258

Buckley, James  100, 101, 306

Buckley, John (Seán)  81, 83, 122, 123, 134

Buckley, William  332

Bullman, Seán  287

Bunce, John Edward  221

Burgatia House  76, 78, 177, 271

Burke, Christopher Henry  363

Burke, Francis  252

Burke, George  367

Burke, Michael  112, 250, 251

Burns, Patrick (Ballincollig)  298

Burns, Patrick  311

Busteed, Frank  58, 59, 65, 222

Butterfield, Thomas C.  20

Buttimer, James  86, 88, 89, 285

Buttimer, John  87, 89, 285

Buttimer, William J.  89

Byrne, James  344

Byrne, James (Upton Station ambush)  188

Byrne, Patrick  314

Byrne, Peter  318

C

Cahill, Peter  290

Cambridge, Robert 162

Camm, Alfred 276, 277

Cane, William Arthur 194

Canty, Godfrey (Geoffrey) 231

Carey, Nellie 207

Carnegie Library 53

Carrigaphooka Bridge 99

Carrigtwohill 113, 223, 229, 239, 248, 264, 282, 356

Carroll, William 136

Carson, Edward 17

Carson, Matthew 256

Carter, Edward Lionel 177

Casement, Roger 15, 111

Casey, Daniel 199

Casey, Daniel (Jeremiah) 334

Casey, Jeremiah 167

Casey, Patrick 224

Castlelyons 10, 105, 211

Castlemartyr 133, 154, 225

Castletownbere 108, 111, 236, 360

Castletown-Kinneigh 86, 89, 171, 205

Castletownroche 208, 218, 288, 315, 323

Cathcart, John 212

Cawley, Sidney 208

Chalmers, Donald 236

Chambers, Stewart 149, 267

Chapman, Charles 256

Chapman, Spencer R. 51, 163, 164

Charleville 131, 183, 184, 207, 220, 226, 244, 262, 270, 271, 317, 348

Chave, Clarence Victor 138, 139

Chetwynd Viaduct 58, 139

Chinnery, John 86–89, 285

City Hall, Cork 38, 53, 140

Claffey, Joseph (James) 313

Clancy, Daniel 280

Clancy, Patrick 127

Clarke, Alexander 278

Clarke, James 66, 68, 205

Clarke, Thomas J. 15

Clonakilty 80, 86–88, 91, 96, 99, 114, 123, 159, 160, 176, 184, 213, 231, 282, 283, 295, 299, 314, 315, 344, 350, 371

Clondrohid 183, 265, 286, 298, 302, 334, 361

Clonmult 33, 62, 64, 192, 221, 241, 242, 252, 278

Cloyne 34, 62, 163

Clune, Peter 354

Coachford 65, 146, 223, 275, 303, 304, 306

Coakley, Denis 347

Coakley, Michael 362, 363

Cobh 21, 33, 37, 63, 64, 88, 107, 112, 134, 206, 216, 230, 239, 248, 250, 251, 264, 282, 293, 316, 323, 338

Coffey, Denis 292

Coffey, James 89, 186, 199

Coffey, Timothy 89, 176, 186, 199

Cohalan, Daniel 20, 25, 122, 366

Coleman, James 150

Coleman, Jeremiah 370, 371

Coleman, Joseph 233, 234

College Road, Cork city 60, 161, 284

Collins, Michael 8, 9, 18, 23, 24, 88, 90–100, 111, 112, 122, 222, 281, 298, 299, 326, 333–335, 358

Collins, Michael ('small') 292, 293

Collins, Patrick 80, 215

Collins, Thomas 226, 227

Collins, Timothy 308

Compton Smith, Geoffrey 222

Condon, Martin 25

Connell, William 190

Connelly, Richard 81

Connolly, John 138

Connolly, Neilus 81

Connolly, Timothy 189

Connor, James 273, 274

Conway, Ralph 306

Conway, Thomas 302

Cooke, William Levingstone 297

Cooney, Patrick 300

Cooper, John 256

Coppeen 46

Corby, Leo 261

Corcoran, Patrick 296

Cork Harbour 33, 91

Corkery, Jack 70, 238

Cork Harbour 280, 363

Corless, Harry 111

Cormyn, Thomas 233

Cotter, Alfred 194, 195

Cotter, Thomas 199

Cottle, Albert Redvers 300, 301

Coughlan (Anti-Treaty IRA) 359, 360

Coughlan, John 33, 34, 126

Coughlan, Joseph 225

Coughlan, Peter 235

Courtney, Seamus 106, 107

Cowin, Edward 141

Cox, William 317, 318

Crafer, Joseph 208

Craig, Inspector 30

Crake, Francis 41, 45, 154

Crawford, Samuel 343

Crean, Cornelius 114

Creedon, Denis 305

Creedon, Eamon 187

Creegan, Frank 323

Cregan, Edward 296, 297

Cronin, John F. 325

Cronin, Patrick 279, 280

Cronin, William 325

Crossbarry 69–75, 209, 232

Crowley, Bryan 110

Crowley, Cornelius 117

Crowley, Daniel 258

Crowley, Daniel (Volunteer) 211

Crowley, Florence J. 83, 84

Crowley, John 121

Crowley, Michael 70, 123, 124, 237, 299

Crowley, Michael J. 179, 300

Crowley, Patrick 178, 179

Crowley, Sonny Dave 40

Crowley, Tadhg (Timothy) 164

Crowther, Frederick 267, 269

Crozier, Frank 39, 50

Culhane, Jack 30

Cullen, James 231

Cumann na mBan 15, 179

Cumming, Hanway 201, 202

Cunningham, Jack 55

Cunningham, Laurence 350

Curragh 82, 337, 365, 366

Curtin, Mary Ann 294

Curzon, Lord 92

Cusack, Maurice 273

Cusack, Michael 349

Customs House, Dublin 99, 100

D

Daker, Harold 276, 277

Dalton, Emmet 95, 97, 98, 100, 101

Daly, Charles (Charlie) 196, 197

Daly, Charles James 268

Daly, Con 209

Daly, Jeremiah 55

Daly, Madge 327

D'Arcy, Finbarr 168

De Róiste, Liam 25, 93

De Valera, Éamon 24, 91, 94, 96

Deasy, Liam 70, 71, 81, 83, 91, 96, 129, 337

Deasy, Pat 42, 43, 46, 47, 49, 155

Deasy, William 115, 211

Delaney, Cornelius 54, 163

Delaney, James 329

Delaney, Jeremiah 54, 163

Dennehy, Daniel 319

Dennehy, Donal 192

Dennehy, Thomas 211

Desmond, Daniel 327

Desmond, David 192

Desmond, Jeremiah 342

Desmond, John 348

Desmond, Michael 62, 192

Devitt, Patrick 57, 176

Devoy, Jimmy 369

Dillon, John 16

Dillon's Cross 51, 53, 54, 164, 267, 269

Dillon, William 133

Dinan, Jeremiah 361, 362

Dinan, Thomas 361, 362

Dineen, Michael 266

Dixon, William Alfred 144, 145

Donoghue, James 157

Donoghue, William 188

Donovan, Daniel 'Sandow' 30, 194

Donovan, Denis 214

Donovan, Denis 'Din Din' Finbarr 217

Donovan, Patrick 170

Donovan, Stephen 310

Donovan, Timothy 164, 165

Dorgan, Patrick 187

Dorman, Stephen 244

Dove, George R. A. 285, 286

Dowling, John 22

Downey, Michael 345

Downey, Thomas 155

Dowse, Bishop 60

Doyle, Constable 80, 115

Dray, Ernest 165

Dripsey 65–68

Driscoll, Jeremiah 315

Driscoll, John 108

Driscoll, Michael 260, 261

Dublin Castle 10, 16–18, 112, 117, 151, 196, 246, 255, 267, 269

Duckham, George 265, 266

Duggan, John 361

Duggan, Patrick 326

Duggan, Peg 26

Dunmanway 43, 53, 54, 76, 79, 83, 85, 86, 146, 164, 258, 279, 310, 314, 347, 354, 362

Dunne, Edward 114

Dunne, Margaret 357

Dwyer, John 337

Dwyer, Michael (Denis) 171

**E**

Eady, Robert 184

Egan, Mary (Molly) 324

Ellis, Alan 51, 52

Elton, William 208

Entwistle, William 372

Essex Regiment 28, 69, 70, 72, 82, 84, 91, 122, 123, 129, 139, 140, 144, 157, 171, 176, 179, 193, 195, 231, 232, 237, 245, 246, 256–258, 260, 261, 278

Evans, Frederick 252

Evans, Joseph 131

# F

Falvey, Batt 188

Faraday, Lieutenant 80

Feehely, Katherine 341, 342

Feeley, Michael 27

Fermoy 62, 105, 109, 110, 121, 124–126, 137, 143, 144, 146, 153, 154, 204, 207, 245, 294, 300, 323, 334, 339, 343, 358, 359

Fielding, Norman 220

Finn, William 188

Fitzalan, Lord 18

Fitzgerald, Daniel 372

Fitzgerald, Henry 249

Fitzgerald, Michael 143, 144, 359

Fitzgerald, Ned 30

Fitzgerald, Thomas 249

Fitzgerald, Timothy 129, 130, 368

Fitzgibbon, David 258, 259

Fitzmaurice, Francis 86, 88, 89, 285

Fitzpatrick, Frank 80, 215

Flanagan, Inspector 31

Fleming, John 161

Fleming, Paddy 24

Fletcher, George 192

Flood, Matt 137, 141

Flood (National Army) 292, 294

Flynn, John (Bandon) 355, 356

Flynn, John (Timoleague) 114

Flynn, Patrick 187

Flynn, Richard 238

Foley, Cornelius 202

Foley, James 198

Foley, John 275

Foley, May 37

Foley, Michael 108

Forde, H. F. 47–49

Francis, Bernard 234, 235

French, Viceroy Lord 27

Frongoch Internment Camp 15, 20, 90, 176

# G

Gallagher, Ellen (Lily) 317

Gallagher, Thomas 320

Galvin, Denis 351, 352

Galvin, James 192

Galvin, John 157

Galvin, Laurence 339

Galvin, Michael 130, 131

Gammon, Walter 153

Garvey, Denis 115

Genochio, Henry 283

Gibbs, William George 137

Gill, William Alfred 68, 195

Glavin, Jimmy 63

Gleave, James Chubb 45, 154

Glengarriff 116, 117, 131–133, 308, 326

Gloster, William 284, 285

Goggin, Patrick 219

Good, John 170, 204, 205

Good, William 213

Gordon, James 156

Gorman, Michael 350

Grace, Michael J. 27

Graham, Philip Noel 45, 154

Grant, Frederick 288

Grant, James Seafield 194

Gray, Alfred 208

Gray, Bernard 306

Greenfield, James 87, 89, 285

Green, Montague 149, 267

Greensmyth, Joseph 56, 57, 176

Greenwood, Hamar 32, 37, 164, 200, 229, 254

Grey/Gray, David 86, 88, 285

Griffin, Daniel 319

Griffin, Maurice 141, 142

Griffith, Arthur 92, 95

Guthrie, Cecil James 42, 47, 154

## H

Hales, Seán 70, 93, 111, 130, 140, 264, 295, 314, 334–336

Hales, Tom 88, 149, 264, 289, 335

Hall, Ernest 153

Hall, May (Mary) 69, 188

Hallahan, Michael 63, 192

Hall, Charles Edward 133, 134

Hallinan, Major 71

Hampshire Regiment 62, 64, 67, 140, 147, 168, 246, 252, 253, 264

Hanley, Patrick 150

Harbord, Ralph 87

Harford, Patrick 351

Harold, Charles 70, 72, 74, 75

Harrington, Daniel 115

Harrington, Peter 108

Harrison, Arthur Joseph 223

Hart, Vernon 51, 164

Haugh, Matthew 131, 132

Hawkes/Mahony, John (James) 146

Hawkins, Edward 242, 243

Hayes, Ellen Patricia 350

Hayes, Michael 312

Hayes, Patrick 235

Hayes, Seán 93, 365

Haynes, Frances 307

Healy, Charles 25

Healy, Daniel 30, 115, 243

Healy, Patrick 329

Healy, William 305, 352, 353

Heffernan, William (Liam) 154

Hegarty, Batt 272, 273

Hegarty, Denis 170

Hegarty, Patrick/Liam 135, 136

Hegarty, Richard 63, 192

Hegarty, Sean 188

Helen, R. J. 89

Henderson, Kenneth R. 286

Hendy, Ronald A. 285, 286

Hennessy, D. 27

Hennessy, Jack 41–43, 46, 47, 49, 195

Hennessy, Thomas 206

Hennessy, Timothy 224

Henry, Denis 32, 116, 238

Herlihy, David 203, 204

Herlihy, James 128, 129

Herlihy, Jeremiah 139

Hesterman, Frederick 252, 253

Hickey, Michael 352

Hickey, Patrick 245, 246

Higgins, Mary 33

Higginson, Colonel 52, 206, 246

Higgins, Patrick 62, 64, 221

Hill, Arthur Wilfred 242

Hill, Private 68

Hoare, Liam (William) 216, 217

Hodnett, John 228, 229

Hodnett, Leonard Douglas 67, 195, 268

Holland, Jeremiah 311

Holman, Joseph 255

Holmes, Philip Armstrong 174, 175

Holyome, John 182, 183

Hooper-Jones, Stanley 45, 46, 154

Horan, James 224

Horgan, Andrew 320, 321

Horgan, George 53, 162

Horgan, Patrick 284

Horgan, William 269

Hornibrook, Samuel 85, 285, 286

Hornibrook, Thomas Henry 85, 285, 286

Hotblack, Geoffrey 72, 73, 129, 130, 208

Hourican (Hourigan), Jeremiah 293

Hourihan, Dan 43

Hourihane, John 300

Hourihan, Timothy 205, 206

Howe, Robert 86, 87, 285

Howell, John 320, 321

Hudson, Colonel 81, 82, 83

Hugo, Frederick 45, 154

Hunter, John Alexander 236

Hunter, Thomas 23

Hurley, Charlie 69, 71, 188, 209

Hurley, Daniel 334

Hurley, Frank 123, 173, 231, 232

Huston, Fred 52

**I**

Inchigeela 106, 130, 310, 361

Inch Strand 33

Ingerton, Michael 66

Innishannon 114, 129, 214, 238, 255, 309, 312

Irish Parliamentary Party (IPP) 16, 17, 21, 23

Irish Republican Brotherhood (IRB) 20, 90, 94, 358

**J**

Jagoe, William 86, 89, 279, 280

Jays, Henry Clement 150

Jerrum, Herbert Charles 373

Johansen (Jolinsin), Carl 157

Johnston, Charles Penrose 188

Johnston, Thomas 167

Johnston, William 181

Jones, Albert 45, 154

Jones, Samuel 321

Jones, William 109, 110, 358

Joyce, John Joe 62, 192

**K**

Kanturk 126–128, 141, 169, 203, 204, 210, 215, 262, 280, 296, 297, 327, 329

Keany, Michael 184, 282, 283

Kearney, Peter 70, 73, 86, 193, 236, 237

Kearns, Charles 313

Kearns, Richard (Dick) 301

Keating, Patrick 246

Kelleher, Dr 46

Kelleher, Michael John 179

Kelleher, Seán Jeremiah 256, 257

Kelleher, Tom 70–73, 255

Kelly, Denis 359, 360

Kelly, John 132

Kenefick, William 218

Kenna, John 237

Kennefick, Timothy 303, 304

Kent, David 105, 366

Kent, Richard 10, 105

Kent, Thomas 10, 15, 105

Kent, William 105

Kenure, John (Patrick) 253

Kenward, Arthur 208

Keogh, Tom 99, 100, 306

Keohane, Tim 43, 49

Kidney, Alfred 179

Kiely, Joseph 27

Kiely, Michael (Timothy) 203, 204

Kiernan, Katherine (Kitty) 90, 91

Kilbrittain 62, 110, 129, 174, 179, 181, 189, 232, 267, 287, 299

Kildorrery 125, 152, 218, 266, 267, 296

Killarney 32, 99, 101, 146, 162, 183

Kilmichael 9, 39, 40, 44, 47, 49, 155, 156, 159, 201

Kilpatrick 123, 129

King, Alice 56, 176

King, Thomas 115, 116

King, William 147

King, William H. 56

King's Liverpool Regiment 81–84, 166, 278, 328

Kingston, Thomas 76, 78

Kinsale 69, 70, 84, 178, 260, 287, 292, 307, 312, 340

Knight, James 193

**L**

Lack, James 321

Lane, Tom 231

Langtry, Eugene 65

Larter, Edward 276

Leahy, Michael 33, 34, 250, 368

Lee, Cyril 298

Lehane, David 351

Lehane, Denis 368

Lehane, James 142

Lindsay, Mary 65, 66, 68, 205

Listowel 30–32, 158, 174

Lloyd George, David 21, 23, 28, 29, 92, 94

Lockyer, George 166

London 9, 15, 16, 23, 28, 35–37, 47, 60, 91, 94, 183, 236, 282

Long, Jeremiah 309

Looney, Cornelius 236, 237

Looney, Michael 187

Lord, Frederick 215

Lordan, Denis 70, 81, 82, 177, 181

Lordan, John 41–43, 46, 47, 49, 70, 171, 214

Lorton, Harry 27, 28

Lowe, William 15

Lucas, Ernest 45, 155

Lucey, Christopher 148, 149

Lucey, Daniel 170, 171

Lucey, John 259, 260

Lucey, Michael 133

Lynch, Daniel 368, 369

Lynch, Fionán 93

Lynch, James 226

Lynch, John Sullivan 250

Lynch, Liam 19, 25, 109, 203, 204, 270, 334, 345, 358, 359

Lynch, Michael 135, 136

Lyons, John 65, 195

**M**

MacCurtain, Tomás 10, 25–28, 35, 58, 93, 113, 115, 219

MacDonagh, Thomas 15

MacDonnell, Patrick 24

MacEoin, Seán 93

MacKenzie-Kennedy, Ian 292–294

MacNamara, Edward 238, 239

MacNeill, Eoin 16, 20

Macready, Nevil 66, 68, 221, 225, 251

Macroom 20, 40, 47, 65, 70, 73, 86, 96, 99, 100, 106, 120, 121, 128, 136, 137, 146, 150, 161, 167, 183, 202, 215, 257, 260, 265, 286, 296, 298, 301, 320, 342, 351, 360, 361, 366, 371

MacSweeney, John  169

MacSwiney, Áine  35, 37

MacSwiney, Christy  25

MacSwiney, Máire  35

MacSwiney, Muriel  36

MacSwiney, Terence  9, 35, 36, 38, 93, 145, 182, 264

Madden, James  292

Maddox, Thomas  122, 123

Madell, Roland  233

Magner, Canon Thomas  164

Maguire, Patrick  292

Mahony, James  358

Maligny, Harold  201, 202

Mallow  55, 57, 137, 141, 151, 176, 187, 204, 244, 249, 262, 274, 288, 289, 298, 315, 327, 351, 361, 366, 367, 373

Malone, James  337, 338

Malone, Thomas  24

Maloney, Daniel  179

Maloney, James  293, 294

Mangan, Patrick  308

Manning, Tom  306

Marquis, John  220

Martin, Cyril  208

Marum, James  317

Maultrahane  81

Maunsell, Daniel  130

Maxwell, John  15

McCall, Reginald  252

McCann, James  302, 303

McCann, Thomas  328

McCarthy, Ben  353, 354

McCarthy, Cornelius  189

McCarthy, Daniel  247, 248, 267

McCarthy, Denis  299

McCarthy, Donal (Daniel)  300

McCarthy, John  86

McCarthy, Michael (Clonakilty)  114

McCarthy, Michael (Kilmichael)  40–43, 46, 47, 49, 155

McCarthy, Patrick (Millstreet)  151

McCarthy, Patrick (Skibbereen)  289, 290

McCarthy, Timothy  65, 195

McCarthy, William  244

McDonald, Jeremiah  295

McDonald, Michael  344

McDonnell, John Cyril  219, 220

McDonnell, Thomas  119, 120

McGarry, Seán  24, 337

McGoldrick, Patrick  114

McGrath, Daniel  119, 120

McGrath, John  189

McGrath, Joseph  93, 336

McGrath, Patrick  27, 28

McGrath, William  32, 118, 119

McGuinness, James  99

McKelvey, Joe  19, 336

McKenna, Frederick  292

McKenna, Gerald  292

McKinley, Alexander Gerald  87, 89, 285

McLean, Hugh  239, 240

McLean, Michael  159, 160

McMahon, Francis Leo  243

McMillan, Robert  236

McNamara, John  132

McNeice, William  333

McNestry, Patrick  143

McPherson, William  274

McWilliams, Melville  27

Meade, Edward  145

Meara, Harriet K.  161

Medaile, Sarah  163

Mee, Jeremiah 31, 32

Meihigan, James 152

Mercy Hospital 100, 109, 161, 218, 243, 257, 290, 305, 317, 322, 324, 330, 332–334, 338, 342, 344, 346, 349–352, 355, 356, 360, 361, 363

Midleton 34, 62, 63, 133, 134, 152, 154, 165, 169, 211, 216, 234, 238, 239, 242, 248, 249, 255, 272, 316, 317, 353, 357

Millbank Hospital 47

Millstreet 20, 126, 132, 151, 171, 176, 182, 201, 202, 262, 265, 266, 272, 316, 317, 327, 345

Milroy, Seán 24, 93

Minogue, Denis 347

Mitchell, Lionel 149

Mitchelstown 119, 120, 261, 276

Mohally, William 191

Moloney, Jack 55

Monaghan, Peter 73, 208

Monahan, Michael 361

Montenotte 67, 350

Mooney, Thomas 338

Moore, Maurice 64, 221

Morey, Richard 172

Morris, Henry 276

Morrisey, Joseph 192

Morris, Henry 277

Morrison, William 86

Morrissey, Christopher 153

Morrissey, Patrick 113

Mountjoy Prison 24, 94, 365, 366

Mourneabbey 62, 187, 203, 221, 244, 254

Moyles (Miles), John 174, 175

Moynihan, Bernard 272

Mulcahy, Arthur 210, 211

Mulcahy, Denis 55

Mulcahy, Liam 153

Mulcahy, Richard 101, 335

Mulcahy, Thomas 187, 220, 221

Mulcahy, William (John) 148

Mulherin, William 121, 122

Mullane, Daniel 57, 176

Mullane, Jeremiah 210

Mullen, Martin 165, 166

Murphy, Abina 363

Murphy, Bernard 309

Murphy, Cornelius (Millstreet) 175, 176

Murphy, Cornelius (Timoleague) 232, 233

Murphy, Daniel 211

Murphy, Denis 316

Murphy, Desmond 37

Murphy, James 322, 323

Murphy, James 'Spud' 44, 76, 78, 123, 176, 197, 231, 271, 350

Murphy, John 264, 265

Murphy, Joseph 35, 145

Murphy, Michael Francis 160, 161

Murphy, Mick 58, 59, 149

Murphy, Ned 55

Murphy, Patrick 304

Murphy, Seán 83

Murphy, Ted 98

Murphy, Timothy (Patrick) 271

Murphy, Walter Leo 139, 151, 198, 209, 247, 248, 250, 267, 268

Murphy, William (Clogheen) 107

Murphy, William (Cork city) 360

Murphy, William (National Army) 306

Murragh 86, 87, 231

Murray, Constable James 123, 124

Murray, James 301

Murray, Michael Joseph 206, 207
Murray, Patrick 348
Murray, Victor B. 197
Murtagh, Joseph 25, 27, 113

## N

Nagle, David 209
Nagle, Michael 341
Nagle, Robert 87, 89, 285
Nagle, Tom 87, 89
Nathan, Matthew 16, 17
Neary, Francis 301
Neenan, Michael 111
Nevin, William 292
Newcestown 85, 106, 140, 231, 239, 260, 348
Newman, Richard 206
Newman, William 112
Newmarket 127, 141, 207, 262
Nicholson, James 58, 60
Noble, Bridget 200
Nolan, David 318
Nolan, James 345, 346
Nolan, Thomas 333
Nolan, William J. 278, 279, 291
Noonan, Richard 313
Norway, Arthur Hamilton 16
Nunn, Albert Edward 126, 127
Nyhan, John 'Flyer' 123, 124
Nyhan, Kate 89

## O

O'Brien, Art 36, 37
O'Brien, Bernard 355
O'Brien, Constable Daniel 149
O'Brien, Dan 306
O'Brien, Daniel 241
O'Brien, Denis 200

O'Brien, James 16
O'Brien, John (Anti-Treaty) 305
O'Brien, John (Cloyne) 163
O'Brien, John (Cork city) 32, 118
O'Brien, Michael 218
O'Brien, Michael (Grenagh) 356
O'Brien, Seán 198
O'Brien, Stephen 81
O'Brien, Thomas 65, 195
O'Callaghan, Daniel 65, 195
O'Callaghan, Daniel (Carrigtwohill) 264
O'Callaghan, Donal 36
O'Callaghan, Fr James 240, 241
O'Callaghan, James 315
O'Callaghan, Jeremiah 65
O'Callaghan, Jeremiah (Mallow) 298
O'Callaghan, John 136
O'Callaghan, Leo 55, 203
O'Callaghan, Peter 369
O'Callaghan, Stephen 369
O'Connell, Eugene 150
O'Connell, James 24
O'Connell, J. J. 'Ginger' 30, 95
O'Connell, John 250, 251
O'Connell, John (Jack) 127, 128
O'Connor, George B. 277, 278
O'Connor, Patrick 175
O'Connor, Rory 18, 95, 336
O'Daly, Paddy 99, 100
O'Donnell, Denis 152, 153
O'Donoghue, Florence (Florrie) 27, 28, 96, 111, 112, 155, 245, 278
O'Donoghue, James 150
O'Donoghue, Patrick 152
O'Donoghue, Seán 30, 310, 312
O'Donovan, Daniel 312, 313
O'Donovan, James 291

O'Donovan, John 'Jack' 362

O'Donovan, Matt 260

O'Donovan, Peter 27, 28

O'Driscoll, Cornelius 355

O'Driscoll, Eileen 323, 324

O'Driscoll, Michael 72, 116, 133

O'Driscoll, Patrick 181

O'Dwyer, Con 108

O'Halloran, Daniel 316

O'Hanlon, Daniel 311

Ó hAodha, Seán 23

O'Hegarty, Seán 30, 260

O'Hurley, Diarmuid (Jeremiah) 248, 249

O'Keeffe, Michael 223, 230

O'Keeffe, Patrick 23, 93

O'Keeffe, Thomas 259

O'Kelly, Seán T. 23

Olden, Christie 295

O'Leary, Cornelius 333

O'Leary, Daniel 331

O'Leary, Jeremiah 209

O'Leary, John (Cork city) 186, 187

O'Leary, John (Macroom) 301, 302

O'Leary, Seámus 348

O'Leary, Sonny 64, 221

O'Leary, Timothy 287

O'Leary, Timothy (Tadhg) 320

O'Mahony, Daniel 183

O'Mahony, Jeremiah 201

O'Mahony, Sergeant Major Jeremiah 345, 346

O'Mahony, Michael John 195, 196

O'Mahony, Patrick 65, 195

O'Mahony, Thomas 316

Ó Máille, Pádraig 335

O'Malley, Ernie 33, 368

O'Meara (Mara), Daniel 330

Ó Muirthile, Seán 94

O'Mullane, Jeremiah 211

O'Neill, Jeremiah 189

O'Neill, Michael 85, 88, 144, 285, 286

O'Neill, Stephen 43, 44, 123, 124

O'Reilly, Charles 207

O'Reilly, Daniel 174

O'Riordan, Daniel 256, 257

O'Riordan, Denis (Din-Din) 58, 155

O'Rourke, Patrick 306

O'Shaughnessy, Thomas 27

O'Shea, Ambrose 79, 80, 215

O'Shea, John 211

O'Sullivan, Aileen 37

O'Sullivan, Andrew 366, 367

O'Sullivan, Christopher William 247

O'Sullivan, Cornelius 30

O'Sullivan, David 306, 307

O'Sullivan, Denis (Denny) 156

O'Sullivan, Gearóid 91, 94, 313, 331

O'Sullivan, Geraldine 37

O'Sullivan, Jack 44

O'Sullivan, Jeremiah 319

O'Sullivan, Jim 42, 43, 46, 47, 155

O'Sullivan, John 342

O'Sullivan, Michael 211

O'Sullivan, Michael Finbarr 191, 192

O'Sullivan/Sullivan, Paddy 63, 221

O'Sullivan, Padraig 27

O'Sullivan, Patrick (Scott Lane) 180

O'Sullivan, Patrick (Upton Station) 188

O'Sullivan, Robert 307

O'Sullivan, Tadhg 27, 218, 219

O'Sullivan, Timothy 91

O'Sullivan, William 290

O'Sullivan, William (Cork city) 185

O'Sullivan, William (Droumdrastil) 364

O'Toole, Christopher 292
Ovens 85, 247, 248, 256, 369, 370

**P**

Pallester, William 45, 49, 155
Parker, William 234, 235
Parnell, Mary 266
Parsons, William Edward 291
Peacocke, Warren John 254, 255
Pearse, Patrick 312
Pearse, Patrick H. 15
Pearson, Horace 45, 155
Percival, Arthur 28, 70, 72–74, 82, 122,
    135, 140, 141, 178, 189, 193, 225, 232,
    233, 246, 256–258, 260, 278
Perrier, Frederick 193
Perrott, Thomas 188
Perry, Patrick 292
Perry, Wilfred 27, 28
Phelan, John 188
Pincher, Private 369
Pomeroy, Henry 345
Poole, Arthur 45, 155
Pouladuff 111, 129
Powell, Albert 276, 277
Power, Francis 312
Prendergast, Joseph 192, 193
Prendergast, Nicholas de Sales 158
Prenderville, Maurice 158
Pring, Gerald Oswald 169
Purcell, William (James/John) 227

**Q**

Queenstown. *See* Cobh
Quinlan, Denis 106
Quinlisk, Timothy 111, 112
Quinn, Henry 292
Quinn, Timothy 154

**R**

Rathmore 20, 99, 219, 351
Rea, Patrick 172
Redmond, John 16, 17
Redmond, William Charles Forbes 100
Regan, Denis 159
Reid, Charles 144
Reid, Joseph 107
Reilly, Alfred Charles 58, 181, 182, 277
Richardson, Gurth 140, 141
Ring, Denis 152
Riordan, John 306
Rippengale, Bertie 145
Robertson, Robert 140, 141
Roche, James 339, 340, 343, 344
Rochestown 59, 60, 95, 182, 277, 293,
    296
Ross, Gibbs 289, 290, 300, 311
Rosscarbery 76, 177, 197, 215, 271, 295,
    315
Roughley, F. 262
Rowe, William 10, 105
Roycroft, Thomas 370
Roynane, Patrick 187, 220, 221
Rundle, Albert E. 145
Rutherford, David 146, 149
Ryan, John 238, 239
Ryle, John 235

**S**

Saunders, James 254
Savage, Michael 282
Scannell, Josie 263
Scully, Timothy 112, 113
Searls, Edward 309
Shanley, Thomas 266, 267
Shannon, Samuel 142

Sharman, Frederick 128

Sheehan, Cornelius (Long Con) 209

Sheehan, Denis 65

Sheehan, John 210

Sheehan, Patrick 239

Sheehan, Patrick J. 269–271

Shepard (Sheppard), Francis 236, 237

Sherman, Mr 27

Shinnick, Fr 65, 66

Shortall, Francis 167

Shorter, Frederick 262, 263

Simmons, George 252

Sisk, John 188

Skibbereen 80–82, 84, 96, 146, 181, 190, 240, 278, 289, 295, 299, 325, 347

Smith, Christopher 348

Smith, William 225

Smyth, Gerald Brice Ferguson 30–32, 118

Snewin, Philip William 373

Soady, Clive 194

Somers, Nicholas 203

South Gate Bridge 60, 140, 285

South Infirmary 185, 189, 191, 195, 227, 294, 296, 354, 367, 369

South Mall, Cork city 30, 32, 68, 167, 182, 228, 302

Spiers, John 188

Spike Island 91, 197, 251, 252, 280

Spillane, William 289

Spriggs, Denis 274, 275, 277

Squibbs, John Gordon 140

St Finbarr's Cemetery 38, 93, 110, 130, 143, 148, 244, 283, 287, 290, 313, 366

St Patrick's Bridge 21, 52, 319, 352

St Patrick's Street 21, 51, 52, 68, 106, 110, 138, 143, 152, 161, 174, 247, 279, 283, 341, 360

Stack, Austin 24

Starling, Percy 148

Starr, Patrick 224

Statton, Edward 372

Stenning, Frederick 214

Sterland, Frederick 227, 228

Steward, Stanley 208

Stokes, John 225, 226

Strickland, Peter 66, 68, 70, 177, 206, 286

Stringer, Henry 327

Stubbs, Herbert 193

Sullivan, Christopher 192

Sullivan, Daniel 312

Sullivan, Daniel (Burgita) 315

Sullivan, Frank 271, 272

Sullivan/O'Sullivan, John 269–271

Sullivan, Patrick 33, 221

Sullivan's Quay 52, 140, 186, 302, 303

Sullivan, Tom 86

Swanton, Edwin (Eugene) 255

Swanzy, Oswald Ross 21, 27, 28, 58, 106

Sweeney, V. 371

Sweetman, Mathew 190

**T**

Tarrant, Patrick 164, 165

Taylor, Francis (Frank) 45, 155

Taylor, Percy 157, 159

Taylor, William Henry 177

Tehan, John 288, 289

Thomas, James 57

Thompson, Harold 216, 233

Thompson, Joseph 151, 267

Thompson's Bakery 58, 59

Thornton, Frank 90

Thornton, Hugh 99, 299

p(e), Arthur 165

on, George 58, 60, 61, 190

on, Richard H. 61

moleague 114, 129, 159, 170, 179, 204, 213, 232, 313

Tinker's Cross 123, 129, 130

Tobin, Miceál 108, 109

Tobin, Robert 346

Toureen ambush 40, 144

Tower, Lieutenant 72, 73

Trahy, Patrick 152

Tralee 32, 99, 174, 175, 204, 293

Travers, John 338

Treacy, Seán 24

Tudor, Henry Hugh 31

Turner, Edward 373

Turner, Harold 201, 202

Twomey, Edward 203, 204

**U**

Union Quay Barracks, Cork city 53, 138, 167, 174, 192

Upton 121, 312, 330

Upton Station 69, 71, 188, 191

**V**

Victoria Barracks, Cork city 10, 21, 51, 65, 66, 95, 105, 111, 124, 145, 176, 186, 187, 216, 224, 241, 259, 268, 283, 291, 294, 309, 334

Vincent, Seymour 245

**W**

Wainwright, Christopher 45, 155

Walker, George 134

Walker, William 201, 202

Walsh, David 241, 242

Walsh, Fr Dan 37

Walsh, J. J. 23, 24, 93, 94, 143

Walsh, John 328

Walsh, John J. 272

Walsh, John (Patrick) 314

Walsh, Michael 189–191

Walsh, Patrick 183, 184

Walsh, T. J. 147

Ward, Nicholas 301

Ward, Private H. 368

Washington, Frederick 252

Washington Street, Cork city 161, 169, 218, 247, 318, 346

Waterfall 70, 139, 172, 209, 267, 268, 370

Waters, Edward 203, 204

Watkins, Ernest 125, 126

Watling, Thomas 157, 159

Watts, Edward 208

Watts, William 149, 267

Webb, John 225

Webster, Benjamin 45, 155

Western Road, Cork city 123, 124, 169, 277, 317, 346

Whichlow, Louis 252

Whitear, Alfred Edward 67, 195

White, Patrick 251, 252

Whooley, Timothy 213

Wilkins, William 208

Williams, Edward 305

Williams, Michael 287, 288

Williamson, William 330, 331

Wilson, George 80, 215

Wilson, Woodrow 23, 24

Wise, Thomas 68, 195

Wolfe, Eric 340

Woodford Bourne 58, 59, 138

Woods, Henry 258

Woods, Herbert 85, 285

Woods (Wolfe), Michael  320
Woodward, George  218
Woulahan, William Francis  326
Wyatt, Major  82

**Y**

Yates, James  302, 303
Young, Ned  41, 42, 46, 49, 160

Thor
Til
Til
Ti